. . . And I Haven't Had a Bad Day Since

. . . *And I Haven't Had a Bad Day Since*

FROM THE STREETS OF HARLEM TO THE HALLS OF CONGRESS

by
CHARLES B. RANGEL
with LEON WYNTER

Thomas Dunne Books/St. Martin's Press
New York

THOMAS DUNNE BOOKS.
An imprint of St. Martin's Press.

www.thomasdunnebooks.com
www.stmartins.com

Library of Congress Cataloging-in-Publication Data

Rangel, Charles B.
    And I haven't had a bad day since : from the streets of Harlem to the halls
of Congress / by Charles B. Rangel ; with Leon Wynter.
        p. cm.
    ISBN-13: 978-0-312-37252-1
    ISBN-10: 0-312-37252-3
    1. Rangel, Charles B. 2. United States. Congress. House—Biography.
3. Legislators—United States—Biography. 4. African American
legislators—Biography. 5. African Americans—Politics and government—
20th century. 6. Korean War, 1950–1953—Personal narratives, African
American. 7. United States—Politics and government—1945–1989.
8. United States—Politics and government—1989– 9. Harlem (New York,
N.Y.)—Biography. 10. New York (N.Y.)—Biography. I. Wynter, Leon E.
II. Title.

    E840.8.R36 A3 2007
    328.73092 B 22

                                                                    2006053094

                                                    First Edition: April 2007

                                        10   9   8   7   6   5   4   3   2   1

I dedicate this book to my beloved mother,
Blanche Mary Wharton Rangel,
and to my dear brother,
Ralph J. Rangel, Jr.

To Tom

John really loves

you

Charlie

Contents

Preface

November 13, 2006

At the time of this writing, I expect to be named chairman of the Ways and Means Committee of the U.S. House of Representatives—the only committee specifically mentioned at the drafting of the Constitution of the United States—when the 110th Congress begins in January 2007.

What has amazed me most about becoming chairman of Ways and Means is the deep pride my constituents have shown in my achievement, and the resounding cheers I've already received from so many Americans from every corner and walk of life in this great country. And that's all without them *really* knowing what the Ways and Means Committee actually *does*. People have been stopping their cars in the middle of the street and blocking traffic to hail me. I'm flattered, I'm honored, and I'm humbled by the confidence they seem to have in knowing that I will be playing an important role in shaping our domestic policy.

Day and night, wherever I go it's been "Welcome, Mr. Chairman." Walking through an airport, a woman came up, grabbed me, and planted a great big kiss on my cheek. I couldn't help but believe that I must have known her from somewhere and had forgotten who she was. But when I tried to recover, she looked me in the eye and said, "You son of a gun. You don't know me. I'm just so damn happy that you won!"

For decades I have hoped to gain the chairmanship before I retired from the Congress, but I had no idea how I would actually feel once I finally got the privilege, after thirty-six years of service. So no one is more surprised than me to find that I'm more elated about the opportunity awaiting the voters for giving Democrats the leadership of both houses of the Congress than I am about the fact that I will get the chairman's gavel placed in my hand. Today, even before all the campaign posters have come down, rather than celebrate in triumph I feel more inclined to make sure that we don't disappoint the people who trusted us with their votes. To be certain that we do not act to get even with the Republicans, but rather that we try to come together with them to get some things done for the common good.

I am prepared to share with my colleagues in the House and Senate and even the president of the United States our willingness to stop the hemorrhaging of taxpayer dollars to service our national debt. I am ready to invest more of our national treasure in education and job training to pull people out of poverty and prevent them from going to jail. To encourage youngsters to make careers instead of unwanted children. To fill the gap that exists between the public school system and a job opportunity. I am convinced that all of these things are not just social issues that Americans would be proud to support, but are in fact issues that, if they continue to fester, pose a real a threat to our national security.

No nation, no matter how wealthy, can survive if it not only ignores two million of its citizens who are in prison, but also remains indifferent to the *reasons why* they are incarcerated. I will be working with mayors from across the country and pulling together members of Congress from big cities to explain why there has been a spike in the possession and use of firearms and an increase in violent deaths, especially in the inner cities. I hope I can encourage Republicans and Democrats alike to take a look at the profiles of who is being shot and who is doing the killing. I will ask them: "Why is there a connection between high school dropouts, lack of job training, drug use, incarcerations, ineligibility for the military, HIV, and poverty? What are we doing wrong, and can we find a way to have people from the private sector come in and use their business-world experience to assist us in training these young people to break the cycle of ignorance, incarceration, poverty, and death?"

I want to lead Ways and Means toward the right package of business incentives to address these pressing questions. For decades, the Republicans have held up reliance on the private sector—and scorn for government action—as the highest guiding principle for the public good. The results of the 2006 midterm election have proven that the voters found more than a little hypocrisy, if not outright corruption, in how this principle played out in practice. But I will not let Democratic faith in the power of government to do good be an obstacle to forging public-private partnerships that make sense. I'm an old poker player from Harlem. For this hand, I will see the Republican faith in the private sector and raise the stakes to a wager that will cut more average Americans in on the winnings of globalization and a robust free market.

American business has learned how to go overseas and teach Indians and Bangladeshis to run call centers and even speak on the phone with American accents. It has developed the genius to make previously uncompetitive people some of the most competitive in the world. I have seen them do the same thing here at home in certain industries, but I don't see it enough. Take the hospitality industry. Las Vegas is growing so fast that it has had to learn to train all kinds of people to become cooks and such. The biggest problem, from my point of view, is that the jobs pay so darn well that the young workers don't want to go on to college. If they can do it in Las Vegas, why can't it be done right here in New York, where we've got hotels going up in Harlem?

So I ask you private sector entrepreneurs, as you begin lining up to get my attention with visions of tax breaks dancing in your eyes: Have you ever thought, "If I can go to India and Singapore and train people for the global economy, couldn't I train Americans, too, if they were drug free and had a greater government investment in their health and fitness for work behind them?"

When I ran for the Congress in 1970, we still looked to the greatness of Franklin Roosevelt's New Deal, and Lyndon Johnson's Great Society was still offering a great leap forward for many Americans left out of the benefits of the postwar prosperity. But I was not in office five minutes before the discrediting of that Democratic legacy of activist government began. In the Republican view, those issues of equity and economic justice were not supposed to be federal responsibilities. So under decades of partial or total Republican rule, Social Security, Medicaid, Medicare and government support for housing have slowly but surely been targeted for privatization or outright extinction.

I have no illusions about bringing back the Great Society. But I believe that in order for America to be strong we will need strong young people, and we need to start their education and training sooner. We have to be aware of globalization, and recognize that our toughest competitors' employees receive full health and education benefits as a matter of national policy. We can't afford the luxury of ignoring the needs of the poor in this country simply because helping would fall under the category of social improvement. The tragedy of Hurricane Katrina teaches us that a natural disaster can cause a loss of life just because people are poor. Certainly there would have been no difference if Katrina were a terrorist attack instead of a hurricane—the victims would have been just as dead, or just as homeless. Can anyone challenge the fact that if the victims of Katrina had been better educated and more affluent they also would have been better able to protect themselves against death and homelessness—and could have had the resources to flee from danger?

I understand that expectations for the new Democratic leadership are high, and I also know that meeting these expectations will not be easy. For the past twelve years it's been abundantly clear that the Republican leadership in the House never sought bipartisanship. They didn't really want to pass bills; they wanted to make political statements on which they could run for reelection rather than demonstrate that they had cooperated with Democrats on anything. Many Democrats, meanwhile, have dug themselves into trenches against the Republican siege, and occasionally gotten the taste of blood in their mouths as the battle raged. By my count, over half the members of the Ways and Means Committee have never had a real opportunity to work together across the aisle. Notwithstanding the voters' clear demand for cooperation, it seems to me there remains a profound lack of trust between Democrats and Republicans alike. There are still a lot of young Democratic members who want to get even, but I will continue to impress upon them the truth: Getting "even" means they will not be getting anything done. The Republicans no doubt have felt the sharp barbs from Democrats when we were in the minority—out of our frustration—and perhaps they have no real reason to believe us when we say bipartisanship is good for the Democratic party, good for the Congress, and good for the country. I personally hope the president will assist us in dispelling this distrust. It's the right thing to do, it's the patriotic thing to do—and I hope everyone will see that it's also the politically practical thing to do.

In this spirit, I am prepared to forget how we got *into* Iraq, if there are Republicans prepared to work with us on how we get *out of* Iraq. There is no one single "Democratic way" to resolve this conflict, but one thing is clear: There is no *military* way to victory. That said, Democrats now have a special responsibility to work with the administration to define what victory really is, not in terms of what the president has articulated, but what the American people are demanding. Democrats don't have the obligation to establish our course in the Middle East, but we do have the oversight responsibility to evaluate the president's course, and then to inform the people. In my opinion it is not just an issue of the United States and Israel being the victims of terrorism. We have to find a way to regain the confidence of our international friends and leaders, and we have to ask and demand that countries in the region assume more responsibility. Whether it's Egypt, Saudi Arabia, or Jordan, we need them to assist us in better understanding the cultures we're dealing with, not just for face saving or diplomacy behind the scenes but in open actions to bring stable, viable government to the area.

I was proud to be one of four people in our Democratic caucus to second the nomination of Nancy Pelosi for Speaker of the House. That day, I shared with the group how historic it was, not only that a woman was elected, but how twenty-three Hispanics and forty-three African Americans elected in the Democratic party have shattered the imagination of the framers of the Constitution, who ignored the rights of minorities and women in its drafting. And at the unveiling of the portrait of Congressman John Conyers, Jr.—who will become the first African American to chair the House Judiciary Committee—I was powerfully struck by how the framers, who considered African slaves as mere chattels, could never have imagined that one day the chairman of the very committee that *cradles* the Constitution would be a descendant of slaves. But, again, there is nothing to be gained by gloating. The mere fact that I'll be sitting in that chair with the gavel in my hand will be enough for most people to say that we did get even, or rather, that the voters got even for us. But the voters will also be watching, and wondering, "Okay, now that we've given you a chance to govern, what are you gonna do with these two years?"

For one thing, we're going to do whatever it takes to pass some positive legislation. Unlike the recent Republican leadership in our house, we Democrats *actually believe* in our legislation. I think that's one difference that all legislators can appreciate, regardless of policy. Recently on the floor of the House, I noticed three Republican members of my committee talking among themselves. Because of the way I caught their eyes, and their awkwardness when I caught them, I knew they were talking about me. They talked a bit more and then came over as a group. One of them said: "We're sorry we didn't win. Each of us wanted to come over and congratulate you, and to say how much we really look forward to working with you. We just want to let you know that we're Republicans, but we're looking forward to you bringing us together. But we didn't want to do it individually, because you might think we were sucking up!" I was deeply moved by this. But we still haven't been tested yet. We haven't had one meeting; I am not the chairman yet.

Recently I met with a group of twenty CEOs, who, now that I will be chairman, came down to Washington to find out "Who is Charlie Rangel, and what will it mean to me and my company?" Here's what I've told them: "Right now your companies get tax breaks for investing and creating jobs overseas. And as long as you keep your profits overseas, and reinvested in China or India or Mexico, you won't be taxed on them. But if you want to bring those profits home, and invest them here in the United States, *then* you have to pay the IRS. I think that's wrong." Today we are encouraging CEOs to drain capital and jobs from within our borders. I have told them I'd like to see them get benefits for reinvesting in the United States, but I will need them to support some things that they traditionally have not supported.

First of all, I would start where I always start: education. The CEOs would have me believe that education is a state and local concern. That's their party, their tradition, and so forth, but for the people they're competing against, education is a *national* responsibility. Compared to us, India and China are sending their kids to school for math and science in overwhelming numbers that pose a threat to our future as the world leader in technology.

Now consider health care. The head of General Motors once told me that the company spends more per car on workers' health insurance than on steel. But its competitors don't pay for worker health benefits. In the economies we're competing against, everyone comes in educated, and all the workers have health insurance.

The same pattern holds with what we call Social Security. The cost of private-sector retirement benefits have become crushing at the very same time our Republican legislators want to dismantle Social Security, the main supplement to private retirement benefits. So I ask CEOs: "If you knew there was a solid supplemental Social Security system—one that the workers could believe in—behind whatever retirement benefits you're offering, wouldn't that make your struggle with the costs of such benefits a little easier?"

Of course it would. Then I go to the hospital executives and say, "There are forty-three million Americans who don't have health insurance. Yet they go to your hospitals, get treated, and they don't pay. But the people who have insurance, they're paying, because you've got to make a profit. So you're charging your paying customers to carry those who can't pay. And every day the health insurance companies cut a little closer to your bone with onerous reimbursement rules and regulations to prevent you from passing these costs on to them. Why don't you help me get some kind of insurance for those people?"

So the way I can reach my agenda is by explaining to the CEOs that this philosophical and political wall between what Republicans insist the framers intended government to do and not to do, and what actually needs to be done to address these very real threats to our national security—this wall must come down. Globalization demands it, and it's the right thing to do. And, if the CEOs don't want to listen to me, let them listen to economists about the cost to American business of holding two million people in prison today. The taxes used to build and maintain prisons are part of every business's payroll. When a kid is in the street, and feels he has to shoot another kid—without health insurance—and he goes to intensive care, that's the most expensive health care there is. And if the victim is young enough, and is permanently disabled, the tab might be $2 million per kid. So much potential wasted, and all because we failed to engage the shooter in productive society in the first place.

Economists will explain that not only are the shooter and his victim not contributing to our economy, but they are a drain on it. None of this is new; the United Negro College Fund made "A mind is a terrible thing to waste" into a catchy slogan decades ago. Hillary Clinton helped popularize the African proverb that says "It takes a village to raise a child" back in the nineties. But we are long past the time to make the truth of these slogans a reality. Education, health care, and criminal justice are not under the direct jurisdiction of the Ways and Means Committee. But providing the tax incentives to encourage the corporate sector to get the job done is. That's where Chairman Charlie Rangel wants to go.

So the CEOs will be leaving my office knowing what I want to do. But that's not the same as knowing me. They will come away understanding that I'm a legislator, that I want to be successful and that I want to work with Republicans to get something done. They have begun to see that there's more to me, a traditional Democrat from the Tip O'Neill school, than "tax and spend." They will leave my office thinking: "This is a guy we can do business with." But believe me, so far this new corporate courtship is not an engagement. It's a good first date, with a promise to go steady. Passing the legislation, with their strong support—*that* will be the marriage.

To tell the truth, I really don't need the CEOs to know me. What I need is those jobs they're creating, and I need them here. When they're bringing in those profits, the shareholders are not going to ask them who Charlie Rangel is. It's my job to help them be successful, but it will be *their* responsibility to demonstrate not just the return to shareholders, but the benefit to the common good.

Take international trade, which is very much under the jurisdiction of Ways and Means. They say Democrats are against trade. I say that it's not that Democrats oppose trade. Our problem is in making a case for the benefits of trade, and we need your help, Mr. CEO, to do it. When a plant is closed, people are put out of work and there's a hole in the middle of somebody's congressional district, and they will make their anger known. But when trade creates jobs here, people don't run around saying, "I got my job through the Peruvian Free Trade Agreement." Why? Because, to the extent those jobs exist, or extra profits are made, they are spread out in geographically dispersed, white-collar industries like banking, insurance, and high technology. Worse, the gains from trade may be concentrated in fewer, wealthier hands. If you want more trade,

Mr. CEO, you've got to get these people out of the woodwork and talking to *their* representatives about trade. Because, as the money keeps pouring in on the top, and dispersing among Americans near the top of the ladder, I've got to deal with the representatives of people way down in the economic middle who are stuck in free trade–stricken communities across this country.

I hope those CEOs who really do want to know me are reading this book right now, right along with you, dear reader. I was born seventy-six years ago and raised in my grandfather's house, by the tough corner of 132nd Street and Lenox Avenue in the heart of Harlem. I still live less than a hundred yards from the house once owned by my namesake, the late Charlie B. Wharton. To know me, it's important to know that I have been in office for thirty-six years because of the support I've received from my constituents—my neighbors—and that my predecessor, the late, great Adam Clayton Powell, was in office for twenty-six years. He was the first congressman from Harlem and I am only the second. It should not go unnoticed that Adam, who by his seniority led the powerful House Education and Labor Committee to push through the historic legislation creating Lyndon Johnson's Great Society, was commonly referred to as "the Chairman." How pleased I am for the people of Harlem, East Harlem, and Washington Heights that I will be able to continue in that tradition as "Mr. Chairman."

Harlem is where I learned to play poker. Now, if you're playing poker with some of the boys on the block, or you're playing poker with international leaders, or you're playing poker with national CEOs, it's still the same game. When you're dealt a hand with the boys on the block, the ante is low, the betting is low, and the winnings are low. But when you're playing for big stakes, with that same hand, you still have to play by the same rules and logic.

The stakes today are huge. Where the pot may have been five bucks on Lenox Avenue, for a chairman of the Ways and Means Committee it is now trillions of dollars. The country has to find a strategy by which we can build the economy, raise revenues to run the government, and have programs that provide for the health and welfare of the people. And we only have fifty-two cards to do it with. It's the same game, and in the pages to come I invite you the reader—CEOs and block boys alike—to discover how I came to play it the way I do.

One thing I've learned is that you can't win by folding your hand and walking away from the table. I learned that a long time ago, and it's just one of many, many reasons why I haven't had a bad day since.

Introduction

Every day is a good day. People are going to see me sitting up in a nursing home one day. They're gonna say something like:

"Who's that guy?"

"You don't know him?"

"Nope."

"That's Rangel. He used to be a congressman; he was very important in Washington."

"Oh, yeah? But why does he have that damn silly smile on his face?"

"I really don't know. Some people say that he swore he'd milk every day of his life for everything it was worth, before time caught up with him."

And there I will be, just smiling and thinking to myself: "Sometimes the day gets rough, but I can't screw this one up, because it's the only day I've got."

Even if that guy doesn't remember the name of this book— . . . *And I Haven't Had a Bad Day Since*—I will still be grinning.

And it will still be working for me.

It's often been said that everyone has a story worth sharing with others. Some lessons from one life may inspire initiative in another. Other lessons may simply help people avoid making unnecessary, possibly tragic mistakes. My story is really no different from most people's, except that I did discover a way to always turn what could have been bad days into good days. It could be as horrific and life-transforming a day as the one I had at Kunu-ri, North Korea, on November 30, 1950. Or it could be any number of everyday setbacks that can become etched in the mind, causing devastating emotional harm if you refuse to release the pain and move on.

What's my story? I'm Charlie Rangel, only the second person to represent Harlem in the Congress of the United States, succeeding the legendary Adam Clayton Powell. The district was created in 1944, and Adam represented it for the first twenty-six years. I was sworn in in 1971, giving us combined service of sixty-two years. After thirty-six years in office, only three representatives have more seniority than me. I don't officially speak for the Democratic Party, but as a Democrat I certainly don't hesitate to allow my views to be heard.

Every chapter can (and often does) end with "And I haven't had a bad day since," because I came up from nothing, with almost nothing, on Lenox Avenue and 132nd Street. I was a fatherless high school dropout with a gift for living by my wits and hiding my inadequacies behind bravado. At age twenty-two I was pushing a hand truck in the gutters of New York's garment district for a living. I had missed the train to the expanding post–World War II American Dream, or rather, like so many African-Americans, the train had missed me. Yet somehow, by age thirty, I had acquired three degrees in six years, and was a newly minted lawyer admitted to the New York bar.

My story doesn't mean you can be a screwup your whole life and then expect to get a break and turn the whole thing around. As a role model, I can't tell kids to screw up, do everything they want, and everything is going to be all right. You can't depend on it happening— though it did happen with me. I want them to know they have to do everything I didn't do—get started early, set goals, have ambitions, stay out of trouble, and stay away from people who will get them in trouble. I have to say it, even if it makes people who really knew me when laugh out loud. But life is still about making choices. My story is about what can happen when you're blessed to get a second chance to make one of life's primary choices: to get an education.

At age seventy-six, I've outlasted almost all of my political generation, and I'm still a step ahead of the one that followed. I'm a witness to the old saying about the race not being to the swift or the battle to the strong: time and chance rule them all. After eluding me for all these years, the chairman's gavel of the Ways and Means Committee—the committee that writes our tax laws and approves our trade deals—will finally come into my hands as a result of the November 2006 midterm election.

I was elected to succeed the late great Adam Clayton Powell, not to be him, or to be a "black leader" in the model of any of the well-known African-American leaders. I'm a successful politician who more than happens to be black. Not that I have a problem with Jesse Jackson or Al Sharpton. It's just that, at the end of the day, I don't have to take as many barbs as they do. All I have to do is be the congressman from the capital of black America. I deal in the art of the possible, and represent the best of the American Dream on behalf of a community that's seen the worst of it. It's a job that lets me take my responsibilities a lot more seriously than I take myself.

I can make the case that life, at least for me, is really not that competitive. It's not that I'm so much better at it than everybody else. It's that when it comes down to a fight, I've usually got one less opponent than my opposite; I'm never struggling to overcome my own ego's sense of entitlement.

The idea behind "And I haven't had a bad day since" is that no matter what obstacles you come across in life, if you can pause and count your blessings, or recall difficulties that were far more serious, you can avoid the emotionally draining trap of viewing present circumstances as unbearable. The attitude of gratitude is a gift that truly keeps on giving. It affords me the opportunity to take a better, clearer look at the obstacle in front of me. You don't have to be in fear for your life, as I have been, to have your mind concentrated in this way, every day. You don't have to be in the frying pan to appreciate how much worse it would be in the fire.

Calling it liberal optimism would make me out to be more hopeful than I really am. Call me an emotionally healthy political animal. Hope, liberal or otherwise, is hard to find these days. As we've gone from an industrial to a postindustrial service society in a global economy, education is no longer something to which everyone can aspire. Health care is being parceled out, with one system for the very rich, a very different one for the poor, and a fast-shrinking middle ground for all those in between. War today has now taken away the face of the enemy. Instead of fighting another nation, or even an ideology, we're now spending blood and hemorrhaging treasure in mortal combat against a tactic: terrorism.

We face so many new challenges today. After eighteen years of Reagan Bush Bush, despite the eight-year respite of Clintonism, the American house that the New Deal built, the GI Bill renovated, and the Great Society extended to Americans regardless of race or class is nearly a ruin. Yet, as a politician of what Howard Dean called the Democratic wing of the Democratic Party, and a member of Congress, I simply can't afford to let Republicans give me a bad day.

I've had to negotiate on behalf of my constituents, and in many cases on behalf of my country, in areas of foreign policy and trade. I've never seen a situation where having the confidence of knowing that we have faced more serious obstacles and overcome them doesn't sustain me. I've seen enough to know personally that in every generation we have been confronted with tough problems. Knowledge, resources, management tools, and technologies are necessary but will not be sufficient to carry the coming days. I sincerely believe that one's attitude in facing the problem is just as important as one's ability to overcome it.

Going into a negotiation without an emotional agenda, knowing that at the end of the day you're not going to leave feeling hurt or overly elated that you succeeded, is like dealing yourself an ace or two in a poker game. To know that other people are usually bringing emotions concerning their own ambitions to the table is to know that their cards are always exposed.

In poker, sometimes you win when people merely *think* you have the best hand. Sometimes in life it's pretty much the same thing.

If there was one legacy I could leave, one thing I wanted to be remembered for, it would not be the Purple Heart or the Bronze Star I earned in Korea. It would not be the Empowerment Zones, the "bloody" Rangel Amendment, or other legislative and political accomplishments described in these pages. My legacy would be a deep and abiding belief that the investment we make in education yields the highest returns to our national security. An educated American has a better chance of having a job, and coming home not only with a paycheck, but perhaps, more importantly, with the dignity and pride of knowing they are somebody. They have access to health care, and resources to extend more productive, rewarding lifetimes. An educated American has too much to lose by gambling on crime or drug abuse.

When I got out of the army, every black professional I knew was a beneficiary of the GI Bill. My life shows that when America became just a little bit color blind—for a minute—for veterans, and tried to compensate them for their service with access to education, it worked no matter what the background of the veteran was. And if it worked for veterans, it has to work for all Americans. Education is the independent variable in my life experiment that separates me from the guys I grew up with on Lenox Avenue and 132nd Street; it's amazing how many of them didn't make it to the nineteen-eighties.

When I say I haven't had a bad day, it doesn't mean that I haven't had some heartbreaking experiences, few as they may be. I lost my brother—who was a father, a brother, a friend, and everything to me—in 1975. Somehow I managed to thank God for having a brother in the first place, because we always used to joke about people who never had a brother, or brothers who were so distant from each other. And when I lost my mom—and we were inseparable—all I could talk about was how few people had a mom as a buddy for ninety years. Setbacks I've had; bad days, no.

My mom used to say it was because I looked like her. She said sons who look like their mothers are blessed, and that I'll never have a problem in life. Thank you, Mom, for never teaching me the words *woe, woe, woe.* Instead, she never tired of saying "God is good" at times when our life was the roughest. For years, I never understood the connection she made between "God is good" and hardship. But as I got older, I found myself adopting her expressions as my own, and saying "God is good" during the hard times instead of cursing Him. As I became older still, I realized that if I thought about what I was saying, I'd have to ask myself: "Why is God good?" And the answer would be in how good God has been to me. The answer lies in how fortunate I am to just have whatever problem is before me, to be able to recognize it and try to address it, instead of saying "woe, woe, woe."

Without really getting religious about it, if it isn't that God is good, it's that I have been so darn lucky in avoiding the train wrecks of life. When there have been dramatic delays in reaching my goal, no one can say that I got so frustrated, or blinded by ambition, cynicism, or greed, that I lost sight of it. Those blinders come from a sense of entitlement that, like the love of a father, I grew up never knowing.

My daughter remembers so well how I proved to her that whenever we turned the pages of a family photo album together, the only time she would stop was when she saw a picture of herself. I've challenged her to take the album and test it on the whole family; it never fails. When negotiating in politics or in life, if you go in only looking for your picture, and you don't realize that the other party is only looking for theirs, more often than not you'll lose.

As far as I'm concerned, I don't have a picture. The album was handed to me, and I enjoy going through it. Having lost the tendency to look for myself the hard way, I spend my time focusing on the other person's picture, and I'm OK. Even if I do see my picture—and I knew it was in there—I can do better at the end of the day talking about somebody else's picture. It's so simple, and so amazing how this works.

And I haven't had a bad day since.

*. . . And I Haven't
Had a Bad Day Since*

1

My Beginnings
Family Roots Through Junior High School

My family hails from miscegenated roots in Accomac, the seat of Accomack County, Virginia, on the rural DelMarVa peninsula. If the peninsula is a stubby thumb of land sticking 180 miles straight down the coast, right below the point where the borders of Maryland, Delaware, and Pennsylvania meet, then Accomac is smack in the middle of its overgrown fingernail, the last 75 miles that encloses the mouth of the Chesapeake Bay. By the map, Accomac is just 180 miles from the U.S. Capitol, but by road, history, and economics, it's much closer to Richmond, the ex-capital of the Confederacy.

Then as now, the wealth of Accomack County comes from the land and the accumulated labor of African-Americans since slavery times. The tiny county raised 5 percent of all Virginia's chickens and grew almost half of Virginia's cash vegetable, corn, and melon crop in 1992. The 2000 census also said it was 32 percent black, 63 percent white, and just under one percent any kind of mixture. But everybody knows the numbers don't tell the real story.

Accomac, Virginia, was a very strange place. It had a lot of relationships that were a lot stronger than anything you could get by getting married or in court. They had a lot of respect for people who simply had children and took care of them, whether they were married or not. And, from slavery times, a lot of those children were fathered by white landowners on black women. I think that attitude made it easier for everyone to live together, separate and, of course, unequal, bound to the same isolated piece of land, without a great need to ask a whole lot of questions about who was what to whom.

In Accomac everybody was related to one another. My great-grandfather Frazer Wharton, who the pictures indicate I favor the most, had a white father. Frazer had his first child, my grandfather, by his first wife, Mary Dye, around 1893. Then he married another lady and had four-

1

teen children. I'm not sure how Frazer managed to get all this land in Accomac, but I assume it came from the white Wharton clan that gave him his name. Except for a couple of uncles of mine who later passed for white, I still don't know much about the white Whartons. I grew up assuming that my grandfather was a scion of a proud black landholding gentry. Oh, was my mother proud of being a Wharton, hot damn! "Blanche Mary Wharton Rangel," she'd reply when formally asked her name.

As a child, from the time I was seven to about age fifteen, the family would have me and my sister down there for the summers. They called it Whartonville, because the Whartons ran everything. I remember the farm people who would come into town and get drunk, and Frazer Wharton would get them out of jail. It was another world, the rural Deep South in the late depression years, or maybe two worlds away from Harlem. In Harlem, fruits and vegetables came to you, rolling by your house on a paved road, on a cart pushed by some European immigrant shouting in a foreign accent. In Accomac, you went down dirt roads to get your food from the land, with no whites of any kind in sight.

In Harlem there were corner bars and rent parties and dance halls for celebrating the end of the workweek, or to get away from having no work at all. In Accomac there were county fairs. Oh, those fairs! It was just like in the movies—think *Giant* with Liz Taylor and Rock Hudson, or, better still, the movie version of the musical *State Fair.* Except everything and everybody was black. Oh, the pies, the crabs, and the corn— all that food and entertainment and all the drinking! I'd go there with my granduncle George, who liked to squire his little nephew from the big city around town. He was really the bad boy of the whole clan. He ran a little social spot in town, a kind of cross between what we called a candy store in Harlem and a nightclub. And he drank a lot of liquor. He'd get drunk at the fair and then forget where he left me. You know, something about drinking and then misplacing your kids must run in my family, because years later my uncle Herbert would sometimes do the same thing to me up in New York.

In Accomac it seemed as if everyone but Uncle George worked the fields. When my sister and I were down there, everyone got up at five o'clock in the morning. If we wanted to eat with them, we had better be up early, too. Actually, they'd leave a cold ham on the table, maybe some fried apples in the frying pan. But then everyone hit the fields, and they worked hard. They took it very seriously, and they had us out there taking it seriously, too. I remember how we weren't supposed to eat any of the strawberries we were picking. They'd get angry with you if you were talking or fooling around, and they'd raise hell. Of course, once the day was over, and we'd come back in out of that sun, they'd love us to death. But when they were working, they didn't give a damn where you were visiting from; if you were there and you were eating, you worked hard in the fields.

If only for that reason, I made sure I spent my time hanging with Uncle George.

Uncle George used to visit a lot of people at night, and leave me in the car. One time I ran the damn car into a tree while I was waiting. But he was so bad, he just said, "Forget about it." He didn't give a care about nothing. Uncle George! He had this place—I guess you'd call it a road-house—that served hot dogs and beer but no hard liquor. They had music going, and people would come, buy their cigarettes and soft drinks, and socialize. I don't recall thinking much about it at the time, but it must have felt a whole lot like the action on a Harlem street corner, and that was damn sure more my speed than picking produce.

And Uncle George thought my coming from Harlem made me something special, gave me what we now call street smarts. And then I caught some guys stealing money from him one time, and that did it. He fired the guys, and bragged about how it took a kid from Harlem to get these thieving sons of bitches out of his business.

So these are my grandfather's roots, but he didn't like the farm life that Accomac offered him. His name was Charlie Wharton, and I guess he could have stayed and staked a claim to some of that land. But one day when he was sixteen, he reached down, picked up a good handful of that dirt, and let it crumble through his hand. Then he looked up at his father and said he didn't want any part of it. That's the story he told me about getting out of Accomac, over and over through the decades. He basically went a couple hundred miles up the coast, to Atlantic City, New Jersey, and found work as a waiter. Later on he met this pretty gal, Frances, my grandmother, whom I never knew. She was from Savannah, Georgia. He brought her to New York, and had two children—my mother and her older brother, Herbert. They were living someplace in Hell's Kitchen, because that's where the blacks were at that time, before they started moving up, and uptown. My uncle was born in 1902, my mother in 1904. When my mother was two years old my grandmother died giving birth to a third child, who didn't survive. About 1923 my grandfather left Hell's Kitchen and moved to 132nd Street, where he bought a brownstone.

Now, for the longest time he would have me believe that he didn't have access to any money to afford to buy that house, but his father, Frazer, came up to New York and signed a note for him. My grandfather put a down payment on the house, and he had to pay off that note.

These are stories my grandfather told me in the kitchen, when he'd be drinking. Often, from down in his cups, he would go on about all he had done for my mother and my uncle Herbert, and how neither one of them appreciated it.

My grandfather would never learn how to use the word *love*. Ever. But he did talk a lot about how he had to fight the authorities to keep his kids. Apparently the child welfare officials of the day were always trying to take my mother and Uncle Herbert from him because he wasn't married. Years later he would tell me stories about all the girlfriends he kept around the house when my mother and uncle were children. He'd go on about how they all had boyfriends, and he knew it. But he tolerated them, because all he cared about was having someone around to take care of those kids. Hell, he wasn't even around half the time, because he was out trying to make ends meet for them. To hear him tell it, the gals thought they were working him over, and he thought he was working them over. They may have thought they were cheating on him. But all he was concerned about was maintaining a minimum acceptable domestic environment for his children's sake. He wasn't looking for love; he was looking for someone to be there for those kids so he could go out and work.

Somewhere along the line he met this lady, Miss Indie, we called her. I don't remember where she was from, but she was the force that straightened him out. He married her, and she really structured his life. She got him to take a civil service examination, which at the time involved picking up dumbbells, to qualify for an elevator operator job. She also got him to join a political club, and then to go for the job running an elevator in the Criminal Court building downtown. He put in about thirty-five years on that job before he retired. In fact, it was trying to help him keep that job just a little longer that caused me to take my very first step into politics.

When he turned sixty-five, and they were trying to force him to retire, I had to go hat in hand to the neighborhood Democratic political club to plead for an extension. What happened was that I had signed a petition supporting an insurgent candidate for party office, someone who was not part of the regular organization. I didn't know what the hell I was signing. I was in law school, and I had not a clue about how clubhouse and Democratic machine politics worked. But they made a big deal out of it. It just happened that insurgents were the only guys who came by the house, always bearing petitions and asking us to sign. So I had signed. But the local captain made it abundantly clear that he had checked the names on that petition, and it looked like I was an upstart who was going against the regular organization. Nowadays, in most places in New York, it seems like nobody knows who is who, much less who signed what, at the precinct level of politics. But back then, in Harlem, precinct- and club-level politics were like church-congregation or family-clan politics—no disloyalties went unnoticed or unrecorded, and people had memories like elephants. Even I remember it like yesterday. It was then called the New Era Democratic Club, and a few years later I'd make my first mark in politics by going up against its leader, Lloyd Dickens.

My grandfather had actually signed the right petition, because he knew the precinct captain. And so he was right pissed at me for making waves that might sink his civil service job early—for no good reason. They would not give it to him until I came to the club—contrite—and asked forgiveness for my transgression. But it didn't stop there. They actually made me go to the Democratic leader of New York County, Carmine DeSapio, for the extension. They sent me to a guy who had something to say about making presidents of the United States, just to let one old black man in Harlem keep running an elevator for a few more years!

The whole thing really teed me off, until I saw how petty it all was. That's just how disciplined they were back then, because for generations they maintained power over people down to the smallest detail—even a menial job—by counting every vote. It wasn't entirely about me at all. But there is also no question that once I showed up, going to law school and all, and voting in their precincts, they felt they needed to send me a message: "We've got our eye on you, son." They knew I was going someplace. I got that extension, and later, for years after I became friends with Carmine, I had something to tease him about. I also had my first taste of how dealing with powerful people gets things done, and might make you powerful, too.

———

Miss Indie opened up a little bakery-restaurant on Lenox Avenue. I never knew her well, but I understand that she was an entrepreneur. Ironically, after all those years of Grandfather keeping girlfriends as nannies for his kids, Miss Indie didn't really get along all that well with my mother or Uncle Herbert. Family history has it that Uncle Herbert once threw a brick through her store window, because he was mad about something or other. Uncle Herbert must have had a chip of some kind on his shoulder from puberty on. He ran away from home at least once as a teenager, and had a reputation as a street fighter. He joined the army at fifteen, and soon went up to Peekskill, New York, where he was trained. He served in the legendary 369th Infantry Regiment, the "Harlem Hellfighters," though he did not get to go overseas. Grandfather eventually convinced him to settle down and get a civil service job. They ended up working one block from each other, Uncle Herbert running an elevator in the New York State court building at 80 Worth Street, and my grandfather at the New York City Criminal Court building at 100 Centre Street. Uncle Herbert was married to one woman, my aunt Mariah—and had that elevator job and drank hard on the weekends—until the day he died. He had a bad relationship with his father, but in some ways he ended up doing the exact same thing with his life.

My mother met my father in that brownstone on 132nd Street, where she lived with her father and stepmother. My father was working in the building as a handyman; she was fifteen or sixteen years old. She ran off with him and got married, though she was forced from time to time to return with me to the house she was raised in. My grandfather never, ever forgave her for that. While Uncle Herbert waged an open war for independence from grandfather's control, my mother went back and forth between cowering under her father's intimidation and slipping away on her own. It's hard to say who won most of the time, but I know who was always in the middle of their fight: me.

My mother would buckle under a tongue-lashing from him, calling him "Father" and pleading with him. He'd cuss her out, and then I'd jump in and say "Don't you talk that way to my mother." She'd say, "Charlie, that's my father, you shut up." Grandfather would just laugh, because he just liked to piss me off. "I'll slap you to the floorboards, Blanche. I'll slap you to the floor," he'd go on. "No, you're not," I'd say, and run over to her, as he would be backing her down, jabbing his fist at her. "Oh, Father, please don't," she'd cry. But all it was was him showing me that he was in charge. He never hit her; he didn't have to to make his points. In fact, most of the time *I* was the one who got my behind whipped—by my mother, for interfering.

Grandfather was content to simply scare the hell out of her, yelling and balling up his fist at her. He was short and my mother was short—he would have so much fun just intimidating her. And I would really go at him. I know he didn't dislike me for doing that, but it created an atmosphere of unpleasantness. Grandfather was forever giving me chores to do—clean the steps, sweep the street, march up to the Bronx over the Madison Avenue bridge to buy day-old bread, go downstairs to get coal for the fire, gather horse manure from the street for his backyard garden. On reflection, the fact that he would raise hell with me showed that he really cared. It just wasn't in him to say it or act like it. Like I said, he was not on speaking terms with the word *love*. It was the language of intrafamily power and control that my grandfather spoke, as much as a man like my grandfather could actually have power and control in his life.

My beloved brother, Ralph, who died in 1975, was the oldest of my mother's three children. I came seven years after, on June 11, 1930, and my sister, Frances, three years later, in September 1933. Shortly after Ralph was born, my grandfather kidnapped him, after a fashion, and, along with Miss Indie, took him to Canada. I don't know a lot about it, except what my mother would tell me. Grandfather wanted to keep Ralph away from our father; in his mind, taking him to Canada at birth was somehow providing a safe, albeit temporary, haven. Grandfather was also determined to show her that she'd made a mistake, running off like that with my father so young, and then turning up with a baby at age nineteen. And my mother was just too weak to resist him.

It was no more than a visit to Canada, probably to see some relatives for a few days, but it was vintage Grandfather sending a message. You know how grandparents are. They love their newborn grandbabies to death, and they just *know* they would do a better job raising them than their own children will. My mother may have given birth, but mother or not, a grandfather's daughter will always be his child. He looks at her with that newborn in the bed and what does he see? His baby holding another baby.

When my daughter Alicia gave birth to her son, my grandson, in 2002, and I visited her in the hospital, she caught me staring down at her as though my mind was somewhere in the clouds. I had this great big smile on my face.

"Why are you smiling like that?" she asked. I said that I was thinking about how I used to grill my mother about Ralph's "kidnapping."

"How could you possibly allow your father to take your firstborn, just take him like that?" I used to ask her. "Didn't you fight? Didn't you scream? Didn't you yell? And what kind of guy was he to believe he could just take your child?"

Now my daughter looks at me, concerned.

"Well, why are you thinking about that here?" she asked.

"Because I'm thinking about taking your child right now!"

And, boy, did we laugh. I didn't snatch the child. But I could see for the first time what Grandfather was thinking. You just can't help feeling that a child is too important a thing to leave in the hands of a young mother. Especially, as in my grandfather's view, when you don't think the mother has too much on the ball. Of course, I'd never think that of my beloved Alicia, but there are those parents who do. It just took me until age seventy-two to understand them.

My mother must have done some amount of growing up in the seven years between having Ralph and having me. One thing is for sure, nobody was taking me away from her, though she did kind of ship me off to live with Uncle Herbert for a couple of years. Mom used to make it clear to me that whatever happened, she was stuck with me. Not that I was stuck with her, but she with me. We were always based in Grandfather's brownstone at 74 West 132nd Street—we called it "Buckingham Palace" like the one in England, or just "Seventy-four." By the time I came along I think she'd gotten enough legs under her to skip out of there on a regular basis to do her things, working or whatever. And when my mother would leave, maybe get a new boyfriend or something, I was the one who would always be with her. We looked alike, unlike my brother or my sister. She'd joke about it, in terms of how I was always around her apron strings.

My father was absolutely no good, but my mother loved him. In my earliest memory of him, and of being stuck to her, I must have been about five or six years old. My father was hitting my mother on the steps of some apartment-type building. I went and got a broom to hit my father. He started laughing at me and then just walked away. I guess I've hated him ever since. When he died, my sister asked me if I was going to the funeral. She said she wouldn't go unless I went. I really didn't want to, but because my mother still loved him, I agreed. My brother got along with my father a lot better, for some reason, but I never did. I belonged to my grandfather's home, to "Seventy-four," not my father's. I lived there all the time, except when my mother would leave the house and take me with her.

One thing is clear: My grandfather jumped right over me in terms of falling in love with my mother's kids. He fell in love with my sister, Frances, and he raised her. And he cared about my brother, Ralph. But I really couldn't get along with that Wharton clan, though it was the only family I had. I think a lot of it had to do with the fact that I was so tied to my mother, and she was so often going in and out of Seventy-four for the sake of love or a job—she often lived upstate while working as a maid in a Catskills resort hotel. I think each time she fell from grace, I had to fall right along with her, in some people's eyes if not my own.

But then again, I truly didn't get along with a lot of people when I was a kid. I remember so clearly visiting my uncle John, my grandfather's brother, who drove trucks for the U.S. Postal Service. He had his home in Long Island—Jamaica, Long Island. That's Queens, of course, but back then people still thought it was the same as Nassau or Suffolk County, the suburbs. He was the big shot in the family, with this big house, and when we kids would be visiting, they'd ask Ralph to dance or some such thing. And they'd give him a dime for dancing, and they'd point to me and say, "Well, he ain't gonna do nothing." And I wouldn't, either; I never got the dime. I just knew I wasn't getting that dime.

I guess they would say I had a mean streak in me. Once, I remember making Uncle John turn his car around on the Triboro Bridge—you could do that in those days—because I wanted to go home. He had to do it, 'cause I was raising so much hell, and I don't think he ever forgave me for it. I have to think that would be my attitude, too. If I were taking my daughter's kid somewhere and he raised so much hell I had to turn around, I'd be pissed for a good long time. So I can understand why I was not well liked. What I don't understand is if it was just that I was disliked and was responding to it, or whether I was responsible for being disliked. That's why I'm very tolerant of children today, even little bastards of children.

Everyone, of course, wants to be liked. But I think even then I figured that if I wasn't going to be well liked, I would be respected, or at least have my desires respected. The exception to this that stands out in my mind was a time I wasn't tied to my mother's coming and going for a couple of years. She was working upstate in a hotel as a maid, doing what they called "day's work," where she got paid by the day, some kind of contractual thing. All I know is that she decided not to take me for a change. She cut a deal with Uncle Herbert for me to live with him and his wife in the Bronx for two years. That had to be the roughest two years of my goddamn life. But I had big fun.

Poor Uncle Herbert. He didn't drink anything during the day, or at night for that matter, but there wasn't a weekend that he didn't get drunk. He was married to a very nice lady, Aunt Mariah. For the life of me, I don't know how she tolerated that guy. Damn, he was nice during the week, but he was rough on the weekends—definitely a Jekyll and Hyde situation. If it were today, Social Services would instantly intervene in the case of a kid caught up with an uncle who would get drunk and wash his own face with powdered chlorine bleach. He'd whip my ass on the weekends just to be whipping my ass. But he was always so ashamed of himself on Monday when Aunt Mariah told him what he had done.

Nobody got away from Uncle Herbert on the weekends. Nobody. He'd get drunk and go visit all his relatives. He'd go and embarrass everybody—I mean *everybody!* He'd get out to Uncle John's in Long Island. Uncle John used to make this homemade wine, and they'd caution Uncle Herbert, "Now, don't drink too much, Herbert." Shoot, Herbert had his own bottle on him. Nobody could figure out how Herbert got drunk so quickly, but I knew; Herbert carried his liquor with him.

The good news about living at Uncle Herbert's was going to school in the Bronx. He lived at 1478 Brook Avenue, in what we now think of as the poor black and Hispanic South Bronx. But back then it was an almost entirely white, working- to middle-class neighborhood. I don't remember ever having a black friend there. Everybody on the block knew us, and I guess we must have fit in. In those days people didn't always have telephones, so you'd give people the number of your closest candy store. The phone would ring and they'd shout the message up at your building: "Hey, Mr. Wharton, telephone call for ya nephew Chahlee—it's his motha!"

I did pretty well in school there. Later, when I returned to P.S. 89 and Junior High School 139 in Harlem, I had enough going for me, in terms of confidence and good work habits, that studying was really no big deal. I really didn't appreciate it at the time, but that Bronx sojourn left me with some things that would work for me for the rest of my life. Among them, I have to assume, is what some people call my trademark New York accent.

Honestly, I never notice it. I was really amazed when I first went to Congress, and served on the Judiciary Committee, that they referred to me as the guy with the New York accent. Because I had no idea what a New York accent was. To me, it was just me. It was a Jewish neighborhood, and a predominantly Jewish school. I remember, after I got back to Harlem, the kids would just laugh and laugh at me for the way I talked. They'd say I talked like a white boy, a Jewish white boy. And I had no idea how I was talking. But it would be clear, from what older people would say, that I had picked up all of their accents, and all of their mannerisms, in what would have been my formative years, maybe age seven or eight or nine.

I'm convinced that my stay with Uncle Herbert, from an academic point of view, had to be a big plus. Aunt Mariah *always* made me do my homework. Before I got to that street, I had to get my work done. Now, when I did hit the street, apparently I was running with a pack of white boys. To hear Uncle Herbert tell it, I was leading a little gang of Jewish kids called the Black Pirates. He would laugh and say, "He's in charge of some white boys called the Black Pirates, can you imagine? This black kid, in charge?"

Uncle Herbert later said that back then I didn't know black from white. Maybe I didn't, but he damn sure did. Uncle Herbert was quite the black nationalist and Pan-Africanist in his day. He would take me with him when he was doing the bars in Harlem on Saturdays. He'd take me in the bar with him, they'd tell him I couldn't stay, so he'd put me outside to wait for him. Shoot, that bastard once went on about his business and forgot he had left me out there. As an adult, I used to rib him, and say, "Uncle Herbert, how could you do that to me?" And he would just laugh.

He was a rebel—he'd be out there with those people on 125th Street and Seventh Avenue in the 1940s, where people would show up for political speeches, the old Garveyites and, later on, the Black Muslims. Some of the things he did! He would go and put all this thick grease into his hair, then go to a white barbershop and raise hell because they couldn't cut it. There was no way in hell they *could* cut it, mind you, because it was harder than lard. He would go down to Atlantic City, and order glasses of beer. Back then these places would break the glass after he drank from it, because he was black. So he'd go down there just to see how many glasses he could get them to break out of spite. He was a big supporter of Haile Selassie and Ethiopia against Mussolini and the Italians in the run-up to World War II, always bragging on how Selassie fought back against Italians—then a force in Harlem—in Africa.

And yet he was living in this white neighborhood in the Bronx. He damn sure didn't socialize with any of them. He didn't have a white friend. Of course, I don't remember him having any black friends either. All Uncle Herbert needed in life was Aunt Mariah, a job, and picking up those jugs on Friday. During the week, though, he was "Mr. Personality" down there in the New York State Court building. I used to go down there and hear him call out to whoever was the attorney general, welcoming him into the first car in the bank—his privilege as the senior elevator operator—"Hey, General," he'd shout. He'd laugh at me, hanging out with those white kids around Brook Avenue in the Bronx. But I was getting good grades, and he was thankful that his wife was doing such a good job guiding me. One sure thing in my life back then was that I *knew* Aunt Mariah loved me. And boy, oh boy, could that woman cook!

Uncle Herbert used to tell my mother that he wasn't gonna give me back. Jesus, did I hope he was joking. Of course he was, and when my mother did take me back she moved me to a place on 137th Street that was more or less my home until I joined the army. I don't think there's a lot to be gained talking about the rough life with my mother and her boyfriends during that time. Suffice it to say that I knew when I was sixteen years old that it just wasn't working. Even though I was getting pretty good grades in DeWitt Clinton High School, I was torn between life tied to my mother and being on my own. I guess all teenagers go through it, but I knew I really had to get out.

My brother knew he had to get out of that mess, too. I loved my brother so much; I still do. His way out was the army. In 1941, probably in the summer, definitely before Pearl Harbor, he volunteered. We'd write each other all the time, and he sent my mother an allotment from his pay. When he came home in 1945 I was fifteen, and we started hanging out, big time. I have so many photographs of us together with "his gang," and "my gang," and "our gang."

What I do want to say about life after Uncle Herbert and the Bronx is that I tore it up at P.S. 89 in Harlem. Because Harlem was still such a mecca at that time, every successful black who grew up there went to P.S. 89. Put another way, if you were in Harlem it was also the only place to go. So we had commissioners, doctors, judges, and the like, everyone who survived Harlem and went on to Columbia and places like that started off in P.S. 89.

As I said, something about going to that school with all those white kids, and holding my own, instilled a lot of confidence in me. Maybe too much for my own good, as I would learn in a hard lesson about arrogance after I got out of the army. But for the rest of grade school I was bright as hell, and mischievous. I was taking a lot of stuff from other kids about the Bronx mannerisms I'd picked up, but one teacher at P.S. 89, Nettie Messenger, fell absolutely in love with me—and my intonation.

It probably wasn't love at first sight. She was a substitute teacher, and we prided ourselves on finding ways to send them packing, in tears. She left her purse on the desk, so we took it—not to take anything in it but to give her a hard time. But after I returned it without taking anything, she acted like nothing happened and stuck it out. Once, after she became permanent, she caught me drawing dirty pictures—I had a little talent for art back then—in a kind of booklet made from notepaper stapled in the corner. She grabbed it from me, and said I should be ashamed, but she didn't tear it up. Later, at the ice cream parlor where we went for milk shakes and such and the teachers ate lunch, I caught her sharing my book of nasty pictures with her friends.

As a young teacher she just assumed we were disorderly kids, and we were. Before I left her class, she got me to use my talent to draw a whole set of transparencies on the history of flight—from Daedalus and Icarus to the Wright Brothers. She used them to teach that unit until she retired. We kept in touch (years later we even laughed when I told her I knew what she did with my dirty pictures) and became close friends for the rest of her life. When I was in the army we exchanged letters, and when I went back to school in the fifties she was so proud of me. On one of her postretirement visits to my home in Washington she returned those transparencies to me. I went to her funeral in Los Angeles in 1994.

———————

I always had a job. I had been working since I was eight or nine or ten years old. I don't know if my grandfather made me do it or not, but I know I didn't mind doing it. One of the first jobs I ever had was at the Model Drug Store, on the corner of 133rd and Lenox Avenue. It was a big deal, and I was a little big shot for having that job. My arrogance was in full effect. Then one day I tried to ring up a sale and got the register tape all screwed up. My grandfather was so embarrassed he cursed me out.

The Model was one of those luncheonette and pharmacy combinations that were popular in the day, with a lunch counter with stools and such on one side, pharmacy and drugstore items on the other side, and a storage room behind that. I swore I ran it all. I was so damned good, or so I thought, that whatever came up with customers, for either side of the store, I just assumed I could handle it and jumped right up. Most of the time the pharmacist who owned the store—everybody called him Doc—would just sit on a stool, killing time at the counter, and let me run the show.

Once this pretty lady comes in. Doc is sitting on a stool at the soda fountain, flirting with some gal. I'm behind the pharmacy counter, and the lady asks for some sanitary napkins.

"Uhhh, we don't carry that," I said.

"Yes, you do," she said, "they're all ready, wrapped in boxes in the back."

So I yell to Doc, at the counter, "Hey, do we have any clean napkins, this lady says she needs some . . ."

See, I hear "sanitary" and I thought she meant napkins that were clean. I just assumed she was in the wrong place—you bought napkins in a grocery store. Women just didn't talk openly about such things in those days. In fact, the boxes were all prewrapped in plain paper—you never even saw pictures of the product. People forget, but back then, and to this day, black folks are very conservative in some ways. We're always hearing this garbage about moral values, and how Democrats and urbanites don't have them, but most parties to this debate have no idea how conservative black folks are. I think it has more to do with being from the South, especially back then, than being black. When I was in the army I remember so many Southerners complaining about constipation problems, because they just couldn't bring themselves to squat alongside other men on the rows of open toilets in the latrines. Some of them would wait until the middle of the night to catch a shower alone, rather than be naked in a group. Meanwhile, they insisted that New Yorkers were some kind of perverts regarding body functions and sex practices, accusing us of actually letting women put their tongues in our mouths. I remember this one guy from Georgia whose mantra was "I wouldn't suck nobody's titty but my mama's."

But I had already seen it all, starting at the Model Drug Store. Talk about body fluids! We used to bleed people, with leeches! Oh, did I love doing that. Somebody comes in with a black eye and we'd bleed them, for a quarter. We had a big jar full of leeches. You reach in, take out the leech, "OK, now put your head a little closer," bingo! I'd watch that leech suck up that bad blood, puff, puff, puff up, and then fall down. They let me do everything. I'd make up the castor oil bottles, breaking it down from the five-gallon cans and putting it into little bottles with the Model Drug Store label on them and the dosage. If you needed a dose on the spot, then I'd go over to the other side and tell "The Greek"—that's what we called the man running the lunch counter side—to give you a milk shake. I'd spike it with a little castor oil, clean up the bottle, and make an extra quarter on the deal.

All the people running the drugstore were white, but there were so many black folks—real characters—involved when I first started hustling to make a little money. I was a paperboy for a newspaper that Adam Clayton Powell was putting out. You'd go to his headquarters at Abyssinian Baptist Church, buy the newspapers, and then sell them, at a terrific markup. When I started, I remember Mr. Newbie, the West Indian tailor, telling me, in his thick accent: "Baye, ya can't sell newspapers unless ya have a newspaper bag, ya got ta have a bag, baye." He made me go home and get some old clothes for him to stitch up into a right sharp sack for serving newspapers. I'd go back to the Bronx, in the area where I used to live, and sell the papers.

One of Adam Powell's guys—I think it was Acy Lennon—ran the newspaper. We sold them on consignment, and I remember one day it was raining, and I hadn't sold many, and he wouldn't give me my money back. He was a big guy, one of Adam's longtime right-hand henchmen. I had to go get my grandfather—all five-foot-something of him—to get me back my damn money. I also sold the old *New York Post* up there, going door to door and in and out of the candy stores. I don't remember making any money, but I did win a bicycle. Grandfather had no fear of the powers that had been in Harlem. He wasn't a man of means, but he did have that brownstone, and that family name—Wharton—and underneath all his common workingman front he was so damn proud of it. He would never admit it, but he was effectively cut off from the family wealth in Accomac, such as it was.

The wealth was primarily in agricultural property, but when his father, Frazer, died, Grandfather didn't inherit. He was the oldest of the fifteen kids, remember, and he had a different mother than the rest of them. It wasn't so much that the gang didn't accept him as it was that he had left them so early on and come to New York. Half of his half-brothers stayed on the farm, and half of them got the hell out of Accomac and went on to do pretty well for themselves. Clifton Wharton Sr., whose father got all the way to Boston, was a big State Department guy as far back as the forties. He became the first "Negro" ambassador to represent the United States of America. His son, Clifton Jr., was a deputy secretary of state under Bill Clinton, and ran TIAA-CREF, one of the largest retirement fund companies in the world, for many years before that. Cliff Jr. lived across the street from us, in the newly built, fashionable Lenox Terrace Apartments, in the fifties and sixties. But his grandfather, a cousin and good buddy to my grandfather, was uneducated, from right off the farm.

To tell the truth, my great-grandfather Frazer Wharton was a wealthy man, a truly bad dude, running all those county fairs I remember from childhood. But with all those kids, who were never able to consolidate and leverage the value of that land, it didn't amount to much after he died. Still, my grandfather never felt dispossessed of the family glory, probably because, uneducated elevator operator that he was, he always had an important place in the family geometry, the point where all the lines, lighter-skinned and darker, richer and poorer, professional and menial, often met.

My grandfather had three sets of clothes: the clothes he felt comfortable in, his overalls; his uniform as an elevator operator; and when he got sharp, the clothes from the attic that made him look like Beau Brummell. But most of the time he wore his overalls. I remember him in those overalls when his cousin Cliff Wharton Sr., the State Department big shot, would sometimes show up in this big black Cadillac limousine. Whenever I saw that thing pull up, I just knew I was getting a dollar, which was like a hundred dollars in those days. The movie house on the corner where we lived only cost eleven cents. A whole dollar! I just knew this guy was rich. He and Grandfather would go into the kitchen, overalls and ambassador suit, close the door, and just talk and talk. And every time he left, and that Caddy pulled away, the boys would say "Hey, Charlie, who died?" Because that's all a black Cadillac meant to them—a funeral.

———————

Whenever somebody actually did die, or the Wharton clan had some other reason to gather in New York, they stayed at "Seventy-four." Grandfather was the grand host: sending out for food, like rotisserie chicken from the place on "36th" Street—that's 136th Street if you're not from Harlem—or the place on Seventh Avenue for fried oysters. As with all families, funerals put all the eternal family lore, and all the outstanding family grievances, onto the living room couch and back against the kitchen sink for debate. And in my family that debate was lubricated by alcohol. One thing you could depend on at a Wharton clan gathering: There was gonna be liquor and there was gonna be an argument. Usually, the argument was about who Grandpa Frazer loved the most. But sometimes it was about which Wharton kin they knew, or at least suspected, were passing for white.

One time they all came up to New York because one of their relatives was dying, and they wanted to see him. They sent my overall-wearing grandfather to the hospital to see a pharmacist cousin, who was passing for white. Grandfather was about the only one in the family who even kept up with this man. He would visit with him like he was some old colored hand, and they would talk. So now that he was dying, the family asked Grandfather to let him know that the family had come up from Accomac because they heard he was sick as hell. I was in the living room when Grandfather came back and told them that the cousin apologized and said he really wished he had lived his life differently. He asked Grandfather to tell them he appreciated their coming, but the whole thing was too much to explain; they should just go on back to Accomac. Poor bastard was buried and they couldn't even go to the funeral. But my grandfather could, and did, in the role of the "colored fellow" who always used to come up to see him. The colored fellow who knew the family.

Boy, did Grandfather dress up sharp for those funerals.

Passing Whartons, some verified, some merely suspected, were just another part of the family lore. They'd tell the stories, and point the fingers, but there wasn't really any tension—the whites were the whites and that was that. There was a John Wharton who became the superintendent of this big post office in Manhattan, the same post office that my uncle John who lived in Queens worked out of. Uncle John drove a U.S.

Postal Service truck, a very prestigious job for a Negro in those days. But because he was so fair-skinned, his black co-workers would tease him that he looked just like the white superintendent, who just happened to have the same name. "John, that must be your brother," they would tease. Of course, as it turned out, they were in fact distantly related, but Uncle John couldn't ever let them know!

I think my grandfather, as the oldest of Frazer's kids, saw himself as a kind of reality check on the far-flung, sometimes alienated reaches of the Wharton empire. One summer, when I was in law school, he insisted that I accompany his brother Roscoe, and Roscoe's girlfriend, on his annual vacation pilgrimage by car from Baltimore to Martha's Vineyard. Uncle Roscoe was a dark-skinned, untrained elevator operator in Baltimore, who was somewhat cut off from a bunch of well-educated Whartons who were big-time teachers and administrators in the public schools there. Every year he'd haul out this old Cadillac that he kept shined up, and take his time getting up to Martha's Vineyard, stopping at every relative's house along the way and spending the night. That was his vacation.

"Grandfather," I complained, "this is stupid. Why are you asking me to do this? I got homework to do, I got a job. . . ."

"Goddamn it," he came back at me, "can't you do any goddamn thing I ask you? Listen, there are those goddamn people down there in the family passing for white. They don't even talk to my brother. But damn it, they don't mind black folks if they're going to school. One of 'em is even married to a black guy, a goddamn professor down there."

"What the hell does that have to do with me?"

"Well, goddamn, you're black, and you're going to law school," he says, putting his foot down.

Being in law school made me the perfect calling card to ride shotgun with Roscoe, who, of course, was really standing in for Grandfather. For Grandfather's part, he was standing up for his brother and sending a message: We were black, and he and Roscoe were uneducated elevator operators, but I was about to become a professional, a somebody. Boy, was I in for a ride!

So Roscoe's going to show me off to his white and near-white relatives—who don't talk to his elevator-driving ass—all the way to Martha's Vineyard, starting from New York, where he picked me up. We get to Boston about two o'clock in the morning, and he insists on going to see his brother Sam. So I'm in the car with his girlfriend, Kitty. We wait fifteen minutes, twenty minutes—forty minutes go by. She says go upstairs and get your uncle, but I don't even know where the hell he went. Suddenly he comes storming out, yelling, "That no good, rotten son of a bitch . . ." We ask "What is it?" and he tells us to mind our goddamn business. "Let's go to Cousin Marie's," he insists, and his jaws are tight the whole way. We get to Marie's, who had a brownstone similar to my grandfather's, and she sweetly settles us in for the night. Then, at six or seven o'clock in the morning, there's this big fight in the kitchen. I hear it, and I say, "Kitty, Kitty, what the hell is going on?" Kitty said Roscoe was downstairs fighting with his brother Sam. Roscoe was pissed off because Sam wouldn't let him into his house the night before. Sam was passing for white and his wife didn't know it!

For years in the thirties and later in the forties, when my mother was "in" at "Seventy-four," my brother Ralph and I shared the same bed. In my teens we really were only together for three years—in between the end of his hitch in World War II and when I volunteered for the army. In those three years, 1945 to 1948, we were the Brothers Rangel. He was dating a lot of girls, I was dating a lot of girls. We sometimes even dated the same girl. We were inseparable. I see them as a kind of Golden Age, when my big brother came back from the war and found me worthy and grown-up enough, at age fifteen, to hang tough with him at twenty-two. I had my own crew, we called ourselves Les Garçons, but Ralph and I were a thing unto ourselves.

Even when we fought with each other, we were brothers. Once, when I was discharged, he had a club that was giving an affair at Small's Paradise. This was when I was a brand-new Korean War hero. I had a date, elsewhere, but he wanted me to go in and be with him and his club members, he was so proud of me. And I wanted to go on my date; I just stopped by to say hello. He got a little belligerent with me, pulled on my coat, and we started fighting. Then one of his buddies jumps in and hits me; so we turned around and the both of us whipped the hell out of his buddy. Then we didn't talk for weeks. The game we played was that we just knew what the other was thinking. It was that way from childhood, the same way that married couples can complete each other's sentences.

While I was tied to my mother's apron, he was always running away. He'd show up at "Seventy-four" late at night; my sister, Frances, would let him in; and he'd leave early in the morning. He was a streets kind of guy—that's why he went off to the army. The army, then as now, was a common way out for people who were backing into a choice between risking their lives on the street or in a foreign war zone. When I was a young lawyer, a lot of troubled kids escaped from the streets to the army via the court system. I got a lot of cases just by reputation, but for most of them I wasn't even paid. A kid would get arrested for some petty crime and the family, if there was any, was usually without funds. I'd take them before Judge Maurice Gray, who was a friend. And when it appeared as though there was no father in the house, the mother was working, and the kid was out of control, Judge Gray would always be prepared to accept joining the military as an alternative to going to jail. When they enlisted, the charges were dismissed.

My brother, Ralph, married and had children soon after he left the service, which stopped him from taking advantage of the GI Bill. He simply couldn't work to feed his family and go to college at the same time. He started working for the New York State Department of Employment, where he remained for many years. Looking back, I still marvel at how we made it at all. When I talk to people who grew up in middle-class households, where going to college was a given, I'm just amazed. I mean, college wasn't even mentioned in our house when we were growing up. If it was mentioned, it was for someone else, not for us. This experience of living as "less than" could have been painful for me. But for some reason—call it a quirk—I simply tend to forget the hardest experiences of deprivation or humiliation. Even when I'm reminded, I have never been one to long for the "good old days." There's an expression in the army that sums up my attitude nicely: "Every soldier believes his last base was the best one."

The "good old days" were rough times. I used to *keep* a hole in my shoes. My brother and I used to joke that our shoes were so bad, with the holes in our soles, that we had developed "radar feet." If there was a piece of glass in the street, we never had to look down; our feet would just automatically avoid it. There was a guy with a shoe-repair shop down the street from us. When people didn't pick up their shoes, he'd shine them up and sell them. That's probably how I got my bad feet, but at the time I thought that was where everybody got their shoes.

When my grandfather died, I knew he wanted to be buried next to his mother, in Accomac, and that's where he is. He never saw me take my seat in Congress, or in the New York State Assembly for that matter. But if I had to thank anyone for the fact that I got there I'm amazed to say it would have to be him. It is from thinking about this book that I've come realize that the *only* reason I would one day blurt out that I wanted to be a lawyer was because of him.

If he had worked in a hospital I could have been a brain surgeon. But because he worked in the Criminal Court building, always looking up to the lawyers he was lifting all day long, that's what I ended up wanting to become, a lawyer. So I can't say I got my love of law, or politics, or even people from him. But what I did get from him was a context, a kind of kitchen college, a wisdom from the bottom of the cup. He was so unsentimental, and for the longest time I just saw one mean old man in it. For example, when I was in my twenties, after the army and then going to school, I hung tough at the big-name Harlem nightspots and later worked at the now legendary Hotel Theresa, which catered to the headliners appearing at the Apollo Theatre around the corner as well as other big shots. No one could tell me that Harlem and I weren't hot stuff.

But down in the kitchen, Grandfather would sometimes talk about Harlem's heydays of the twenties and thirties, and he made it clear that they were not any Renaissance for him. The nightspots that were glorified catered to white people from downtown. Their limousines were parked in front, but he couldn't even get a job in many of those places. Talking about me working in the Hotel Theresa—twenty years earlier he couldn't even go into the Hotel Theresa and be served.

Now, this was where Adam Powell came in, at the beginning of the war, and said, "This is wrong." Quite frankly, I don't see how blacks tolerated it all even that long. But Adam is the one who really turned the thing around. I'm very proud of the resurgence of Harlem, all the bustle and new buildings I can see every day from the windows of my district office. But the connection to past black glory is false, because all of these legends—the Apollo, the Cotton Club— weren't built for black folks, like the new Magic Johnson Theatres down the street from me were built for black folks. It was Adam Powell who broke the mold of people accepting a position of inferiority in our own community. He started marching on 125th Street, and picketing stores like Woolworth's, until blacks could work there. It's painful but important to remember that blacks still couldn't get jobs in the best restaurants on 125th Street when I was a teenager, much less eat in them.

So I'd have these conversations with my grandfather, in the kitchen in the forties and fifties, when the history was still recent and still plain all around us if we just opened our eyes. People find it very easy to remember the good times and forget the bad, but Harlem was a racist place. If you want to talk about Count Basie, Duke Ellington . . . the wonderful people . . . the yellow dancing gals at the Cotton Club, you can. But you don't talk about how many blacks could actually go in, order a drink, and see a show. There is no question that Grandfather's talk affected my views coming up. He never allowed anyone to believe he had an easy time in Harlem. Harlem was a rough place for him. As a teenager I remember listening to nationalists on 125th Street, condemning this thing called white supremacy, and lynching, and advocating black causes. But they were so much more entertainment than anything else. It wasn't until Malcolm X came along that what my grandfather had said, what my militant pan-Africanist Uncle Herbert used to go on about, finally made sense.

They really did think we were chattel. They really did take away our identity, so many of my uncles and cousins bumping around, just one and two generations out of slavery. They really did erase anything that would allow us to believe we were somebody from somewhere. And even today the stigma of slavery is still here. It's in the air. Black kids have it, and their parents have had it, and their grandparents have had it. You've got to rebut the presumption that you aren't just as good as a white person, and to do that you have to become better, make more of yourself—from less.

African Americans see ourselves as a minority in our own country, without any sense of Europeans being a minority in the world. How a handful of Europeans could have done that to the entire world, for so long, I'll never understand. Maybe I have to do more reading. In my old age I'm also trying to make sense—moral sense—of the insanity of today's Washington, and what it's got to do with my story and all our stories, our human American story. I want to understand how people are once again so silent, when we're changing the tax laws to put the burden on working people, when we're cutting back on government programs, when we're bombing people senseless without declaring war, when we're coercing smaller countries. And everyone is quiet! The religious leaders, the business sector—everyone is quiet.

Even in the early fifties we were still pretty quiet about the Jews who had recently been exterminated in Germany, and the drunk Senator McCarthy destroying people's lives by innuendo. We were mostly quiet about the lynchings and mutilations of black folks still taking place down South. Still, in my postwar Harlem, the Hotel Theresa, the Savoy, and so many other places that were off limits to blacks opened up to become part of a brief Renaissance that black people could actually enjoy. Unfortunately, some of them made a point of retaining the pretensions of the whites who had preceded them. While I was working at the Hotel Theresa, even people who were not guests of the hotel would ask me to page them, so that people would know that at least they were in the lobby.

Like I said, my people hail from Accomac, Virginia, the land where the seeds of America in black and white were well planted before we were uprooted north. Being half-white meant nothing to my great-grandfather; being one quarter white meant even less to his son Charlie, for whom I was named. Once it was decided you were black, and weren't passing, it didn't make any difference what your complexion was, except perhaps for other blacks enslaved by the mentality coded into the old Negro signify: "If you're white you're right, if you're brown stick around, if you're black get back." These things were said in jest, but when I first went to Washington, D.C., in 1971 no less, the remnants of this mentality were still clear with professionals in my age group. I saw how the neighborhoods—the black neighborhoods—were broken down by wealth and color in a black-majority city that didn't even have the pitiful measure of home rule it has today.

I was forty, and I used to say that I couldn't comprehend how the black mind could be so bent as to adopt these prejudices. But now I understand. It was what Grandfather was trying to tell me all along. But my perspective, coming of age in Harlem in the decade following World War II, didn't afford me a good angle on the truth.

2

Les Garçons

So many people have said that those of us who were raised on Lenox Avenue just didn't have any class.

For generations of African Americans raised in the inner cities, or the other side of the small-town tracks, class was what their mothers or grandmothers or even neighbors brought home from their service in the kitchens and dining rooms of affluent whites. When I was a boy in depression-era Harlem, class and sophistication was Mrs. Daniels, the mother of a childhood friend who worked in the home of some very wealthy white folks. No matter how humble the meal, if it was served in her home the presentation was fit for royalty. Even to eat a sandwich in Mrs. Daniels's home we really had to prepare. Her carriage was consistent with her table; she was always telling her stories of what she'd seen and learned and done in her service with so much dignity and such good diction. She's my original epitome of class; I saw a lot more than table manners in her.

Anyone fortunate enough to eat from white tablecloths on a regular basis can acquire the obligatory etiquette. I think in some ways that's exactly what I've done. Even today I see myself watching closely to observe which fork other people are using at very, very formal dinners. Real class, of course, is much more than the formalities of table manners. It's a set of values placed so deeply in one's character as to become a way of life. You don't have to be born into class, though it helps a great deal. You can merely be exposed to it and have it nurtured in you at an early age. Mrs. Daniels notwithstanding, that was definitely not the case with me.

I really believe I'm so close to being the last person in the world who would ever end up in the Congress. My talents had been so unrecognized as a kid, that whatever people thought I would be, it wouldn't be a college grad and a lawyer, and certainly not a representative in the

23

Congress of the United States. My older brother, Ralph, was my best friend, my dad, my confidant—we slept in the same bed. My sister, Frances—my beloved friend—was raised by my mother's father, Charlie B. Wharton. It always brings a smile to my face when someone refers to me as "Charlie B.," because as a kid people always wanted to remind me that I was named for my grandfather. There was no real family life at all. Mom hadn't finished school, and Grandfather, well, I think he liked me the least but ended up with me the most because, as the last of the grandchildren to leave "Seventy-four," I needed him the most. I heard and learned an awful lot from his mouth, but we never really talked much.

I was blissfully unaware of the existence of class, much less a need for it, well into my teens. I remember hanging out at the Police Athletic League recreation center on "26th" Street and Eighth Avenue—that's 126th Street, if you're not from Harlem—chasing the girls and doing what I did near the end of World War II. I must have been fourteen or fifteen, and my thing was being in trouble and, when I walked into a room, letting people know I was there. I could not go to a place without shaking up something. There was a very attractive woman working at the rec center—I later learned she was a social worker—who took a liking to me, bad-boy persona and all, and invited me to her home for dinner and to meet her niece.

She lived up on Sugar Hill, somewhere above 145th Street on Convent or St. Nicholas Avenue. The "Hill" was just that, a steady climb going north on St. Nicholas, or a steep climb going west on 145th, from the "valley" of Central Harlem where I lived. The most affluent blacks, including celebrities like Duke Ellington, Paul Robeson, and Joe Lewis, lived on Sugar Hill, literally at such altitudes that it was hard not to feel looked down upon. This woman was so very well groomed. I remember my mother scrubbing me up for the thing, but she knew nothing about preparing me for what to expect. When I got there, they had more glass and silverware laid on than I'd seen in my life, much less on one table. I did not have the slightest idea what each glass was for, or how I could possibly use so many knives and spoons at one meal. The lace and the cloth napkins were like something I'd only seen in the movies. I sat down, and they started serving, and I spent the rest of that afternoon just watching which fork and which knife and which spoon the other people were using. That was a painful experience, and to this day, whenever I pick up the wrong fork or spoon by accident, I recall that meal like it was yesterday.

The woman figured I could be cleaned up and possibly be an acceptable date for her niece. She probably thought I wasn't all that bad, but I wasn't nearly as good as she thought I could be. I was really a fish out of water, drowning in the totally unfamiliar atmosphere of class. I couldn't think of going back up there to see them, and embarrass myself all over again.

In telling my story as a politician, I used to talk about how my mother had done "day's work" as a chambermaid in the Catskills resorts for some years. I remember once she saw me talking about it on TV and was very annoyed, because I left out that she later worked in a garment factory and was a member of the International Ladies Garment Workers Union. She was *so proud* to be a union member who made shoulder pads for women's dresses. It was clear that she was not proud of the maid work that she'd done; being a union worker was it for her. But I don't recall ever feeling personally smacked down by such class comparisons. I never felt invested in my class identity. At the same time—I don't know if it's God's grace or my dumb luck—people were always making a little space for me in their lives. I was always blessed with people who were willing to shine a light on my possibilities instead of my liabilities.

Carl Durham, a black salesman at the Adler shoe store on 125th Street, is the first name that comes to mind in this idea of mentorship. He took me under his wing when I worked there full-time as a stock boy after I dropped out of high school. If I wanted to grow up to be anything at that time, it was to be Carl Durham, because in my eyes he had a lot of that Mrs. Daniels in him. He wore vests and shirts with collar pins—he was a classy guy. To this day, I wear a dress shirt with a collar pin every day. From time to time he would invite me to his home at 55 St. Nicholas Place—up on the same Sugar Hill where that social worker lived—for a polite meal with him and his lovely, beautiful, and cultured wife. For a Sunday lunch he would make certain I showed up scrubbed down, with my fingernails clean and wearing my best shirt and tie. Oh, was their house exquisite. Oh my God, the furniture was so polished, the sofas and the overstuffed chairs so plush, with the lace doilies on the arms. And, ever so patiently at the table, his wife would teach me how to eat.

The social worker meant well enough, but introducing me to her niece like that was a test, perhaps one I was set up to fail. Sunday lunch with the Durhams, on the other hand, was no test. I didn't understand it then, but now I see: They simply wanted to bring me into something that was very much like class, but without the pretense or sense of pre-election. They didn't make it feel as though I was stupid and didn't know anything. They cared, and they gave me so much attention. I really enjoyed it, even though I had no place to practice my adopted graces. I would be blessed with many more mentors along my way who would expose me to a little more than I was used to. But it would be a long time before I had real opportunities to actually apply the knowledge, and a little longer still before I felt I owned the "class" that Carl Durham and those that followed wanted me to have.

Even after I decided to go back to school, after the army and Korea, I was, to myself, still nothing but a subway student. I was just a working-class guy, taking the Seventh Avenue train to Hoyt Street every day, to a factory building in downtown Brooklyn that just happened to house St. John's Law School. I came home each night to the sight and smell of collard greens or lima beans with ham hocks or the other soul foods bubbling up from a pot that was always going on the coal stove. It was the aroma of Accomac, Virginia. That was my grandfather. Of course, as far as I was concerned, the hot dogs, hamburgers, rotisserie chicken, or spaghetti-and-meatball takeout I brought home, that was Lenox Avenue, that was me. Accomac and Lenox Avenue never seemed to merge.

———

When I was in high school, and after I left, I ran with a gang—no, I belonged to a social group—that still means something to me that only the few people who really know me understand. We buried another one of the group in 2003, but we are still together, and have been since 1944 or 1945.

We called ourselves Les Garçons—"The Boys" in French. It was Arthur Barnes's idea—I think he got it from studying the language in high school. In our teens in Harlem we were notable, at least to ourselves, if not notorious, as young men on the move. And most of the gang did manage to not just arrive in life but to get there in the style to which we were determined to become accustomed. Arthur went to the famed Bronx High School of Science, so he was pretty smart. He finished high school in 1947, the year I dropped out. He went on to a rather accomplished career in the insurance industry and is currently a senior vice president with HIP, one of the oldest and largest health insurers in the Northeast.

Norman Howard was Arthur's buddy from St. Mark's Catholic Church on 138th Street. He was at DeWitt Clinton with me, and became a police officer after graduation. His dad had a heavy West Indian accent that some of us would mimic for big laughs. Like Arthur, Norman was a great jazz fanatic. They knew every guitar and horn player, every instrument, every blues singer. I was a jazz fan myself. I kept up with some horn players, especially Ben Webster, Johnny Hodges, and Coleman Hawkins. But my real thing was the ballads of the day, and the singers who put them across, like Sarah Vaughn, Billy Eckstine, Ella Fitzgerald, and Arthur Prysock.

Norman and Arthur were also up on the emerging bebop scene—they were digging Charlie Parker before he was a legend. We used to go down to 52nd Street sometimes—before it was legendary—for a beer and whatnot. But, of course, we didn't have the money to be able to actually sit in any of the clubs there. Years later, when Norman was a young officer, as he was leaving the Alhambra jazz club in Harlem with his wife, he spotted some criminal in the act. He collared the guy and was promoted to detective, at a time in the fifties when there still weren't many black detectives in the NYPD. Norman's unfailing sense of humor kept Les Garçons together over the years as much as anything or anyone else.

I met Guy Guyton at St. Aloysius Church, where we both served as altar boys. We would also play hooky together in our high school days. Like me, Guy didn't finish high school, and he, too, eventually wound up volunteering for the army. At that point the group also included Jimmy Taylor and Henry Courtland. Often, when we were supposed to be in school, the four of us hung out at Jimmy's house on 128th Street playing pinochle. After a stint in the army, Jimmy became a successful psychologist. And though we always joked that he showed more potential to be a patient than a therapist, it was another member of our crew who ended up with deep psychiatric problems. This poor fellow received a good Catholic school education back when some of us were dropping out, and made it as far as becoming a CPA before he lost it. He's been homeless, though not entirely out of touch with me, for some years now.

Jimmy, Henry, and I didn't have fathers in the household, but Guy not only had a dad, he had a wonderful family. They lived for all these years in a big apartment at 243 West 135th Street, between Seventh and Lenox, right across from the police station. Guy's parents would go on trips to Miami a lot, and when they did we were home free to party in that wonderful apartment that seemed so large and luxurious at the time. Our Friday-night "grooves" there remain the stuff of our legends. Guy would put these dark lights in the ceilings, and, man, did we party, with his parents' blessing. Mrs. Guyton was like a mother to us. If I had a girl who thought she was being mistreated, she'd go straight to Mrs. Guyton and cry.

On its surface, Les Garçons represented a merger between some kids from St. Aloysius Catholic Church on 132nd Street between Seventh and Eighth, and St. Mark's Catholic Church on 138th between

Fifth and Lenox. Arthur Barnes was the leader from the St. Mark's group and he brought Norman Howard and Trevor Bannister, who lived in an especially rough neighborhood, with him. In a more important sense, for the making of Charlie Rangel, it was a merger between the worst fears—based on where and how I was raised—and the best hopes people had for me, whether or not I actually had them for myself. The sharp contrast between my immediate past and my possibilities could be captured just by walking those three long blocks west on 132nd Street from between Fifth and Lenox, where I lived, over to Eighth Avenue and back again, as I did nearly every day. As I've said, my mom didn't have much to give me in life, but if there was one thing she valued, beside that Wharton name, it was membership in the St. Aloysius Catholic Church at the western end of my world. She insisted on passing it on to me, and from about the eighth grade I not only attended but served as an altar boy there, along with Guy Guyton, Marshall White, and Maceo Williams.

But I didn't attend the St. Aloysius Catholic school. The tuition, though only a few dollars a week, put it out of the question. That three-block walk was from the worst neighborhood, with more hoodlum-minded boys in it, to the best neighborhood, the block lined with trees and the brownstones and the Catholic church. Somehow I lived in both of those worlds, and tried to live both of those lives. I was a bum who went out with the miscreants and future felons on my block, but I also hung out with the guys from St. Aloysius, who were by no means angels but had no criminal intent. These altar boy types, who would become true lifelong friends, allowed me to be the big shot, paying me all due respect for what we now call my "street cred," because I was from the other side of Lenox. At the same time, I was serving the altar at St. Aloysius's 6:00 A.M. mass; none of the guys from my end of 132nd Street had any idea what I was doing around the church because I served and was back home before they got up.

Nevertheless, my worlds would still collide at times, especially when my thugging friends would come up from Lenox Avenue and rob these Catholic schoolkids. They'd show up to take—they didn't see it as stealing—the kind of things that street kids valued, a watch or a pink "Spaldeen" rubber ball, or somebody's lunch money. Then they'd see me and say, "What the hell are *you* doing up here?" And then I'd be the one negotiating a deal to get the stuff back.

"Oh, c'mon, Herbert, give Marshall his damn watch back," I can still hear myself saying. Invariably it led to warnings ("When you get back to the block tonight, we gotta talk!"). I was always being threatened with having to make up my mind about which side I was on, or else. But I don't recall ever having to pay the piper for my dual life. I figured I had it better than all those cats, from either end of 132nd Street, because while I was in all the worlds, they were only in one. I was a hood when I was with the hoods, and I was running after their fine and proper Catholic schoolgirls when I was an altar boy, and I was in Les Garçons. I was living all the worlds at once, so what the hell, I thought.

Learning to explain to my Catholic kids why my hoodlum friends were always picking on them, and answering when the hoodlums asked "Why are you hanging around with those uppity so-and-so's in the first place," probably prepared me well for bridging factions in the army, the Harlem Democratic clubhouses, the state legislature, and ultimately the Congress. But I don't think I ever needed to explain my tacit loyalty to the Les Garçons crew to myself or anyone else. Frankly, after more than fifty years, I don't think I have to explain it. But if I did, it might come back to where we began this chapter: class.

Catholic school was class. These guys were going to finish good high schools, and they were going to go to college or at least become something in life. I don't know how I knew it. We didn't really talk about it, but I knew it. The public school guys on my block were not expected to finish high school. The Catholic school guys were book smarter, if not street smarter, and maybe life smarter, too. And they came from families that had strong, competent mothers and a lot more fathers (though not all) than the kids on my block had.

I didn't have class, and to this day I remain indifferent—at best— to true class membership. But what I did get from my identification with Les Garçons could be summed up in a phrase that's never far from my consciousness: "Assume the virtue, though you have it not." It's actually from *Hamlet* (act 3, scene 4: "Assume a virtue, if you have it not"), though I have no idea where I picked it up. Do I have class? I got enough to fake it. Decades later, in our Les Garçons poker game reunions, in the basements of our respectable homes, ain't none of us would have any class, because when we're together like that we go back to where we were when we started out together. Over the years we've acquired enough class markers—titles, degrees, and some assets—to get by in life and for people to *think* we have it. But only our wives really know if we have it or not. Either way, we've certainly picked something up along the way, because we damn sure didn't inherit it.

Most of Les Garçons were active in the Harlem YMCA on 135th Street. Arthur and I were copresidents of the teen council, which sponsored a basketball game and a dance every Friday night. None of our guys played basketball, so after the other guys got all sweaty and stinky, our crew would be there on the sidelines, with the girls all to ourselves for our own, private parties. One of the guys, Arthur Best, whom we called Barry, had an uncle who was "a well-known Harlem sportsman." I think that meant he was in the numbers business. He had an apartment nearby that he used for his business by day. By night we used it as our clubhouse—we even had keys. This was a big thing. That's where we'd take the girls to party after those basketball games. To keep away unwanted competition, we'd station Norman, who was a big football player, on the door.

Having that clubhouse—at age fifteen or sixteen—cut us up a notch or two in terms of sophistication and brought us a hell of a lot closer as a group. But Les Garçons was really born the day we got the bright idea that we could give the dances ourselves. We went to the Congress Casino, a club on 131st and Seventh Avenue, arranged to rent the place and hired a band. It turned out to be a terrible failure; there were heavy thundershowers all day and into the evening and nobody showed up. At the end of the night, the manager of the Congress Casino came after us for the money. We told him, hell, we were kids, and we weren't authorized to sign any contract, and we don't have any money, anyway. We then decided to take our assumed entrepreneurial virtue over to St. Philip's Episcopal Church on 134th Street, and hold our "pay parties" there. Father Shelton Hale Bishop was the pastor. Our Friday-night soirees began to catch on there, and we started making a little money. Then one night after the party Father Bishop let us know that the church wanted a cut; we sent the cash home with Norman Howard. We honored the Congress Casino precedent; nobody representing heaven or earth was getting our money. We were doing our own money.

To this day, the surviving Les Garçons agree that it was the lesson from the Congress Casino failure, not our later success, that forged our bond. There was no stopping us after that. We had regular monthly meetings and were always looking for opportunities to expand our influence. There were some similar groups operating for girls in those days, and soon we had a few of them "affiliated" with Les Garçons. We told the girls we'd introduce them into the social world, connect them to older, more mature figures in the community. As things got going, we'd actually have them sponsoring affairs for us in return for the value of our mentorship. Some of the things that we did, and things we said about ourselves, were just so silly. But we got by with it. In retrospect, I could be accused by people who knew me then of always running off at the mouth as a kid, and they wouldn't be too far from wrong. But "assuming the virtue," as a Les Garçons, meant believing that with the gifts of superior gab, style, and confidence bordering on arrogance, you could run the game. We would be the players and not the played.

Arthur Barnes's mother, who was a seamstress, eventually made us a set of double-breasted vests that we wore more like an emblem than a uniform; we were tough.

———————

I always look for flaws in my perception on this, but I live in total and consistent disbelief that I actually came from the gutters of New York to this position in the U.S. Congress. What amazes me most, to the point of incredulity, is the kind of support that was always within arm's reach when I was on the right path, even though the road went through some kind of hell. It was not so much with dollars and cents that I was lifted, it was more a kind of moral support that I received from everybody in the community, and the gifts of friendship.

I can still see "Moms" Mabley, the legendary comedian, hectoring the show-business guests and hangers-on in the lobby of the Hotel Theresa when I was night desk clerk, studying for law school during my downtime in the wee hours. And I can still hear her raspy, raucous delivery: "Give the boy some money! Can't you see he's goin' ta school?"

Of course, I believe I've been saying thank you all my life, but only lately have I appreciated how rewarding it's been to do so. The sad fact is that almost all the people I used to say thank you to, from generations past, are dead. So this memoir is yet another gift, a precious opportunity to say thank you not just to Les Garçons but to all the people who were there for me then, and those who would come later. I truly believe that one of the reasons I enjoy each and every day of being a congressman and being in public service is that it allows me to say thank you to my community for giving me this great opportunity to do for others what they did for me.

Among them would have to be Charlie Fried, who had a big hardware store on Lenox between 132nd and 133rd streets. What a fantastic individual he was, along with his wife, Rose. When my grandfather retired, he used to hang around the store, often sitting in the backroom, drinking with Charlie Fried. Charlie let my grandfather work there for a while, just to get the additional quarters of salaried employment necessary to qualify for a Social Security check. And I worked there, too, as did my brother before me. I learned to do a lot of things with my head and my hands—fix lamps, splice wires, lay linoleum—working there. Charlie Fried always had a half-dozen blacks in his employ. There was John Nelson, always the clean-cut one, who used to take me to his house on 145th Street, and always encouraged me to go to school and get an education. But the other workers were lovable characters, once you got to know them—guys who would work hard by day, then drink hard and fight by night. There seemed to be a lot of fighting and cutting going on in Harlem back then. Not a lot of shooting, but, man, people got cut left and right. Guys like the Diggs brothers who were working there—they'd whip somebody's behind in a minute. Charlie Fried would fire them, then rehire them because they worked so damn hard. They drove the trucks; they made deliveries; they installed locks; they did everything.

This cast of characters also included the cop on the beat, Patrolman J. At that time cops had fixed beats, and his seemed centered on the corner of 132nd and Lenox. I had just two suits to my name at the time, and for some reason both were in the cleaners on 132nd Street when it was robbed. I lamented to Patrolman J. that I didn't know what I was going to do without my best and only suits, because style was everything to me in those days. Now, I don't know what Patrolman J. did when he wasn't on his corner. All I know is that later that night he brought me back both of my suits, in a cellophane bag. Police, as Adam Clayton Powell would ultimately be undone for saying, were not always engaged in lawful conduct.

Patrolman J.'s activities were not unusual while I was being raised off Lenox Avenue. Some of the most heroic policemen, who would risk their lives for the people on their beat, did not think twice about taking kickbacks from drug dealers or numbers runners on the same beat. I'd put my Harlem hardware store experience up against any small-town five-and-dime or general store pickle barrel in the country. Charlie Fried's place was formative for me even after the army and Korea. Once, when I was in law school, I was there when some detectives came barging in.

> DETECTIVE: "You Charlie Fried?"
> CHARLIE FRIED: "Yes, I'm Charlie Fried."
> DETECTIVE: "We have to talk to you."
> Charlie Fried tells his brother-in-law to take over the front counter while he ushers the cops into the back of the store.
> "Charlie, you come with me," he says, and immediately these cops want to know what this black dude is doing in the meeting.
> CHARLIE FRIED: "He's going to law school; now, what is it you want?"
> He knew something was going on. The cops ask him if he had a 1957 Ford pickup truck.

CHARLIE FRIED: "Yes, I do."

DETECTIVE: "It was involved in a lumber yard robbery last
night—a lot of lumber was stolen."

CHARLIE FRIED: "Are you sure?"

DETECTIVE: "Yeah. Who drives the truck?"

Charlie Fried answers that Nelson drives, and these other
guys drive.

DETECTIVE: "Well, I'm afraid, Mr. Fried, that we're gonna
have to take him down to the precinct."

CHARLIE FRIED: "Well, I'm afraid you don't really want to
take him down to the precinct."

DETECTIVE: "What are you talking about?"

CHARLIE FRIED: "You don't want to take him down because
Patrolman J. asked to borrow the Ford last night, and I
loaned it to him!"

Charlie Fried had a son my age who would in later years maintain
and tell me that "my dad always wished you were his son." Charlie
Fried just *knew* I had *it*. Yes, it still warms a smile inside me that spreads
from one ear across my face to the other ear, just remembering the
way he affirmed me. I could write poetry and I could draw, and that
really impressed him and earned his respect. Charlie Fried and I really
hit it off. I had a little portable typewriter, and at one time I really
thought I was pawning that worthless thing with Charlie Fried. But
that was just his way of giving me some money—technically a loan—
while making me think he was holding my typewriter for security. He
would challenge me on everything. He would tell me how to fold my
money, teach me how to count the change, the nickels and dimes.
He would talk to me about so many things, as if I was his best buddy.
He'd confided in me about how much he loved his mother, and her
advancing senility.

It was Charlie Fried who told me how sometimes in life you really
can't always tell the truth if lying a little means that you're making someone feel good. When I asked him what on earth that meant, he said:

"Well, my mother grew up poor and feeling insecure in this society.
She always feels she needs more money. So every Saturday I take our
weekly bank deposit and bring it to my mother, like it's a gift. And every
Saturday she says, 'Count it for me, Charlie,' and I count it for her. And
then she says, 'Now put it in the bank, son.'"

And bank it he did. The truth he never told her was that it was
going into *his* bank account, not hers. And he'd do it every Saturday
night.

I didn't understand half of these things until I became older. He would say things like, "You know, you could be a leader of your people, but you've got to stop fighting each other." He was talking about this big rivalry that was obviously going on between West Indians, who have always been a critical part of the mix in Harlem, and the Southern black majority. Now, I never really noticed it, or saw it that way, until I got involved in politics. In our gang we made fun of one another, and fun of one another's parents—mainly those with strong West Indian accents or deep Southern black American accents. But hell, we were buddies, right?

The West Indian kids would call those of us with Southern parents "pork chops" and "country." We'd call them "monkey chasers," a term of derision that goes back to the great West Indian firebrand Marcus Garvey's ill-fated attempt to enlist all of us in his "Back to Africa" movement in the twenties. But Charlie Fried's point, the thing he insisted I take away, was that a minority group in America has to stick together at all costs. To Fried it was clear: We were riven by false rivalries concerning everything from skin shade, to hair texture, to dialect and accent. We even had class warfare of the (Sugar) "Hill" versus the "Valley" variety.

If there was one set of people Charlie Fried hated the most, it was German Jews. Until I got to know him, I never perceived any variation among whites, period. I didn't understand the distinction of Jew from gentile at that time, much less the Germans from other Jews. Fried never tired of talking about how these Jews that came from Germany after World War I thought they were better than everybody else, and really mistreated other Jews. Yet Charlie Fried always made it clear: "You let someone say something about a German Jew to me, and I'll defend 'em to my death. That's what black people have to understand. No matter what colors they are, or where they come from, they gotta be like Jews and fight like hell when somebody attacks one of them." Of course, he was speaking as the horrific revelations of the Holocaust were still unfolding in the news. Charlie Fried personified the emotional response to racist oppression of an American minority group that was not my own.

Charlie Fried really treated me like a son, sharing all of his stories and advice. Things like how I should save money—"spend a dollar, save a dollar," he would always say. I've stayed in touch with his son all these years. But I couldn't argue with him when he would say his dad wished I was his other son. His father used to take me to his fabulous apartment in the South Bronx for dinner sometimes. It's a slum now, but back then it was like a palace. He'd take me—just me from the store—and his wife, Rose, would say, "Go in there and wash up . . . be sure to get under your fingernails . . . and clean that neck of yours, Charlie. And gimme that shirt, I'll wash that shirt and iron it for you, Charlie."

———————

Les Garçons and mentors like Charlie Fried notwithstanding, I still wasn't fooling any of the nuns or priests at St. Aloysius about who I was. You know, today some of those old nuns would swear they remember me actually being enrolled at St. Aloysius, with all their contemporary pride in my accomplishments. But I remember them regularly chasing me away—as I was trying to chase the girls there—just because they assumed I was a bum out of a public school—Junior High School 139— however well regarded. They knew I wasn't one of them because I didn't wear their school uniform. I dressed sharp, by street standards, a style they equated with the worst of the public school kids, right up until I was eighteen and went into the army.

The Franciscan Handmaids of Mary is one of a very small handful of black convents in the country. They started in Georgia during World War I and moved to Harlem in 1923. Anything was better than Savannah in the 1920s, but even New York, and its Catholic hierarchy, weren't quite ready for this black-run institution. To make ends meet at first they actually had to take in laundry, just as they did in Georgia. They started with a nursery, St. Benedict's, and that grew into the prestigious St. Aloysius school that opened in 1941 when I was eleven. Harlem has gone through a lot of changes over the decades, but the Handmaids of Mary are still thriving here. Some of today's nuns were just kids when I was going to school. The Handmaids of Mary were always available when needed to babysit my children. Needless to say, I'm always on the lookout for ways to support the order; we've been in each other's lives pretty much as long as we've both been alive.

In my remarks at a recent St. Aloysius reunion, I joked that if the nuns were in charge, the whole Church would be in better shape. They all laughed, including Sister Cecilia, the guest of honor, who is somewhere north of ninety years old. After I was in the Congress, I'd often hear some of the nuns say, "Oh, Charles, I *knew* when you were young that you would amount to something." But back when I was a teenager there wasn't a nun in the place who didn't think I was going to end up in jail. I may have been an altar boy, but around St. Aloysius I wasn't seen as an "altar boy" altar boy; I was more of a "hoodlum" altar boy. They all thought I was just spending time around the convent to see the girls there. And you know what? I was.

One girl in particular came to represent my entire relationship with the Handmaids of Mary. Sister Cecilia, who was the Mother Superior back then, had come to Harlem and St. Aloysius from Beaumont, Texas. Her sister had fraternal twin daughters and one of them, Erma, was absolutely gorgeous. She sent her girls to Harlem and St. Aloysius for a better education, in a strict environment, under the watchful eye of their aunt, the Mother Superior. I entered the picture at a Christmas high mass in 1946. I was serving the altar and Erma was lined up to take Communion. She was fifteen, and I must have been sixteen. She looked so much like an angel, I couldn't help myself from taking the plate on which the sacred host was served, and gently tapping her under her chin with it as she knelt. The last time I ran into Sister Cecilia on the street she made a point of saying: "Oh, my beloved Charles . . . if Erma could see you now. She loved you so much. We all loved you so much; we knew you were gonna make us proud."

I know she believes every word of it. But it does show you what the mind can do to your memory. The record should show that when she discovered I was trying to see her niece I was quickly banned from the convent. Whenever I went to see her at the school itself I was closely monitored, being the urchin from the other end of the block. Mind you, Erma was not studying to be a nun, but she was boarding in a strict convent environment.

Actually, I didn't really mind being banned that much. It was easy enough to get around it when I needed to—I managed to charm a few of the nuns into letting me sneak back in on occasion—and it made me look a little tougher than the other guys; it gave me a kind of forbidden fruit allure. From then on, everyone assumed that Erma and I were in love, and everyone made it their business to involve themselves in some way, usually in trying to keep us apart. It was rough, but I did have my allies. There was a priest who would be in charge of things—don't ask me why—and sometimes when he'd take all the girls to a movie, he'd call me with the information so I could make the same show and Erma and I could sit in the back and hold hands. There were nuns who became friends of my family—Sister Gertrude and Sister Benedicte—who would let me come over to the convent to take their books to the library, just to give me an opportunity to wave to Erma and let her know I was there.

Once people decide a relationship is a Romeo and Juliet story, they endow it with a public, fictional life of its own. The flame between the lovers in question always burns brighter in their imaginations than in reality. And, as in the Shakespeare play, the more the authorities try to keep them apart, the more the audience—the chorus, really—believes their love to be true. From the time I returned from Korea in 1950, when I was twenty, until all too recently, people who thought they knew the story were always saying, "Oh, Erma and Charlie; their love was made in heaven." On paper—one of many letters exchanged while I was abroad—we were engaged to be married.

From the start of my service, Erma and I would write every day. I would show everyone in my unit her picture; she was so pretty. Erma had finished school, returned to Beaumont, and was teaching school just across the border in Louisiana. When I got into combat, I wrote and told her about all the guys who never received any mail. She set up a project where every kid in her class adopted a soldier in my unit. They not only got letters, but boxes and other stuff on a regular basis. Somewhere in all those letters and longings and parcels I guess we fell deeper in love; I sent her a ring and a letter of proposal.

It's clear to me now that getting married by letter falls far short of being on your knees and looking into someone's eyes. Marrying Erma was of a piece with a larger vision I made up for myself, based on my newfound status as a Korean War hero. I saw myself reenlisting and making a career as an army recruiter, with all the benefits and incentives being offered at that time. I saw myself sporting a crisp dress uniform, every day, with sergeant first class stripes on my arms. Erma would be my career military wife. We'd live off base, with a ration allowance and a $6,000 reenlistment bonus in the kitty.

The great thing about having a vision like this when you're twenty and haven't had a foot in the civilian real world since you were eighteen is that I wouldn't have to go through with it until I was twenty-two, a date so far in the future as to be indefinite. In the meantime, I hoped Erma would meet me in Harlem for a time when I got my first big home leave after Korea. But Erma had other plans. She said there was no way I could head for New York from my temporary base in California without stopping to visit her parents in Texas. It threw me for a loop, but we talked it out and I thought I cut a deal with her. I would come to Texas first and meet her people, and maybe she'd come back with me to New York.

Her parents welcomed me like a son. They were so excited about the engagement that they'd already arranged to have the wedding in the same church where they had been married. They took me around Beaumont and showed me where they planned to build a house for Erma and me, the way everyone in the family had built each other's houses. Even though they knew we'd be traveling around the world as a military family—as per my vision—everyone needed a home base, as far as they were concerned.

After showing me around, they made it clear to me that they saw no reason why we should wait two years to marry. Why wait when Erma already had the ring? It was also clear to me that I wasn't ready. As I said, my vision took shape in the indefinite future of 1952. The love that was born out of all those efforts to keep us apart, and nurtured by all those letters from combat began to crumble that week in Beaumont. I was just twenty years old, and still reasoning like the eighteen-year-old kid I was when I enlisted. It was one thing to imagine myself a properly married career military husband in two whole years. It was quite another to come face-to-face with what that commitment meant in what we now call "real time."

As much as I enjoyed meeting her parents, I left Beaumont with the engagement ring in my pocket. It was over, but never quite done in the imaginations of all who were there when it began. Even after Erma married someone else—a career soldier who rose to the rank of colonel—they never gave up the notion that she was supposed to have married me. Decades later, when Erma occasionally visited New York to see her girlfriends and such, they delighted in arranging what appeared to be clandestine meetings between us. Mind you, we were both happily married to other people and had no intention of having an affair. Erma and I had such laughs together about the persistence of her friends' fantasies of a mad, torrid affair going on between us. The funniest part is that we both knew that if people hadn't been so involved in keeping us apart, our paper love would have folded within six months of that fateful Christmas mass. Like Romeo and Juliet, we were just kids when we met. Yet unlike Shakespeare's lovers, we had the chance to tell love from infatuation before fate caught up to us. Though Erma did die before we could laugh into old age about it, we got to enjoy each other's company as friends, and I can treasure that. I'm still in touch with her mom.

DeWitt Clinton High School, with its all-male campus on tree-lined Moshulu Parkway way up in the Bronx, was considered a very fine school. It was a fortress of advancement for upwardly mobile Jewish boys for at least one generation before and one generation after my high school days. I have never spent a lot of time wondering how and why I dropped out of Clinton after my sophomore year. My brother, Ralph, had graduated from the school, so I didn't think twice about it being good enough for me, too. After all, I had been an exceptional student at JHS 139, which everybody called Frederick Douglass, and P.S. 89 before that. But I was shocked and surprised to find that as good as I thought I was at Douglass, I was not able to compete with those kids at Clinton. The students there were about 98 percent Jewish, and of course virtually all the teachers were white, but it wasn't an issue of prejudice or racist attitudes toward me as a member of a very minority group there. What did me in was the subject matter, especially the science and the math. Truth be told, those other kids seemed so much better prepared for high school than I was.

Clinton taught me a lesson that I didn't really learn until some years after the army. I didn't know how to handle losing a competition that was based on book smarts rather than street smarts. Since it came easy for me all through junior high school, I thought that there would be nothing but constant improvement in my future. But once I was doing badly at Clinton, it just seemed to get worse. I had no clue as to how to turn things around, and what was worse was that I had little or no motivation to get a clue. There was nothing in my environment that demonstrated the direct reward of getting an education. I didn't know anybody well who especially valued it.

I recently reminded a group of young black teenage achievers about how fortunate they were to participate in extracurricular activities that exposed them to African American mentors, people they could consult if their parents had no college or if they had no other access to college-trained people. It is so easy for those of us who can no longer remember not being surrounded by professional people to take this simple truth for granted: You cannot imagine and dream what you haven't been informed of. I don't remember ever seeing a counselor or talking to anyone at DeWitt Clinton about where to go, what to do, or how to get help. And I don't remember asking anyone for help, either. My mother was very loving, but the value of her input on my schooling was very limited. Anything I wanted to do she was happy with. As I've said, my grandfather and I didn't have the best relationship. There was no reason to believe he didn't want me to succeed, but he was a rough guy to talk with. The story I told those young men and women, about my grandfather's attitude toward my academic and professional possibilities, is still very painful to me. On a fateful day in 1954, I came home to the brownstone on the bad end of 132nd Street and declared to my grandfather that I wanted to become a lawyer.

He laughed so hard I thought he'd never stop; it was the funniest thing he had ever heard.

Eight years and a few life-changing experiences after dropping out of Clinton would make all the difference in the world for my drive to succeed in school and in life. It wasn't that I was any brighter, though I was certainly more mature. It was because it was my last chance at something that, at the time I left Clinton, I didn't know I wanted more than girls, or clothes, or an easy way out. It was my last chance to become something in my grandfather's laughing eyes. Eight years later I was driven. If I didn't get the top grade I was disappointed. But in 1946 there just wasn't much in my life weighing in the balance in favor of education. When I dropped out of high school, I really thought I'd have no problem getting a good-paying job and then taking better care of my mom.

My brother returned from the army and the war in 1945. I figured he'd be like an older brother, but hell, he was like he was a Les Garçons. He made every party. Ralph went right back to the block boys he was hanging out with before he went into the army, and I hung out right with them. They were a fast-moving, hip group that didn't play by the rules as the postwar era dawned. That's when my brother and I really bonded, because I could be with his people and he could be with my people, and not one of these guys would even notice that he was seven years older than me. Having Ralph was like having the best of all my worlds again: a big brother and father figure who was just one of the gang. All that was left of family authority over my decisions was my poor mother and my emotionally distant grandfather. Little wonder, looking back, that I wasn't even thinking about a better future for myself.

Besides Ralph, it seemed to me that I didn't need anybody. And it may very well be that I never lost my lack of need for what some would call real friends. Les Garçons notwithstanding, some people have said that when I was a kid I never really developed any true friendships. But I must say that at the time, I didn't think I needed any; I had my brother, Ralph. When he died in 1975, I didn't just lose my best friend, it was like losing my only friend. Of course, Les Garçons were still with me, but more to preserve a static bond from childhood than an organic friendship in middle age.

I was a loner, making my way through the world, and with other people, on my own terms. I spent a lot of time playing pinochle with Guy Guyton, Jimmy Taylor, and Henry Courtland. They had all probably finished high school during the two years after I had dropped out of Clinton, being a year or two older than me. And one day in September 1948 I would follow Jimmy and Henry downtown to Whitehall Street to watch them enlist in the army. I thought they were fools because I always had a job, right there in Harlem; why sign your life over to Uncle Sam? Little did I know that I'd leave Whitehall Street that day signed up for a one-year hitch myself.

I was always working, whether it was delivering Adam Clayton Powell's newspaper, shining shoes, working in the drug- or hardware store, or, as I was at the time, working full-time for the well-known Adler shoe store at 209 West 125th Street. At one point I was making so much money with my regular checks that my mother was complaining she wouldn't be able to claim me as a deduction on her income taxes anymore. I was Herb Adler's main man. When he went around to the stores at Christmas to pass out bonus checks, I was his bodyguard. I was so successful there that Adler himself would dress me up and take me around with him when he was visiting the rest of the stores, to show them what a stock boy should look like.

I got the job through a Mr. Scott, who was an usher at St. Aloysius Catholic Church. Scotty, as they called him there, was the porter. When the war ended, there were young black men coming home from the military with pockets full of money to chase the latest postwar fashions. At that time, at least uptown, there was a great demand for getting your shoes stained in custom colors, various shades of burgundy and darknesses of brown. The salesman would just ask the customer what color he wanted. He'd take them to the window and the customer would point to the color of a sample shoe. Then they would bring out Scotty, with his stained apron and little brush in his hand like a backroom artist. I helped Scotty put the stain on the shoe, run a lit match over the surface to kind of bake on the color, and the rest was polishing.

The black salesmen in the store—Carl Durham among them—just knew I had something on the ball. It was Durham, with all his class, who guided me in my responsibilities, sorting the new inventory and shelving the boxes in just the right order by size and in just the right spots, and keeping the boxes dusted off. Moreover, he taught me the value of looking as sharp as the salesmen out front, even if my duties were in the back. Above all he stressed keeping myself busy, to anticipate and not wait to be told to do something; if I saw a salesman needed something I was to hop to it.

Soon the salesmen would have me get dressed up and come in on Saturdays, when it was busy, and start selling shoes for them. I discovered that I was good at it. I'd sell customers two and three pairs at a time. They'd come through the door saying they didn't need them at all, at first, and leave via the palm of my hand, lathered with soft soap and service. I knew the business from back room to front window. I'd stain the shoes for them—mahogany, oxblood, whatever color they wanted. The sales force was unionized, and it got to the point where some damn union man tried to make me lose my job because I wasn't eligible to be a member. He went to Mr. Sharkey—Leon "Shark" Sharkey, the store's manager—and said I wasn't supposed to be selling shoes. Sharkey complained back at him that I was too good at it not to be selling. The union guy said he didn't care, because I wasn't getting paid union wages, and I wasn't getting the commission. What he didn't know was that I didn't need any commission, because I'd split the commission with the guy to whom I gave credit for the sale. If you were a salesman who gave me a hard time, you didn't get any of my sales. And I would still get more money in my pocket!

―――――――――――

Around this time I was dating a gal named Dorothy. She had a cousin she wanted Ralph to meet. She set up this blind date—my brother was on the heavy side, and so was the blind date—but she had brought along another cousin, and this girl was beautiful. Ralph was pissed off that they brought him a fat girl. And it was the beautiful cousin who fell in love with him. They passed notes, and before I knew it he went and married that girl while I was in the army. When I went into the army, in 1948, Ralph and I were running buddies and he was just dating Delores. When he told me he'd married her I was so angry about it I didn't know what to do, except to be best man by proxy. It was wrong, I thought, because she was just one of the girls, only eighteen years old at the time, a kid like me, only younger. That was my brother; he was supposed to wait for me to come home because we had more hanging out to do!

Luckily for me, when I left the service, Delores and Ralph were right there to open their home to me. They later gave me my wonderful godson Christopher, my lovely niece Patrice (who I can't believe is now a grandmother), and my soon-to-be-retired NBC executive nephew, Ralph Jr. At least a few times a year I pull my late brother's children together with my sister, Frances; her husband, Donald; and their children, Denise and David. I call my daughter, Alicia, her husband, and my grandchildren, Howard and Joshua. Add some good food, laughter, and lots of love, and that, my friends, is what I call an oldtime family reunion.

My Les Garçons friendships persisted in the two years between leaving high school and enlisting in the army. But there were subtle shifts and interruptions in our relationships, as each of us faced the age of making the first real decisions of adult life—or dodging them. My memory of what happened to each guy goes very fuzzy here, and doesn't get clear until sometime after I left the army. The reason is that, to the extent we had any larger life aspirations at all, we didn't share or especially support one another in them at that time. I don't remember anyone saying "Let's all go to college," or even "Let's all seek our fortune in the military." That wasn't what Les Garçons was about.

Personally, it didn't take much for me to have more than my share of self-esteem. If I was in charge of the stock boys, that was OK. If I became a shoe salesman, that would have been OK, too. On their own, I don't know whether any of the other guys who wound up in the military would have acquired the ambitions they later pursued without the impetus supplied by the availability of GI Bill benefits. Their parents, for the most part, didn't appear to have any great plans for their kids or professional accomplishments for us to model ourselves after. Hell, half of us didn't really have fathers. What little fathering we got spilled over from dealing with the fathers of Guy Guyton, Arthur Barnes, and Maceo Williams.

Arthur's father recently passed away. I couldn't make the funeral but I did have someone read my note of thanks and appreciation. Arthur's father really was shared by all of us, in terms of admiring his sophistication, and his taking enough time to realize that we all needed his guidance. He was a sharp dresser—Arthur really learned how to dress through him. I don't recall what business he was in—another example of what was not passed on to us—but it involved handling a lot of cash. He would teach us how to count money; it was very exciting watching his fingers fly, a little diamond ring on one of them.

Everybody had come up poor, except maybe Maceo. He did come from 131st Street when we bonded through serving at St. Aloysius, but then he moved to upper, upper Central Park West, somewhere around 106th Street. That was a big deal for black folks at that time, and we were impressed. Maceo's father was one of the most interesting people I knew then. Years later I was stunned to find out he had actually gone to college—yet another thing not passed on when it might have had an impact, because you could meet and talk with Mr. Williams and never suspect he had any training at all. He didn't dress like it, and he didn't talk like it, as far as I could tell. He was a consummate entrepreneur of the streets; everything was cash, cash, cash. He ran a burial business, a form of mutual insurance association that poor folks used to cover funeral expenses. He also ran fruit stores, the kind that put produce out on street corners just like the Italian vendors did. Maceo had to work long, odd hours in that fruit business—we'd stay up with him sometimes and drink wine all night long.

My world still incorporated the point of view of the guys I ran with from east of Lenox Avenue. Few would survive even the fifties, except maybe in jail. We used to drink wine, smoke cigarettes, and hang out in front of the candy store. We used to go on the subway, get in one of the unlocked conductor's compartments, and blow the whistle. We used to jump the turnstiles. We used to go up to apartment buildings in the Bronx, push the buttons on the intercoms, yell at the people who answered, and then run. Time spent with these characters led to a lot of time spent in the 32nd Precinct. The cops didn't usually bother to fingerprint and process you when you got taken in back then, they'd just whip your ass. It was more like a system of ad hoc corporal punishment than criminal justice. And sometimes they would just send for my grandfather; then *he* would whip my ass all the way home.

In this environment, and the mind-set it instilled, school was the last thing on my mind. I had actually substituted a contempt for those who sought an education for seeking it myself. That was a big part of the arrogance that kept me going. I didn't have any of this stuff about black or ghetto kids equating success in school with "acting white." But I did harbor a sense of class resentment.

What remains of my "east of Lenox" identity became a ghost of Harlem real estate history by the time I returned home from the army. While I was gone they razed everything from the north side of 132nd Street—our house was on the south side—to 135th Street, between Fifth and Lenox avenues, to build the luxurious—for Harlem at that time—Lenox Terrace Apartments. I now live in the very development that erased the grittiest part of my past. There would be no continuity—thank God—with the hoodlum side of my life after the army. But, as I've said, I saw none of this coming at the time. One day Henry, Jimmy, and I were playing pinochle together, the next day I was going along for the ride to Whitehall Street to watch them throw their lives away. The next hour I was in the army.

In 1948, pushed by then Secretary of State George Marshall, President Harry Truman instituted the first postwar draft. If drafted, you served twenty-one months of active duty, followed by five years in the reserves. If you volunteered, as Henry and Jimmy did, you could satisfy your draft obligation with a three-year hitch. But you could also beat it by taking a one-year enlistment, followed by six years of reserve duty. Now, even though Truman could already see signs of the new "cold" war going hot all over the globe, there was no reason for any of us to fear imminent conscription. We were at peace, not three years after the biggest war the world had ever seen. I think Jimmy and Henry saw that the benefits—three hots and a cot, travel and a paycheck—were better than what we were doing, which was nothing. The recruiter may have conned me a bit by saying I was going to be drafted sooner or later anyway. He might also have said something about Truman's executive order that year that ostensibly desegregated the military. But the real reason I took the one-year deal had more to do with the lack of alternatives. It was as though I suddenly realized that the army was the last train smoking to another world beyond Harlem, however unknown.

I really didn't intend to join the army, but in that instant with the recruiter I looked around and saw that nothing seemed to be working for me. I realized I wasn't really doing anything to get anywhere in life; for all my hustling I was simply spinning my wheels. I remembered when my brother was seventeen and I was ten, and he thought he was a burden on the family. He decided to join the army, and soon he was sending money home. I remembered how that check my mother used to get from him made us so damn happy, and how proud she was to say that her son was taking some care of her. I knew I could help my mother with that army check coming home.

This recruiting sergeant, this salesman, was really something. He really reinforced this feeling that I had nothing better to do with my life. Finally he said to me, "For you I have a special package. How would you like to go in for just one year and see how you like it? Then you'll be in the reserves, and you get paid for being in the reserves. You'll get education benefits . . . and you'll be in good shape."

After my first few weeks in the army, I was convinced that I had been conned. But after my first paycheck, I found myself reenlisting for an additional three years.

━━━━━━━━━━

How little did I know, when I was encouraged by the army recruiter to enlist, that these recruiters were no more than salesmen. How little did I know that they had quotas to meet, just like car dealers, to bring in young people. And how difficult his job would have been if, at the time that I enlisted, I had any idea that I would find myself in combat in Korea, a country I'd never heard of, just two years later. At the time of this writing, the war in Iraq has been on for more than three years. Some twenty-five hundred men and women have been killed. Almost half of them would be those who volunteered for the army and on discharge joined the reserves or the national guard. And the other half would be just like me, hailing from rural areas or inner cities, areas of the very highest unemployment where they see little or no future for themselves.

Unlike 1948, today's recruiter jobs are in fact made much more difficult by the widespread knowledge of exactly what recruits are "volunteering" for. For 2005, the army fell 6,600 soldiers short of its recruitment target, its first such failure since 1999. As of May 2006 the army national guard and reserve posted their worst recruitment figures in a year, with new reserves coming in at just 83 percent of its goal. To pick up the numbers, the army doubled enlistment bonuses in 2006, offering up to $40,000 for joining its Special Forces units. Bonuses have soared for some recruits, it's been alleged, who have not even completed high school. The evidence is overwhelming that America has relegated the job of fighting today's wars to people and families and communities without economic or political clout. These are the people, the sons and daughters of the inner cities and rural/small-town America poverty, who are "volunteering" to be our fighting men and women in Iraq. All it takes is a look at the pictures, and the surnames, and the hometowns from which they come, to know who they are. A shockingly large number of the casualties are not even citizens.

In 2006 I reintroduced a bill to reinstitute the draft. When I first proposed it, in the fall of 2004, the Republicans buried it with a parliamentary procedure. It's still not what the Republicans, and perhaps even some more pragmatic Democrats, want to hear, much less vote for. But the downward trend in recruitment, along with the rising level of public skepticism about the means and ends of the prosecution of the war in Iraq, should force them to at least listen. I note at the time of this writing that, despite the dangerous decline in recruitment, President George W. Bush has yet to make an appeal directly to American youth to volunteer to serve their country. He has not called men and women of fighting age to their duty to bring freedom and liberty—as he sees it—to Iraq, Iran, Syria, and North Korea. While he spends a lot of time complimenting those already under arms, he has apparently never perceived that danger to the United States from these nations to be serious enough to urge all American families to make such a sacrifice.

I am calling for a draft that would reach everyone between the ages of eighteen and forty-two, with deferments allowed only for completion of high school, up to age twenty, and for reasons of health, conscience, or religious belief. I updated my bill to reflect the fact that the army itself has raised the top age for volunteers from thirty-nine to forty-two. I'm not just trying to make a partisan political point with this call. The Pentagon's own researchers say there's a crisis in military recruitment, and there's no plan to fix it. I want to make those who support preemptive war either consider putting people from their own families, their own neighborhoods, and their own class in harm's way, or consider themselves hypocrites. With all the evidence that we now have showing why we never should have gone into Iraq in the first place, there is no doubt in my mind that with a draft in place we would have held the president's case for war in Iraq to a much higher standard, and never gone in. But now that we're there, if people still support the war, why wouldn't they support a draft? Why aren't they leading a charge (if the president won't) for service as a patriotic duty?

I have to conclude that the answer is that this is not a patriotic war. And believe me, when it comes to recruiting kids from Harlem, they are not talking about anything like patriotism. They're talking about up to $90,000 for reenlisting active duty servicemen in some special-ties. It's a far cry from the bone of self-respect they threw me to get me to sign in 1948. But, if recent trends hold, it's still not going to be enough.

I didn't hang out too much with Les Garçons after I got out of the army in 1952. I didn't hang out much with anybody in those years. We drifted back together later in the decade, well after I established myself as an older college student. We didn't operate as a formal group but more like an alumni association, graduates of the particular place and time that was our late teens and early twenties in Harlem. It wasn't obvious, at first, but we were really preserving something of intangible value about ourselves in the amber of stories retold and fights refought, over hard liquor and cigarette smoke.

Every year, from the time I entered the Congress or maybe a little before, I held a poker game in my house. In the early years we'd go down to the basement and do a lot of smoking and drinking and cussing and lying about the good old days. That would be all we did the whole weekend, and by Sunday we'd be so fed up with one another that we could never be sure we'd be meeting again the next year. We even did it one year down at my place at Punta Cana in the Dominican Republic. We loved poker—we played all night Friday, went to the beach on Saturday, and stayed up playing all night again.

When you're near middle age—I was forty when I entered Con-gress—but still think you're young, one of the things you do is try to act like you're still from the hood in front of the people who knew you when. It's amazing how you have to go back and talk like you think you talked, and assume the appropriate postures. As we got older the smok-ing and drinking stopped, but not the trash talk. We'd play the "dozens," the endless variations of insult jokes with laughs at the expense of wives, girlfriends past and present, and mothers, our most valued possessions. We would bring up all the old stories almost calculated to cause anger and denial, without ever settling the score.

I'd have to say that at some level, no matter how far we did or did not go in the world beyond our youth, inside we never had much except one another. Our families from childhood didn't gave us a wealth of warm memories to take with us to high school or college or wherever we would go. In a sense, to varying degrees, we had to make up our own backgrounds, and we made them up before one another, like mutual mirrors. And it wasn't like we would go to Oak Bluffs or Sag Harbor or some other redoubt of the black upper middle class, where our families would go annually and we would meet up. Some of us have become accustomed to those places, but none of us were of them. We just held on to what we had.

To be sure, there was a little of what we now call professional networking among us over the years. When Arthur became an executive at an insurance company called Consolidated in the sixties, he brought Henry Courtland and Trevor Bannister into the firm, and they became officers. Arthur went on to form a friendship with our mutual friend, and my political ally, Basil Patterson. They got involved in the negotiation and arbitration profession, under the wing of my dear friend, the renowned labor lawyer Ted Kheel. But, just as it was before I joined the army, Les Garçons wasn't about networking. It was about bearing witness.

We were self-invented, and we felt kind of proud that other people, who knew us only from our positions of accomplishment, would even ask why Les Garçons meant so much to us. When we were kids, we used to borrow an expression from the older people in the neighborhood: "This is my twenty-year buddy." We were saying it when we were just teenagers. Then, when we literally became twenty-year buddies, and thirty-year buddies, and forty-year, and even sixty-year buddies, we joked about still being one another's twenty-year buddies. To say "This is my twenty-year buddy" was to say "This is my main man" from a time in the waning years of the depression when we had nothing to give a friend but loyalty. To say "twenty-year buddy" after sixty years means pledging loyalty to the end. A few years ago I was visiting Norman Howard, who was in Mt. Sinai Hospital with a serious heart ailment. Hours flew by, just talking and talking, and I looked at my watch and said I just had to go.

"Well, wait a minute," he said.

"I've been here over two hours and I'm late," I said, about to be late for an appointment.

"Well, I wanna tell you something," he said.

"What the hell could you possibly have left to tell me?" I replied.

And then he smiled his crooked smile, and said, "All I want to tell you is to take care of yourself, Charlie; they're calling our class."

When I picture our class being called, I see Maceo Williams in the front row center.

Maceo, Maceo, Maceo. He finished Rice High School, a well-regarded, almost all-white Catholic school, and attended Howard University in Washington, D.C., just long enough to drop out and join the marines. He ended up finishing his college degree at NYU, with me, courtesy of the GI Bill. He used to call me "Cat," and he was maybe just the plain nicest guy in our whole gang.

In 2002 I got a call saying Maceo had had a stroke. I went to look for him at some hospital in Queens, where at first no one knew who he was. A black nurse recognized me and took me to him. He recognized me immediately.

"Charlie! Cat, it's so good to see you. What am I doing here?"

"Maceo, you had a stroke."

"Oh yes, Cat, they told me that. But . . . do my mother and father know?"

"Maceo, your mother and father have been dead for over thirty years."

"Ohhhh, man! My mother? My father? Ohhh man! Well, who in my family . . ."

"Maceo, you don't have a family."

"I don't? I don't? So that's why I wasn't able to answer their questions. And I thought it was because I had lost my memory. That's why: I don't have anybody."

"Maceo, you've got your friends," I said. And then I mentioned some of those who had died.

"Jimmy? Jimmy Taylor is dead? Norman Howard is dead?"

I didn't know *what* the hell I was going through with Maceo in that hospital room that day. Gradually his mind came back, though he still complained about forgetting things. Later on I remember asking him:

"Maceo, you know, you have about a half-dozen kids out of wedlock running around, right?"

"Oh Cat! You know I don't have no kids out there."

"Just testing you, Maceo," I replied. We had a big laugh.

"You know I can ask you some questions that these psychiatrists would never think of," I followed up. "Remember those gals that time at the Paradise Inn?"

"Yeah, Cat, I remember the gals," he replied.

A few months before he died, Maceo had recovered enough of himself for me and another Les Garçons, Earl Davis, to take Maceo out of the hospital for a lovely day together. But the moral of the story is this: Here's a man who had a wealth of family and friends when he was young, yet, in the end, he had no wife, no kids, no brothers, no sisters . . . and for a while no memory. After Maceo died, I tracked down his remaining family to tell them what happened, and they shunned me for fear I was going to ask them to pay for the funeral. But Maceo didn't need his family to pay for anything; his friends were there for him. Ironically, he had already signed over his pension and death benefits, such as they were, to these, his only living relatives. His kin may have forgotten him, but it felt good to know we didn't have to beg to bury our friend.

We haven't done our reunion poker game for a few years now. When Norman Howard died, and I spoke at the funeral, I said, "Well, Norm, you've got Henry Courtland up there with you, but we never played heads-up poker. So don't start the game yet . . . unless you're really waiting for one of us." We left the funeral on 138th Street and came right back to my place in Lenox Terrace and played poker all night long. That was for Norman. He made it to being a police detective. Barry Best had a career in the post office before he died. Guy Guyton drove a bus, and retired a manager with the New York City Transit Authority; he's still with us, but his health is poor. Wherever we had reached, whatever hands we were holding in terms of our marriages, our children, our health at the time, whenever the gang would get together, we'd just look at one another and smile, because we knew how blessed we'd been. One wrong turn, on the wrong block or on the wrong evening, could have made all the difference in the world. For any of us.

When I was a kid, my mother used to say "God is good," almost at the drop of a hat. I have memorized so many things from childhood— the Lord's Prayer, the Pledge of Allegiance, the "Star-Spangled Banner"—without having a clue as to what the words meant. They said to say it, and I said it. But saying "God is good" always seemed such a misnomer at a time when we were having such bad experiences. It was always when things were the worst that she said it, and I thought my mom was missing the point. Maybe He's good most of the time, but not when He appears to have forgotten you, I thought. But as I got older, I saw that all she was doing was counting the blessings that she had. It's something I've always done. When I lost my brother, and when I lost her, I was overwhelmed with the feeling of how fortunate I was to have them in the first place, and to have enjoyed their love and friendship all those years. That's how I'd like to keep seeing Les Garçons, right up to whatever ends I'm blessed to see.

As I said in the introduction, I believe I got this attitude I call "and I haven't had a bad day since" from that night on the mountain pass in North Korea. I know that whatever I think my problems are right now, they are a hell of a lot easier to deal with than the ones that came before. I know how lucky I am to have been married, to have my children, to be in the Congress, and to be participating in matters of such importance for such a long, healthy lifetime. Whether you call it luck or God's grace, there's no better attitude to have than gratitude for going through life.

I just don't think I should have had to get shot in Korea to get it, but I haven't had a bad day since.

3

Korea (September 1948–June 1952)

After thirty-five years in the Congress I'm well trained in how to stand up and argue a point until my opponents are ready to make a deal, or try to outflank me from behind closed doors. But I really don't want to debate the question of whether my success reflects the persistence of good luck or the grace of God's blessing. Arguing the latter would be hypocritical—it would be putting the words of my mother's faith in my mouth and spilling them on these pages. Yet the story of my journey— really, anybody's journey—is too amazing in its grace to be luck alone.

Meeting Nelson Mandela, and being a part of the end of apartheid, represents this quality of grace in my life to me. In early May 1994, I was aboard the plane of the first lady of the United States, Hillary Clinton— along with Colin Powell, the poet Maya Angelou, entertainment mogul and activist Quincy Jones, and several other members of Congress—to witness Mandela's inauguration as South Africa's first black president. It was one of the most significant ceremonies I've ever beheld, and certainly the high point of my career to that date. I was awed by the sight and sound of the jets that darkened the skies above us in tribute that day. And I was humbled, as Mandela graciously bestowed thanks on the prison guards who befriended him during the twenty-seven years he spent in jail. It was so unbelievable to me that after all that time he would emerge with such compassion in his triumph, and with so much hope for building a nonracist society for the future. To hear the roar of this crowd, and to have been a small part of the eradication of that former government, left me without words for how I felt.

It was like going to heaven after fighting the good fight, without first having to die. The good fight was for the Rangel Amendment, which denied a very valuable tax deduction to U.S. firms doing business in South Africa to compensate for taxes paid to the apartheid South African government. I was told by a former South African ambassador to the United States that in South Africa it was known as "the bloody" Rangel Amendment because its passage in 1987 made it too expensive for even the most stubborn apologists for the South African system to keep doing business there. In particular, Mobil Corporation, the largest U.S. investor in South Africa at the time, cited the sudden hike in its tax bill as a major factor in its April 1989 decision to withdraw. The oil giant had successfully resisted the moral and political pressure that had previously pushed Coca-Cola, General Motors, IBM, and other major American corporations to pull out. Mobil's departure, under the economic pressure from the bill with my name on it, was seen as the backbreaker for U.S. multinational corporate support for the apartheid government. Mandela was freed from his imprisonment at Robben Island ten months later.

I have to thank George Dalley, my faithful chief of staff for well over thirty years, and Jon Sheiner, my staff tax consultant, for helping me write the legislation that brought all this about. It took ten years to get the Rangel Amendment into law, and seven more for me to see Mandela's inaugural day. In all those years, though, I never thought to lash out from my personal frustration in the matter. Hell, Mandela himself did that seventeen years, and ten more besides, in prison. Moreover, I lost my right to complain about anything again in life more than four decades earlier, as I lay wounded in a gully on a Korean mountain pass during the war. What I went through that night in Korea would resolve itself into a survival technique that I've been honing ever since. Recently I asked my staff, who have been with me far too long not to tell me the truth, if they ever remember me getting angry and raising hell about something. The answer was no. I may not talk to you for a while, but that's about it. And that to me is a hell of a thing to be able to say. A lot of people say I'm always smiling. But I don't always intend to smile. And it doesn't mean that I'm always that damn happy. It just means I'm not aware of any reason why I shouldn't be smiling.

Don't get me wrong, I'm as capable of being outraged about some setback or screwup as the next person, and I might want to pull somebody's head off for a minute. Then I remember the bigger picture of what I really wanted to get accomplished in the first place. And I recall some time from the intermediate past that was a hell of a lot worse than what's before me at the moment. And if that doesn't work, I go back to the bottom of that Korean gully, and remember. Immediately, I'm not having a bad day anymore. I've taken a deep breath, and then exhaled with gratitude for lungs that work and air to breathe.

I guess professionals have all kinds of ways of telling people how to do this. All I'm saying is that being shot in the behind in Korea did it for me.

As I share the stories from my life, I hope that this book might allow other people, when facing what looks like tremendous setbacks, to know you don't have to face a pointless death in a foreign land to realize you've been lucky or blessed. You don't have to return from a battle where thousands were left for dead or captured behind you to be a survivor. All you have to do is say: "Bad times mean take that deep breath. Bad times mean take two steps back for a minute and look again." You can't see the problem you have until you line it up next to the problems you've had before and overcome.

I didn't always have this outlook, and it took a few years after I left the service to mature in me. Nevertheless I'm convinced that the foundation for it was laid in Korea. I went into the army in September 1948, at age eighteen, full of self-esteem based on nothing but my belief that I was making it in the world without an education. I left in June 1952 with that same ego, even more swollen, but resting on a fixed baseline for the worst that could happen, a rock on which I would ultimately build more reasonable, if not humble, expectations for my life.

On September 15, 1948, Henry Courtland, Jimmy Taylor, and I reported to Fort Dix, New Jersey, for induction into the army. But I didn't stay at Fort Dix for long. When I arrived they were still waiting for enough people to come in from the South and some other Northern cities to form a new all-black training unit. They gave the few of us on hand toilet articles and such, but no uniforms. I met some guy who had been in the army with my brother and asked him what I was supposed to be doing here, with no uniform and no unit. I had on this blue vest that a friend's mother had made for me—I was still as Harlem sharp as I could be. This guy gave me a fistful of three-day passes, and said I might as well cool my heels at home for a while. When folks saw me come home so soon after shipping off they thought I'd gone AWOL.

For a long time, I managed to avoid all basic training in Fort Dix. When I got back from my succession of three-day leaves, those who had come in while I was home thought I was an old-timer, because I had been there two weeks before and supposedly knew what was going on. I didn't, really, but when they finally gave us uniforms, these country boys thought I was so much more than I was, and I acted the part. The Les Garçons prime directive was still in effect: "Assume the virtue, though you have it not." In fact, there was a whole group of us from New York that quickly learned how to game the system. It was such a cakewalk for me. We were slicker than grease, and those country boys had no idea how to keep up with us.

After basic training we took a troop train from Fort Dix to Fort Lewis, Washington. There we were, hundreds of GIs with nothing but a little basic under our belts, every one of us just eighteen years old. We tore that train up. The poor second lieutenant in charge of us must have aged ten years on that trip. The train broke down someplace outside of New Jersey, and they said we could get off but we had to be back in an hour. I don't know how much alcohol there was on board when we started, but there was definitely more liquor aboard when we started up again! A lot of guys had guitars, and there was a saxophone or two, and we raised hell all the way to Fort Lewis. I started becoming convinced that success in the army was just like getting over on the streets of Harlem, except they fed, housed, and even paid you for getting away with it.

The army, for me, was summed up by a big sign in the mess hall. It read: "Take All You Want, Eat All You Take." It wasn't "Be All You Can Be," but it was more than good enough for me. I walked around with a cocky confidence in my ability to avoid a whole lot of hard or menial work by slipping between the cracks of the army's vast, overlapping bureaucracy. Officially, I was in the 503rd Field Artillery, Headquarters Battery, an all-black unit that was part of the 2nd Infantry Division based at Fort Lewis. Everyone on base at Fort Lewis thought I had come from division headquarters.

I created this protective illusion almost by accident, the result of two moves I made that proved critical, and perhaps lifesaving, in my military career. As I've said, I originally signed up for a one-year enlistment, with a subsequent six-year reserve requirement, in September 1948. It still made me, like a great number of my fellow buck privates, a draftee with a serial number that began "US-57-xxxxx." But by February 1949 I had decided that the army was good enough for me; to hell with avoiding the draft, I'm going to sign up for three years. When I did that, the prefix on my serial number became "RA—Regular Army—but it was still followed by "57" (followed by 156–282). From then on, wherever I reported for duty, people had a hard time figuring out who I was. To be Regular Army meant I was something more of an insider in this white man's army. To be "US" meant I was just another colored boy trying to beat the draft. As it happened I was both; the confusion created openings I quickly learned to squeeze myself through.

On my own I started going up to division headquarters. I would hang out, under the guise of gathering information on what was going on in the division, the army, and the world and how it would affect us. Then

I'd take it back to the rank and file at different parts of the 503rd. It looked like my job, but in reality I had no assignment at all. No one knew for sure who I was, not even the company commander. I basically made up my own job—the position of being in the know. And from that position I soon learned about an opening for a corporal in the wire section and I decided to promote myself into it. The wire section deals with information and communication. I had no training, but I wasn't going to let that stop me.

Around that time there was a Sergeant Parker at division head-quarters who was part of my made-up information network. He was a black guy from New York, too, and I think he wanted to help me. I remember him asking, "What do you do? What do you do here?" I told him what I was doing, and he said, "Well, there's a school for that." The school was at the Carlisle Barracks War College, in Carlisle, Pennsylvania, about two hundred miles southwest of New York City. The course, "Information and Education," supposedly taught you how to keep the troops up on current events and how to relate these events to their present mission, which at the time was battling the communist threat. There I was, a high school dropout, being sent to learn to be a communicator, even a lecturer on American foreign policy: I said, "Hell yes," that's me!

The class was for commissioned and noncommissioned officers alike, and it was damn near perfect, at first. I got to sit in class in a nice shiny uniform, rubbing shoulders with officers like I was some kind of professional. And I went home to Harlem every weekend, looking sharp in my class "A" uniform, with a good-conduct pin on my chest. Then one day in class, a tall, light-skinned, freckle-faced second lieutenant named Lamar Smith pulled me aside. He was an ROTC graduate of Howard University, from Watertown, New York. He was also in my unit, the 503rd Field Artillery. I'd seen him before, but I didn't figure he knew who the hell I was, because I thought I had succeeded in staying under the radar of straight-arrow officers like Lamar Smith. Boy, was I wrong.

"How you doing, soldier?" he says.

"Fine, lieutenant," I say.

"How did you get into this class?" he asks.

"Oh, I guess Captain Dunn recommended me, sir."

"How would he know who you are?" he asks. "Where do you sleep?"

"Barracks Two, sir, Headquarters Battery," I reply.

"But you're not on the field, you're not in the wire section, you're not in mess hall or supply," he counters. "Where do you do most of your work?"

"I do a lot of work on main post, sir," I say, trying to squirm off his well-placed hook. "I do a variety of things—" I started, but he cut me off.

"Rangel," he says, "I know exactly who you are. You're just shiftless, that's what you are. And you've got all of these people conned. And you know something else? I'm not even gonna blow your cover. But one day your past is gonna catch up to you."

Lieutenant Smith also said something about me being bright and intelligent, and New York slick. I just looked at him and said, to myself, "What the hell—you don't know me . . . jive-ass lieutenant." But I knew he'd peeped my hole card.

He was dead right—I had managed not to be assigned to a damn thing at Headquarters Battery. They did allow you to go to school if they thought you could help yourself, so I had as much right to be in that class as he did. But Lieutenant Smith seemed like the only man in the army who knew that I wasn't doing a damn thing in my outfit. Or maybe he was the only one who not only cared to know, but cared enough to call me on it. He was an officer in the same outfit. He knew that whenever there were troops falling out I wasn't with them. Whenever they went to the field I wasn't going into the field. The only time they'd see me was in the mess hall. He didn't know exactly where I was going or what I was doing, but he knew that I was not soldiering in that outfit. It must have dropped his jaw just seeing me show up like a shiny bad penny at that course in Carlisle in the first place.

It was really awkward, almost chilling, to be confronted by an officer that way. He exposed me—to myself—as a fraud. But rather than proceed to expose me to the army as such, he said to hell with it, he'd give me a break. He would bide his time, keep an eye on me, and see if I hung myself with the rope I was taking. I must have passed his smell test in time, but from then on I kept a respectful distance as I went about my business when we got back to Fort Lewis. About a year later, the day our unit was alerted to be shipped to Korea, Lieutenant Smith sent for me. He said, "Rangel, it's your ass now. What can you do? What do you know how to do? Are you gonna be doing 'Information and Education' in combat? Is that what you're gonna do?"

And then Lieutenant Lamar Smith took me under the wing that would enable me to save my life, and the lives of others, in Korea.

I was promoted to private first class in August 1949, but I'd been putting on the airs of higher rank for some time. When I returned to Fort Lewis after the Carlisle class, I don't think I ever wore fatigues. I got into the habit of wearing nothing but that starched khaki uniform with my shiny brass on. Now that I'd had this training, I really thought I had the power to cloud men's minds like the old *Shadow* radio show. Everybody at Headquarters Battery thought I was just bunking with them but that I was assigned to division rear. And when I'd go to division headquarters, they thought I was there on official business from the 503rd Field Artillery Headquarters Battery. I had such a good time acting like a big shot, asking professional-sounding questions and taking notes. In reality, I was nothing but a very well-dressed PFC—with a clipboard.

I carried an official army clipboard with me the way MPs carry sidearms. I honestly don't know where or how I figured this out, but in life, if you carry a clipboard, people think you're doing something. I remember when Stevie Wonder came to Washington to headline a concert in support of the Congress recognizing the birthday of Dr. Martin Luther King Jr. as a national holiday. Steny Hoyer, who is now the House Democratic Whip, and I walked for what seemed miles through a crowd to get to the main stage for this big televised event. When we got there we saw all these superstars—the late Ossie Davis, Ruby Dee, Harry Belafonte, and so on. Then we looked up saw a little white guy on stage, and I said to Steny, "Is that who I think it is?" He says, "Yes, it sure is." It was Dale Kildee, then a relatively new member of Congress from Michigan. Steny and I had nearly thirty years in Congress between us, but Kildee had this clipboard. He was up on that stage and welcoming people and checking this clipboard as if he were in charge. And he didn't know *anybody!* We kept trying to get his attention, and he kept ignoring us. Kildee stayed on TV for hours that day, checking off famous people backstage on his clipboard as they came in.

Dale Kildee was the epitome of how to use a clipboard. Thank God, he's still with us to tell the tale of the chutzpah he had that day. He assumed the virtue though he had it not. Sergeant Parker had asked, "What do you do, Rangel?" Well, me and my clipboard weren't doing a damn thing, and we looked and felt good doing it, too. Army paperwork can be a deadly weapon in the right hands. I didn't know it then, but I was inventing myself as a Sergeant Bilko before anybody dreamed up the classic 1950s sitcom that starred Phil Silvers as a constantly conniving motor pool sergeant. And I was only a private!

Of course, I wasn't strutting around in the army that you see in standard World War II movies, or the few Korean War pictures that were made. Sergeant Bilko was in the white man's army; I spent almost four years in the segregated black man's army, even though Truman supposedly desegregated the military months before I reported for duty. It really irks me how the truth is often compressed into untruth in the popular recording of history. At the time of the fiftieth anniversary of the signing of the armistice that officially ended our police action in Korea, I watched a History Channel special on the war in utter disbelief. There they were talking about how Truman had integrated the armed forces by executive order in 1948. If that was so, what was my black ass doing in an all-black outfit—besides the commissioned officers—in 1950? What was I doing in an extremely segregated base at Fort Sill, Oklahoma, in 1951?

Yes, in June 1948, Truman did sign Executive Order 9981 that says, in part, "It is hereby declared to be the policy of the President that there shall be equality of treatment and opportunity for all persons in the armed services without regard to race, color, religion, or national origin." But the order, correctly anticipating strenuous military resistance to integration, especially from the army, established a presidential commission to oversee the obstacles of its own implementation. Before the Fahy Committee members were even named—three days after I entered the army—Army Chief of Staff Omar Bradley said that desegregation would not come to the army until it was a "fact" in American society at large. That was the bar set by the general ultimately in charge of the army in Korea, six years before the *Brown v. Board of Education* decision.

Even after the army reached an agreement with the Fahy Committee on a preliminary integration plan, in January 1950, it held on to a tight 10 percent recruitment quota on African-Americans. The army, it seemed, was desperately afraid of being overrun by a disproportionate number of blacks enlisting in an integrated military. Truman then cut a deal with Secretary of the Army Gordon Gray: He would drop the quota but had the option of reinstating it if blacks topped 10 percent of the recruits. That was in March 1950. North Korea invaded South Korea on June 25, 1950; the army began to integrate, unofficially and quite voluntarily, that same month, starting with basic training for new recruits. But as I was fighting my way up the Korean peninsula that fall, there were no plans to break up our all-black units and integrate them into white units. The army's segregationist culture was far too entrenched to turn on that dime, especially in wartime.

A year earlier, in September 1949, my unit participated in a massive war-game exercise called Operation MIKI. It was a mock invasion of the island of Hawaii. Somehow, by the time our black unit got there with our 155mm howitzers, the damn game was over. For most of us, it was our first time ever getting off the mainland of the United States, much less to an island paradise like Hawaii. So we went into town to see what we could get into, and what we ran into was just raw racism.

A black GI named Paul Plummer, a screwup from New York like me, was on the maneuver. In Hawaii, someone told me that he'd been arrested by the MPs for causing a fight at one of the local bars, so I went there with my lawyerlike self to try to deal with the MPs on his behalf. Paul told me that all the white soldiers were going into this club, but they wouldn't let him in. I really didn't believe him. So I decided to try to show him. I was going to check out this club myself, and showing him that the whole thing was a misunderstanding. I got to the door, and the guy said, "We told you: no niggers allowed!" What was worse, this racism was coming from Hawaiians, people whose skin and hair looked like mine. The explanation: The locals were already accustomed to catering to the culture of a segregated white army. The white soldiers were there first, and would have insisted on not letting the "niggers" in.

Just like in Korea, the white boys would call us niggers, so the natives would call us niggers, and a lot worse, thinking that's what we were called, and not knowing any better. It was a profoundly racist experience. Poor Plummer was later put in the 24th Infantry and sent to Japan because he was a screwup, before the war started. He later committed suicide.

The unprecedented bloodshed in Korea quickly disabused the army of the notion that it could fight the semideclared wars of post-colonialism with a "white man's army." They needed warm bodies in large numbers. Whites with means, or at least with GI Bill college benefits, could escape service through too many holes in the draft laws. It was too early in the cold war to convince the average patriotic American family that an attack on a little-known Asian nation on the other side of the world was worth volunteering for. Remember, it took Franklin Roosevelt five years after Hitler broke the Versailles Treaty in 1936, two years after Hitler rolled over Czechoslovakia and Poland in 1939, and then Pearl Harbor to get America to jump wholeheartedly into World War II.

In January 1951, some fourteen months after my Operation MIKI initiation into segregated army life, the 8th Army adopted an unofficial policy of integrating African-American troops into previously all-white units. The reason was simple: Two months earlier the 8th Army was chewed up on a mountain pass near a place called Kunu-ri, when 300,000 Chinese troops entered the war on North Korea's side. Their need for as many replacements as they could get, as soon as they could get them, was suddenly as color blind as it was acute.

I suffered my wounds and earned my medals at Kunu-ri, in a unit that, save the overwhelmingly white commissioned officers, was all black. I've never thought of thanking the Chinese for slapping the U.S. Army into the reality of a postwar, postsegregation America. But the fact is that I should never have been in that damn hole called Kunu-ri in the first place. The army and the U.S. government should have had better intelligence about the Chinese surrounding us. America was really ill-prepared to enter that war in North Korea, even more ill-prepared than for Iraq, if that's possible. While Truman and MacArthur were arguing about whether we should go to China, China came to us, and like it or not they gave us our first post–World War II defeat. It was soon to be followed by our second, in Vietnam.

We should not have been taken by surprise. True, Douglas MacArthur was talking about invading China, but that was only because China was giving material assistance to North Korea. They were not, in our underestimation, capable of direct involvement in that conflict. We were arrogant—with MacArthur occupying the conquered Japanese like he was lord of all Asia—and almost racist in our naïveté about what other Asian nations could do. Historians have their theories and disputes about what Truman knew, what MacArthur knew, and when they knew it. But one damn thing is clear: Someone should have been indicted for manslaughter for not knowing that the entire 8th Army could be surrounded by tens of thousands of Chinese troops. There was just no excuse for that happening to us.

My unit was alerted for Korea on July 9, 1950. Our commanding officer, Captain John Dunn, told us we could go into town for a last taste of stateside liberty. I ended up in Tacoma with a bunch of drunks, taking pictures, signing insurance contracts in case we didn't make it back from Korea alive, and generally carousing. Among my group was my man Willie Jackson, a corporal and a mechanic who worked on the airplanes that lifted the gliders used to spot enemy positions and guide our artillery fire. Lieutenant Smith, who was still keeping a wary eye on me, was always warning me about drinking and hanging out with Willie and Willie's boss, a black pilot and lieutenant named Woolrich.

Some sucker pulled a fire alarm that night and they all got arrested. I went to the precinct with them, to find out what was going on, and then I went back to get Captain Dunn. When he showed up at the courthouse, with me there for support, the arresting officer turned around and looked at me, then turned back to the judge and said, "Hey, he was one of 'em, too." I started sputtering about how "I am the one who is taking these men overseas." Luckily Captain Dunn quickly got us all out of there. Years later, at our reunions, old Willie Jackson would say that "I should have known the son of a bitch was gonna amount to something, because we couldn't figure out how Rangel wasn't locked up in the first place!"

Just as he had promised, when the order for Korea came, Lamar Smith, that smooth, confident black lieutenant who had peeped my hole card at the Carlisle "Information and Education" class, challenged me to put up or shut up about being a real soldier. Jesus Christ, I thought, what am I gonna do? A lot of my self-esteem had come from the fact that I had no self-esteem, and I had developed a cover so that nobody would know I didn't have any. Oh, how it hurt me to be found out for how dumb I really was! But Lamar Smith took me under his wing on that troop ship that took us overseas, and in thirteen days he made me a specialist in artillery operations. He told the colonel that I was working under him as his assistant, taking advantage of the training we received in that Carlisle class. That information-and-education nonsense actually worked for Smith. He jumped into the task of telling the men where we were going in Korea, what a police action was, who the North Koreans were, and why we were going there. And I got to be the guy who was writing it up and putting it on the mimeograph machine. I got to dust off my artistic skills from Nettie Messenger's fourth-grade class by drawing cartoons for our unit newspaper. And I even got to give some of the lectures with him.

But when I wasn't shoveling official information, Lamar Smith was teaching me fire direction, how to plot the maps, how to use the protractor and the slide rule, how to give commands to the guns, and how to direct fire on the enemy. And I enjoyed it immensely! It was the first real military learning experience I had in the army. Poor Lieutenant Smith, God bless him, got killed not long after we arrived in Korea, long before Kunu-ri. I don't know how long I could have faked it in Korea without knowing how to do anything. He really did save my life.

The first American troops in Korea were the 8th Army's 24th and 25th Infantry Divisions that were occupying Japan. These were basically World War II veterans—I don't think they did much training or were well prepared for war. The North Koreans had already crossed the 38th parallel into South Korea. These two divisions got chewed up in July and August, whipped so badly that when we got ready to go over they didn't even know whether it was safe for us to land on the so-called Pusan Perimeter—Pusan being a city on the southeast tip of South Korea.

U.S. and South Korean troops were holding on to that line in the southwest corner of Korea for dear life when my unit, the 503rd Field Artillery Battalion, 2nd Infantry Division, landed in Pusan on August 16. Slowly, as the 8th Army began turning the tide, we started moving north. I'll never forget being on the road north, moving ever closer to the battlefront, because we still hadn't received any ammunition. At one point our convoy was stalled for a long time, but we saw some trucks coming back the other way. Captain Dunn sent me to the front of the line to see what the hell was holding it up. I came back and reported that, according to these guys coming back down, North Koreans had not only chewed them up, but the North Korean troops were out of uniform and in the fields in white peasant clothing. They said the youth we were seeing in the fields were actually the enemy, and they were throwing grenades into the trucks at night. This news came from soldiers in the 3rd Battalion of the 9th Infantry, another all-black unit.

Every truck we passed told the same story. But that wasn't what scared the hell out of us, though we were going north on a road through endless rice paddies. These paddies, by the way, stunk to the high heavens. They're fertilized with human manure—anybody who's been to Korea knows how those rice fields stink in summer. What really scared us was one of the worst sights I ever saw in my life: three truckloads of GIs—dead GIs—on the way to registration. The tarps on the trucks were blowing up in the breeze and we could see them, stacked up just like wood, in their uniforms. And they were black. I don't know whether I cried or threw up, but I knew that the sight would never ever be erased from my mind. Between the stories we heard from the guys returning south, and the evidence we saw in those trucks, we knew the days of boot training were over, and that we were in combat.

On September 15, U.S. troops invaded at Inchon, which was still north of us, a strong strategic move that seemed to break up the North Korean forces and send them running back north. We pursued them across the border, thinking we were just mopping up, with every reason to believe we were going to be home before Christmas 1950. By then we were getting a steady stream of replacements for soldiers we had lost up to that point. I was scared to death that some of these new guys from the States would make some kind of mistake and get me killed before it was time to go home. So I assumed the role of a hard-nosed combat veteran.

Every time I saw one of these new soldiers, I'd ride them about how they should be taking care of their weapon, or making certain they had a good foxhole. And just to scare the hell out of them, I told them to be ready, because the Chinese were going to be landing by parachute. And that scared the living hell out of them. Now, all I knew was that the Chinese were on their side of the Yalu River border, in Manchuria. It never entered my mind that they would actually be prepared to cross it. But I became well known for repeatedly telling these young troops, "Be prepared for the Chinese, be prepared for the Chinese."

Months later, as I lay on a stretcher before some general after my ordeal at Kunu-ri, some of these same young soldiers who survived told the general that I'd told them the Chinese were coming, and that I was the only one who knew that we were going to be attacked. Did I know that? Hell, no; I didn't know a damn thing. But that didn't seem the right moment to talk about my ignorance. To tell the truth, I wasn't ready to talk about much of anything at that point. I needed some time to separate reality from the nightmare of what happened to me in the eternity that was November 29–December 1, 1950.

The 2nd Infantry led the 8th Army charge north and northwest, deep into the mountainous north of North Korea beyond Pyongyang and across the Ch'ongch'on River. By the night of November 24 the forward line was just fifty miles from the Yalu River and the Chinese border. It was a quiet night, but reports were drifting in about a massive buildup of Chinese troops to the north and northeast of the 8th Army positions. When night fell on November 25, Chinese troops came out of the dark in waves that by November 27 made a nearly complete circle—an arc of about thirty miles—around the U.S. and Republic of Korea troop positions. My unit was more or less in the center of the circle, near a place called Kunu-ri, on the road that quickly became the chosen escape route for much of what remained of the 8th Army after the Chinese overran us.

The temperature had fallen to -20 Fahrenheit on the night of November 29. The infantry units that were supposed to protect us had already retreated south past us. We felt helpless not knowing what to expect. Helicopters had actually come in and evacuated some key field officers. For two or three nights we listened to the constant blare of Chinese bugle calls, and stared at the flares they would send up. Loudspeakers screamed unintelligible English at us, all part of a kind of psychological warfare barrage leading up to their attack. We had seen a lot of GIs fall over, frozen to death as they tried so desperately hard to stay awake. It was a waking nightmare becoming a reality, scene by scene, and we couldn't see any possible way out of the situation. Though we knew they were up there, during the day, we never saw the Chinese in the hills above us. When our sorties of fighter planes would come to strafe and bomb them, they seemed to disappear into what we later learned were deep tunnels in the low-grade coal mines in the mountains even higher above us. We knew that our number was up. During the day, when we asked the officers what the situation was, they just told us to pray, or something else that didn't give much comfort. The tension rose to a crescendo with the eerie bugle blare, which seemed to get louder by the hour.

Then they hit. The Chinese poured over that Kunu-ri mountain pass just like ants swarming, from both sides of the road, screaming and yelling and bugling for all they were worth. We were stuck in defensive positions by a long line of trucks just trying to get the hell out of that situation. We were led by a Major John Fralish, who was acting as CO after any number of other officers were wounded, killed, or otherwise missing. I know he later got a Silver Star for his efforts those three days, and for years he showed up at the periodic reunions of Kunu-ri survivors we used to have. He was white, like most of the commissioned officers in our black outfit.

The Chinese attacks seemed to taper off by dawn on November 30. We were supposed to be keeping the road south to Sunchon open for what remained of the 38th Infantry to make its way—and our way—past a succession of shifting Chinese roadblocks. But plans for an orderly retreat fell apart as quickly as they were made, given the tremendous casualties, spotty communications, and repeated breaks in the chain of command between various units. Somehow Major Fralish kept us moving, by fits and starts, down the road toward Sunchon. But the Chinese troops were well positioned on both sides of the road, as it wound through increasingly higher hills approaching a narrow pass in the mountains between us and Sunchon. They were really playing cat and mouse with us, letting us get a little farther, then cutting off one part or another of our ragtag column.

Much of the real fighting took place at night, heightening the sheer terror. The 503rd's Battery B was pinched off and torn up in just such an attack right after dark on November 30. Soon we were taking mortar fire, and trying to throw it back, but nobody knows what, if any, effect it had. Later that night, after making our way a few more miles south, Battery A was cut off, and very few escaped. Around midnight, after one last meeting under fire, the remaining officers decided there was no choice but to split up. One group would attempt to break through the Chinese roadblocks with the trucks carrying the wounded. They weren't very successful. The rest of us, led by Major Fralish and a Lieutenant Douglas D. Grinnell from the 38th Infantry, would try to go through the hills and around the mountain toward Sunchon by foot.

We would move out after midnight but we were trying to collect whatever wounded we could and put them on trailers. The record supporting my Bronze Star medal says I was already wounded myself, but I was still clearing the road of dead and wounded bodies to try and keep the convoy moving. We didn't know what the hell we were really doing, with all the people screaming and moaning around us. We could see some GIs being marched away by the Chinese. I had given away my wound kit, but it wouldn't have made any difference; it was so unbelievably cold that the blood was frozen in the wounds.

There was a tractored vehicle, like a small tank, that seemed to be going someplace. I guess it was an ammunition carrier. Something hit that damn thing, maybe a mortar, and all I saw was orange. Everything seemed to be orange, and I was thrown into a gully that was deep enough to make it seem that all the action was happening far above me.

It was there, seemingly below the action in another time zone, that I prayed to Jesus. I told Jesus that if I ever got out of that mess, if I could somehow survive that night, which I never thought I could, that I would never be a problem to anybody, ever again. In that moment, you see, I suddenly saw that I had caused a lot of problems. Somehow, I felt that I heard Jesus say, "Boy, if you want any help you'd better get out of that hole." It could have been five minutes, or it could have been an hour as I started to pull myself up. I could see hand-to-hand combat, and the outlines against the moonlight of some of our soldiers being led away with their hands over their heads. And above and beyond it all, like some kind of natural fortress framed by the full moon, was that mountain. From the rim of that gully it just looked like everything had to be better on the other side of that damn mountain.

I don't know how I could have been more frightened. At one point I thought about acting like I was dead, but I was too scared to do that. I knew I had to get the hell out of there. My heart was beating so hard, I remember thinking that people could hear it. I really don't remember feeling any pain, just fear. I realized that the ditch was beside a little hill, a mound that could have been a grave or burial mound—some Koreans bury their people in mountainsides. I crawled to the other side of that road on my stomach. When I got there, there were other GIs there, and they were screaming and yelling at me: "What should we do, Sarge? What should we do?"

Sarge. It was a title whose virtue I had assumed—really appropriated—even before we had gotten to Korea. If any of them had any doubt about me being something other than the simple PFC that I actually was, those doubts were washed away when the Chinese hit, because I was the one who told them they were coming. I was the one who always gave the impression of knowing more than I did, of knowing a little more than what the average black soldier in a white man's army was supposed to know. I didn't have the slightest idea what we should do or who they were, but I knew we had to get the hell out of where we were. There I was, scared to death, with these young soldiers thinking I could lead them somewhere. I call them young because I was twenty and they were closer to eighteen or nineteen. Of course, when you're in combat your age doesn't make a difference, you're so much older and more experienced then someone who's never made combat. But they were depending on me, and I acted like I knew what I was doing.

Why? You know, there are so many things I do as a congressman simply because I'm expected to act like a congressman, because I've been trained to respond to legislative issues, trained to give speeches and to be long-winded. Training does that; you don't have to think about what you're going to do. The fact that I didn't know was irrelevant; they didn't know what I didn't know. Only I knew what I didn't know. And I guess that whether I was imitating a master sergeant or an officer because I admired the way they took charge, or whether I actually thought I was in charge, all I knew was I was too damn scared to take myself too seriously. But I also knew I couldn't afford to let them know that I was scared.

I didn't have a rifle. I picked one up—an automatic carbine with a double-magazine bullet holder fixed to it—but my hands were probably too numb to fire it. I didn't even know if it would work, anyway, because in that cold a lot of those rifles just froze up. The mountain's crest—sanctuary—loomed in the moonlight. I heard so much moaning and groaning and screaming, and machine-gun fire. Somebody was machine-gunning that whole side of the mountain. I remember clearly, so very clearly, a guy by the name of John Rivers, who was the top sergeant, yelling at us hysterically, "You better get the hell out of where you are, because they're sending in bloodhounds to find us!"

I thought old top kick had lost his mind. We always thought he didn't have far to go. He was an old man, to us, because he was over thirty years old. When we were getting ready to leave for Korea he gave us a little speech: "Men, I understand that some of you have me on your hit list for when we get into combat. All I want to tell you is: I've got my list, too!" Now I saw this long-legged, decorated World War II veteran racing across this hill like a mad spider on a hot rock. I thought that would be the last time I'd see old top kick. As it turned out, he would beat us to the other side of that mountain.

Getting to the other side of the mountain was almost a spiritual obsession for me. We checked out our guns and ammunition—we had no food. I heard some saying, "Sergeant's gonna get us out of here," and away we went through the night, desperately afraid of sunrise catching us anywhere near where we had been. There were hundreds, maybe thousands of us, all trying to get away, praying for the moonlight to hold back the dawn. One of these guys had a map, someone else had a compass. As far as they were concerned I was in charge—I just didn't know where the hell to go. When it finally did light up, we looked down on the most awful and amazing sight. We saw dead GIs hanging out of vehicles. We saw dead Chinese, and Chinese pouring over these vehicles like ants, trying to take rifles and everything they could off the trucks. We saw more GIs being marched away by Chinese soldiers. And we were so scared that they could look up and see us like we could look down and see them.

It wasn't like trying to scale a truly vertical mountain, it was more like walking up a hill. We were still low enough to see what was going on below, but too high to hear the terrible sounds we knew went with the carnage. One of the saddest, strangest sights I've ever seen was air force fighter pilots strafing and killing our own men as they were shooting the Chinese, and bombing the area. What made it surreal was that we had just been there. From our vantage point it was like watching a horror film on television with the mute button on. Or trying to scream in a nightmare. We couldn't yell, or signal to them that they were strafing our own troops along with the Chinese, because we were so scared that the Chinese would find us.

I think we must have been spotted by those returning jets anyway, because by midday one of those gliders used to assist in direction of artillery fire came by and dropped food—busting up a lot of cans of C rations in the process—and other supplies. The glider also led us to the direction we needed to go. We were starving, and we were frozen. When we got to the river, there was the biggest raft I ever saw in my life waiting for us. Damn, that was a good sight! The river itself, the Taedong, wasn't that wide, you could see to the other side where they had all these fires burning there for us. There must have been some kind of deal with the Chinese, because they were not attacking on that side of the mountain. When we got over there was a field hospital and medics waiting for us. They put me on a cart and there was a general congratulating me for leading the men through enemy lines. But in my first moment as a war hero I felt nothing but the shock of fleeing for my life, and the awe that

I still had life. And because I appeared to be less scared than the forty-three enlisted men who followed me, I received the Bronze Star with the "V" device for valor.

———

Believe me, I have been so blessed that God never gave me the nightmares about my combat duty that so many soldiers have suffered. It helps that I've made a point of avoiding the kinds of war movies whose gratuitous violence thrills everyone but those who've actually been to war. I've been lucky that, until now, I've never really had to dwell on what happened in this kind of detail. The only time I've ever suffered the mental pain of revisiting Kunu-ri was when President Clinton asked me to lead the delegation of veterans back to Korea in 2000 for the celebration of the fiftieth anniversary of the war. Of course, it wasn't the anniversary of a victory, or even a decisive battle. It was just the fiftieth anniversary of the damn communists overrunning the South Koreans. It was hard—very, very hard—on me to think that I went through all that pain and misery and terror for a goal that doesn't even sound patriotic or make me feel like I was a warrior. "Armistice" sounds like we didn't win anything. Even though we technically never declared war on North Korea, the war is still technically on. The situation with North Korea today is still as bizarre, and as tragic, as our ordeal at Kunu-ri.

And it brings my mind back to Iraq.

Why was my voice so lonely out there in 2003, when I questioned our invasion and the new doctrine of preemptive war? On that trip back to Korea in 2000, my fellow veterans and colleagues looked to me and asked, "Charlie, how did we get here in the first place?" It felt like a flashback to those young soldiers looking to me for answers because I had "assumed the virtue." Except now it's not a pose to cover my lack of self-esteem, nor is it my instinct for self-preservation—mortal or political—kicking in. I told my traveling companions that they really didn't want to know what I know about how we got there. All that matters, I said, is doing all that I can to see that no one else gets caught like that. And my answer, as usual, was greeted with silence.

When they tell you you're pulling out on July 15, your job is to stay alive until July 15. When they tell you you're not leaving on July 15 after all, they are messing with your mind, and your life. After I survived the battle of Kunu-ri, I was scared to death I was going to get killed on a "humble"—something out of left field like a hit-and-run accident with one of our own jeeps—in a war that now had no clear direction. That's one reason our troops are suffering so terribly in Iraq; they keep getting told that their service there will be limited in some way, but they keep sending them back, holding them in place with stop-loss orders and the like. This mismatch between the clear duty to serve one's country in time of war and the cloudy objectives— military and political—of this war is taking a toll on the junior military officers we may desperately need ten or fifteen years from now, when a real war comes along. An essay by screenwriter Lucian Truscott IV, published in the *New York Times* (June 28, 2005), captures this point in the frustration of a young West Point graduate on daily combat duty in Iraq.

> I feel like politicians have created a difficult situation for us. . . . I know I'm going to be coming back here about a year from now. I want to get married. I want to have a life. But I feel like if I get out when my commitment is up, who's going to be coming here in my place? I feel this obligation to see it through, but everybody over here knows we're just targets. Sooner or later, your luck's going to run out.

Put another way, without an honest and true statement of who the enemy is, and a definite yardstick for measuring his defeat, our soldiers are to some extent just sitting ducks—one unfortunate jeep accident or helicopter crash or roadside bomb away from becoming another casualty to our president's determination to wage what could be perpetual war in the name of thwarting terrorism. Exposing the fallacy of making war on an "ism" is near to the heart of what I think must be done to stop another generation from being caught up in a surreal war as I was caught up. It's been forgotten that we went into Korea not to defeat communism but to defend the South against aggression by the North. It's also forgotten that we didn't go in on our own, but under the authority of the United Nations: Korea was the fledgling UN's first war.

We have come a sad long way in our leadership of the free world since then. The preemptive strike on Iraq has been a historic watershed for the United States of America. It's established a new precedent in our putative role as a leader of the UN. Under our new doctrine, you don't have to go to the UN to determine your right to go to war when you haven't been attacked. All you have to do is convince a majority of citizens that such a war is in our self-interest; consent or cooperation from any and all nations is welcome but not required. Dissent or opposition may not be tolerated.

The stalemate in Korea did kick-start our military buildup for the cold war. But Harry Truman never confused our national security with a preemptive war against communism, even when it seemed to some that we had the unmatched power to wage such a war. Truman rightly saw our security interest in countering Stalin's Russia, with its clearly expansionist designs, massive ground forces, and new atomic bomb. But he saw no need to paint China and North Korea with the same brush because they were communists, too. He did let MacArthur convince him to cross the 38th parallel after Inchon, with the unstated aim of crushing Kim Il Sung and reuniting the Koreas by force. But after our recovery from the rout at Kunu-ri, MacArthur publicly campaigned to strike back at China, with nuclear arms if necessary, arrogantly asserting his brand of "might makes right" anticommunism. Truman fired MacArthur for insubordination, in publicly objecting to the policy of his commander in chief.

Truman correctly realized that restraint in the face of potential combined Chinese and Russian power preserved our national security, especially at a time when we were still recovering from World War II. We never did go to war with China or Russia. Cold warriors, and their allies in the military-industrial complex that Eisenhower warned us about, would eventually succeed in committing us to a massive thirty-year nuclear and conventional arms race, and involvement in proxy wars culminating in the loss of fifty thousand lives in Vietnam. But the war on communism wasn't won on any proxy war battlefield. In fact, the war on communism wasn't even won. The Soviet Union merely collapsed, a victim of its own contradictions and inability to compete. China, poised to become the dominant power of the twenty-first century, is still a nominally communist nation. War on ideology turns out to be a dodge, a very convenient cover for a failure of vision—moral and strategic—for our place in the history of a diverse world.

Sometime early in 2005 the serious questions about how and why we got into Iraq really began to penetrate the American consciousness, and not just in New York. Near the end of June, with polls showing public support for the Iraq war hemorrhaging, President Bush delivered a speech before dress-uniformed elite Army Airborne soldiers at Fort Bragg, North Carolina. He stressed his determination to stay the course in the war on terrorism, which he equated with the fight against the Iraqi insurgents, repeating the logic that it was better to fight them "over there" than on our own shores. Rhetorically, he asked how we should be certain that Iraq is now the primary battlefield in the war on terror. His answer: Because Osama bin Laden said so! Nearly four years after 9/11 and bin Laden is still alive and well and calling the tune, and the president insists we must dance.

The speech, reluctantly televised in prime time by the major networks, was met mostly with stony respect by the gathered troops, who interrupted only once with applause. The next day, in a roundup of national reactions to the speech, one vignette from a twenty-three-year-old Iraq combat veteran, who had been wounded in one of the nearly daily roadside bomb blasts, sent chills of recognition through me:

> Specialist [Nicki] Worrell . . . said Iraq had come to look a lot like South Korea, where she served for a year with the Army before going to Iraq. She is now in the inactive reserve.
>
> What she saw in both places, she said, was a kind of battle between factions, with the United States stuck in the middle. Korea has become a hardship post across a no-man's-land of tension, Specialist Worrell said, and she thinks the same thing will happen in Iraq.
>
> "We are just protecting good Iraq from bad Iraq, and that's always going to be there," she said.

Those young soldiers in Korea, especially those who followed me over there, were ill prepared to be there. Their rifles and their clothing were as vulnerable to the cold Korean winter as Specialist Worrell's Humvee was to these so-called improvised explosive devices that kill our soldiers in Iraq nearly every week. I don't know if any polls were taken when the Korean armistice was signed in 1953, but if the American people didn't feel any more secure when the Chinese and North Koreans withdrew above the 38th parallel, I would not be surprised. We are still paying the price for sweeping the contradictions of the Korean War under the rug. There are still 37,000 American troops, including my old 2nd Infantry, committed, yet now we actually face a nuclear threat from North Korea.

Something was wrong with the Korean War. The same thing is wrong with Iraq. We are indeed "stuck in the middle," between the idealism to "pay any price . . . to assure the survival and success of liberty," as John F. Kennedy said in his inaugural address, and the accumulated shortfall of our ideals in practice around the world since the United Nations was founded.

I insist that we can't afford to wait for the judgment of history to recognize the bad taste it has left in our mouths, and to do something that is right to cleanse it.

———————

The orange flash that blew me into that ditch was indeed an exploding mortar shell. I carried shrapnel from that blast all the way to the field hospital where I was first treated after the retreat. Later I was removed to a more permanent hospital, well to the rear of the U.S. lines in South Korea, where I spent some time recuperating from the entire ordeal. I stayed on the lookout for anyone black, hoping they would be from our outfit. One day I did see a guy, a corporal I knew. We had just gotten out of combat, but he was strutting around in this class "A" uniform with all these medals, his cap under his belt, on his way to and from the mess hall. I couldn't even get out of the bed. I'd call out, "Hey, Brown, hey, Brown—it's Rangel!" He looked at me, and squinted, and kept on going. Finally, when I was ambulatory and on crutches, I waited until he came by and I pulled up to him. I said, "What's wrong with you, you crazy son of a bitch; why aren't you talking to me?"

He said, "Rangel, please don't talk to me, or say anything to me. I'm getting the hell out of here; they think I'm crazy." I asked him who thought he was crazy, and who said he could go home. He said he had gone to the chaplain and told him that after Kunu-ri he didn't trust himself to be in combat anymore.

"I told him, 'I didn't know who the hell I'm gonna kill, but I'm gonna kill some sons of bitches—I'm just a killing machine,' " he said. "He told me I wasn't fit for combat anymore," Brown added.

Well, I couldn't wait to get to that chaplain. I made arrangements, and went to see this black Baptist chaplain. But he said he couldn't help me, because I was a Catholic. I tried to convince him it would be OK—hell, we were all black, right?—but he wouldn't budge; I'd have to see the Catholic chaplain.

Of course, they didn't have any Catholic chaplains in a black unit. So they put me in a jeep, and bumpety bump bump took me to some white outfit. When we got there they pointed out this old white man with mud all over his face, dirty khakis, a 45 on each hip, and they say that's the chaplain. Man, oh man: The black Baptist guy was so clean and organized . . . and here this guy looks like Audie Murphy or John Wayne or something. I said:

"Father, I'm having some problems, and combat fatigue . . ."

"Do you want to go to confession?"

"Yes . . . uhh, that might be what I want."

"Well, go ahead and confess," he says. Now, in church, you're in a box, and it's dark. Here I'm looking at him, and he's looking at me in broad daylight. So he turns his back and kneels, and puts the sacred cloth around his neck, and says, "Go ahead." So I kneel, and I tell the weirdest story about how I wake up thinking about killing somebody . . . and I didn't know who I was gonna kill. He doesn't say anything, so I kick it up a notch, about how my mind's not right. He still doesn't say anything.

Finally he says:

"You finished?"

"Yeah . . . I'm finished."

"Well, son, war is hell, and we all wish we could get out of here. Say five Our Fathers and five Hail Marys."

They put my ass back in that jeep, and I said to myself, "Well, I'll be damned. I'm gonna go back and get killed and go straight to hell for lying to the damn priest!" I mean, we're trained that if you're gonna die the priests give you last rites—and what had I done? Lied, on the way to hell. It's a bad feeling to tell a lie to a priest. But I had already lied to the Baptist, so I didn't mind doing it again, if I thought it was going to get me out of there.

I spent my remaining days in combat scared to death that one of those young guys was going to get me killed. I didn't go straight back to the front lines, because the outfit they sent us to had retreated and was still replenishing its strength. There were so many new people, and I didn't know many of them, so I just stopped talking to them altogether. I'd eat alone, stay alone, and they'd say, "Oh, that's that crazy-ass sarge, he got hit by the Chinese and hasn't been right since." The more they thought I was crazy, the more I just stood apart, knowing my day was coming for rotating back home.

———————

Fritz Hollings, my good friend and recently retired senator from South Carolina, called me up back in 2003, after I first called for restoring the draft.

"You know," he starts, "you ought to run for president, and I'll run for vice president. And if you don't wanna do it, then I'll run for president and you can run for vice president. But you gotta promise me one thing."

I said, "What's that, Fritz?"

He says, "You gotta stop talking about these minorities catching hell in the military."

"Why?"

"Because nobody out there knows what my rednecks are going through!"

We got a big laugh, but there's so much truth in this joke. What the people who are fighting our wars are going through today is really not a racial thing; it's an economic thing. His "rednecks" have no opportunities—their farms are shutting down, they can't get an education, they're stuck in the low-wage South—but when they put on that uniform they are ten feet tall; they're warriors. The people Hollings was talking about finished their military service in the bases and camps all over South Carolina. All they wanted was a little pension and a little status, but they're getting called up for combat two and three times as reservists. That's a double whammy for all of us, because if you've seen some of those reservists, you wonder how we can ever win these wars so easily. Same thing with the national guard. I saw some of them recently and I was crying. They thought it was because I loved them, but to be honest it was because I felt sorry for them.

Hollings's joke about military rednecks takes me back to the troop ship that finally brought me home from Korea in July 1951. It was a stinky, funky, overcrowded troop ship, with lousy food. Talk about a caste system—the officers' mess had good silver to eat with, and white uniforms, while if some hungry son of a bitch GI opened a can of sardines in our quarters, people would damn near want to kill him because it stank so bad where we were. The fact that we were going home didn't stop the rising tensions and complaints. And there was a lot of liquor on that ship. I knew we weren't going to dock without a fight. And my worst fear was not just a fight, but a riot. There was a whole lot of "black motherfucker" this and "white motherfucker" that going around. There was also the kind of 1st Infantry versus 15th Infantry stuff, and a lot of war talk. But I just knew that when it blew it was going to be racial.

Well, it did blow. There was a huge fight, and it lasted half the night. And would you believe it: It was North against the South!

It was the first real culture shock I had had after nearly three years in the army. There were blacks from the South fighting against black New Yorkers and black soldiers from New Jersey and Philadelphia. They were fighting alongside white Southerners, and we were fighting alongside white Northerners. It was the most unbelievable thing I'd ever seen. They called us "sex freaks," "New York pimps," and other disgusting things. And we called them "country ass hicks," and worse. Years later my personal experience would reveal that blacks and whites in the

South lived and worked much more closely together than the races did in the North. The cultural ties between blacks and whites in the South are much more binding. I also learned that our true common interests are not always clearly outlined in black and white; they have much more to do with class than race. Those same blacks and whites would return to the South and do battle over integration for the next twenty years. And black and white Northerners would be down there together on the black side.

The troop ship landed us at Camp Stoneman, about forty miles northeast of San Francisco. We were the first combat veterans to come back from Korea, and boy, did they turn out for us. There was a big parade, and we had on our class "A" uniforms, decorated with brand-new medals and ribbons. And guess who was waiting for us at the end of the parade: members of the original 503rd Field Artillery who had not gone overseas with us. They would soon be boarding the same troop ships, and heading to Korea. They were crying, as they asked what happened to different guys they had known in the outfit. Nine out of ten of those guys had been killed or captured, which scared the hell out of them. But hey, what could I tell them?

These guys had begun at Fort Dix and then went to Fort Lewis with me, but hadn't gone overseas because they had only taken one-year enlistments, while I had reenlisted. They trained at Fort Lewis for all of a couple of months, and then we left them behind when we took off to Hawaii in Operation MIKI, taking all the officers, commissioned and noncommissioned, with us. We left them on post in that summer of '49 just waiting to be discharged. They thought they were avoiding the draft, even before the war started. Little did they suspect they would be recalled to active duty while serving out their six-year reserve requirement. Suddenly they found themselves bound for what was left of the front lines without enough real training under their belts. It's a sad story; somebody should write a book on how unprepared they were for combat duty.

Having been promoted twice in as many months shortly after Kunu-ri, I really was a sergeant when I stepped off that boat, and for my remaining two years of service I gladly let the army convince me that I was a big, new man. I was stationed at Fort Sill, Oklahoma. The base was still basically segregated, but they only had one noncom officers' club, and I was entitled. Remember, I was one of the first new war heroes they had seen since World War II, from the very first U.S.-based division, the 2nd Infantry, to go over there. I had survived the biggest defeat that the U.S. Army had suffered in anybody's memory at Kunu-ri, and lived to tell the tale. Boy, did I tell that tale! I had no military responsibility but going to mess at the officers' club. No drilling, no marching, just lording it over the black troops and even some of the white officers who had to respect my medals, even if they didn't especially respect me.

All this attention convinced me that I'd make an excellent salesman for the army. I dreamed up a plan to reenlist one more time, and make a career of the army as a recruiter. I'd get six thousand damn dollars, an additional stripe to sergeant first class, and live in my own place with clothing and ration allowances. I'd be a fit husband for Erma, my sweetheart from St. Aloysius, to whom I was betrothed, at least on paper.

Of course, as I explained in the last chapter, none of this came to pass. I still had a lot of growing up to do, and one long dark night of the soul to go through before I was ready to really become Charlie Rangel. One last army story suggests just how much I still had to learn about the arrogance still covering my insecurity, and what Jesus had really spared me for that night at Kunu-ri.

Old Willie Jackson, who had survived that night in Tacoma as well as Korea, was also a sergeant stationed at Fort Sill. We used to hang out together, drinking and talking trash with our crisp uniforms and medals at the noncom club. There was a gorgeous woman who would be in there. It turned out she lived on base, in what they called the Guest House, where people visiting the GIs could stay. Unfortunately, she was the wife of a recruit, who was still in the field. She got special treatment because her husband was a boxer on the division boxing team. I got to know this lady a little bit while her husband was in the field, and Willie Jackson used to see me with her.

One night the YMCA gave a dance. Willie and I didn't have any dates, so we were just drinking at the bar. Willie says to me:

"Isn't that your girlfriend who just came in?"

I look over, and there she is . . . with this huge son of a gun. I'd heard he was big, but I'd never seen him before. They sat down.

"Why don't you go over and say hello to your girl?" says Willie.

"Will you shut up!" I say, trying to be cool.

"Hell, no," he says. "You're the big veteran—just go over there and tell that recruit to step aside, because this is your girl!"

"Willie, will you leave me alone!" I say, but by now Willie is kind of drunk.

"You're not gonna dance with her? Well, I'll go dance with her," he says. And Willie goes over there and asks this big dude, "Do you mind if I dance with her?"

This guy jumps up and knocks Willie all the way across the dance floor with one punch. He yells at Willie, "You curly-haired son of a bitch, you haven't asked for permission all this time, why start now?"

Willie and I were both sergeants. We had the same complexion and curly hair. We were both in the 503rd Field Artillery and had gone to Korea and returned alive. Clearly someone had given him a description of me, and what I was up to, and figured he had finally caught the son of a bitch spending time with his wife. Poor old Willie Jackson, my man.

And I haven't had a bad day since!

4

Sergeant Rangel

The last time I saw Sergeant Rangel, he was following the activities of recently retired army general Wesley Clark with great interest. Clark had become a regular on the television talk shows, and had some hard and critical things to say about the role of the military in the Bush administration's foreign policy. His critique of the Iraq war before and after the invasion as a CNN military analyst was so devastating that, according to him, the administration tried to get him kicked off the air. The fact that he was a general, and a Democrat, really made him unique.

I was so impressed with the general that I picked up the phone and asked him to consider running for president. Knowing that he was going to accept my call made me smile to myself, because it reminded me that Sergeant Rangel had reached the point where he was confident that even a general would promptly return his call. When it came, to put what might have been an awkward moment at ease, I said:

"This is Sergeant Charles Rangel, RA-57156282. General, I'm reporting for duty, and so are you."

He laughed and laughed, and as we spoke we dodged the big question for a little while. But I knew he would be coming back to it. I knew it like I knew First Lady Hillary Clinton would come back to the prospect of running for the Senate from New York on my first "date" with her on the subject. It's like the guy that dated his wife for ten years; when he finally proposed marriage, he really thought it was his idea. In that same way, there was no question in my mind that I had not been the first one to put the Senate in play with Hillary, and I certainly was not the first to discuss the presidency with Wesley Clark. At first he kept insisting that he just couldn't move without reaching agreement with his beloved wife, Gert. But I just knew that meant it was only a matter of time before he would be in the race for president. And this should not be taken as coyness or hypocrisy on his part, or Hillary's before the 2000 race. Before anyone makes the decision to hold themselves out to high elective office, especially for the first time, they have to make certain they have fallback positions; they have to know where they will land, and how hard, should their bids fall short. Just as Hillary's staff inquired intensely about labor support, the backing of the New York congressional delegation, and fund-raising, General Clark would ask repeatedly, "Do you really think we can do it?"

I told him, in the summer of 2003, that it looked like Howard Dean was the only candidate who was dealing honestly with the question of whether our engagement in this war was moral or lawful, and the only one addressing what the American people really thought about it. At the same time, I said it was my impression that too many people saw nothing but the liberal-left wing of the Democratic Party in Howard Dean. But the same people would see something very different in a general who graduated from West Point and served as Allied Supreme Commander of NATO, a decorated war hero with an international reputation who could bring together our allies' generals. When a general like Wesley Clark debates the wisdom of this war against a president with no clue about what military service or combat is, I told him, I could not see how he would not soon be called President Wesley Clark.

When I met Gert Clark, I immediately realized that there were more than questions of polls, support, and money holding up the decision. I have never met a more attractive, dynamic, and exciting personality in my life; I should have known she was from Brooklyn. General Clark was no general with Mrs. Gert Clark; they were partners, and he could not have been as successful as he was without this extraordinary woman behind him. I still don't understand why he didn't do better, and why he didn't capture the imagination of every Democrat. He did have a tremendous setback after he told the *New York Times*'s Adam Nagourney that, if he had been in Congress, he would have voted to give President Bush the authority to invade Iraq. The media ate him alive after that one, and I can see why. How could be against the war, and then say he would have voted for it in the Congress? It just seemed so inconsistent.

Asked to explain his answer, he told the news media that he was inexperienced in dealing with the press and had gotten very relaxed during what he thought was a friendly, off-the-record campaign plane chat with the reporter. I really, really wished I could have given him the better answer: The president had given Congress and the American people misleading information—linking Saddam Hussein, 9/11, al-Qaeda, WMDs, uranium from Niger, and so on. This was the same problem John Kerry had; he just could not say he was misled into voting for the war. I can't imagine how a heroic Vietnam veteran being challenged by Bush and Cheney—with no war records between them—felt he had to defend himself about whether or not it was his medals or his ribbons that he threw over the White House fence. Who cares?

The 2004 presidential campaign—like the upcoming 2006 congressional campaign—seemed to be our election to lose. I never thought it would turn out so badly for our candidate. Early in his bid for the nomination, long before Wesley Clark came into the picture, Senator Kerry came to visit me in my congressional office. I was really surprised that he would make the trip all the way from the Senate just to talk with me about his candidacy. Before he could even start soliciting my support, the bells rang calling me to the House floor for a vote. I said, " Senator, you'll have to walk me over to the floor. But before you do, I want to make it clear: I can't find myself supporting any candidate for president who actually voted for the war." I went on to tell him that my very dear friend Dick Gephardt, the Democratic minority leader, would be the candidate I'd really want to support, but I couldn't consider backing him either, because he, too, had voted for the war.

As the time remaining for me to cast my vote was running out, and the elevator arrived, Kerry started with "Oh, Charlie, come off of it . . ." I entered the elevator, the doors closed, and with them closed my interest in John Kerry. Then along came General Clark. I must admit that Kerry has come a long way in explaining his position on the war in Iraq. After his speech at Georgetown University in October 2005, in which he called for a quick withdrawal of twenty thousand American soldiers and a clear timetable for removing the remainder of our forces, most Democrats could only wish that he had been that forceful and critical during the campaign, instead of waiting a year.

I really thought General Clark made a good recovery from his stumble about voting for the war; take my word for it, we haven't seen the last of Wesley Clark. Of course, for me personally, there's always a chance that his future ambitions may one day collide with those of my friend the junior senator from New York. I told him as much at my annual birthday fund-raiser in 2005 at Tavern on the Green in Central Park. It was a spectacular event that Senator Clinton capped with her version of how I "drafted" her for the New York Senate seat. Concerning my solicitation for her to run, she said:

> I told him no, and he said reconsider. He'd call. He'd haunt me. And I would say, "I don't believe I can do it, I don't think there's support there."

"No, no, no," I said. But in the end, like so many
women before me, I just couldn't say no.

The audience went wild. The papers said I blushed, and she
blushed. Then she hastened to add: "Oh, and men, too!"

It made for a wonderful big photo of her hugging me in the *New
York Post*.

———————

Today I feel blessed and humbled to count four-star generals like Wesley
Clark and Colin Powell as friends. General Powell, for one, never lets
me forget the "humbled" part. He seems to get a kick out of demanding
a salute from Sergeant Rangel, often at the most awkward times. A few
years ago, on that Air Force One flight to South Africa for Nelson Mandela's inauguration, Powell found another way to put me in my place. If
anyone ever warns you about playing poker with Colin Powell, please
believe them; he is *good*. I was at the table with him, along with Quincy
Jones and some others, and General Powell cleaned me out! I was so
embarrassed—that just doesn't happen to me—that all I could do was
mumble something about how it was merely politically expedient for
me to let the general win.

Looking back, however, I really have to smile whenever I think
about the Charlie Rangel who joined the army in 1948 going on to
become a friend of generals. I have to smile, because none of the guys I
trained with at Fort Dix or Fort Lewis, or saw combat with me in Korea,
would ever believe it. Generals were giants who lived in a different world
from privates and sergeants. When I came home from Korea, there
were so many people from Lenox Avenue who would come up to me
and ask, "What was General MacArthur *really* like?" I would smile and
say, "Oh, we got along just great." And they would say, very seriously, "I
thought so." Mind you, I had never even seen General MacArthur,
much less talked with him: such is the distance—two different worlds—
between a sergeant and a general.

Not that the distance mattered much to me at the time. I had done
so well in the army that the need for advancement, or an education,
never entered my mind. I had the uniform, a pocket full of money,
sergeant's stripes, and a chest full of medals; I really didn't think it could
get any better than that. I left the army in 1952 the same way I went in—
a poor high school dropout. I came out clinging to my medals for dear
life. The worst part, however, was that you couldn't tell me I wasn't at the

top of my game. I had no clue as to what life might have in store for me, but after Korea I really believed I was in peak form at being a successful human being.

The army has a way of making you feel important through rank and tenure. All I could see were the four stripes on my arm, and the promise of a fifth. I had my ribbons and my army pay in my pocket. I had everything but a vision of something more in life than what had gone before. I didn't know any lawyers or doctors or engineers, much less people who could credibly see themselves in the Oval Office. The need to lay a new foundation for my life had simply not occurred to me, much less having an ambition for that life. I had no basis to dream.

And that is something that's tragic in this country. Immigrants can arrive here not just with American dreams, but with blueprints of the monuments they want to build to their talent, hard work, and the sacrifices their loved ones had to make in order to get them this far. But so many African-Americans, who have been here for generations, never have their sleep sweetened, or disturbed, by a recurring American Dream. They don't know the dream, and they have nobody and nothing in their lives to implant the idea that they can and must become something better than what they are.

My ambitions were so limited. The closest my grandfather ever came to giving me direction for my future was his admonition to "Stay out of trouble and get a civil service job with a pension." But I wasn't thinking about taking even that humble advice. I thought of nothing more than survival, one step at a time—that was my dream. Not retirement with a pension, not recognition for some great talent or deeds. Knowing that I would come home to Harlem from Fort Sill, Oklahoma, as Sergeant Rangel was good enough for me. I was looking forward to going on being Sergeant Rangel for as far as I could see, which wasn't very far at all. My plan for marrying Erma was dead, but the rest of it, based on the fluke of having wandered into the army and then surviving Kunu-ri, was still in effect. All I could see was the reenlistment money— $6,000—the additional stripe, a civilian clothing allowance, and not having to live on base. I saw myself posted to the very same recruitment office at Whitehall Street in lower Manhattan that snagged Jimmy Taylor, Henry Courtland, and me four years earlier. I'd live at home, and the army would give me an allowance for that, too. All put together, I'd be making almost as much as a lieutenant—not bad, considering I hadn't gone to Officer Candidate School. I'd make sergeant first class one day, and after twenty years, I'd finally be following my grandfather's advice to stay out of trouble and, at only thirty-eight years old, retire with a government pension. That was going to be it, for me.

But my brother, Ralph, had another idea. He was working for the New York State Department of Labor at that time, along with his best friend, Bill Julien. Their jobs were helping unemployed people find positions, of all things. Somehow, I let them talk me out of reenlisting. They convinced me that the best thing was to get out of the service altogether. In hindsight, of course, they had no idea how right they were. But at the time it wasn't long before I woke up every day cursing Bill Julien and my brother out, to myself, and wondering why the hell I ever listened to them. Now, of course, I know why. My brother had brains; Bill Julien had brains and class. Bill was a college graduate. My brother wasn't, but he was as smart as any college graduate. He just decided to have a family instead of seeking college degrees.

Nevertheless, between the two of them, they convinced me that there was a civilian world out there that was mine for the picking. When I resisted, they would goad me with taunts like "You're a hero in combat, but a coward in facing life." And while they worked on me, the time ran out on my reenlistment plan. The three-month window of opportunity closed. If I went back in, it would be as a private, and I'd be starting from scratch. Maybe I was just vulnerable to their arguments, having nothing in civilian life to mask the insecurities I'd learned to cover so well in the army. I just knew one thing for damn sure: they were in the New York State Department of Labor, so they were going to get me a job.

At first, however, I thought I found the ticket to success on my own. I saw a newspaper ad with the headline "Make $10,000 a Year: Become a Health Consultant." That would be about $100,000 today, so of course I went downtown to this big-time hotel where they had a suite and were recruiting salesmen to demonstrate a sophisticated machine that they called the "health unit" door to door. About a hundred young men—black, white, and everything in between—had responded to the ad. Many of them were Korean War veterans. We were met by almost as many older men who did all the talking. They looked so sharp that it seemed they had been dressed by consultants. And they were so articulate, with hundred-watt smiles that never dimmed as they spoke. All in all, these guys put on a road-tested Broadway show that made what I'd learned about selling at the Adler shoe store look like summer stock.

It was actually a great vacuum cleaner, but it was sold as everything *except* a great vacuum cleaner. They even changed the title of "salesman" to "health consultant," making all of us "experts." From the start, everyone who talked reinforced the idea of how successful they were. How they went on monthlong vacations to places like Hawaii and all over the world. And how you could not be successful as a salesman unless you believed in the product, and its power to save so many people's lives. And we sat there thinking "show us the product, already," but they just kept on teasing us with their testimony, pumping up the room like a Baptist revival meeting:

> "Joe, how many did you sell?"
> "Oh, I didn't sell any, really. I just allowed people to buy them!"
> "Ho, that's the stuff! And you there, what do you do?"
> "Well, I've been here ten years, and my biggest problem is paying the taxes on all this money I'm making!"

Then someone comes out with a white lab jacket on, carrying a "unit" that he said was being used in atomic bomb plants to cleanse the air of dangerous radioactive particles. Units were also purifying the atmosphere in hospitals and sick rooms, we were told. The Filter Queen, we were assured, pulled the germ-laden dust particles out of the air by centrifugal force, and prevented them from returning to the atmosphere.

> "Why can't every household enjoy the benefit of a unit like this?" they asked. "Why do we have to have children— some with asthmatic conditions—breathing this, and not knowing what they're breathing?"
> "Joe, can you show these people what they're breathing?"
> "I certainly can."

Joe then picks up a very bright photographer's lamp, takes a piece of cheesecloth and puts it over the intake of the machine and turns it on. We hear the roar of the machine, and when he removes the cheesecloth there's this big black spot on it. He takes the lamp, taps it lightly against the cheesecloth, and under this bright light we see the black dust just falling down.

> "Joe, is that what we're breathing?"
> "Yes, that's what we're breathing."

Then they brought out a crib, and explained how babies are sleeping in piles of sloughed-off dead skin. They take the cheesecloth, put it on the intake hose, vacuum the crib, scrape the particles into a little pile, and light a match to it.

"Doesn't that smell like flesh? We don't want to talk about it, but that's exactly what it is."

"You know," they explained, "you guys may not be doctors, but you certainly are medical consultants, because you're gonna help people live longer."

There was a lot of money to be made, they said, but we were not salesmen—we were demonstrators. That was code for the real game, which was just shy of a full-blown con that would probably be illegal today. We offered the customers a token gift for letting us into their homes to demonstrate a vacuum that we said was about to come on the market. If we hooked them, after a bit of cat and mouse we could be persuaded to offer it to them at a big prerelease discount price, but only if they qualified as "friends or family." Of course, when we were ready to close the sale, we'd call in the order, and with a wink to the hopeful customer, explain that they had convinced our boss that they were distantly related to us.

Despite the morally shaky selling proposition, I have to admit that some of the things I learned from this company will never, ever leave me. Sincerity and honesty, they stressed, were the most important thing in selling a product. You cannot be successful if you don't believe in what you're selling, they said, so get to know it well. More important, first thing the potential customer will do is size you up, so you have to find something nice to say about that person. Sometimes it may be very difficult, but you know that if you get into the apartment, you cannot even start your presentation until you find something pleasant to say. As my dear friend the late Ann Kheel, wife of the labor lawyer Ted Kheel, would say, "If you can't find anything nice to say about somebody, think harder."

Look at the walls. Any baby you see is cute and beautiful. Look at the carpet. Find something, anything, but don't say a word until you're able to disarm that suspect and make him or her a prospect as you start your demonstration. The only caveat: It's got to be sincere, something that has some truth to it, because if it doesn't they will know it. And I'll be damned, as I reflect on all the compliments I've received over the years, I always come away thinking, "What a wonderful person." All I can say is try it, you'll see how well it works.

Except perhaps when the marks are a bit *too* close family.

I first tried my pitch on my grandfather. "Hell, no," he shot back, "I'm not gonna buy any vacuum cleaner. I don't have any damn rugs. Go over there and sell one to your cousin." That would be my cousin Clifford Wharton Jr., the son of perhaps the most successful of all the

Wharton clan to that point in time, Clifford Wharton Sr., who I remembered showing up in a Cadillac limousine when I was a kid. The elder Clifford Wharton was serving as the U.S. consul general in Lisbon at that time. The younger Clifford, who graduated from Harvard in 1947 and became the first "Negro" to get a master's degree from the Johns Hopkins School of International Studies in 1948, was working on Latin American development issues for some Rockefeller family philanthropies. My cousin Cliff Jr. would go on proving himself incapable of accomplishing anything that wasn't amplified by the prefix "first black" over the next forty years, including:

- President of a predominantly white major university, Michigan State, in 1970
- Elected chairman and CEO of a Fortune 500 company, the giant TIAA-CREF retirement insurer, in 1987
- Chairman of the Rockefeller Foundation in 1982
- Deputy secretary of state, the number-two position in the State Department, in 1993

And here I was, his high school dropout war-hero cousin, trying to sell him an overdressed vacuum cleaner in 1952!

He had already made it to Lenox Terrace, then a new luxury apartment complex between Fifth and Lenox, 132nd and 135th streets. He and his lovely wife, Delores, lived there with some pretty ritzy black folks for neighbors. Harlem is a big small world—Delores is the sister of Jack Duncan, a prominent Harlem undertaker who would one day bury Adam Clayton Powell. I gave Cliff my twenty-minute pitch on the health and welfare benefits of the Filter Queen. All the while he was focused on what turned out to be a big family tree chart on the floor, with his father and grandfather on it, and all this stuff about the slavery thing. He was more interested in asking me what I knew about my relatives than buying a vacuum cleaner.

"Did you sell it?" asked my grandfather when I got back home.

"Noooooo," I said. "As a matter of fact, he spent all this time asking me about who your father was, and who your mother was, and about my father and his father and his grandmother—it was very confusing," I said. Grandfather looked at me and said, "He really wants to know more about the Wharton family, does he? Well, you just go right back and tell him that I have the answers to every one of his questions, and believe me, he doesn't want to know them!"

Poor Cousin Cliff soldiered on anyway, finding time amid his triumphs over the decades to finish that family tree. What he finally put together, with the aid of today's computer software, traces our connection back to a great-great-grandmother named Tabiatha Wharton (1820–1906), who must have been the property of one Peter Wharton, our great-great-grandfather and the source of the family name.

I recovered from that rocky start, and, like most initiates, I was successful as long as I was actually prospecting among my real family and friends. Downtown they called me Pep, because I'd gotten off to a quick start. Soon even I had a line of testimony of my own in the sales-revival meetings. It brought me the attention of another new salesman from Harlem named Eddie Ruiz. Long, lean, black, handsome, slick-haired Eddie Ruiz. Eddie had a smile and a set of teeth more sparkling than anybody in the room. He favored these long European-style overcoats, and had the manicured nails of a real Romeo type. He was so smooth that he could have been giving us those classes, and I was really impressed. Eddie was knocking off two and three machines *a day* in sales. At that rate, Eddie would be making his $10,000 a year in six months! I just couldn't see how he was doing it. Somehow we hooked up—he saw something in me, and I thought that if I was already good, he could only make me better.

I ended up following him around the edges of a whole host of activities, almost every kind of hustle *but* selling vacuum cleaners. He had this swagger about him—a Jack Palance type of guy. He listened to my war stories, and told me about all these girls he had. Before I knew it, without going into details, I was sucked into his image of success. I later found out why he never wanted me too close to his Filter Queen sales: he was pawning those damn machines, putting in false sales contracts and getting that money, too. Luckily, I never witnessed any of it. And he never went to jail, though they could have easily prosecuted him for it. When they caught up with him, Eddie said they could throw him in jail, but they'd never find out where those machines were. They let him off the hook for just turning over the pawn tickets; all they really wanted was to get these brand-new machines back.

That wasn't the end of Eddie's hustles. He had a phony apartment brokerage business, where he would take money from people looking to rent, then go to the apartment listings in the *Amsterdam News* and try to hook them up. When they caught up to him that time, a bunch of angry marks chased his ass to the police station. Eddie had a wife who was much older than he was. He basically took the woman's house after he married her, and ran the lower floor as an after-hours joint some nights, with party girls and everything.

I remember his wife calling out, "Eddie, are you coming home tonight?"

"No, I won't be home tonight, darling. Charlie and I have some business to take care of."

Or, "Eddie, what are you doing down there?"

"Oh, were just conducting some business, darling—don't come downstairs. . . ."

I've never told my Eddie Ruiz story before. I did a lot of things with Eddie, but I never forgot that if I ever decided I wanted a civil service job after all, I would have to stay out of trouble. Thank God, nobody has called me Pep since those days with Eddie Ruiz. It has allowed me to completely delete that period of my life from my memory. When my legal Filter Queen sales went flat, as they inevitably would, instead of following in Eddie's corrupt footsteps, I chose to humble myself back to the New York State Unemployment Office for help. I wish I could claim the virtue, but I really don't know why I finally put myself at the mercy of the job interviews my brother, Ralph, and Bill Julien could arrange. All I do know is that's when reality really hit me in the face; I was not the big shot I thought I was.

———————

I don't know how many times I cursed them out because the jobs they sent me to were so totally unfair. The stories of the work they found me could fill their own book and tell what an unlettered black man could do to feed himself in the early 1950s. I remember unloading trucks at a warehouse on 117th Street and Pleasant Avenue, among any number of menial, manual labor jobs I took. Me, who had come through four years of the army without doing a lick of KP!

How I left that job on Pleasant Avenue says a lot about the positions I tried in early 1953. In the warehouse they had all the syrup that was used to supply soda machines around New York. They also had these big lead tanks of CO_2 for the the carbonation. I would come to the truck, they'd give me the big boxes of syrup, I'd put them on the skid, and when it was full I'd drive it into the warehouse and the salesmen would come in, tell me what they wanted, I'd check their order and put the boxes in place. I still had more ego than I deserved. I'd come into that office every morning with a shirt and tie on, before changing into these stinking work clothes. Fortunately they had a shower, so when you saw me leaving the place, you saw an executive. But when I was actually on the job I was just so afraid that some of the boys from the block would see what I was really doing.

You never like to quit a job if you don't have a backup, especially if you need the money, even if it looks like a dead end. Without a backup, I suspect that many times I was just waiting for something dramatic to happen in order to make the decision to leave. When these heavy lead cylinders of gas were unloaded from the truck they were grabbed by the receiver and guided toward a big cushion of hemp. It's thrown off the truck, hits this big pillar of hemp, bounces up—and then you grab it on the bounce and roll it in. Very professional. I'd never done this part of the job, because any false move and whammo. Sure enough, one guy didn't know what he was doing one day, and he bounced the cylinder off his foot. The ambulance came and took him to Metropolitan Hospital. And before they knew it, Rangel had showered, put on his shirt and tie, and was on his way back down to the New York State Unemployment Office. I did not come home alive from Kunu-ri to get killed on the job unloading a truck!

When I was in the army, still brandishing my clipboard, one of the few jobs I actually did do was give the high school equivalency exams to new recruits. At that time, I really thought that if you had a Southern accent, you were less sophisticated than those of us from New York. I thought I was so smart that I didn't need any damn high school diploma as Sergeant Rangel, even though I was the one giving the high school tests. Someone once asked just what kind of so-and-so was I, to actually be giving people high school equivalency exams when I didn't have one myself? Today I'd have to say I was a so-and-so who was learning about power. I've been learning to be clear about which side of the table—or clipboard—I wanted to be on all of my life. But I never thought about the fact that early on, all I had learned was how to cheat the system. I never thought about the hypocrisy: being in charge, with no credible basis for being in charge.

I had never really admitted to myself that I was a high school dropout. Suddenly it occurred to me that Sergeant Rangel had never dared to sit for his own test. Oh, I'd like to blame it on the army again. But the truth is that it was my ego that had blocked my limitations from consciousness, to such an extent that they never crossed my mind when I checked out of the army and into civilian life. It didn't hit me until I had to write the damn truth of it on job applications, over and over again. I still wasn't ready to do anything about it, though. Despite my friendships with the high school graduated and partially college-bound Les Garçons crew, I still harbored something close to utter contempt for educated people whom I didn't know personally—that is, for educated people as a class.

Recently, while accepting an award from the alumni of City College, I admitted as much. As a young fellow in Harlem, I said, I would see white kids pouring out of the subway at 135th Street and St. Nicholas Avenue and head up the hill through St. Nicholas Park to this "castle" called City College, high above central Harlem. I wasn't quite certain as to what was going on up there, but I knew by looking at these white kids that it didn't include me. I guess for me it was a case of "Don't ask, don't tell." I never asked what they were doing and no one told me what they were doing. It turned out all right, however: City College and the City of New York have announced plans to create the Rangel School of Public Service, right up there at the college on the hill.

In the summer of 1953, I finally thought I had found an opportunity in a garment business in a long, long loft space down on Thirty-sixth Street and Sixth Avenue. I was told that these two young white guys had just started this business, and it would be a good fit because they had gone to DeWitt Clinton, where I had dropped out. It sounded good, and professional, to me. I dressed up, went down, and interviewed. I would be opening and closing the place, acting like a floor manager. They had about twenty mostly Hispanic women tearing strips of lace off huge bolts of the material, wrapping it around a hunk of cardboard and putting the smaller rolls into a box. No machines, no nothing. I would get the coffee and the lunches, go over the invoices of the lace when it came in, and keep track of the outgoing orders. My job was to make certain the women had enough work—keeping them supplied with uncut lace material—and to really act as though I was in charge. I also put the boxes of finished goods on a hand truck and pushed them all over the West Thirties to the jobbers who used the stuff to make dresses or whatever. Now, the lace itself was light in weight. But the boxes were big and awkward.

The salary was low, almost nothing really, but they kept telling me about how smart and articulate I was, and that they would eventually make me a partner, after I had learned the business and they expanded. I believed this just enough to keep coming in every day, and to keep up the appearance to myself and others of being Sergeant Rangel in action. Every morning I would dress up nicely for my walk to the subway to catch the train downtown, so that no one would suspect I was back working in the garment district, as I had for a time before the army. I'd put on my real work clothes when I got to the loft, and change back into my nice clothes before heading home at the end of the day. Part of my job was sweeping the floor and cleaning up at the end of the day, but that was not the worst—they actually were good about making it not look like I was just a gofer. The worst part was pulling that hand truck through the streets with those bulky boxes on it.

For me there was no pride to be found in pulling that damn hand truck through the streets. It was the epitome of failure; if you couldn't get a job anywhere else, you could damn sure get one pulling a hand truck through the street. And there I was, representing the opposite of success. I'd hold the hand truck as these white boys I worked for stacked it high with boxes. Then they'd almost jump-start me, pointing me in the right direction with a shove, and I'd just push past the people on the street until I got where I was going.

One day it was raining like hell. I was pulling that hand truck through midday traffic around Thirty-sixth and Sixth, which was even more hellishly jammed than it is today, with horns blaring and people cursing all the more for being caught in the downpour. Everything was so rain-slick. In an instant I just lost my grip on the handles, and the damn thing slipped out of my hands. It wasn't that the truck was so heavy, but it was just so awkward. And I couldn't see where I was going, because it was piled so high with boxes. That hand truck flipped over, scattering the boxes all over Sixth Avenue.

I remember so vividly the way some police officer cussed me out. I can still hear him screaming, "Get those goddamn boxes up! Look what you're doing to the damn traffic!" I stared down through the pouring rain at the boxes in the gutter. All I saw was a scene from a waking nightmare. Sergeant Rangel getting cussed out by a mere civilian for messing up the equivalent of a garbage detail. I had never forgotten Sergeant Rangel, because Sergeant Rangel was all I had. No one was supposed to be talking to him like that. And oh, did I curse my brother for talking me out of going back into the army. There is no regret like the kind that grips your gut in a nightmare. Oh, what a terrible decision I knew I'd made. Four damn years in the army, gone, bang, just like that. I had crawled out of a ditch at Kunu-ri and lived, only to die this indignity in a garment district gutter.

Once again, time stood still. And when it resumed, I looked up from that gutter and I began to walk. I was soaked, and I was stripped of the notion of being Sergeant Rangel, war hero. I wasn't anybody anymore, or anything. I walked straight to the Veterans Administration office at Twenty-third Street and Seventh Avenue. I don't know what came over me; all I know is that I left those boxes and that hand truck on the street, and I never went back to that business again, not even to get my last check.

There was a line at the VA. I took a number and waited. When my turn came I told them that I was Sergeant Rangel. I told them I had the Purple Heart, the Bronze Star, four Battle Stars, and I was in deep trouble. I went looking for the VA even though there was nobody to tell me what the VA could do for me. All I knew was that I was in a lot of pain, and it didn't have much of anything to do with the shrapnel I'd taken in Korea. It was my pride that ached. I was shot at and eventually hit in Korea, but my pride was never wounded in the army. In fact, I'd built up a layer of ego there from the things I had gotten away with that was damn near impervious to assault, at least within the closed system of the white man's army. I had come home with a carefree swagger, but something about tipping that hand truck on the street that day turned my stride into a bitter limp. As my pride ran down that gutter with the rain, I swore that somebody was going to catch hell for what civilian life had done to Sergeant Rangel.

At the VA there were all these old white men doing the intake. They didn't seem overly impressed with my story. Now, by old, I mean they were all World War II veterans. I was twenty-three, and they were thirty, thirty-five, forty years old, old enough to have gone into the service before I'd gone into kindergarten. That not only made them *old* to me, it really dated them, and not in a good way. A lot of them were disabled, including many amputees and cripples, from fighting against the Japanese or in mortal combat against the Germans. These veterans had entered the service before the American armed forces had even *thought* about considering the black man an equal comrade in arms, with an equal investment in the causes of freedom and the American way of life.

If they had a collective personality, it would be akin to that of Archie Bunker in the television show *All in the Family*. Their general mentality held quite simply that if you had not been in World War II, you were not really a veteran. Even when my brother and his friends were talking about war, they meant "the Big War," World War II. When they talked about Korea, it wasn't even the "little war." It was the "police action," just as Truman called it. Vietnam, and its veterans, would suffer a similar disrespect in the 1970s. Even today, with the World War II veterans mostly dead, we still talk about the "great war" and the "good war" and the "greatest generation." We still place that war and the cohort that I missed by just a couple of years above all others. It's hard sometimes to escape the feeling that the culture of American veterans has been a semiclosed society since Japan surrendered.

I mention all this because I think it explains why they were none too sensitive to me down at the VA in 1953. I didn't feel a lot of sensitivity toward them either, despite their missing limbs, their wheelchairs, and their scars. But what I did feel was a kind of shame for all I had gotten away with in the army, all my arrogance without admitting to anyone that I was a dropout. My shame left me vulnerable to their condescension, and sometimes outright contempt for me. I couldn't articulate what I wanted from them, but I knew Sergeant Rangel deserved better than he was getting. There were a whole lot of other black Korea veterans down there looking for something, too, and they also felt there was no helping hand being extended to them. Since I didn't have a job, I just kept going down there every day and raising hell.

Eventually they told me they could help me after I took an aptitude test. That made sense to me. They gave me a choice of venue—Columbia University or Catholic Charities. So of course I picked up my rosary and I went to Catholic Charities, reasoning that if I took it there I'd have to come out ahead. I really wanted to talk to somebody about my future, and how I was being treated. I reasoned that if they were going to help me with this testing and counseling business, then they would have to talk with me. But all they did was put me in a room and give me a test. Nobody talked with me about anything. I was also scared and utterly alone in trying to figure out the next move in my life. I didn't know what the hell I wanted to do. There was no teacher figure in the back of my brain reminding me that "when you grow up, you should be this."

From the test results they concluded I was fit to be trained for one of two things: mortician or electrician. I could not have been more outraged by their assessment. A *mortician?* I had seen my share of dead men in the war these old men dismissed as a police action. It was not unusual in Korea to see bodies piled on the side of the road—Korean bodies—that were all bloated up and blue and stinking. And I'd never forgotten the sight of those three truckloads of dead black GIs, stacked like cordwood. The very idea that I should be an undertaker, handling dead people for a living, was more than an insult or a bad joke; it was torture. And, in my mind at the time, it could only be racist torture. I told them flat out: When it came to me being a mortician, they must have been looking at someone else's test.

As for concluding I should be an electrician, it was true that I'd gotten my promotions in the army by putting myself down for a vacant position in the Wire Unit. But I didn't know one piece of wire from the next. I was just skating around before facing combat, because that's where the vacancies and promotions were at the time. I knew that because I typed most of my promotions myself. Moreover, there was nothing on the aptitude test that had anything to do with being a damn electrician. So I just assumed that this offer was somehow racist, too. I continued raising hell. Of course, there were no blacks doing any work consulting with any of the veterans coming in there, so I made it my business to wise up any other blacks who came down there looking for help, and tried to enlist them in our common cause. Instead of just bitching about the test conclusions, I made the counseling and testing process *itself* the issue. I'd come at them with:

> You show me any question that I answered that would
> tell you that I have an aptitude to be a mortician or an elec-
> trician. You just show me where it is. I want you to tell me
> what I said on this test that allowed you to reach this
> damned racist conclusion!

Playing what we now call the race card and organizing other blacks in my position didn't seem like a very big or dramatic thing for me to do at the time, a few years ahead of the civil rights revolution. They were all white and we were all black; it was just that obvious and simple to me. The integration of the armed forces was all new and shiny somewhere in the world, maybe on an air force base in Germany or something. But the army never got integrated for me, and it definitely hadn't caught up to the VA, as far as I could see. It was all old World War II white men. Mostly Irish and Italian-American, which was not much different from being Southern, to my mind.

Looking back through the mirror of my years, in the young man raising all that hell at the VA, I see the natural prepolitical Charlie Rangel, unimpeded by deliberation or any thought of consequences. I knew then by nature as I know now by experience that if you're being mistreated, you've got to let them know they're making a big mistake by not treating you fairly. Once you know you are right, and that it's really happening to you, you've got to call their asses on it, whoever they are. You've got to, as Frederick Douglass said, "speak truth to power." I just knew this was my big chance to expose the VA for what it really was, because there was no way for them to justify the results of that test to me. I had their asses. Oh, they tried to explain to me that being a mortician was really about personality and people, rather than corpses. I don't even remember the rest of the bullshit they tried to get me to take about being an electrician.

I must have gone back and forth with the people at the VA for weeks. I can't say exactly where it would have gone had it continued this way, but it was probably downhill. Then along came a VA counselor named John Becatoris, who must have inherited me after all the hell I was raising around there. Either he liked me or he just got tired of my complaining; either way he was determined to cut through to the heart of the standoff between me and the VA. For me that heart was emotional, but Becatoris figured out that it was really pragmatic. He was a short, bald-headed guy with a bushy mustache who seemed a little older than the rest. He looked over my file, and quickly concluded that the mortician or electrician referral was not about the aptitude test. It was about the fact that I had not completed high school. The VA, he said, had a time limit on educational benefits; they were simply trying to make me employable before the benefits ran out.

It took me awhile to accept that this wasn't more bureaucratic runaround. Emotionally, I didn't understand why they weren't talking about sending me to college. Then one day Becatoris just hit me right between the eyes with it:

"What do you *really* want to be, Rangel?" he demanded. I told him that I really didn't know, except that I didn't want to be no damn undertaker, or no damn electrician, and that the whole VA was just full of shit, and my boys out there knew it.

He'd heard that before. He came back with: "Stop and just think about it; you haven't even finished high school. You've got a limited amount of time here as far as your education benefits are concerned. You can't go to college, because there's not enough time." This was news to me; nobody down there had ever told me anything about any time limits on what I could become. Now I understood that because I had quit DeWitt Clinton two years shy of my high school diploma, there wasn't time to prepare me for anything requiring four years of college.

Then Becatoris said, "But suppose none of the limits existed. What would you want to be?" I tried to stall him at first with "Wasn't that what the aptitude test was for?" He said to forget the test, tests are for lab rats; this is for your real life. That was when we *really* started talking. He forced me past my tactic of exposing the racism at the VA. I had no clue as to what profession I could possibly fit in. He said I couldn't just go on complaining like that and expect to get anywhere. He said I had to help them if I wanted to help myself. "Just tell me," he said, "where do you wanna take this?"

Up to that point what I thought he meant was: You tell me what you *want* to be, and then I'll tell you what you *can* be. But now I saw that he really wanted to get at what the hell I wanted to be in the world. There was no room for making up anything to bullshit Becatoris anymore. As luck would have it, something inside me picked that moment to speak up for itself, from someplace I'd never looked before.

"I want to be a lawyer," I said.

Where the hell could that have come from? I tell you with my whole heart, I could have said brain surgeon in that moment, or ambassador to France. That's how unconscious I was of any motivation beyond saying something, anything, to get me out of that damn box of being a mortician! I used to laugh when my mother insisted I wanted to be a lawyer when I was a child. Decades later, however, I came to realize that lawyer wasn't some wild guess; it came from my grandfather. Lawyer had nothing to do with what he saw in me—as far as I knew he never saw anything but trouble in me—but it had a lot to do with how I saw him, and something I wanted to see in his eyes when he looked at me.

My grandfather, who I always loved but would never say "I love you" back, was just a rough guy on the outside. In his work as an elevator operator at the criminal court down at 100 Centre Street he operated the machinery that took the judges and the district attorneys from the street to their aeries of power and back, all day long. On so many Saturdays I'd go down there with him, sometimes with my sister, riding up and down on that elevator.

He was a big shot on the block. He kept that uniform on, with a little round badge pinned to his chest, as if it made him an officer of the court. We didn't have many black lawyers back then, but there were the Jewish lawyers who would handle our cases, and he knew them all. He also knew Cornelius McDermott, one of the very first of the few black lawyers practicing in the criminal courts at that time. *Everybody* in the neighborhood knew Charlie Wharton, and where he worked. And I knew Charlie Wharton's unqualified respect for lawyers.

Challenged by Becatoris to look inside and to see past my anger and resentment, I had to have been thinking about who was and was not impressed by whom in my world. Nobody in my immediate family had gone to college. I must confess that when I came home in those days and saw my kid sister in her starched white uniform going off to school, it didn't go unnoticed that she would soon be a registered nurse, while I, the Purple Heart veteran, was still unloading trucks or pushing carts. Becoming a lawyer was still not really what I had gone to the VA to do. But discovering in my heart the wish for my grandfather's approval put the ball in my court; now Becatoris was determined that I should return it, somehow.

When I said lawyer, I'll be damned if Becatoris didn't start probing me, to see how this could be done. He finally came around to what almost sounded like an offer, but it came out something like, "You can't become a lawyer unless you have already graduated from college." I couldn't understand why, if I wanted to become a lawyer, I would first have to graduate from college. He explained, again, that law school required an undergraduate college degree and that I still had two years of high school left to do. "You've got two years of high school to make up and four years of college, that's six years," he said. "How are you gonna get six years into four years?" I said I didn't know. He said, "We can do it, but it depends on how serious you are."

I must have been pretty serious, because the doors to opportunity seemed to fly open after that. He found some high school that took the two years I needed and rammed it into one. He later got me into NYU and we figured out how to do four years in three by going to school year-round and carrying up to 18 credits most terms. I needed 130 credits for the degree, and somehow I got them in three years. He told me the courses to take and the courses not to take. Becatoris also told me I was eligible for a stipend, disability benefits, and a special program for disabled veterans that no one in the VA had bothered to tell me about before. Together they allowed me to get my full tuition and all my books paid for, and even put a little cash money in my pocket.

From that day in 1953 until I was admitted to the New York State bar in 1960, apart from my amazing assortment of part-time jobs, becoming a lawyer was my only business. College was a breeze, and finishing high school was less than a blur. In fact, all I recall about my high school career was a terrible scare I had following law school, when I had to answer the character and fitness questions for admission to the bar. I had already passed the exam, but now they wanted to know things like whether I'd ever been thrown out of any schools along the way.

It's funny, now, the kinds of things that put the fear of God in you at different points in your life. I was damn near thirty years old, a St. John's Law and NYU graduate. Now comes one silly little question, and I damn near panic: I could not remember exactly how the hell I left DeWitt Clinton! I recall my mom had nothing to say in the matter. She couldn't chastise me about going to school anymore, because I was seventeen, cocksure I was a man, and busy hanging out with my guys. I doubted that I had bothered with a formal withdrawal. As white and elite a public high school as DeWitt Clinton was at the time, I just knew they must have thrown my ass out. But I had to be sure.

Hoping desperately against hope, I took the Jerome Avenue train from Harlem way up past Yankee Stadium to Moshulu Parkway near the end of the line. I told some people in charge there that I was a disabled veteran who had been wounded in Korea.

"What do you want?" they asked.

"I'm a Purple Heart, and I've got the Bronze Star, too," I said.

"But what do you want?" they asked.

"I attended Clinton, and I went to law school," I said, almost pleading.

"That's nice, Mr. Rangel, but can you tell us *what do you want?*"

"I want to know," I blurted, "how did I leave DeWitt Clinton? I may never become a lawyer. I don't know what I want. Look at this paper; look at what they're asking me!"

They looked at each other for a while, and then they said they had to go in the back and check the records. Actually, they just wanted to see me sweat a little longer, because they came back laughing and said, "Mr. Rangel, we don't have any record of how you left. We know you came here, but we don't know how you left."

"Is that true?" I asked. "You don't have any record?"

"Yes," they laughed; they didn't have anything on me.

And that was the last time I left DeWitt Clinton High School; I was one happy warrior!

———————————

Before I went into the army, I can remember just how much I despised those colored kids who went to college. Especially the ones who would run around flaunting that Greek black fraternity stuff. How I detested every damn one of them—from the Alphas to the Omegas. And then there I was, saying I wanted to be one of them, and setting myself up to do it, all without knowing what the hell they really were.

When I was a teenager, and even before, I didn't know anyone who had gone to college except the teachers. I'm not just talking about knowing someone who graduated from college, I mean I knew no one personally who had set foot in college. My lack of acquaintance molded my attitude; I was satisfied to scorn college-trained people. I delighted in saying things like: "You see that black guy there? He says he belongs to a Greek organization, and the guy can't speak English." Or about the educated elite who frequented the high-class clubs like Jock's or the Red Rooster: "They think they got more degrees than a thermometer—but they only know how to talk to each other."

So, for a guy with all my built-in prejudices, my emotional break-through to seeing myself as a college graduate and then some was really quite something. And it made quite an impression on everyone around me, too, especially people who had known me when. After I made the decision, at the relatively old age of twenty-three, to go back to high school with something as high as law school in my sights, I was humbled, if not a bit amazed, to see how people who knew me really pitched in. They saw that I really wanted to do something and thought it damn unusual, not just for me but for anyone who came from my world. It was as if they all went home and said around the dinner table, "If this street hoodlum thinks he can make it, well, I just gotta help him." There were also people like Nettie Messenger, my old teacher who was still at P.S. 89, and Charlie Fried from the hardware store. They were always available to say how proud they were, and to reinforce what I was trying to accomplish. You can't just do it all yourself. You have to have people who know what you're doing with your life.

To my hating-college-trained-blacks way of thinking, reaching for college meant risking rejection from my untrained peers. But once I made my move, my attitude was turned on its head; I found myself embraced. Because attending college is so widely expected now, it's hard for me to imagine what a young person, even from a poor background, could attempt today that would be similarly remarkable. It was as though I said I was preparing for the marathon, or the Olympics. Me, a guy from the street with holes in my shoes, suddenly in training and seen running around and around the block every morning and evening. I became a local legend. Even when things weren't going that well, I was still known as the guy who was going to go to law school. Except for certain strategic or ceremonial occasions, my Sergeant Rangel persona was comfortably retired.

For the VA, I put down "business degree" as my objective for going to college. But I knew from day one that getting into law school was my job. And I knew that I had to look for scholarships like nobody else had ever looked for law school scholarships, because that's where my GI tuition benefits ended. And I knew that I had to get the grades to prove that I could be a lawyer. I had to get A's. One of my greatest nightmares was to be left holding onto my bachelor of science degree with no way to get to law school and without any skills or hope of getting a job. I had to get into law school, and I had to do it in three years.

I have to say that managing my NYU education by objective—law school–worthy grades—worked pretty well. My hard work in carefully selected courses got me on the dean's list. I also received an occasional helping hand for poor old Sergeant Rangel. For example, I recall screwing up badly in an accounting course. But the teacher knew I was a Korean veteran, and he had lost a son in Korea who had been a pilot. Damn, if this teacher didn't always go out of his way to ask how I was doing whenever I walked into class. He gave a test once, and I didn't know what was going on. He was proctoring, and he kept looking at me as I struggled. And he looked and he looked, until finally he said, "I want you to see me after class." Boy, did he give me a talking to, about how combat veterans must have some kind of psychological block about reaching out to ask for help when we need it. He complained that I wasn't responding in class, which was true enough because I didn't know what the hell was going on. "But damn it," he concluded, "you served your country, and that's what counts!" He gave me a B and I stayed away from accounting for the rest of my life.

Then as now, going to NYU, one of the largest private universities in the nation, could be an impersonal, almost anonymous experience. The classes were so big that you were given a number and that's who you were. If you weren't in class, you were nothing but an empty seat; they didn't say "Mr. Jones was absent," they just opened up a book and pulled out your number—that was you. The student body was not only vast but so diverse in terms of where students were coming from as to geography, life experience, personal circumstances, and objectives, that you were more likely to have a meaningful relationship with the subway that brought you there than with the school itself or any particular classmates. Everyone had too much else going on in their lives—especially jobs and just being engaged by the beating heart of New York City—to participate in some larger camaraderie. I was the typical subway student. I never got a chance to form any friendships, and it seemed like nobody else wanted to have any friends either. I was part of no fraternity or any other group; if my life depended on it I couldn't think of one person I either went to class with or graduated with out of all the thousands that were in the school with me.

My anonymity at NYU led to an unforgettable graduation day story. As I've said so many times before—because the more I reflect on it, the more it bears repeating—my gruff grandfather was almost incapable of showing that he cared for people. It didn't mean he had no interest or concern about a lot of people; he just never showed any affection. So it must have been extremely awkward for him when I asked him to attend my graduation from NYU. His immediate response was, "Why the hell would I want to do something like that?"

I half expected it, and I wasn't really hurt by his answer, or the fact that there was nobody emotionally invested in my graduating. So I went on down there by myself and did what everybody else did. There must have been seven thousand graduates from all of the schools walking that day. When I finally got home, my grandfather, who kept his good clothes wrapped up with mothballs upstairs in a cedar closet, was sitting by the kitchen coal stove in a derby hat and Chesterfield coat. He even had spats on his shiny shoes—and he was as drunk as Billy B. Damn. When I picked my jaw off the floor, I asked him what the hell this was all about.

"You curly-haired son of a gun," he started. "I went down there looking for your ass, and nobody knew you. They didn't know where you were. You come up here trying to act like you're a big shot in this school, and nobody knew who you were!"

There was nothing for me to say and only one thing for me to do: get out a glass and start drinking the rest of graduation day away with my poor old grandfather.

I ended up getting six law school scholarships to choose from, including NYU. Most of them offered partial support with no stipends, something I couldn't afford. But the mother of them all granted me three years tuition, books, and a stipend—a full ride. It was called the Catholic Scholarship for Negroes, from the Putnam family philanthropy out of Springfield, Massachusetts. I'm still in touch with the family on raising money for the fund. It was specifically targeted for St. John's University, so that's where I went.

I remained a subway student, riding the same Seventh Avenue line a few more stops past Greenwich Village and into downtown Brooklyn, where St. John's University Law School was located at the time. I've always found it interesting that both of my schools, now housed in relatively new, palatial campuses, were sited in old factory buildings at the time I attended. The parallels, however, ended there. After four years with my head down, I had reached my destination. I looked up, and a voice in my head said, "You've really gotten in over your head this time, Charlie." For the high school and undergraduate part of the journey, I had a clear advantage as a mature veteran, on my own and on a mission. It was a cakewalk. At St. John's the classes and the whole school were much smaller and more intimate than NYU. The kids were much smarter, and not appreciably less mature than I was. There was no question that I was going to stand out among them; the only question was how.

I was scared to death. But by the end of my first year I was tearing up St. John's. I didn't exactly do it with the books, though I kept up my grades and made the dean's list. I tore up St. John's in terms of politics. Looking back, I think I rediscovered my instinct for the nature of institutions that was first awakened in the army. But where the army was a bureaucratic autocracy, law school was more of an academic democracy. In the end both are political, but unlike the army, the law school was always taking votes, appointing representatives, and holding elections. I had found my meat. Before long I was embedded in the center of whatever was happening. I was running slates of students for various offices. I organized the handful of blacks there to make coalition with the Italians, who in those days were not treated as well as the Irish. I found ways to bring in the Jews, and other marginal groups, orchestrating the ethnic politics of St. John's like Toscanini conducting Beethoven's Ninth. In this way I ran the moot court, and had a hand on the levers of the student government's discipline machinery.

I learned a great deal about New Yorkers who weren't like me—Jews, Italians, and Irish—from those students at St. John's. I got much more out of my experience than someone who might have gone to a historically black university, whose parents were professionals and belonged to one of those black fraternities I resented so much. At St. John's, a group of us actually started our own national fraternity—mainly to stick it to the dean, because we thought he catered to one Irish fraternity. And who was in our fraternity? Everybody except the preferred Irish majority. You see, when St. John's started, Catholics were not as readily accepted in Ivy League schools as they are today. Italians were still finding it difficult to get into those schools, and other groups were still having a hard time, too. St. John's opened up to all of them then, as it remains to this day. But back then it needed to open a little more for Italians and other non-Irish ethnic groups. I formed friendships that I still maintain, with kids who didn't come from families of great social standing.

I would guess that a great many kids from my era at St. John's later entered politics in some fashion. The reason, I think, is because their parents were civil servants or low-level elected officials. As I said earlier, I myself took my first step in politics during these law school years because my grandfather needed a city government dispensation for his pension. My classmates were the seedlings of the new postwar middle class, born into the New Deal, watered and fertilized by the GI Bill. They didn't give me the kind of "class by association" that poor, aspiring students can acquire by going to an Ivy League school, or even an elite black school. But I honestly believe they gave me my whole way of speaking, and my basic education in getting things done through working with people.

Sometime near the end of my first year, a new professor, J. Walter McKenna—he had come from NYU Law School—approached me saying he'd heard a lot of good things about me. At NYU he had run something called the Criminal Law Institute. It was like a law review with an elite internship attached. He said he'd talked with another professor—Edward Re, who went on to distinguish himself as a judge—and ticked off all the things I was running at St. John's. Prof. Re, who has been a good friend of mine ever since, had put me in charge of the moot court. "Would you consider stopping all of this," McKenna asked, "and starting a criminal law institute here at St. John's?"

He explained that I'd be the founder and president, able to select the students who'd be assigned to DA's offices throughout the five counties as interns for course credit. They would work with the DAs on real cases, and even sit with them during the trials. "You have to be kidding," I said. "They'll never let me do that here."

"Oh no," he seemed to agree, "but they will let *me* do that here; and I want you to be the one to do it."

Already beginning to think like a lawyer, I took this offer under advisement to another professor, Charlie Sparacio, who was very well known at the time because he gave the Sparacio bar review courses in addition to teaching there. He was always excited about me. A dark Italian, he used to like to drink with me, perhaps because I was a war veteran or something. His best buddy was the dean, Harold McNiece, a real straight arrow who was very strict yet beloved by the institution, especially by its Irish students. My agitating and organizing among the left out groups never did sit well with Dean McNiece.

When I ran the criminal law institute idea by Sparacio he said, "You wouldn't want to take that—it's too stable. You couldn't cause trouble; you'd have to be responsible." I said, "Aw, come on, Professor." He said, "Nawww, you'd never do that in a million years. That would be too responsible for you to do." By the time we finished talking, I went back to McKenna and said, "If you can get this past McNiece, I'd love to do it."

And doggone if I didn't become the first president of the Criminal Law Institute, which is still there at St. John's. And five years after I blurted out "lawyer" to John Becatoris at the VA, because my grandfather respected them so much, I was an intern in the very same office where he ran the elevator. There I was, a big-shot intern, not even out of law school, and I was Mr. Rangel in that building, hot damn! And they had come to me! It wasn't as though I had put the pieces together from scratch. It should have been no surprise to anyone that I appointed myself to New York County DA Frank Hogan's office. I was this close to being exactly the same as any prosecutor riding Grandfather's elevator. In the end, after I graduated, racism stopped me from even getting an interview for an assistant district attorney job there, much to my dismay. But as you'll see, soon after that door closed, an even bigger door was opened to me.

———————

Today, when the children of the New York "ethnics" can go to law school almost anywhere they're qualified, with the support of parents who stand at least a few rungs above mere civil servant on the status ladder, many are still attending St. John's Law School. I think it's because their parents have a deep attachment to the idea of continuity—they want their kids to go where they went. I was proud to send my son Steven to St. John's Law. But I'd be damned if I let him work the kinds of jobs I worked while I was studying there. As I've said, I always had jobs as a young man, often simultaneously. I remember working for the post office at some point during my law school career, and of course being an intern in Frank Hogan's office. But my biggest money, and fondest memories, came from working the desk in two Harlem hotels.

I worked first for a hot sheet place on 132nd and Lenox called the Riverton Hotel. The guy I got the job from, Earl Smith, had gone on to robbing banks, so there was a vacancy. A lot of prostitutes went through that place. Frankly, without going into details, some of them were very nice to me. I worked from four to twelve, taking over from a guy named Rio, who worked eight to four. The hotel was over a bar nicknamed the Bucket O'Blood, and across the street from the Baron bar; between the two of them that place really jumped in the summer. Now, on Thursdays, the standard maids' night off, a lot of the gals who worked live-in in Long Island would come to New York and check in at the hotel for a good time, hanging at the bars and partying, before going back to their jobs. There was this big, fat, pretty girl who used to come in every Thursday. She used to flirt with me, but I was pretty serious about my studies. One week she comes in with this guy, and says, "Well, you didn't want to give me any, so I got someone prettier than you." The guy looked a little awkward.

"Where do I sign?" he asked.

"She already has her room," I said.

"Well, do I pay you anything?"

"No, sir, she's already registered."

"You got any liquor I could buy?"

"No, sir."

"You got any condoms?"

"No, sir."

"Is this one of your girls?"

"No, sir."

Finally, he gives me a three-dollar tip. They go off to the room, and about forty minutes later he comes out saying, "Boy, was that good, she was right; you sure missed a lot. What do I owe you?" I said, "You don't owe me anything, mister." He leaves with her, and she's all happy. He comes back about a half hour later. I'm studying.

"Gimme my fuckin' three dollars back," he demands. I turn around and he's standing there with another guy in plain clothes, showing me badges and declaring that they're cops. I ask them what it's all about; they demand to see the registration book. Of course, the name to which the room was registered wasn't hers. You see, the guy on the desk before me was renting "hot sheets." He had a deal with the housekeeper that if someone checked out early in the same day, that room would be his to control until the next day. He'd rerent the same room at a cut rate, pocket the money, and pay off the housekeeper to change the sheets. The cop accused me of pimping and running a whorehouse. I said, "Mister, I'm no pimp, I'm going to law school." He said, "You know, we arrested that whore." I said, "Mister, that woman is just a maid."

The hotel called in a black lawyer who told me the thing turned on whether they arrested her on the property or in the street. I said she didn't walk out of there looking like a woman under arrest. Based on how they were trying to shake me down, they probably tried to shake her down, but she didn't have any money. If they arrested her at all, I told him, that's probably why. He asked me to sign an affidavit that she wasn't arrested in the hotel. But I couldn't sign anything saying she wasn't arrested there. I could sign one saying nobody *told me* she was arrested there, but that was about it. They threatened to fire me but I said I was in law school—I had to think about what I was signing now. I had been accustomed to corrupt policemen all my life growing up on Lenox Avenue. I never thought I could still be caught in their net when I was so close to completing law school. It was a lesson I would never forget.

I was such a damn good desk clerk, and the reason, I think, is because I did every shift in its moment, and gave that moment the best I had to give. I try to tell kids today that if they can dream, and believe in their dreams, then they can tell themselves that each part of their life, each shift, is only a step away from moving on to something better. If you can believe in yourself, you can commit to that shift, and do it for all you're worth. Knowing I'm going to do better tomorrow through the benefit of what I do today has become habit for life with me. I honestly feel that whatever I may be going through today is no big deal, no problem at all. I trace this attitude back to those years of law school when my life really began to take off. From those days on, you couldn't get me angry, no matter what you said to me as the desk clerk. Because, the way I processed it, I would think that you were probably trying to get some satisfaction out of making me angry, and me getting angry because of *you* would be the dumbest thing in the world for me to do. This approach has worked for me with everybody from irate johns on the other side of the hotel desk, to irate Ways and Means chairmen from the other side of the aisle, as I'll explain in a later chapter.

From that hot sheets place they actually *recruited* me for the legendary Hotel Theresa. A guy named Lawrence Browner came to the hotel where I was working, hung out in the lobby checking me out, and then recruited me. Was that a move up? Man, that was it! The official Harlem Renaissance of the 1920s and early 1930s had been over for decades. But for the black people of Harlem, the real renaissance had begun in the 1940s, when a combination of the changes brought by

World War II and the activism of Adam Clayton Powell, among others, opened employment for African-Americans at the major retail and service businesses on 125th Street, and forced the integration of all of the most fabled nightspots, restaurants, and other places—including the Hotel Theresa itself.

So I was privileged to be a desk clerk when Harlem was most truly the cultural and social capital of black America, and the Theresa was its Waldorf-Astoria. Everybody black who was anybody in America came through Harlem, and stayed at the Theresa, just steps away from the Apollo Theatre in its heyday. The Apollo was the top venue on the Chitlin' Circuit of theaters catering to African-American audiences, and the primary venues available to black icons like Billie Holiday, James Brown, Dick Gregory, Duke Ellington, Pearl Bailey, and Louis Armstrong. And at nights, when I worked, it was Grand Central Station for the biggest black stars of stage and screen, the top athletes, the highest rollers, and all the inevitable low-life hangers-on.

Within six years, by the time of the Harlem riots of 1964, the glory that was the Hotel Theresa in 1958—it closed in 1966—would seem like a cruel illusion. But what an illusion it was. When I got there the dress code was shirt and tie. William Brown, the father of the late former commerce secretary Ron Brown, was the manager. Harlem royalty, including Thurgood Marshall, then the NAACP's top lawyer, Paul Robeson, and Langston Hughes, were regular guests in Bill and Gloria Brown's lovely penthouse suite on the twelfth floor. He loved to play poker, and I soon made money on the side as a gofer during the games. I made so much money that I'd come home counting it. My grandfather would see me and say, "What exactly the hell are you doing down there! You must be up to no good." Of course I wasn't playing; there was no way I could afford to play in those games. I was rolling in cash just from the tips I got for bringing back the liquor and the food and everything else those guys demanded. It was my reward for taking the guff that made these big men feel bigger when they had a few drinks in them.

By hook or crook, I was taking in so much money going to law school in my Hotel Theresa days that it seemed like I would be losing money by going to work as a lawyer when I graduated. As I said earlier, the legendary comedian Jackie "Moms" Mabley lived at the hotel. Some people say we have the same gravel-throated delivery. I'd be studying while I worked my shift—midnight to eight—and she'd come downstairs sometimes when the shows were over and the hustlers were in the lobby cussing and raising hell. She'd jump all over them with, "You see this boy trying to get an education, and you bums are raisin' hell. If you wanna help yourselves, give the boy some money, damn it!"

The Theresa had other fringe benefits. There were always a lot of girls—dancers, acrobats, and singers—who were working the Apollo staying there. They were in town to work, and weren't looking for any hanky-panky. But they did want to step out in black New York, to see and be seen at Smalls' or the Baby Grand. In those days, real ladies still didn't feel comfortable going to high-class spots unescorted. I was in the know, and looking pretty good, so they'd always let me know when they were coming to town. Damn, if they didn't think I was the cat's meow! I'd get all dressed up for a night on the town. Mind you, I might not have a spare nickel in my pocket, but I'd be right up there at Jock's or the Red Rooster with one of these beautiful girls. I can never forget the look on the faces of the guys at the bar as they wondered how the hell a desk clerk/law student managed to hold onto the kind of gals I was taking out. How little they knew that that was all I was doing.

Sometimes this escort service of mine got pretty complicated. One of these gals would come into New York without notifying me, and I was already doing the town with somebody else. I was friends with a long-time barmaid at Jock's named Fannie Pennington—now a very active member of the Abyssinian Baptist Church. When she saw a "complication" coming up behind me, she'd pull my coat and say, "Charlie, I think you want to go in the back," because she could see who was coming in the front. And I'd go on in the back. She was very good to me. As an aside, she really loved Adam Powell, and hated me when I beat him. But she loves me now, again. I still joke with her about how so many years after our Jock's days, she found Jesus and I found Congress.

Whenever Billie Holiday played the Apollo, I'd play hooky from school. I'd be sitting up there in the balcony, swearing that she was singing only to me. Imagine my surprise one night at the Theresa, when the chance to assume the virtue of a knight to her Lady came my way. I was working my usual shift. She came in the lobby in such disarray and staggered to a seat on the elevator operator's bench. My heart was so broken at the sight. And then this fellow who was with her comes up to the desk, says he's Billie Holiday's husband, and asks for a room. I said, "Mister, we don't have any rooms." He demanded to see the manager. "Mister," I said, "for all practical purposes, I am the manager!" And that was that. Hot damn, I was somebody! I wasn't letting this fool take *my* woman upstairs, husband or no husband.

One of the wannabe politicians who hung out at the Theresa was a tough-talking character who shall remain nameless here. He went on to become pretty well known around Harlem because he hung out with Adam Clayton Powell. But when Adam got in trouble, he was one of the first guys to turn against him, politically. Nobody, including Adam, ever took him seriously. But when he died, Percy Sutton and I were sitting together at the funeral at Abyssinian. And there was the Reverend Licorish, an assistant pastor, conducting the service. You have to hear this in his strong West Indian accent:

> Well, we're here to bury this fellow. I want you politi-
> cians out there to build a shrine to the man. A monument,
> a statue, or something. I know: a lot of you people think
> that all he did was drink liquor, go to the bars, chase the
> women. You didn't know . . . he was coming to see me to
> learn about Je-suss, did you?? Yessss, I was teaching him the
> gospel! His wife knows it—not his first wife or his second
> wife, but his third wife right here; she knows that he was try-
> ing to get the gospel!

Percy leans over and says, "Charlie, you gotta promise me something: If I die before you do, please, do not let that son of a gun anywhere near my funeral!"

The spring of 1960 came and found me a new man. Seven years earlier, Sergeant Rangel walked out of the rain and almost crawled into the VA at the bottom of his game, looking to get one last break out of the white man's army. They told me I had only two tickets to choose from, electrician or mortician—neither a place I wanted to go. With the help of old Becatoris, I ended up writing my own ticket. For years, long after I finished law school, I would occasionally drop in at the VA office just to talk to him.

When I say "I haven't had a bad day since," I really mean it's the theme for the story of my life. Ever since Kunu-ri, life for me has resolved its meaning to the having of my days. Dale Carnegie, the father of self-improvement, said people should "live in day-tight compartments," segments that may be full of challenges but sealed against regret for what is past and fear of what is to come. Anyone who has ever recognized the day of their own death, as I did at Kunu-ri, and then somehow summons all they have, gets up and walks away from it, knows this truth. Like the man Jesus met at the Bethesda pool, I picked up my mat and I never stopped walking.

Those guys in law school just knew that Rangel was going to become something. They thought maybe I would become Manhattan borough president, probably because at the time we had the first black borough president, Hulan Jack. They weren't even thinking about Adam Clayton Powell and his congressional seat. Neither was I. There is something important about focusing on where you are, while knowing that you're not staying where you are, that allows you to do a better job than anybody in the world. And I do that today in the Congress.

I've worked so damn hard at everything I've done. But, as you might now begin to appreciate, I have not been much of a planner. You don't make a plan to be tested in a ditch in Korea, or in a gutter on Sixth Avenue, and then be found worthy. You live life, you work hard, and, if you are blessed with the opportunity to get an education, you open your eyes and seize it. Then you learn how to live a little better. I didn't plan on going into the army to become anybody. I didn't try to succeed, and I didn't succeed. And yet, with what I learned about living and staying alive in the army, I came out with medals, but no direction.

I went to the VA to beat the rain, and I came out a guy on his way to tear up law school. And I haven't had a bad day since.

5

Harlem Lawyer

"All things from eternity are of like forms and come round in a circle."
—Marcus Aurelius, *Meditations*, Bk. 2, Ch. 14

The truth that is in the things you do, and the things that are done to you, cycles through your life and the lives of all you touch, like a system of planets on intersecting orbits around a sun. These truths, deflected in their arcs by the sway of what is right over what is wrong, have been proven to me over time. What goes around really does come around. And if you're blessed with humility and enough years to see these things through, you get a front-row seat on the most amazing second comings.

So it was with a full sense of sweet irony that I stood before the cameras in the fall of 2005 to defend my friend Robert Morgenthau—the model for the original Manhattan district attorney on the popular *Law & Order* television show—against a scurrilous and false charge of racism in hiring and promotion in his office as he sought an unprecedented eighth term. The charge was made by an African-American who had been an assistant district attorney in the eighties. In a campaign ad for Morgenthau's opponent, he had nothing good to say about her, but hit Morgenthau on how few black senior attorneys there were when he began there. The knife in the tagline was "It's been thirty years and nothing has changed."

When I jumped at the chance to help him, I told Morgenthau that nobody knows better than me the truth about the racism of the New York County District Attorney's Office in the sixties and early seventies. But that was *before* Bob Morgenthau took office. Here's how I know. When I was graduating from law school, and students were getting interviewed for jobs, there was no question, in my mind anyway, that I was going to be interviewed and hired as an assistant district attorney under then DA Frank Hogan. Remember, I had assigned myself there as an intern under the St. John's Criminal Law Institute that I co-founded. The assistant district attorney I worked for was the now famous Jay Goldberg, Donald Trump's lawyer. He had treated me more like a kid brother than an intern. I sat with him at trials, and he helped me prepare for every step on the way to becoming a New York County prosecutor. If anything, my write-up was inflated by the relationship I had with him; he even let me help write my own reference for him to sign.

It wasn't just my dream; it was my only dream. Arrogantly, perhaps, I thought I was already living it. I just knew that if I played my cards right—and I was sure I had—I'd reach the top of my game as an assistant DA in Frank Hogan's office. But Hogan's chief of staff was in the way. When the interview for the position was overdue, I went to him to find out why.

I said to him, "I haven't been interviewed."

"No," he says, "and you're not going to be."

"Why?"

"You didn't make the cut," he says.

I reminded him that I'd interned there for two years. He shot back that "We told you people that you weren't getting your foot in the door." I said I had the grades, and was well written up.

"And besides," I added, "there's a vacancy for a minority."

Oh, did he not want to hear that! He hit the damn ceiling so hard it could have cracked. But there *was* a vacancy. I knew every black in there, all five of them. They all became judges. When the chief of staff peeled himself from the ceiling, he dared me to say they had a quota for black prosecutors. I said they had something worse than a quota, and proceeded to raise hell with him and Hogan's office. The mess made it to the *Amsterdam News*. "Rejected" was the headline.

A year later, in 1961, I was sworn in, not as a New York County prosecutor, but as a *federal* prosecutor. Technically I was appointed by then Attorney General Robert F. Kennedy, but I was there mainly because Robert Morgenthau, who was the U.S. attorney for the Southern District of New York, gave me an opportunity. At the time, being a bit less seasoned on the wheel of karma than I am today, I couldn't wait to go back to Hogan's office, just to rub it in while saying "hi" to everybody.

When Bob Morgenthau said in 2005 that minority employment in his office went from 5 percent when he took office to 22 percent, that was good enough for me. But it's hard for even the best-intentioned white public official to weather a charge of not doing enough for minorities. Given our history of racial distrust it's especially hard to disprove a negative, and easy to be assumed guilty until proven innocent. He was deeply wounded by the charge, and a little shaken. I had to remind Morgenthau about all the times over the years he came to me looking for minority ADA candidates. I would tell him over and over how easy it was to find talented minority lawyers to jump at a chance to be a Manhattan prosecutor when I was trying to get into Frank Hogan's office, because there were so few opportunities for us then. Today, the kind of minority candidate the New York DA's Office is looking for—the most talented tenth of the talented tenth—have career options that far exceed the ability of the DA's Office to pay them.

A few weeks before the primary, the *New York Times* opined that thirty-plus years is long enough for anybody to be in office, no matter how beloved, and endorsed Leslie Crocker Snyder over Bob Morgenthau. Fortunately for me, as I anticipate my nineteenth run for Congress, the *New York Times* editorial board does not vote in the 17th Congressional District! As I stumped, I told Morgenthau that if I wasn't proud of his record, I wouldn't be "with him." You know, as much as I and other politicians talk about being "with" one another, the phrase and its meaning never appear in media coverage of how we do what we do. The closest thing to it in popular culture is when the captain or the lieutenant in some military adventure mission says: "Mr. O'Brien, you are with me." It's a much more personal commitment and professional obligation than a newspaper endorsement. To be with someone is to be bound to him for the battle, and at his disposal. Together "with" Bob Morgenthau, we put a lot of people in jail who were victimizing my community during my time as a federal prosecutor. We remained friends and worked together as I made my way up the ladder of public office. He still tells the story of how, while I served in his office, he didn't believe me when I told him that there were a lot of New York policemen taking bribes to look the other way on gambling and narcotics. But, he says, he trusted me enough to let me prove it to him, and his office went after them with vigor. Morgenthau was "with" me when I took my narcotics fighting to Congress in 1970.

Soon after I went to Congress, in 1973, I learned that the same guy from Hogan's office who had denied me the opportunity to be interviewed was challenging my old friend Robert Morgenthau for district attorney of New York County. I couldn't wait to join Bob's campaign. I wanted to let this man know in no uncertain terms that the position was filled. The message was delivered in the form of Bob's decisive victory. That was my first front-row seat for the coming around of what I did and what was done to me in 1960. And so, in 2005, it came around again, with a newly humbling wonder to it. So I stepped to the microphones, and I didn't dignify the blowhard who let himself be played as the race card in the attack on Morgenthau by calling his name. Instead, I pointed out the hypocrisy of the challenger hitting Morgenthau's record on diversity when she is a partner in a law firm with no black attorneys out of forty-four working there. I should have asked if she planned to make her race card surrogate an offer, but that would have been uncharitable. I felt too good, as I did in 1973, for that. Then as now I could only laugh and say how good God is, and how good He has been to me.

And, on September 13, 2005, Bob Morgenthau thrashed Leslie Crocker Snyder in the Democratic primary, virtually assuring reelection to his eighth term.

People get where they're going not for where they say they're going, but by dint of what they do. In life there is this funny way that faith in yourself, or in something more than yourself, eventually gets you around the people who try to stand between you and your goal. As it turns out, it's almost impossible for someone to effectively block you for long, because it's highly unlikely that they really know what your goal is—especially your ultimate goal. And, as I've said, I really wasn't planning my route, anyway. All I was doing was riding a wave that began to crest when I got to law school. Yet I had no idea that it was not a wave at all, but a wheel that was turning. Still, almost by nature, I have never wanted to get even with those I thought treated me unfairly. I tend to forget them—although when they do come back around, boy, do I remember!

One of my greatest experiences while serving in Hogan's office was meeting two other black interns who showed great promise. J. Bruce Llewellyn was just a few years older than me but had already studied to become a doctor before becoming a lawyer. Bruce later was very helpful to me politically, and went on to become one of the most successful African-American entrepreneurs of all time, with holdings that included a Buffalo, New York, television station and one of the nation's largest Coca-Cola franchises in Philadelphia. Clifford Alexander, who would soon be appointed an assistant district attorney, was not only well liked, but with degrees from Harvard and Yale he had a running start on an astonishing record of success in both public service and the private sector. His career would have a habit of weaving in and out of my own story. While I was at the U.S. Attorney's Office, Cliff called me about an opening running the city's Hamilton Grange community conservation program, which maintained the Harlem home of Alexander Hamilton as a national historic site. He had been its first executive director. It was based in a lovely building just outside the City College of New York campus at 270 Convent Avenue on Sugar Hill. Taking that job doubled my U.S. attorney salary, to $12,000, and also put me in a position to become a true confidant of the late great political mastermind J. Raymond Jones. I'll return to Ray Jones shortly.

Through a Harvard connection with Kennedy and Johnson administration national security adviser McGeorge Bundy, Cliff was called to Washington as a foreign affairs officer in 1963, and subsequently became an adviser to President Lyndon Johnson. Not long after that, he had my name put on a short list of people recommended as counsel to a presidential commission on Selective Service. Joe Califano, who was a special assistant to Johnson for domestic policy, later showed me that list, with Johnson's sign-off—"OK, LBJ"—next to my name. Califano's been a good friend ever since. So when I talk about the draft today, it's from knowledge I began building forty years ago, when we had a draft *and* a shooting war that was escalating and inciting a broad-based peace movement. Well before the war became a driving force behind the youthful upheaval of the late sixties, Johnson saw the need to study the system that manned the armed forces. Once you start getting large numbers of self-interested college kids involved in the question of who fights, and what we're fighting for, you start getting a different view on the stakes of war, which was then Vietnam.

Speaking of the sixties, despite my previous employment by the Justice Department as an assistant U.S. attorney, the federal government was a land far, far away for me at that time. On one of my earliest trips, however, I was accidentally shocked to discover that Uncle Sam was operating a lot closer to Harlem than I thought. I had gone to the Old Executive Office Building next to the White House to be interviewed by the members of the commission. Vernon Jordan, now an esteemed Washington rainmaker and friend of Bill Clinton, then a noted civil rights lawyer, was a member. But when I entered the building, the security guard, seeing I was black, thought I was part of another meeting in the building, and ushered me into a big room where a group of about two hundred to three hundred blacks were being addressed. I opened the door and immediately knew I was in the wrong place, but I sat down and checked it out anyway. They were being briefed by a black Justice Department official. This group was made up of people from all over the country who were employed as the undercover eyes and ears of the Justice Department in black communities. They seemed to be charged with monitoring the community pulse, a kind of covert, tension control mission. Some of them didn't live where they worked—I heard one of them say he lived at the Hotel Theresa and go on about who all he had seen doing what, on which street corner. This, of course, was near the height of the civil rights movement, and the era of the urban "long hot summers." But it had nothing to do with civil rights; this was all about law enforcement. And for the privilege of spying on their fellow blacks, they were being paid the princely sum of $100 per day!

Cliff Alexander went on to have a charmed career in and out of public and private nonprofit service and the practice of law, including secretary of the army under President Jimmy Carter. Like me, his circle went around and came around through Adam Clayton Powell. In 1963 Adam ousted Cliff from the top job with Harlem Youth Opportunities (Haryou), one of the pioneer "poverty programs" of the "Great Society." Adam, who had spearheaded the legislation creating the program, eventually got his own man, Livingston Wingate, an articulate lawyer with plenty of street smarts, to run the show. This is the same Adam who didn't know I was alive, up and coming in the heart of his district, and treated me with contempt when I did make his radar. In the end, however, none of this stopped Cliff Alexander or Adam or me from getting where we were going. Cliff's ouster from Haryou opened the door to his post with the Johnson administration, which led to my first Washington appointment. One of Cliff's other jobs in the Johnson administration was to find military field officers with general potential; one of them was a guy named Colin Powell.

Even Wingate got where he was going, as far as his circle through my life was concerned. In 1973 Percy Sutton and I made him a judge. But that is part of the next story.

Wingate was a name partner in *the* black law firm in New York, Weaver, Evans & Wingate. Every one of the partners went on to become a judge. Every one of them was a fantastic human being. When Hogan's office wouldn't interview me for assistant district attorney in 1960, Weaver, Evans gave me my first job after passing the bar. They were located down on Wall Street, at 160 Broadway, which was quite something for any kind of black firm at the time. Back in the sixties that didn't mean they were getting rich, but they were doing well by black standards. The practice included a full range of civil matters—deeds, negligence, mortgages, wills—and a little bit of criminal law. Most of their clients were successful, if not prominent, black people. Billy Strayhorn, who composed for Duke Ellington and wrote the Duke's theme song "Take the A Train," was a client, and he brought in a lot of musicians and entertainers.

My first encounter with the firm was in law school. I was doing research on some court of appeals case for a project with a guy named Altman, who happened to be Jewish. It was Good Friday, and the library at the very Catholic St. John's Law School was closed, but I had gotten

Wingate to let me use the firm's membership card with the New York County Law Library. Wingate wasn't there, but another partner, Bruce Wright, knew about St. John's and our project, and, boy, was he expecting us. The colloquy went something like:

> WRIGHT: "And you, Mr. Altman, are you black?"
> ALTMAN: "No."
> WRIGHT: "Are you Catholic?"
> ALTMAN: "No."
> WRIGHT: "Then what are you doing here, and why are you going to St. John's?"

Well, Altman was just dumbstruck. Bruce was this overpowering personality who just played on people's inability to keep up with his intellect as it leaped. He never laughed while he was doing it, so if you didn't have a clue as to where he was coming from, like poor Altman and me, it was simply devastating. He gave us the card to go across the street to the library, and then he continued:

> WRIGHT: "Tell me, how do you two work together? Rangel, do you believe in Jesus?"
> ME: "Yes."
> WRIGHT: "Now, who do you believe in, Mr. Altman?"
> ALTMAN: (Gives some stumbling explanation of his faith)
> WRIGHT: "Now, Rangel, today is Good Friday. Your Jesus Christ died today. Now, when He died, did people's rights die with Him? Did crime die? Did the poor die?"
> ME: "I don't understand what you mean."
> WRIGHT: "Well, you closed the school while you were studying, even though you want to provide service to people. There's some inconsistencies with what you people say you believe and what you do. But I'm here to help you, so you go on across the street and do your work.
> "Oh, are you black, Altman?"
> ALTMAN: "No, sir."
> WRIGHT: "Well, don't look at me in total disbelief. In this racist country, all you need is one drop of black blood and you're black, you know. You could ask me whether I'm white, because I've got some white blood. But somehow white blood is not as powerful as the black blood that would make you a Negro."

All this just to pick up a library card! I thought the man was crazy. But I got to know and love him during my time at the firm. I really did more learning than working there, because these guys were professors, people who had been there and done that in law. Bruce would lecture to me, in a humorous way, but I always walked away learning something. What I *didn't* know about Bruce Wright when he confronted Altman and me that day was that he really did have "white blood"—his mother was a devout white Catholic—and that after he was accepted and then denied entry to Princeton he was also turned away from Catholic Notre Dame. And after he had clerked with the prestigious Manhattan firm of Proskauer, Rose, Goetz and Mendelsohn, he was again told he would not get a position because he was black. That's where he was on his road when we met him at the black law firm of Weaver, Evans & Wingate.

Of course, his razor-sharp rhetorical method was not widely appreciated in the seventies and eighties when, as a judge, to the great chagrin of police and prosecutors, he became nationally known for releasing criminal suspects with little or no bail. The police union, abetted by the tabloid press, demonized him as "Turn 'Em Loose Bruce." But, until the day he died in 2005, he never stopped his slashing defense—for Bruce that meant offense—for equality for all under the law. The truth is—and there's nobody black or white who practices law who doesn't understand this—there is only one criterion for setting bail. It's not to punish anybody. It's not to say that the person has committed a crime; they've been charged with a crime and that is all. The purpose of bail is to provide enough security for the court to believe that when that person is called to stand trial for the charge, they will appear. And if there's every reason to believe that person will appear, you don't need any bail. So "Turn 'Em Loose Bruce" was really a scholar, not someone who gave the benefit of doubt to criminals. He didn't give that benefit to anyone; he simply made the judgment that he wasn't going to throw away the key because someone was merely arrested, not convicted. And, having survived the landing at Normandy on D-day, earning two Purple Hearts and two Bronze Stars, he wasn't about to back down for fear of what the cops thought. Bruce had six children, including Geoffrey, a Manhattan civil court judge, and veteran Harlem state assemblyman Keith Wright. Keith has certainly followed in the steps of his father and mentor. They shared a remarkable physical resemblance, and if you close your eyes, you would think that the judge were speaking.

Wright was probably the only partner in the firm at that time who was not politically connected. They were all about ten years older than me—the older generation to my thirty-year-old eyes at the time—and I only knew them by reputation. Most of them had gone to school on the GI Bill right after World War II. By 1960 they were big men, at least in Harlem, who hung out at Jock's and The Rooster, the elite bars where professionals, entertainers, sportsmen, and the "wannabes" hung out.

Herb Evans gave me my first real opportunity to practice law. He was part of the J. Raymond Jones political family, and went from the firm to a seat on the City Council and then an appointment to the New York City Housing and Redevelopment Board before becoming a judge. Evans had a large negligence practice, cases that begged and screamed to be settled. But to force that settlement, if the insurance company lawyers didn't believe you had enough evidence to prove their client was liable, you had to be prepared to go to court. Now, a real lawyer can't tell opponents he is ready for trial when he's not. But I could, baby-toothed law pup that I was, because I was just trying to bluff them into settling. Anticipating his elevation to bigger things, Evans turned a great many of these cases over to me to wind down, and I made us *so* much money. I would call them all, and say something like:

"This is attorney Charles Rangel . . . we've had this case pending in our office for some time. I've been looking it over and I just want to say that the firm is ready to go to trial on the matter. I'd like to see whether we can fix a date today or as soon as possible. I'll be trial counsel."

They might say, "Oh, this isn't that much of a case . . . we'll offer your client $1,500." To which I'd respond, "I'm sorry, sir, we're not prepared to discuss that kind of figure." Of course I wasn't prepared to go to any damn trial. I just figured that if one of them called my bluff, I'd get someone who knew what they were doing to sit with me in court. But I also knew the insurance firm lawyers weren't prepared either. Once, while haggling on the phone, one of the opposing lawyers said of our black client, "You know, he's a colored kid, Mr. Rangel, and the possibility for loss of income is really quite limited for these people."

"Well," I said, "I tell you what—maybe if you'd like to come in and talk it over with me and the senior partner, Tom Weaver, we could take it into consideration." Then I run over and tell Tom that "A white guy is coming over from the insurance company, and he thinks we're white!" We got a rather substantial settlement on that one. A year or so later, when I was an assistant U.S. attorney, I was trying to get a guy to come to trial, and the lawyer kept postponing and postponing. I told him that we were going to send the marshals out and have his client arrested. He said, "Well, you know, the guy is Negro, and you know they lie a lot. I can't prepare for trial because he just won't tell me the truth, these coloreds just lie, and lie, and lie." I said, "I know that, but I can't tell the judge that he's colored and that he lies a lot. You gotta bring him in. If you don't, we're gonna arrest his ass and knock off his bail." He reluctantly agreed to bring his client in, and to meet me in the courtroom a little early before the hearing. "Look for me, Rangel," I told him. Now, I had a half-dozen white assistants working for me. I told one of them to walk in the courtroom that day and sit at the prosecutor's desk while I acted like I was the assistant. The defense lawyer comes in.

"Rangel?" he says to my white assistant.

"I'm Rangel," I lean over and say; he knew immediately he was dead meat.

Afterward, in an effort to get another adjournment, he asked his client to share with me why he was failing to keep his appointments in court. I felt obliged to share with the defendant why *his lawyer* thought he was not showing up in court.

By 1968, Weaver, Evans, Wingate & Wright was effectively closed, a victim of their great success. Judgeships, appointments, and other political opportunities that would have been denied them just a decade before came in a flurry in the early 1960s. Credit what you will—the Kennedy optimism, Lyndon Johnson's Great Society, Martin Luther King Jr. and the civil rights movement—but every year things got better for black lawyers, a trend that continues to this day. I am not one to wax nostalgic about the good old days when racism and segregation bound black people into a tighter social and professional community. But it is true that during those heady early sixties when I first became a lawyer, racism had positioned an amazing cadre of brilliant black legal and political minds for takeoff on the Harlem and national scene, and I had put myself into position to benefit from it.

Tom Weaver, the firm's disciplinarian and anchor—and a Republican—became a judge. Livingston Wingate, who was called Roy, began as a skycap and worked his way up to be one of Harlem's most respected and political lawyers. He would be in Jock's every night playing Socrates among the many leading lawyers and intellectuals of that time and place, always talking, always challenging, always interesting. You could learn a lot from these people as they debated race, law, politics, or whatever was current. He was black, proud, and what people would call militant years before it came into fashion. Dark-skinned, he was fond of saying things like "The day of the mulatto is over." Ironically, however, his advancements came as a very loyal and trusted part of Adam Clayton Powell's political machine. Adam, of course, could almost pass for white. As I said, Adam placed Roy at the head of the youth and poverty program that came to be known as Haryou-ACT, in a move that was calculated to make the program as much a political power base as community resource. Roy kept this base after Adam's fall and used it to give me my first and only

serious challenge for Congress in 1972. Roy Wingate was eminently qualified as a lawyer, if not as a politician. Recognizing that he might hound
me for the rest of my congressional career, it made a lot of sense to have
him on the bench as a judge, rather than on the streets as a candidate.
Right after I defeated him in the 1972 primary, a vacancy came up on the
state supreme court, and once again a perfect circle, from my point of
view, was completed.

Adam Clayton Powell, as I will say many times, was a force of nature and
a law unto himself in Harlem. But political Harlem itself, as represented
by this emergent roster of world-class black talent, was the work of J.
Raymond Jones. He built and ran the launching pad from which the
majority of these people took off.

A large, formal oil portrait of Ray Jones sits over my right shoulder on
the wall of my Harlem office. It's not because I wouldn't be here without
him, though that's definitely true. And it's not because I loved him,
almost like the father I never really had. Ray Jones has hovered over me
for decades to remind me of how Harlem itself arrived, politically, from a
minor Manhattan black fiefdom controlled by the Irish and Italian-
American politicians of Tammany Hall to the base of black power in New
York City projected onto the national stage. The deal that put Adam Clayton Powell in the chair of the House Education and Labor Committee
(where Adam could then make Roy Wingate his chief of staff) was made
through Ray Jones. And it was through Ray Jones that so many less historic
moves were made to cut African Americans into the game of political
power and influence and to advance them for the good of all concerned.

He was never really comfortable with his nickname, "The Harlem
Fox," because it spoke more to his cunning—and deservedly so—than
his principles. Ray Jones on my shoulder will not let me forget that
Harlem was not built on favoritism for the fortunate few. Ray Jones was
not the only African American leader of his generation to deeply believe
that the only way for blacks to advance as a group was to lift up individuals who were simply too good—professionally and ethically—to be
denied. But as a seminal black politician—eventually the first black boss
of Tammany Hall—Ray was uniquely disciplined and consistent in following this principle for himself and applying it vigorously to the mission of black empowerment. In my introductions it is often said that
Harlem has had only two congressmen. But Harlem has had only one
Ray Jones; all the rest of us are just disciples and heirs.

In 1963 I had gone no farther in politics than to join a local political club, following my adventure securing Grandfather's pension benefits from Carmine DeSapio's Tammany Hall. Before moving on, I must briefly explain the basic structure of New York clubhouse politics. In general, winning the Democratic primary nomination is tantamount to winning the general election because this is an overwhelmingly Democratic town. As a result, the long tradition of sometimes vicious competition for political leadership has been within the Democratic Party, with the political club, the election district, and the state assembly districts as the basic units of organization.

The first political club I joined was the New Era Democratic Club, which was led by State Assemblyman Lloyd Dickens. He was also the Democratic Party district leader and a longtime supporter of Adam Clayton Powell. Dickens was in real estate, and purportedly one of the wealthiest businessmen in Harlem. I joined right after law school with the encouragement of my dear friend Basil Patterson, who was a member. He said it was the place to be if I ever had any political ambitions. Well, I didn't, but I listened to him anyway. I also listened to a guy named Archie Seal, Lloyd Dickens's nephew, who always praised me and my potential value to the club, even before I came in. I didn't know much about how these clubs were structured or how they operated. But I'll never forget one telling conversation we had:

> SEAL: "Did my uncle ever call you in privately to talk about your ambitions?"
>
> ME: "How did you know that, Archie?"
>
> SEAL: "What did he ask you?"
>
> ME: "He asked me whether I was interested in politics, whether I intended to stay, and told me about how I was doing such a good job in the club."
>
> SEAL: "He didn't ask you whether you would want to become an assemblyman, did he?"
>
> ME: "As a matter of fact, he did."
>
> SEAL: "You didn't tell him yes, did you?"
>
> ME: "I think I did—"
>
> SEAL: "Oh, hell! Damn it, he asks every ambitious newcomer the same thing; he's gonna be watching your ass for sure now!"

Sure enough, Seal's understanding of the situation was wiser and more prophetic than he knew. In the stunted and limited universe of black Democratic politics at the time—really all politics—entrenched politicians tended to see rookie talent as more of a threat than an opportunity. Not so Ray Jones: He looked right past the potential threat posed by the bright and ambitious to see an opportunity to advance his own short- and long-term goals. Sometime in the spring of 1963, Bruce Llewellyn, accompanied by a lawyer and real estate developer named John Edmonds, told me that J. Raymond Jones wanted to see me. Already a legend for his twenty-five years as a rare black insider with considerable influence in Tammany Hall, Jones had just gotten himself appointed to a seat on the City Council that was being vacated by Herb Evans, who was taking an appointment to the Housing and Redevelopment Board. Evans, of course, was also part of Jones's Carver Democratic Club, and Ray had a hand in all these moves. The big picture was that in 1963, after decades of pulling levers inside the party machine, for the first time Jones saw a strategic need to run for legislative office himself. Among other things, he accurately foresaw the splintering of the Democratic Party organization in New York due to rising factional infighting and the likelihood of Republican John V. Lindsay taking City Hall in 1965.

Ray could feel early tremors of a coming quake beneath his political feet. Two years earlier his successful support for mayor Robert F. Wagner's reelection—against the Tammany Hall slate headed by State Comptroller Arthur Levitt—had put Ray in an excellent position of influence in City Hall. The ensuing ouster of longtime Tammany boss Carmine DeSapio brought Ray within a whisker of becoming Tammany chief himself. But looking two years forward, Ray correctly saw major obstacles to Wagner winning again in 1965. The increased feuding among the Reform, Liberal, and Regular Democratic factions meant a lot of blood on the floor in the primary fight. And Ray could see the star of the attractive, liberal Republican John Lindsay rising above the Democratic fray. As a district leader without a Democrat in Albany or City Hall, his power could be greatly diminished for some time to come. But as a leader on the Democrat-dominated City Council, his power would be enhanced—especially if Lindsay were elected, because he would need Ray to get things done.

This, of course, is now the record of history. But as a political neophyte, just three years out of law school, I knew almost none of it.

So I go up to see Ray Jones. He's got this lilting, royal West Indian brogue from his native Virgin Islands. "Well, young man," he said, "I understand that you want to run for Democratic district leader against Lloyd Dickens. What makes you think you can beat Lloyd Dickens?" Now, I don't remember ever saying publicly that I was going to run against Dickens. All I had said—in private, I thought—was that I thought I could do a better job.

Me: "Well, everyone is saying that, Mr. Jones, but I never—"

Jones: "What do you mean 'everybody is saying that'?"

Me: "Well, the club captains and—"

Jones: "Ohhhh, the club captains, eh? They think you're something?"

Me: "Oh yes, they think a lot of me. I was in charge of the youth group and the newspaper. I was even collecting the dues until Mr. Dickens stopped me."

Jones: "Oh, so you were already acting like the district leader?"

Me: "Well, that's what Mr. Dickens was saying but . . . I was really just trying to—"

Jones: "Trying to build up the club, eh? Build up your own constituency?"

Me: "Well, I wouldn't say that, Mr. Jones. But, Mr. Jones, if you were with me, I could beat—"

Jones: "No, no, I didn't say 'if you were with me.' I heard that *you* think that you can do this."

Me: "Well, there's no question that most people in the club would believe that if—"

Jones: "No, no; do *you* think you can do this?"

I remember hearing myself stammer, "Yes, well, ummm, I, uhhh—yes." He said he was prepared to endorse me, but asked me about the support I had among the precinct captains. As he casually ran down the names, and I faked my way through counting them in my corner, I realized that the son of a gun had already figured out exactly what cards I did and didn't have protecting my bluff. I raised, saying something about how his endorsement would bring out a lot of covert support from people who were afraid to risk supporting an upstart like me against a big man like Dickens. "Well," he called, "why don't you bring those captains together, and I'll meet with them. I'll tell them I'm supporting you for district leader. Just bring them together."

I walked out of his office with the same feeling in my stomach I had had that day in July 1950, when my unit was activated for Korea and Lieutenant Lamar Smith had said, "Rangel, it's your ass now." My mouth had once again brought me to the edge of a fall that my behind might not be able to handle. "Damn," I thought. "How the hell did I get up here lying to this man? What the hell am I going to do?" I only had my brother. I was still living at my grandfather's place—he had passed away a few years before. I had one room, with a little sink in the room, one pullout sofa and one La-Z-Boy chair. How the heck was I going to have a meeting?

I told Charlie Fried, my friend from the hardware store. "*The* J. Raymond Jones?" he asked. "Well, damn, we gotta do it," he said. "How are we gonna do it, Charlie," I wailed. "I've gotta have some food or something. I got no money, and I can't call anyone." "Don't worry about it," he said. He went to Sam Broad, a grocery store guy on Lenox Avenue where my family had always bought "on the book" because we never had cash. Grandfather always swore he was giving us a "fast count" on our purchases, but Sam and Charlie got together and said they were going to give me a reception like I'd never had before. "Where?" I asked. A black undertaker, Dave Noble, had agreed to open up his nearby parlor. I said, "I can't have a meeting in the funeral home." They said, "Yes, you can." They put those bodies in the back of the funeral parlor, and they put up all these screens to make the room look something other than what it was. They had beer and soda, and even hors d'oeuvres that Sam Broad made, these little sandwiches with thick slices of meat in them. Damn, if Charlie Fried wasn't running around passing out drinks. Ray Jones came, and couldn't escape the impression that I actually had white guys working for me. To build up the numbers beyond the half-dozen people who came from the club, I got some boys from the block to clean themselves up and stack the meeting, and say things like, "Yes, Mr. Jones, Rangel is a great leader; I'll follow him straight to hell!"

That was the beginning of my political career. Somehow, I thought, I had gotten away with it. I thought I had loaded the deck, and was the smartest SOB in the world. But, of course, it was Ray Jones who was really dealing the cards. He didn't give a damn whether I won or not. His interest was winning election to the City Council seat, which turned out to be highly contested, and my candidacy played a small but useful role in his strategy. Ray's interest in putting me up against Lloyd Dickens for district leader had almost nothing to do with me. Lloyd Dickens's Assembly district was in the center of the 21st City Council district seat Ray was contesting. Dickens had his own candidate, Henry Williams, in the fight. So it just made sense that Ray needed somebody, *anybody*, to wage a good campaign against Dickens himself, just to distract Dickens from full-time support for Williams. That somebody was me. At the end of the day, Ray must have calculated: Dickens wins, Rangel loses, Williams loses and Jones wins. That indeed was the verdict at the polls. Ray thought that would end the story, but it didn't.

Of course I knew none of this as I eagerly set off campaigning. In my ignorant bliss, I thought it was just like the stuff I'd been pulling since law school, just on another level. One of the reasons I decided to run was because Percy Sutton, who for years had been running and losing against Dickens for district leader and the Assembly seat, was finally not running. So I figured I could pick up all the pieces. Fatefully, during the campaign, I ran into Sutton at Rosenberg Printers on 125th Street. Everybody in politics got their literature printed at Rosenberg's in those days. We were both picking up posters. I admired him—he was older than me, an accomplished lawyer, and an NAACP big shot. He was very pleasant, but I was being very mean, because I was insecure and all I had going for me was my arrogance. He said, "When this is over, we should be on the same side." "You're right," I said, "when this is over, you should be on my side." After more bragging about how I was going to win, he said, "Maybe you will, maybe you won't, but we should still get together afterward." And like almost everything else about my first foray into politics, I had no idea that this chance meeting with Percy Sutton would be the most important result of the entire misbegotten first political affair. Of course I lost, but true to his word, Percy Sutton got together with me soon after the election, and from that point, in that alliance, we rolled forward and have never looked back.

Another thing I didn't know was that Sutton wasn't in Rosenberg's for his health that day. He had his own stealth candidate—George Miller—in the race. Miller and I together actually got more votes than Dickens, but of course Dickens won. One thing I did get for my pains running interference for Ray Jones in that election was my own little club as a base for my campaign. It's now known as the Martin Luther King Jr. Democratic Club, probably the best organized and most influential political club in Manhattan. It was a combination of some of the most exciting political people from three different Harlem clubs, who came together in the wake of George Miller and me losing to Dickens. Sutton brought his John F. Kennedy Reform Club to our partnership. The remnants of Dickens's New Era Democratic Club, which began draining toward me when I left it to run against him, also fed the King club. When Percy Sutton defeated Dickens for the Assembly seat the following year, the rest of New Era was quickly absorbed. The third club was this little outfit I inherited from Ray Jones. It was headed by Dave Stewart, a perennial loser Jones had been sponsoring for a number of years.

The key thing about this club, whose original name escapes me, was that it was entirely West Indian. When I came in I was surprised to discover that its leaders had already relinquished their titles to me, because Ray Jones had told them to. It was then that I first came to understand the social dynamics between Southern blacks and West Indians, and the impact on Harlem politics. In my generation, you'll recall, kids would make fun of one another over where their parents came from—West

Indian "monkey chasers" or Southern "pork chops," and the like. But behind the schoolyard taunts were adults with real resentments, and real prejudice that existed between the extremely ambitious and successful West Indian minority and a Southern black majority that was not, on average, as accomplished. You could see it in who was the tailor and who was the carpenter or skilled tradesman. You saw it in the prominence of West Indian politicians like Hulan Jack and Ray Jones. When Sutton's club merged with my West Indian club, we would open our doors to expand political participation beyond identification with one group or the other. The Miller-Rangel-Dickens race itself had energized voters in the district. It gave us the opportunity to bring a lot of new people—including a lot of younger people—into the political process through our club, making it a resource that would prove invaluable in defeating Adam Clayton Powell less than seven years later.

George Miller became disgruntled with Percy Sutton after his loss, and was so put out when Percy and his club joined with me that Miller went and joined Lloyd Dickens and New Era. Miller, as I've said, would prove to be the closest thing I've ever had to a political enemy after that. Talk about things going in circles. I was still running the Hamilton Grange community conservation program, in that landmark building at 270 Convent Avenue. That building, by the way, is the one that's slated to become the Rangel School for Public Service at City College. But at the time it was just steps from Ray's home at 250 Convent Avenue. I made myself a frequent lunch guest.

Losing that election was one of the best things that happened to me, because I was now perceived as Ray Jones's man. When I went to visit his club, the Carver Democratic, with all of these seasoned and experienced politicians, including David Dinkins, I was a heavyweight among heavyweights because I was one of Ray's candidates. Even though I lost, I was Ray's man in Central Harlem—the heart of Harlem—and it was assumed that I was being groomed for bigger and better things. But even though I "assumed the virtue" of being Ray's man in public, in private I was constantly telling him how this thing wasn't working out worth a damn. I'd go over to his house, and complain that I wasn't getting anything for my loyalty. The first thing that came up was an opening in the State Senate that was created when my friend James "Skiz" Watson was elected to a civil court judgeship. I just knew Ray was going to offer it to me. I just knew I was his fair-haired favorite. Everyone knew I had jumped the line because I ran against a big man for district leader. I was somebody; I didn't have anything, but I was somebody.

But Ray gave the appointment to Constance Baker Motley, who had followed Thurgood Marshall as general counsel to the NAACP Legal Defense Fund. Over the next few years he would move her from the New York State Senate through the Manhattan borough presidency and finally to the federal bench for the Southern District of New York. Each move was a historic first for a black female, but it didn't cut that much ice with me at the time. How was I to know that Ray had cut a deal with the Kennedys early on to make her a federal judge, and wanted her to pay dues? As far as I was concerned, she wasn't from the street. But when I complained, Ray would throw his real problem with me in my face: my alliance with Percy Sutton and his brothers.

He hated Sutton because Sutton had joined the Democratic Reform movement, which at the time was dominated by white Jews with considerable money from the Upper West Side and the Village. Ray deeply distrusted Sutton and all the reformers because they tried to act like they were liberals, but in the end they were all about taking care of their own. When he first found out I was with Sutton his verdict was, "They're gonna eat you alive," and I couldn't budge him. For years, Sutton had been running against the regular Democrats, while calling himself a reformer. I still laugh about how they were the only black "reformers" in the New York Democratic world.

While Sutton's club called itself "reform," Ray Jones hated all reformers, white or black. Jones had spent his political life getting inside the "regular" fortress; reformers were the barbarians at the gate. Everything blacks had they'd gotten from the regulars. You fought regulars to get in, not to be part of the reform movement. That's really what I thought I was doing, with Ray Jones's help. But as I spent so many lunch hours bitching and moaning at 250 Convent, I slowly realized that I had to find a way to get Ray Jones to adopt Percy, too. I said, "Look, Ray, you may hate this guy, but he's all I got. I'm out there, down the hill every day, and I don't see where I fit anywhere on your agenda." He'd come back with, "The Suttons are gonna eat you alive." I'd say, "What's the difference in how I get eaten alive? You don't even know Sutton; why don't you just meet the guy?"

And indeed, once he really met Sutton, he fell in love with him. He supported Sutton for the Assembly, drew me a district leader position, and made Sutton borough president, clearing my appointment to Sutton's Assembly seat. That was the beginning of our political victories. Whether or not Percy was ever a reformer was moot at that point; we were all regulars under Ray Jones's sponsorship. If Dickens had been a thorn in his side, he damn sure got rid of Dickens when he inherited Sutton and me. He would always say, when it came time for judgeships and whatnot:

You see that young fellow, that's Charlie Rangel. Now
watch, I'll ask him if he's "OK" on the judgeship—he'll say
he's with me 100 percent. And then I'll ask him about his
friend Percy Sutton, and he'll say he can't speak for Sutton.
Of course, sometimes Sutton shows up, and he's with me
100 percent. But he can't speak for his friend Charlie
Rangel. Oh, do I long for the day when I have 100 percent
of those two, 100 percent of the time.

When Ray was sick, it was Percy Sutton who brought him back from
the Virgin Islands where he had retired. And it was Charlie Rangel who
stayed with him until he died. His nursing home was on 138th Street,
and I lived on 135th Street, making it very easy for me to visit and take
him out from time to time.

You will not believe this, but I can count the number of times I've
had dinner or just gone to the bar to socialize with Percy Sutton. God
knows we've done political events and campaigned together and eaten
in the streets together, but ours has really been the deepest kind of
purely political friendship one can imagine. What began that day in
Rosenberg's was consummated in one long meeting right after the campaign, on a bitter cold night in his broken-down car as he drove me
home. We spent hours finding out who the other was, and what was driving us. When it was all over, we just had to laugh, because we saw no col-
lisions at all between us in the paths we wanted to take from there.
There was nothing to stop us from standing back to back and taking on
all comers. There was so much out there, for everybody—district leader,
State Assembly, borough president, mayor. The Congress never really
came up. I don't think we've ever had any strong differences of opinion,
politically, at least none that I can remember. We'd be out there on the
street every weekend with the bullhorn "Support Rangel. Support Sutton," up and down the alleys talking to people, and working at our clubhouse.

In adopting us, Ray Jones was saying, "I'm with the organization,
but when young people with talent come knocking, I have to go with
change." His willingness and ability to identify and insist on tapping
qualified people—often overqualified people—for promotion to
political positions set him apart. Call him "Boss" this or "Boss" that, but
when you look at the quality of the candidates he selected, it becomes
clear that it was only racism that had prevented them from being
snapped up by any number of private or public sector institutions
before Ray put them in play. He knew these people, and they were
attracted to him. Even today, when you look at the string of high-pow-

ered African Americans appointed to cabinet positions during the Clinton administrations, you see that they didn't start by running to the White House personnel office; they came running to the Congressional Black Caucus to be validated and promoted. We're not geniuses for selecting an Alexis Hermann, the former labor secretary, or a Ron Brown for major posts; they're drawn to us like iron to a magnet. I think that's near the heart of what political leadership should be all about. Donald Trump once asked me if I knew why he was so smart. He said he's smart because people *think* he's smart—he has the best developers from all over the world coming to him with projects, because they know he can make the biggest and best of their ideas a reality. So he has the ability to take the very best that's coming from the best, and put his name on it. In the end, it's not about being smart, it's about having the integrity not to skip over the best of the best in favor of promoting your friends. It is recognizing that if you're going to continue to enjoy this reputation for being smart, you have to work at it and keep it up. Ray Jones had that kind of consistency, even when it dictated taking an unpopular decision. Putting Connie Motley up for the State Senate—over me—or making her borough president was not the popular thing to do. But it maintained the consistency that made Ray Jones a legend.

Only in my political maturity did I fully appreciate the story of how he put Connie Motley into the first black leadership hall of fame. When that State Senate opening came up, right after Ray's own election to the City Council in 1963, he had initially committed himself to supporting any qualified candidate put up by the leaders of the constituent assembly districts. But when the West Side reformers of the 7th Assembly district came up with an unqualified black guy who had been busted three times for involvement with illegal numbers, it was clear to Ray that the liberal reformers had a much lower standard for black candidates than they did for their own. Ray would have none of it.

So Ray goes into this meeting about the nominees with Connie Motley against their black guy. The white reformers said, "Ray, how could you? You gave us your word, you said . . ."

"Yes," he began in his Roman senatorial cadences, "I did give you my word. But I had assumed that you would have selected a candidate that had honesty, integrity, that would meet high standards for public office. But what did you bring me? You brought me an unqualified convicted felon! Someone who would bring shame to my community. And what did I bring you? The general counsel to the National Association for the Advancement of Colored People, the Legal Defense Fund. Now, ask me: Am I just?"

Those liberal reformers looked at him, and there wasn't a damn thing they could say. They knew that their candidate couldn't stand in the shadow of Constance Baker Motley. Ray's lodestone for excellence and personal integrity was the late Dr. Kenneth Clark, the esteemed psychologist whose studies were given great weight in the landmark 1954 *Brown v. Board of Education* Supreme Court decision that underpinned the civil rights movement. When it came time for me to approach Ray about running for Congress against Adam Clayton Powell, Ray insisted that the meeting be held at Clark's home. He was with me politically, but before he would sign off on me he wanted to make certain that all the questions of my integrity were answered before Dr. Clark. Mind you, I had been in Ray's political family for seven years, and elected to the Assembly twice! Ray didn't have much formal education, and for something he deemed as important as Adam Powell's successor he wanted the eminent Ph.D. of the race to have his chop.

I point this out because it's so easy to say that a "boss" decided an appointment—and he did—but the boss had standards. It's so important to be in a position of power when you make these decisions about appointments and such. But it's more important to have standards that you're proud of and that people would agree with. A good and competent boss is a good thing. It makes it much easier to substitute the word *leader* for *boss* in that equation should anybody care to challenge it. I didn't learn to be a boss from Ray Jones, but I like to think I learned to be a leader.

Like Adam Clayton Powell, I don't expect to be remembered as a civil rights leader. But I did end up making the historic Selma-to-Montgomery march in 1965. Adam, of course, was raising hell about discrimination and organizing protests in Harlem before anyone ever heard of Martin Luther King Jr. But by the time King was large on the scene, he was also too large for Adam's ego, and besides, Adam was on a mountaintop of his own, near the height of his powers as chairman of the House Education and Labor Committee. He couldn't see how what he was achieving in Congress would end up a footnote in the received history of the Movement.

While Adam Powell deliberately distanced himself from Martin Luther King Jr., Percy Sutton was a real freedom fighter—he spent a lot of time in the South. I can't think of anyone in Harlem, certainly among our political leaders, who was as closely identified with these marches.

We were watching on TV and reading in the newspapers like everyone else in the country, but Alabama was basically very far from Harlem. Southern-rooted blacks were a majority at that time, but unlike Detroit or Cleveland or Chicago, black New York has never really been "up South," with a direct and active cultural, family, and highway links to the Deep South. Our black concentrations were not only distributed across four very different boroughs, they were well mixed with large numbers of people from all parts of the African Diaspora, especially the Caribbean.

I was five years out of law school, and one of the counsels to the Speaker of the New York State Assembly, due in no small part to Percy Sutton's recent election there and his immediate impact on the process of selecting the Speaker. The economy was booming and Lyndon Johnson's Great Society was about to go into high gear, bringing unprecedented opportunities for Negroes in position to take advantage. However sad it was for folks struggling down South, things were really beginning to open up for me here. But Percy Sutton, after much kicking and screaming on my part, convinced me to go down to Selma for the kickoff of the march. I had a round-trip ticket. A black guy who worked for New York governor Nelson Rockefeller and a Rockefeller cousin named Aldrich met me at the airport. They were all dressed up to march. I was sharp as Billy B. Damn. I had on my shades, my stingy brim, my cashmere coat, and my Florsheim pointy-toed shoes. The truth is, I never intended to march anywhere. I just wanted to get down there, have my picture taken, and get on back home.

I knew Andrew Young and John Lewis, who were then big men with the Movement, but nowhere near as well as Percy did. Because of Percy they embraced me, thinking I was going to march with them. They made fun of the way I was dressed, and kept trying to push me up to the front. I was trying to stay in the back so that when they started marching I could track my way back to the airport. Then it started to rain, and these poor miserable souls lined up to march were actually putting plastic around their worn and torn shoes. I said to myself, "God, I can't just walk away. I'll just march a little bit." There was another black guy from Governor Rockefeller's office, a tall thin fellow named Johnson, who happened to wear the same shoe size as me. He had come prepared to march with sneakers but decided to wear shoes. Since I had not come prepared, we agreed to exchange footgear. But I still didn't intend to march the whole fifty-four miles. I had bad feet—they were bad even before they froze in Korea—bad enough for me to be collecting disability from the army for them. But what I didn't realize was that when you're in Alabama and decide to march, you're marching through it all—darkness, bad weather, you name it. There are no blocks to just turn off if you feel like it, and there's no subway to jump on when you've had enough. You are *in* it.

I cursed every step of those fifty-four miles, wondering how the hell did I start marching with these redneck national guard troops for an escort. People in every house we passed along the way called us everything under the sun, and threw things at us. Every store played "Bye-Bye, Blackbird" from loudspeakers. We had been sleeping in the fields without a change of clothes, and we stank like hell. One marcher, a one-legged man whom everybody knew as "Sunshine" and who I later saw again at Dr. King's funeral, asked me if I wanted to get a shower, because we would be passing some kind of school and arrangements had been made for a handful of people to get showers. We met and climbed into this broken-down car on a dirt road, and as this overcrowded car took off in the darkness we saw that we were being followed. Damn, were we scared! We sped up, turned around, and gave up all thoughts of showering—all we wanted to do was get back to our group.

Looking back on how I groused, focused only on the pavement before me, I'm impressed with how oblivious I was to the context and consequences of the action I had joined at Selma. I did not appreciate who Dr. King really was. I did not know I'd become a member of Congress, or the impact that the voting rights we marched for would have on my tenure. I did not know that the number of blacks in Congress would swell from nine to thirteen to twenty-six in ten years, and to forty-three in the House and Senate today.

I did not know we were making history out of the moral duty on the road immediately before us.

Today we have the morally suspect war in Iraq, and the threat of the doctrine of preemptive war spilling over into Iran. So many of our soldiers are being killed or maimed every day. These policies are being financed with spiraling deficits, piled up by an inequitable tax system, while we fail to meet domestic priorities like protecting the people of New Orleans, before and after Hurricane Katrina. One day, dear reader, someone may ask you: "During the time our nation was pouring out its blood and treasure in these conflicts, and committing these atrocities abroad and at home, what were *you* doing?"

I know one thing: As much as I complained during that fifty-four-mile march, when my grandchildren ask me what *I* was doing, the Selma story is going to be told much differently. If somehow we can appreciate what we do each day as making a little history—especially election days—every day is exciting because every day can make a difference.

I formed a friendship on the march with a great guy, Dr. Mike Holloman, who kept my spirits up in that cold, wet weather. He was the doctor for our group. Between the constant damp chill and the sneakers, my feet had shriveled up. When I took off my socks for him, he took one look and said, "You're going back home." I said I was sorry, but I'd already come too far to turn back. The feet looked a lot worse than they actually were. But Holloman made much of my courage in going on with my feet falling apart. We became such good friends that when I became chairman of the Ways and Means subcommittee on health, he came to work for me as chief of staff.

When we got to Montgomery, Dr. King and Harry Belafonte were there. They had a big celebration, but I think I slept through it. We have pictures of me when I came back to New York in this orange safety vest that we all wore in the march. Percy called it the "orange vest of courage." You wouldn't believe the number of people to meet me at the airport. Percy Sutton and my brother, Ralph, of course, led the cheering group. My brother appeared to be the happiest, because he had serious reservations about my going on the march in the first place. He had been even more concerned by the fact that Percy, whose encouragement was the main reason I went, did not go himself. (Percy and I still laugh about that.) I felt more proud on returning from that march than I did returning home from Korea. To be sure, all I had suffered was the discomfort of the march itself, from well back where, I suppose, lawyers, political operatives, and other moral supporters were supposed to be. I didn't get my head cracked, like my friend John Lewis of Georgia, in the Bloody Sunday confrontation trying to cross the Edmund Pettus Bridge at the start of the march. But I was there, and the march did galvanize Lyndon Johnson and Congress's resolve to pass the Voting Rights Act later that year.

Percy Sutton also brought the other great comet of the race and rights revolution at that time into my orbit: Malcolm X. Again, it was mainly by association. Malcolm was bigger than day for me, but Percy was Malcolm's lawyer and friend. I sat next to Malcolm when he attended the swearing-in when Percy went to the Assembly. Malcolm always found ways to provide a kind of covert support for his friend Percy when he could. I've never met a more charming guy in my life—his smile was so disarming. Of course I never knew Malcolm as well as Percy, but after Malcolm was assassinated, his wife, the late Betty Shabazz, emerged as a charismatic leader in her own right. Her tragic death remains painful to those of us who knew and loved her.

Though I only knew Malcolm X from afar, if I had to define his lasting impact on me and my community it would be that he took a very serious subject that descendants of slaves have wrestled with forever and subdued it with that charm and the force of his intellect behind it. More than any one person, or group of persons at the time, Malcolm made black a color that people should not be ashamed of. He did it with a smile, he did it with a joke, he did it with anger, and sometimes with a sense of meanness. But when he would spell out all of the reasons why black folks hated other black folks, how we were programmed to think like white folks, when he deconstructed the idioms that reinforced our self-hatred—a dark day, a black Friday, pure as snow—he'd have you laughing, and in that laughter you finally understood that the greatest evil of slavery was not the harm to the body but the harm to the mind. Malcolm freed a great many minds in his amazing short time on the Harlem stage. He won't be remembered as a civil rights leader, but there's nothing wrong with that.

The Selma-to-Montgomery march was about a year before I found myself succeeding Percy Sutton as assemblyman for the 11th A.D. I have to assume that Percy, thinking ahead, wanted me to have my credentials as a civil rights man in order. My ticket was punched in other ways, too. The way Ray Jones set it up, I moved into Percy's seat, and Percy into the Manhattan borough presidency, without an election. Ray had become the boss of Tammany Hall in 1964. When Connie Motley finally got her federal judgeship—the only post she really wanted—in the spring of 1966, Ray's influence with Manhattan's representatives on the City Council, of which he was one, secured Percy's appointment to replace her until the fall elections. At the same time, Percy's leadership in the Assembly secured my appointment to his seat until the fall, when we were both elected outright.

When Percy initially went to the Assembly in 1964, one of the first things he did was organize the growing number of African American members into a caucus. At the same time, for the first time in thirty years, the Democrats had swept both houses of the legislature in Albany. The immediate result was a mad scramble to select the powerful Assembly Speaker and State Senate Majority Leader positions. There were so many Democratic factions vying for power that none of the candidates could get a majority vote. Eventually, Governor Rockefeller weighed in, lining up enough Republican votes to make Anthony Travia, the candidate of Mayor Wagner, Ray Jones, and the regulars, Assembly Speaker. But Percy's black group said they wouldn't go along unless Travia, who was from Brooklyn, made some African Americans part of his leadership team. This would be a real breakthrough for black political interests in New York State. Though I was just a district leader at the time, I was there when Percy got all these black politicos in

Travia's office for a showdown. For the first time in the history of New York State, a black, a very conservative Brooklyn assemblyman named Bertram Baker, was selected as Assembly Whip. Ironically, I don't think Bert Baker even supported the Sutton revolution for minorities in Albany.

Percy went on to be an outstanding legislator, playing a leading role in passing reforms of the divorce law and legalizing abortion in New York. His influence enabled my appointment as part of the team counseling the Speaker. Later, the joke on the staff was that I shouldn't even have been in the room when the deal was made that cut us into power in Albany. But most of the time I was really working closely with Percy Sutton; in a sense I was his man, and the black group's man, in the Speaker's office. That's when we really began to spend a lot of quality time on our political friendship, sharing those long car rides back and forth from Albany, running the same club, and preparing for the next election. He was a great assemblyman, and when I took his seat everybody let me know it, and what they expected of me. Bobby Garcia, an assemblyman from the Bronx who would later go to Congress, jokingly tells the story about how he expected me to do nothing less than to walk in Percy Sutton's footsteps.

When I was still a counsel to the Speaker, Percy used to drive us to Albany in that same beat-up little car of his—a very small Chevrolet—early every Monday morning. The other passengers were David Dinkins, who served briefly in the Assembly, and an aide of Percy's named Al Jenkins. One Monday, as we were traveling speedily toward Albany, a tire blew and, according to Percy, the car was pulled toward oncoming traffic. Somehow, in avoiding a collision, our car turned over several times and ended up with the wheels in the air. We managed to crawl out of the car in one piece, though Jenkins was taken straight to the hospital. When we showed up in Albany, we discovered that word of our demise had preceded us. When we walked into the Assembly chamber we were met by a standing ovation, just for being alive. Percy jokingly said later that while we all initially lauded him for the skill he displayed in executing what he called a life-saving maneuver behind the wheel, as soon as we checked with our lawyers in New York—and Percy's lawyer—his "skill" was described as "gross negligence" for purposes of settling with his insurance carrier.

The Assembly days were good days. My new best friend was Governor Nelson Rockefeller. Just as Rockefeller had made the Speaker with the extra Republican votes, he saw merit and some advantage in making me an almost immediate impact player. Frankly, I really needed his help. Though I was Ray Jones's guy, at least in Manhattan, I wasn't

My official parting army photograph, autographed to Mom upon shipping out to Korea, 1950.

My multiethnic Phi Alpha Delta fraternity chapter, which included Jews, Italians, and blacks, started at St. John's University Law school, circa 1959.

My graduation from St. John's Law, 1960.

With Assemblyman Lloyd Dickens, circa 1961.

Marching,
Selma to
Montgomery,
1965.

An oil painting of J. Raymond
Jones, Harlem inner office.

At my desk,
New York State
Assembly, circa
1967.

Campaigning on 125th Street, 1970.

My campaign headquarters, first congressional campaign, fall 1970.

President Ronald Reagan, signing my low-income housing bill, May 1987.

With President Jimmy Carter.

With Vice President Walter Mondale
during the 1984 campaign.

©UPI

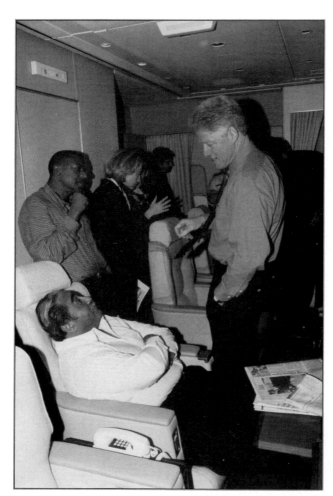

Aboard *Air Force One* for the African trade mission, with President Bill Clinton and BET founder Robert Johnson, March 1998.

©Timothy A. Clark/AFP/Getty Images

Hamming with actor Cicely Tyson, President Bill Clinton, and Senator Chuck Schumer and welcoming President Clinton to his Harlem office, July 2001.

With President George W. Bush.

At a birthday fund-raiser with Senator Hillary Clinton ("Nobody can resist Charlie Rangel"), July 2005.

With David Dinkins, Basil Paterson, Percy Sutton (the Gang of Four), circa the early 1970s.

With David Dinkins,
May 1987.

With
Governor
Nelson A.
Rockefeller,
accepting his
endorsement
for Congress,
1970.

I was the first
elected Democrat
to back John
Lindsay for mayor
against Mario Pro-
caccino, 1969.

Endorsing Hugh Carey for New York governor, 1974.

With Representative Hamilton Fish, New York Attorney General Robert Abrams, and City Councilman Ted Weiss, April 1980.

Governor Mario Cuomo, making an announcement at the Harlem International Trade Center.

Assemblywoman Geraldine Daniels, future mayor David Dinkins, and Mayor Ed Koch, June 1988.

With my mother, Blanche Rangel, and my sister, Frances McDermott, at a party, circa 1955.

With my mother, Blanche Rangel.

My brother, Ralph
Rangel, circa 1971.

My daughter, Alicia Haughton, and my
son, Steven Charles Rangel, circa 1978.

With Tip O'Neill in Morocco, circa 1982.

With Tip O'Neill.

The Congressional Black Congress, with Representatives Parren Mitchell, Bill Clay, Ron Dellums, George Collins, Louis Stokes, Ralph Metcalf, John Conyers, Walter Fauntroy, Roscoe Nix, Charles Diggs, Shirley Chisholm, and Gus Hawkins, circa the early 1970s.

With Representative Robert "Bobby" Garcia.

With Representative Dan Rostenkowski, at the annual Ways and Means alumni dinner.

With HEW secretary Joe Califano. He autographed my copy of his antismoking book (I had just quit), circa 1977.

Graciously conceding contest for Whip, with Representative Tony Coelho, 1986.

On the eightieth birthday of Representative Claude Pepper, along with Representative Pepper, Representative Mario Biaggi, and Senator Alphonse D'Amato, September 1980.

South Africa trade mission with Commerce Secretary Ronald Brown. We are leaving the home of President Nelson Mandela.

My audience with Pope John Paul II.

With Haitian president Jean-Bertrand Aristide, in Washington, D.C., circa 1992.

Welcoming Nelson Mandela in New York, June 1990.

exactly well received by the larger body of regular Democrats who had not forgotten my taking on Lloyd Dickens. And in Albany I was known for being with this reformer Percy Sutton, who was stirring up trouble by organizing the blacks and Hispanics and generally playing the game by no rules but his own. Though I had been counsel to speaker Travia, I had not made as many friends among the Democrats—regular organization or reformers—as Percy Sutton. I had to earn my own stripes. That's where Rocky came in, pouring concrete between the cracks to form a legislative and political platform for both of us to stand on. Many of the bills that came to the floor from the governor's office were my bills. It seemed strange to many that I would become a factor in Albany so quickly. But that's the way the cards were dealt. In retrospect, learning to play with both parties was excellent preparation for working with people in the Congress.

Roy Goodman, a longtime Republican senator from Manhattan, and I carried many of Rockefeller's bills through our respective houses in Albany. Some years ago, he was celebrating his thirty-second year in the State Senate with a banquet. There was a hush in the essentially Republican crowd when I walked into the hall. He beckoned me to sit at his table with his lovely wife. When Goodman spoke, he thanked a long list of people by name, except me. The crowd seemed to be trying to find some way to signal him about it, looking at him, looking back at me, pointing. It was so embarrassing. Everyone assumed he had forgotten me, or worse, that he had deliberately omitted me. When he tried to conclude with, "Well, I think I've covered all the politicians here . . ." The crowd yelled back, "Noooo . . . Rangel . . ."

"No, no," Goodman said, "Charlie Rangel is not one of the politicians here. Charlie Rangel is my brother, a part of my family. He's one of the few people who go back thirty years with me, when we walked shoulder to shoulder carrying the Rockefeller legislation, when I was chided for being friends with this Democrat and he was chided for befriending me, a Republican."

I have some good memories from working with Roy Goodman. There's a picture I have of Roy with my two-year-old son in the State Senate chamber, holding the gavel with my boy looking on. Goodman came up as an heir to the fortune built from the popular laxative Ex-Lax. I grew up a poor black kid in Harlem. But somehow we clicked with each other and with Rockefeller to make things happen. I only spent four years in Albany, but I managed to get my name in the middle of some of the biggest fights. I got the most attention for the bill that added a fourth shift to the police department workday. We got that through despite the kicking and screaming of the police union. By tradition and by law the New York City police had worked in three shifts—8:00 A.M. to 4:00 P.M., 4:00 P.M. to midnight, and midnight to 8:00 A.M. Being up from the streets I already knew what studies had shown for years: Most crime takes place between 6:00 P.M. and 2:00 A.M. There were two shift changes during the peak hours for mayhem in New York, especially in Harlem, mainly to suit the convenience of the cops. The "fourth platoon," as it was called, from 6:00 P.M. to 2:00 A.M., let the police commissioner match his manpower to the job for the first time. The cops were furious with me, but that was nothing new. I began taking them on about drugs, corruption, and brutality almost as soon as I got to Albany. And soon after I got to Washington, as part of my drug-fighting crusade, I started firing away at police involvement in the narcotics trade.

Here's how close and easy it was between Rockefeller and me. On one occasion he asked me to do something—perhaps be a floor leader on a bill or something—and I stalled, telling him I'd really need some time to study the matter first. The truth was that I was facing my first re-election campaign in 1968, and I didn't know if I could run and be effective carrying his water at the same time.

"Well, who's running against you?" he asked. I said it was a Republican named Charles Johnson. "Is he important?" he asked. I said I didn't even know him. Rockefeller picked up the phone and called Vince Albano, the Republican county leader for Manhattan. I had to listen in: "Vince, who the hell is this Charlie Johnson. . . . Why does he have to run against Rangel? . . . 'Cause I got something I'm working out with Rangel. . . . Yeah, he's a good man. . . . What, you don't know Rangel? . . . Oh, you'll like Rangel. . . . Well, good—thank you so much, Vince."

"What the heck did you just do?" I asked. "You just got the Republican endorsement," he says. "You don't have to worry now." I was stunned, and tried to insist on at least visiting each and every Republican club in the district, though I think I knew only one leader. But they called a meeting, brought together all these old men, and Vince Albano got up and said, "This is your candidate." As it happened, Albano's daughter was married to a good friend and classmate from St. John's Law School. So I not only had a friend in the Republican county leadership, but in his daughter, too. Two years later, when I was getting ready to run for Congress, I knew I would have a good shot at getting the Republican nomination because Rocky made that call. That meant that, in going up against the formidable Adam Clayton Powell, if I didn't win the primary I would still be on the November ballot. On reflection, people would have had to be mad as hell with Adam Powell to vote for me on the Republican line!

Rockefeller was at the height of his might then; accepting the vice presidency during the brief Ford administration, for all the prestige, was definitely a step down in power. When I first ran for Congress, sometime in the summer of 1970, someone told me the governor had a birthday present for me. I went to this huge office in the statehouse, and there were all these guys on the floor poring over a map of the state of New York. They had slide rules, and string, and grease pencils, and data about the population of the various counties and cities from the recent census. They were actually drawing the congressional district reapportionment lines for the 1970 elections. All this is done by computer now, of course.

I said "Hi, Governor." "Happy Birthday, Charlie," he replies. I thanked him and said, "I hear you have a present for me." "We certainly do," he says. "We're drawing the congressional lines," he said. Then he hands me a grease pencil, and says with his trademark gruff voice, chased by the twinkle in his eye, "And you better not touch Manny Celler's district, either!"

Emanuel Celler was the dean of the New York delegation in those days. But he was safely over in Brooklyn. I proceeded to draw myself a *wicked* district in Manhattan. For the last decade, of course, I've been the delegation's dean, and the people in Albany make no bones about it; the first district cut is Charlie Rangel's, everything else has to fall in place around it. It's almost embarrassing, the unanimity of the leaders from both parties on this score. But the bottom line is that I'm the only New York congressman whose district has always remained entirely on the island of Manhattan. As I've said a few times earlier, God is good.

Bipartisan love does have its awkward moments, though. In 1972 there was a huge campaign billboard on Broadway that read: "Re-elect President Nixon and Congressman Charles Rangel—both Republican. Paid for by the Committee to Re-elect the President."

I could have died on the spot when I first saw it. And soon after, when I was sitting on the House committee looking into Watergate, I *really* prayed that no one would bring that thing up. They were doing that to pull in the votes, and I was being used. But I can't complain too much, because in my first campaign for Congress in 1970, Alton Marshall, who was then a top aide to Rockefeller, brought together the cream of the New York real estate industry and a number of Republican financial backers in a big fund-raiser for me. Many of them remain my friends today.

I was the first Democrat in office to endorse Republican John Lindsay's second campaign for mayor, in 1969. Being first to go with Lindsay, who was running as an Independent on the Liberal line, seemed like an act of political courage then, but it was really just gut street smarts—and the right thing to do. His Democratic opponent was Mario Procaccino, the comptroller who presented himself as a conservative Democrat just in time to capture the spreading backlash against the progressive political upheavals of the 1960s in general, and black civil rights gains in particular. Within days of Procaccino's win in the Democratic primary a lot of Democrats were looking for any available window to bail out; all I did was open one.

My backing Lindsay would not have been big news or carried that much political weight if I had not been a "colorful" if unsuccessful candidate for citywide office in the primary myself. I ran for City Council president—really a quasi-executive rather than legislative office in those days—on a ticket with former Bronx congressman Jim Scheuer for mayor and former police commissioner Vince Broderick for comptroller. I had served with Broderick in the U.S. Attorney's Office. I got a call at home from a colleague, Assemblyman Sy Posner, who was connected with the Scheuer campaign. I vividly remember the call and the day because I was celebrating the baptism of my son, Steven, when the phone rang. He said that Jim Scheuer, a member of Congress, was running for mayor and wanted me to run with him. I told him he must be crazy, and that I didn't have any money to run for a citywide office. He said Scheuer wanted me anyway; his supporters felt I'd be an attraction to the ticket. He insisted that I at least hear out Scheuer's campaign manager, Dick Brown, and asked if he could send him over that very afternoon.

I told him the family was gathered in my small apartment for the occasion of my son's baptism. All I had were two bedrooms—the living room doubled as the kitchen. So I had to take him to my bedroom, where Dick Brown tried to convince me that I could write my own ticket. I didn't make it easy for him. He said I could run for comptroller, president of the City Council, anything I wanted, and get any money I needed to do it. I said I needed my own campaign manager, my own press person, my own office, and my own general independence. I sounded like a guy who was desperately trying to give them an excuse to pass on me. But they weren't taking or giving no for an answer, no matter what I asked for. Dealing with Brown that day taught me what it meant to receive "an offer you can't refuse." I did have to be checked out, though, by a screening team that included Jim Scheuer and his father, who quickly let it be known that they would not be responsible for my debts.

It was a wild campaign season, and so much fun. I had nothing to lose, really, and the characters who weren't already legendary would soon become so, at least in their own minds. Bella Abzug was shaking up all New York politics by bringing the fervor of anti-Vietnam activism into local elections for the first time. Hugh Carey was running for mayor, along with former mayor Robert Wagner, who entered the race late trying to make a comeback and then ended up running against me for City Council president. So was columnist Jimmy Breslin, on the ticket with Norman Mailer for president. All in all there were about six different Democratic slates in the primary.

Being the only black candidate running citywide—the *Daily News* said I was the first black to run for the number two spot in City Hall—I made news every time I stepped out of the limousine, especially in conservative, predominantly white Staten Island. Because Jim Scheuer had his own mayoral campaign, we were able to go wherever and whenever we wanted to go. But when the Fourth of July rolled around, we didn't have anyplace to go. Nobody on my team had planned to do anything. Watching television, I saw that Hugh Carey and all the other candidates were going to be in Coney Island for the Fourth. I gave my staff hell. They said we didn't have money for the bands and floats and other things the competition was doing. But I insisted; we were going to Coney Island, too.

We got a couple of cars, the posters, and so on, and there we were, campaigning behind somebody else's flatbed truck with a band playing on top. We got to Nathan's, and the campaign bought hot dogs and sodas for everybody. I don't remember having so much fun in anybody else's campaign, but I sure had fun in mine.

Let's face it, before I got to the Assembly hardly anyone in Manhattan knew who I was, much less citywide. A subway token would have gotten me closer to City Hall than my glorious run with Scheuer. But it did raise my profile for a while, and perhaps my stature, at least with black New Yorkers citywide. You would not believe how many people stopped me and said, "Hey, are you Charlie Rangel? Didn't you run for something?" Lindsay, who started thirteen points behind Procaccino in the polls, needed every early strong endorsement he could get to beat Procaccino by the general election. After I endorsed Lindsay, a parade of Democrats followed. I've got to think my leadership, plus newfound visibility, helped him quite a bit.

Procaccino was not a very bright man. But he did coin the term *limousine liberal* to bash Lindsay and all the "radical chic" coddlers of black and progressive causes—everything from the Black Panthers to the fight for community control of public schools that had triggered a bitter two-month teacher's strike in 1968. No less a prophet of white resistance to change than Alabama governor George C. Wallace hailed

Procaccino's primary win as a victory for "law and order" and proof that a hard line on blacks resonated with some Northern whites, too, even in the capital of liberal elitism. Wallace's endorsement, of course, did not stop the conservative Procaccino from assuming, as the Democratic nominee, that he had a right to some black votes. At one point, after having said something offensive about black people, he held a press conference in Harlem, surrounded by all these black district leaders and such, to show some brotherhood under the skin.

"I just wanta you to know," he said, "my heart is just as black as anybody's."

It's easy to laugh at Procaccino for running what would prove to be one of the worst mayoral campaigns in New York history. But in the hindsight of nearly thirty years of Reagan-Bush Republican rule, Procaccino's unlikely candidacy was a major turning point in the family drama that is New York politics. From that election on, the plot began to parallel a larger story in American society, after so many decades of New York not really being America. In a sense, Wallace was more right than he knew. His "Southern strategy" didn't work, but Nixon's version tested very well in 1972, showing the way for Ronald Reagan to change the fundamental equation of political power in Washington to this day. Absolutely nobody expected Procaccino to beat the legendary Bob Wagner in that primary. The opportunity to trade on the resentments of the white working and middle classes that Procaccino sensed but was too crude to exploit in 1969 would be fulfilled in small part by Ed Koch for three terms in the seventies and eighties and by Rudolph Giuliani writ large for two terms in the nineties. Procaccino didn't just beat Wagner, he beat a political tradition and a social consensus that, however flawed, had held New York's ethnic house of cards together for generations. He beat the thing that let John Lindsay roll up his sleeves and calmly walk the streets of Harlem in April 1968, while other cities burned. I believe the political seasons of 1968–69 were a major fork in the road, where the hope somehow branched into the politcs of fear that have brought us to where we are today.

For my support I was rewarded by an extraordinary relationship not only with John Lindsay but with his staff. His staff—the blacks I dealt with—were very political. People like Eleanor Holmes Norton, who would become my colleague in the Congress representing the District of Columbia, and his welfare commissioner James Dumpson. A lot of blacks in the police department were also advanced under Lindsay. But boy, oh boy, did Lindsay have a lot of street black folks in his operation! These were the get-out-the-vote—cynics would call them the hand-out-the-money—folks who were very savvy with street canvassing. They seemed to function in another world from the elite, integrationist intellectual circles Lindsay was always identified with.

When Lindsay agreed to support me for Congress, less than a year later, this group was so tied into Adam Powell and the regular organization that they were outraged. I told Lindsay that he'd never get them behind me, that they were bad-mouthing me, and he kept telling me I could depend on them. Finally, he called a meeting at City Hall, where he laid it out to them about supporting me. Then he was called away for a minute on some matter. As soon as he left the room they made it clear to me that no matter what Lindsay said, they would be supporting Adam Clayton Powell. I couldn't believe my ears that they would allow Lindsay to think they were supporting me when he was in the room, and sing an entirely different tune behind his back. When Lindsay returned I told him exactly what they said, and I was never more proud of him for the way he handled it. He told them that as long as they worked for him, they did not have the luxury of making their own political decisions. He was supporting me for the Congress; either they were supporting me, too, or they were out of business with him. Believe me, they understood, and proved to be my best campaign workers.

Lindsay's support of my candidacy didn't end there. I arrived in Washington with his strong support, along with that of Governor Rockefeller, for a seat on the Ways and Means Committee. Lindsay had already been on the phone with the chairman, the late Wilbur Mills, lobbying on my behalf. Our political paths diverged after that; he was never elected again. Maybe it's the way that memory rounds off the rough edges, but in seeing my support going around to come around again I can't recall wasting any motion along the arc of my career. In the telling, sometimes, I fear that my journey sounds effortless. Nothing could be further from the truth. From the time I entered college I trained myself to work as hard as I could, at whatever I was trying to do. But what is even closer to the truth is the wonder that the results of each day, each month, and each year of hard work inspired in me.

As work dissolves into wonder, at the end of any given day, it stops being work at all.

It's the wonder of arrival, from so far below in the streets. My first day in my new office as an assistant U.S. attorney, I heard the sounds of chains coming down the hall. Here I am in this big office, with mahogany walls and the smell of the leather binding on my new law books. I open the door to see this little black guy bound in chains being pulled past my office by four great big white U.S. Marshals. At that moment, the black guy turns his head to look back at my office door:

"Shorty-Bo?" I asked, incredulous. He was a guy I knew from the block. Shorty-Bo cocks his head to the marshals and says, "See, I told you I knew the son of a bitch!"

There are a million and one stories about the people who didn't know about me going back to school. All the people who only knew me as a bum in the street. I've had a lot of bad dreams, as perhaps a lot of people who come up from the streets do, about what would have happened if I hadn't gone back to school. And to think of all the black kids who did get caught pulling the same capers I used to pull, and ended up career criminals. How easy it was for smart little sons of guns like me to get caught up in these things.

It's the wonder of affirmation, the antidote to the arrogance covering low self-esteem. Even when I arrived in Congress I still had a little bit of a Harlem street chip on my shoulder. I remember a member of Ways and Means knocking the hell out of Adam Clayton Powell once, and lauding me for beating him in the election. I made it clear to him not to get too comfortable about my replacing Adam, because the only difference between us was that Adam was a gentleman and I was not. My problem was the claim all the things I had done—both before and after the army—still had on my psyche. It's really strange how when you're involved in conduct you're not particularly proud of, it never occurs to you that one day somebody will review it. I had a heads-up on this wisdom because, as a Catholic, I knew what it was like to enter a black box, confess everything I did to someone I couldn't see, and wait to hear what my punishment would be. But even then I couldn't tell the truth, because I didn't want to hear myself saying the things I had done. So you can imagine the fear that I had when I was told that the awesome and powerful Federal Bureau of Investigation was going to scrutinize my record for all the reckless years of my life up to age thirty-two, in order to get my appointment to the U.S. Attorney's Office. I was scared to death.

The FBI questionnaire asked me to give some personal references. I assumed they were looking for professionals who could put in a good word for my character. I didn't know any professionals except numbers runners, and I knew I couldn't put them down. I thought about the small businessmen who had helped me up to that point, but I didn't think the FBI would be overly impressed with Charlie Fried and Sam Broad. But I did remember my law school buddy Ned Frank, whose dad, Judge Harry Frank, always enjoyed reminding me how much he resembled Adam Clayton Powell, and how he had had this great "colored" friend in the navy. So I wasn't reluctant to ask Ned to ask his father for a reference, and I was greatly relieved when Judge Frank agreed. But a few weeks later, I got an urgent call to meet him in his chamber. Still in his robes, he looked at me sternly and said:

"Charles, one of the lessons you will have to learn when you're dealing with the Federal Bureau of Investigation is to always tell the truth. Even if there's something wrong, they can take care of it. But always tell the truth." Well, I had done so many things that I had no clue as to what he may have been talking about, and I didn't feel myself in a position to volunteer anything I thought they didn't already know. So I said, "Judge, I want to tell the truth—can you give me any idea as to what the FBI's problem with me is?" He said he wasn't supposed to tell me, but the problem was determining exactly where I lived. I said, "Judge, there must be something else to this. Take my word for it, I have been very honest with them about where I live, because I have never lived anywhere else."

I left his chambers so worried on the ride from Chambers Street to 135th. The three blocks from the subway station to 132nd Street were the longest I'd ever walked in my life. I couldn't stop wondering, with all the things I had done wrong around there, which one the FBI had discovered. My worry was disrupted near the corner of 132nd and Lenox. There was the usual crew, guys I'd gone to school with, guys who had never gotten a job, guys just hanging out. They had been so proud of me, struggling with my books those years when I was going to law school. Finally, one of them, Charlie Williams, calls out, "Hey, there's Charlie Rangel." They all turned around, looked at me, and said, almost in unison: "Where the hell have you been and what the hell have you done? The FBI's been looking for you for over two weeks. We told them we didn't know who you were, and we knocked on every door on this block to tell these people to tell the FBI that they didn't know you either!"

I could not believe my ears. I will never forget knocking on all the doors on my block and saying, "I'm Charlie Rangel, Charlie Wharton's grandson. I'm not in any trouble; the FBI wants to help me." And so many of them would all say, "Of course, son, there's only two decent families in this block, you Whartons and us." As I talk with young people today about getting somewhere in life, I'm always reminded of how much a person is a part of his community. Whether they like it or not, they are who people think they are.

I could see the pride swelling in their eyes when I told the boys on the corner that I was not being investigated to get thrown in jail, but for an appointment to become assistant U.S. Attorney. They may not have known exactly what it meant, but I knew how good it made them feel. As far as the FBI is concerned, it was then that I realized it's not nearly as efficient as I'd always assumed. I thought the FBI could find out everything you ever did. I can't begin to tell you what this epiphany meant to me.

When the FBI gave me a clean bill of health, I passed into legitimacy. I don't know what born-again means to Christians, but I know what it means to me: I was born again. I knew that there would be nothing that could ever tempt me to break the law from that day forward. When I got to Washington I was audited six times by the IRS. I had no idea that it was because I was on Nixon's enemies list, but it didn't matter. I had already been cleared by the FBI. I made up my mind that I would never, ever do anything that would cause me to fear a future investigation.

When they were investigating the House Members' Bank scandal in 1991, I flat-out refused to cooperate with the FBI. I knew damn well I hadn't done anything wrong. They investigated five years of my transactions—making me one of the cleanest politicians in the world—but they only did it because I told them I was not going to cooperate when there were no accusations against me, or a scintilla of evidence that the Congress itself had done anything wrong. They were saying, in effect, that we were all guilty until cleared. So my attitude was, "Go ahead, fire your best shot."

Perhaps I wouldn't have done it if I had known I'd end up being the next to last member cleared in that mess. Seeing "Rangel Not Cleared Yet" and my picture in the paper was hard on my family. But where I was scared to death by that very first FBI check, I probably enjoyed myself too much with the Members' Bank probe, because I knew that, unless they made something up, I hadn't made any mistakes. I can't tell you how good it feels to be seventy-five years old and to know that they can investigate all they want; if it's post-1960, I'm clean.

After arrival and affirmation, the wonder that remains is the wonder of it all, as so many amazing people's paths crossed mine. By the time I hit the Assembly, everyone wondered who that Rangel guy was. Even Governor Rockefeller wanted to know. From where I stood, coming out of law school in 1960, moving to the U.S. attorney in 1961, to the Assembly in 1966, and to Congress in 1970 was no bad deal. I didn't have to plan for where I was going or how I would get there; I was in my thirties, and amazingly it seemed as though it was all coming to me. Throughout my political career I've never consciously placed myself on a particular track. I just wanted to be on the train when it left the station. I never knew where it was going to stop, or where it was going to end up. But I knew the pain of poverty. I knew what it was not to have. I'd never forget the holes in my shoes, but I knew I didn't want to look back. Charlie Rangel wanted no part of the "good old days." There were so many opportunities opening in politics that I had no need to decide exactly which political road I would take.

I never knew that the road would head for Washington. But it's all about the journey, not the destination—and I still haven't had a bad day since.

6

Encountering Adam

I had never even heard of the tiny Bahamian island of Bimini before Adam Powell decided to exile himself to it, and I certainly didn't know how I found myself face-to-face with him there that night in 1969. I sat on a bench at one of the long rough-hewn picnic-style tables covered with bedsheets in a beachside restaurant and bar. It resembled a summer camp mess hall, except the floor beneath my feet was covered with sand, and the whole place reeked of rum and the sea. And there was Adam, presiding, a bottle of vodka at one hand and a cigar in the other.

Adam was surrounded by a dozen locals whose sole job was to crew, catch, and clean the fish, and then sit around drinking rum all night, talking about the one that got away. Adam had made up his mind that he was going to embarrass me in front of the loyal subjects who shared his tropical days and nights.

"Well, now—look who is here," he started in. "Is this my lawyer coming from Harlem? Or is this the lawyer from the State Assembly? Oh, no—this is Governor Rockefeller's lawyer. The governor has sent him down here. And since the governor is rich, I assume the governor has told him to pick up the check."

Boy, did they kick up their legs with laughter then. "Order what you want," he told them. "You're eating with the governor of the state of New York!"

What could I do? What could I say? I had to listen to all those fish stories all night long, until, finally, Adam was about to retire for the evening. "Congressman," I said, "I have to talk with you before I leave." "C'mon, Assemblyman. C'mon, counsel for Rockefeller, let's talk," he said. As we walked back to my stinking hotel room, all I could think was, "How do you tell a powerful congressman that he should come home?" I can give you the answer now; you tell him with great difficulty. I shared with him that I had no desire to run for his seat, but there was a great sense of frustration in the district that we were not being represented in Washington. I said Governor Rockefeller was prepared to remove any legal obstacles to his return. And I told him quite frankly that if he didn't return, there were people lining up to challenge him and me too, because I was seen on television as one of his biggest defenders.

Adam looked at me and smiled. Quite frankly, he said, he didn't care *who* ran against him. All of the would-be candidates were "nothing but a bunch of Mickey Mouses," and if I wanted to run against him myself, I should just go ahead and do it. And with that he gave me a little clap on the cheek, as if I was a kid in short pants. "Do what you have to do, baby," he said.

My Bimini trip began in Albany, where Governor Rockefeller was briefing a group of legislators on an upcoming trip to Washington. He'd be meeting with members of the New York state congressional delegation. Knowing that Adam Clayton Powell had a host of legal impediments barring his return, I felt cocky enough to stand up and say, "Hey, Governor, what about my congressman? You're going to meet with the delegation and my representative can't even attend because of these legal problems," I popped off.

I should have known then, as I learned later, that you never take that attitude when you have to give back the microphone. Especially when you're returning it to someone like Nelson Rockefeller. By the time Rockefeller got finished with me—telling everyone that if I really wanted to get him back, he would take care of the legal problems if I could convince the mighty Adam Clayton Powell to come home—the bottom fell out of my bravado.

The Adam Clayton Powell saga had become a tragic farce by the fall of 1969. For over six years he'd been playing a game of cat and mouse with the New York City police, who were looking to arrest him for defying a 1963 court order to pay civil damages to a woman named Esther James. For years his only public appearances in New York came on Sundays from the pulpit of the Abyssinian Baptist Church, when and where, by tacit agreement with authorities, he would not be touched. Being scarce in New York was just the most visible symbol of the decay that had nearly consumed him personally and politically. In April, to our great relief, it appeared as though he'd finally been vindicated: The Supreme Court ruled that Congress had improperly expelled him in January 1967, and ordered him returned to his seat. And so he was reinstated. But, stripped of seniority and the power of the chairmanship of the Education and Labor Committee, Adam quickly retreated again to his self-imposed exile on Bimini.

Rockefeller had outfoxed me by saying that no one wanted Adam to return to Harlem and Washington more than he did. As a result of my mouth going faster than my brain, I soon found myself bouncing over the waves in a little inflatable "duck" boat going from Paradise Island to this speck in the Caribbean called Bimini. And believe it or not, the comforts only went downhill from there. Just forty-eight miles east of Miami, Bimini is the foreign island that lies closest to the mainland of the United States. But as soon as I landed, it was clear that I was in another world, more a tropical hell of Adam's making than a tropical paradise.

I was greeted by Corrine Huff, a former beauty queen, Washington aide, and Adam's mistress. An object of congressional inquiry herself during the long investigation of Adam's office, she had shared his exile on Bimini since 1967. But, according to *King of the Cats,* the excellent biography of Adam Clayton Powell, Huff had recently broken off with Adam and taken up with an islander. Huff, however, was apparently still acting as an aide and liaison between Adam and the outside world. She was very gracious and explained that the congressman was expecting me, but she didn't know when I could see him. Huff escorted me to a fleabag hotel that wasn't air-conditioned, and I had to cool my heels in that stinking hot room, waiting for my congressman to summon me.

I must have gotten to the hotel well before noon, but it was evening before Huff returned to say that Adam Powell would see me. I was so angry, but she was so charming. She led me to the end-of-the-world fisherman's restaurant-bar. At the main table were about thirty Bahamians, with Adam Powell sitting at the end, toasting a day of fishing with tobacco and alcohol and the adulation of cronies. It wasn't long before I became the object of Adam's toasting, and for the next couple of hours he just berated me, laughing and smoking his cigar.

Before that night in Bimini, I didn't have even the slightest ambition to challenge Adam Clayton Powell. But after that meeting, and that clap on my cheek, I didn't see how I couldn't run against him. When I returned to New York, and Percy Sutton asked me how it went, I said, "Percy, we've got to do it."

I want to make it clear that things were happening for me so well and so fast that I didn't need anything like Congress to be happy with myself. We're talking about a guy who was a dropout in 1953, a lawyer in 1960, but without a clue as to who else was a lawyer. I was immediately associated with a premier black law firm. I became an assistant U.S. attorney—

a prestigious, high-profile job—working with my now lifelong friend Bob Morgenthau. In the space of six years I became a confidant of Joseph Califano and the Johnson administration, John Lindsay, and Nelson Rockefeller, among others, and a public official.

When I reached the Assembly, my salary hit a new high of $15,000 a year. You know, I was still broke, because I remember every raise so well. It was not a bad salary, but what was more important was that I was a lawyer who could make an additional living practicing law. The Assembly met for all of three months a year, for three days a week, and the rules said you could practice all you wanted in between. In the little practice I was doing I was damn good. And even if I wasn't good, just being an assemblyman made the judges deferential. Whenever I went into court, the judges would stop what they were doing and ask, "Yes, Assemblyman, do you have any issues before me?"

At this point, sometime after coming in last in the primary race for City Council president in mid-1969, a well-known lawyer and state senator asked me to meet him for a drink at Jock's, to talk about my taking over his law practice. He was being moved up to a judgeship, and said he chose me in appreciation for my support over the years. I was flattered, because this judge-to-be personified the dignity of a Wall Street lawyer—the pipe, the glasses over the bridge of his nose, the great eloquence with which he spoke. I had assumed that upon taking over his practice, coupled with my influential Assembly seat, the road to success was a red carpet rolling out before me.

My new associates had been part of the legal team that defended the Scottsboro Boys, and were well known in civil rights circles. They were active members of the National Lawyers Guild, which had a strong left-wing agenda. One of them even had a daughter working in the sugarcane fields of Fidel Castro's Cuba. But they were generous in sharing their extensive knowledge and experience with me, and I would learn a lot from them. Our offices were downtown in the civic center area near Wall Street. My share of the rent of the classy building on Vesey Street was $2,000 a month.

I thought I'd reached the peak of success. Then I started seeing the type of clients I'd inherited, and quickly realized that I would not have a political future if I continued representing them. Many of them were actually people I had prosecuted. Even with the presumption of innocence, representing them would be incompatible with holding public office. This really came to a head when I was invited to get to know one of my new clients by spending a Sunday afternoon on his yacht. My excitement—I'd never been on a yacht before—quickly melted into despair when I recognized the owner as a well-known Harlem numbers banker whose activities had attracted the attention of the Justice Department. Right then and there the whole dream began to fall apart, even though I'd already signed that expensive lease. There was nothing for me to do but wind down the outstanding cases, and eat the cost of the overhead until I could get out of it.

My signing that lease, knowing that the rules of the House forbid practicing law on the side, should dispel any doubts that going to Washington was not on my mind in 1969. In the weeks after I returned from Bimini the logic would become inescapable, like being overtaken by a fast-moving storm. But until that unforgettable trip the capital under my blue skies was in Albany, not Washington. From 1966, when I went to the Assembly, Adam Powell didn't have a darn thing to do with my political career. And believe me, I liked it that way. At that time, my ego seemed to sing "watch my smoke—I'm gonna become the next Speaker of the Assembly" to anyone who cared to listen.

But, of course, Adam changed all that.

Before I bonded with Percy Sutton I had no political direction, just a drive to be against whoever was "in," because I wanted to be in their place. That's what going for district leader was about. After I succeeded Percy in the Assembly, and became a trusted son in Ray Jones's political family, I wanted nothing more than the most that being in that body had to offer: a lucrative law practice and eventual speakership. Now, you might think that representing a larger chunk of Harlem as a state senator would be my next political objective. But you would be wrong. I had one of my best legislative periods in the Assembly when Basil Patterson was in the state senate from Harlem. We formed a great legislative team and a great friendship. I never envied any of my colleagues in the state senate, just as I have never aspired to be a U.S. senator. It always seemed to me that the smaller my political base, the better I could serve it, while retaining my ability to get involved in matters outside of my narrow district.

With most jobs, the better you get to know how to handle the problems in your own backyard, the better you feel when you venture outside your own community. Yet sometimes, when you leave your home turf, you learn that you're not nearly as good as you think you are. I remember so well campaigning for Hugh Carey in a rural county upstate one year. Filling in for him at a fund-raiser, I was hailed as a great Democrat and a great congressman. In my talk I shared my experiences with Carey and expounded on what a great governor he would be. I woke up the next morning to the smell of fresh coffee, and had a real old-fashioned breakfast in the country fresh air. My host, who was the county Democratic chairman, and his wife told me how great I had been the night before, and that more of my "kind" should come up to their community because there was so much opportunity for Negro people. And then they made a point about how much they enjoyed watching *The Jeffersons* situation comedy, about a black family "moving on up" in the world. I really felt so insulted. I had to remember that I was there for my friend Hugh Carey. But it convinced me that I could do a hell of a lot better representing my congressional district with every sincere feeling I have, than to go up to that county and try to share with them what a good U.S. senator I could be.

Then as now, I'd much rather deal with the representatives of the diverse American people beyond Harlem than represent all those people directly. In the Assembly, I could make the people of central Harlem first among equals in New York. I didn't have to worry about representing any larger state or national agenda. That was Adam's stage, and while he held it there was no thought in anyone's mind about replacing him. He wasn't my idol, and he wasn't in my way for anything. I would have loved to go on being an exciting member of the Assembly, thriving not in the shadow but in the shade of the giant Adam Powell.

But Adam operated in another universe, at the head of a parade, literally, in which Percy and I were just part of the crowd of local politicians bringing up the rear. I remember occasions on which the two of us would gauge the roar of the crowd, or the lack thereof, as Adam went by, but it was just an academic exercise. If anything, I thought maybe Percy might be the candidate against him one day, since he was better known. But the line of succession, in our conventional wisdom, would make him shoot for mayor, as he did in 1977, after being borough president. My run for citywide office, eight years before Percy tried, was an anomaly, a free wild card I couldn't afford not to use. Adam Powell was not a player in that card game, and I never intended to beat his hand.

Adam Clayton Powell came with the territory of Harlem. You didn't talk about when is Adam leaving, or who was going to replace Adam. Adam was part of when Harlem was being born. Adam was there. A. Philip Randolph was there. The NAACP under leaders like Roy Wilkins was there. But where the spotlight hit center stage, where lightning struck the status quo of social and political relationship among the races in New York, there was only Adam Clayton Powell. It was Powell who, after taking over the reins of the Abyssinian Baptist Church from his father, pulled everyone from diehard Garveyites to NAACP members to pro-labor and anti-Nazi Jews to communists into his crusade against employment discrimination in Harlem. From the pulpit of one of the largest churches in America he launched an army of picketers that eventually broke the will of retailers on 125th Street, insurance companies, and even Con Edison, which until 1938 refused to hire blacks. When Adam came in he toppled the existing leadership by moral authority—A. Philip Randolph's long struggle to organize the successful Brotherhood of Sleeping Car Porters union—and replaced it with what can only be described as the authority of his own personality. He took certain of the gifts of Marcus Garvey—oration, charisma, and drama—and put them into service of something larger and perhaps more appropriate for the time than ideology: activism. There he was, making the perfectly timed impactful entrance—whether it was a street rally, café society downtown, the Rooster uptown, or a meeting in the corridors of power—in his trademark light-colored suit. He made making change through direct, decisive, and unpredictable political action an end in itself.

Or rather an end in *himself*. A 1942 civil rights rally at Madison Square Garden perfectly captures the force of nature that was Adam Powell, and the ultimately fatal way it set him apart from black leadership throughout his career. It was intended as a salute to Randolph for his long battle to bring the federal Fair Employment Practices Commission into existence, as well as recognition for many of the disparate progressive forces in New York that Adam had convened a few years earlier in his own antidiscrimination crusade. Adam had just been elected to the New York City Council, the first African-American to be seated, under new rules aimed at increasing minority representation. More important, reformist governor Herbert Lehman had signed a law cutting black Harlem's first congressional seat, which would be filled in 1944. With Randolph near the peak of his acclaim as a black Harlem leader, there was a feeling that the seat would be his for the asking. But to Adam it wasn't a question of asking, but taking.

As reported in the newspapers, and the letters of Langston Hughes, Adam took the podium to thunderous applause, and launched into a review of recent protests against discrimination in New York, most of which he had led. He reminded the packed house, reportedly twenty thousand people, that their protests played a direct role in making him the first black to sit on the New York City Council. And before anyone knew what hit them, Adam declared it his duty to run for the Congress, in the seat everyone, including the thousands of proud Pullman porters in the crowd, expected Randolph to get by default. The shocking announcement caused such an uproar that Randolph never got a chance to speak!

I was a kid at the time. Even though I never knew exactly what this Adam Clayton Powell did, there was always excitement when his name was involved. Adam was a high-profile theatrical figure whom everyone knew was fighting for black folks on 125th Street and beyond. When I went into the army that year, if they asked me who my congressman was, I would certainly have known, but the whole idea of what the Congress was, or public service, wasn't clear to me. Years later, hanging out with my Les Garçons buddies, in my very earliest years in politics, every time there was a dispute and I tried to broker a resolution, they would rib me with: "Oh, there's Young Adam, at it again." It wasn't necessarily a compliment.

What Adam deployed that night in 1942 was the particular strength of his personality that was his willing ability to take criticism that was often unfair but rarely unprovoked. He had no fear of the response when he stood up and declared, in fact, that now that he was there Congress would never be the same. Adam was the first person to attack the racist structure of the Congress, and more particularly the House of Representatives. His presence, his attitude, and his actions backed up his claim to wield "audacious power" for himself and his people.

Adam was not merely a leader of Harlem, though Harlem was in his title. He was a leader of the black world. When Adam Powell was sent to Pan-African meetings on the mother continent, even though he had the reputation of being a renegade, he became an American, albeit a black American. He would not tolerate attacks on our country, by anybody. On domestic policy he was really a pain in the ass to any administration. But on foreign policy he was quite a spokesman on behalf of the United States. Most of us don't know enough about all that our predecessors did to remove the obstacles to our advancement. With Adam Powell, had I not succeeded him, I'd just be among those who said he was one of those who had the courage to speak out when it was not popular to do so. I cannot tell you how deeply I feel about the moral imperative of bearing witness to injustice, but I will remind you of the tragedy of silence while Jews were massacred by the millions, while Senator Joseph McCarthy, drunk with power, destroyed people's lives, or while people in the civil rights movement were beaten or lynched and mutilated. Whether we're talking about early postwar America or present-day Iraq war America, in every era there are so many good people who are silent, until someone breaks through.

After that, of course, it's hard to find anyone who'll admit that they knew anything bad was going on, much less that they looked the other way. Suddenly nobody in Europe knew the Jews were being killed. Nobody knew people were being blacklisted in New York and Hollywood. Suddenly, all the good folks were for Martin Luther King Jr. against lynching and for voting rights.

Adam broke through on the Holocaust and McCarthy and lynching. He even pushed Eisenhower to integrate facilities at Fort Sill, Oklahoma, the year after I left the army. I am proud to say that there are people who believe I've taken some courageous positions from the seat that was once Adam's. But they really don't compare to the stands that people like him, and Malcolm X and Martin Luther King Jr., took, because they took them when we didn't have a place to stand. After all, there were just three other black members in Congress when Adam was expelled in 1967. I say Adam was a black world leader because for a long time it was just him and William Dawson of Chicago. Dawson was elected in 1942, one term before Adam, to what was the first and only black seat in America after Reconstruction. But as soon as Adam came it was "Dawson who?" As Adam was one with the aspirations of Harlem, Adam and Harlem became one with the aspirations of all black folks in America. He was, in fact, just the first black from the Northeast, but he might as well have been the first black from the whole United States.

As unique and self-created as he was, Adam owed a critical political debt to Ray Jones. Their relationship blew hot and cold over the years, but it was Jones who cut the deal when Adam was caught between supporting John F. Kennedy or Lyndon Johnson for the Democratic presidential nomination in 1960. Adam was playing it coy about whom he was backing in the months before the convention. That led the powerful House Speaker Sam Rayburn to summon Ray to Washington to make a deal on behalf of his fellow Texan, then-senator Lyndon Johnson. Rayburn's straightforward offer for Adam's support of Johnson as far as Johnson went at the convention was to make Adam chairman of the House Education and Labor Committee, regardless of what other Southern Democrats thought.

Speakers were far more powerful than they are today, and so were chairmen. This was an immense promise that Rayburn could certainly keep. At the time the "smart money" was on Kennedy getting the nomination. But Ray had already made the calculation that there might be more to gain by going against conventional wisdom, and took the deal. The way he saw it, he and Adam had more to gain by being among the few in the best seats on the Johnson bus than two more among the many on the Kennedy bandwagon. No matter who ultimately won in November, in what would prove to be one of the closest elections in American history, Sam Rayburn would still be Speaker of the House, and in a position to guarantee the chairmanship of Education and Labor for Powell. It was the kind of no-lose politics that Ray preferred.

That bit of vintage Ray Jones is why he hangs above my right shoulder in my Harlem office. In a sense, it may be the most historically significant of the many hundreds of deals that marked his career. It certainly was the most important for Adam. Two years after he hit that chair, with Johnson in the White House after Kennedy's death, Johnson made Adam his legislative general in his long-dreamed for war on poverty. No congressman of any color was better prepared to receive that kind of power than Adam Powell. Among other things, he reorganized the committee for maximum effectiveness, decentralizing the subcommittees for the first time to allow their chairmen to become legislative leaders in their own rights—under his leadership, of course. The net result was the passage of hundreds of pieces of legislation in the space of a few years. It was perhaps the most productive period of legislation for "poor folks" in American history. I say "poor folks" because so many of the beneficiaries were the white rural poor as well as the blacks and other racial minorities who are always most identified with the war on poverty.

Once, when I was still new as a district leader and before I reached the Assembly, I got a call from somebody saying that the congressman wanted to see me. Hot damn, I thought, "The congressman wants to see me! This must be it; I was going to meet the congressman." I know it would have been my first meeting, because I remember being so excited about it. When I got to the Abyssinian Church at 138th Street, there was such a big crowd waiting outside the church that I thought there must have been a funeral going on at the same time as my meeting. As it turned out, Adam had invited everybody he knew—and didn't know—to witness and ratify another public display of his audacious power.

There were hundreds of people there, responding to the call from our congressman. Adam was on stage, with the lawyer Henry Williams officiating. Williams appeared to be reading procedure from the civil laws of the state of New York. But the part he was really playing was straight man for the pastor. He recited the part of the law describing the designation of a church board of trustees. Adam, of course, had just fired the entire board for their failure to give him the backing he thought he deserved, and was replacing them with his most faithful political friends. One of them was a big community liquor store owner, C. B. King, and another was his female Democratic district leader, Lillian Upshaw.

Well, the ousted trustees, along with members of the church, were in an uproar. All they could see were political people like me, who never went anywhere near the church, standing with Adam in a leadership coup. "Pastor . . . what are you doing to us?" they called out. "You know this is wrong . . . these people voting are not members of the church!"

And Adam looked them straight in the eye, and pointed that finger at them: "See, I *told* you to keep the records. I told you that we should know who is and is not a member. But you didn't do it, as the shepherds of the church. That's why I'm getting rid of you. We're gonna have records from here on in. But you cannot challenge anyone in this church as a nonmember, because you just don't know." The new board was installed with what Adam called "audible votes" from the crowd—members or not—supporting his move.

Audacious power!

I remember him speaking once on a platform at 145th Street, with all the elected officials there. I was sitting up in front. He just went on about how powerful he was, how great he was. He never acknowledged me or anyone else in the crowd. Percy Sutton always tells the story about us being at a Powell rally somewhere when an awestruck bystander exclaims about Adam: "Look at him, just look at him—and he doesn't even have to *be* one of us!"

And there it is: Adam's white "blood" is as much a part of his story as Bimini. The way Adam used his looks set him far apart from the long tradition of fair-skinned black leaders. Where the old guard seemed to project by their light skin the virtue and merit of the unseen black masses they claimed to represent, Adam found the power in projecting unapologetic blackness through the privilege encoded in his nearly white skin. Much of his audacious power, I think, flowed from putting white people off balance as they struggled to reconcile the dissonant image that was Adam Powell.

I wonder sometimes, though, how well his combination of color and arrogance would have continued to serve him within the black community had he lived a bit longer into the black-conscious seventies. Roy Wingate, who was Adam's chief of staff near the end and very dark-skinned, talked loudly about "We've gotta get rid of the mulattos," when he ran against me in 1972. He took pains to include Percy Sutton and Adam himself. I really don't believe Wingate would ever have mentioned color if Adam was alive and well, but we'll never know.

To hear me tell it, every time I ever met Adam is recalled as the first time. That, I believe, is because to meet him, no matter how many times you did it, was not to know him. One of my memorable "first time" audiences also began with a summons from Adam, delivered via Lillian Upshaw.

Adam held forth at the Rooster, on the west side of Seventh Avenue between 137th and 138th, right across from the Abyssinian Church. He had his place at a table in the back, with his crowd of cronies saying "Yes, Congressman," as he smoked his little cigars. I'd gone alone, which was stupid. He had all of his Rooster crowd surrounding him, like a chorus that seemed to be assembled just to ridicule me. I was still brand-new as a district leader, and I was once again overly impressed with the invitation. I thought Lillian, as a fellow district leader, had invited me so that Adam and I could sit and talk in private. But the meeting was all about "So . . . you're the new guy on the block. . . . You're the smart one . . .," you're this, and you're that. I learned a lesson from that meeting, and I remembered everyone who was there.

The humiliation haunted me over the next few years, but it was more than offset by my rising political fortunes, and the moral and strategic blunders of the white people in and out of Congress who were out to get him. As I said before, my political limit was the sky above my own backyard; whatever Adam did or did not think of me, he cared even less about where I was going. Adam was still an untouchable myth. I respected his arrogance, even as I was embarrassed by his conduct. I couldn't be considered a friend of Adam's. If you took all our conversations before I announced against him, excluding Bimini, and added them up, you wouldn't get three minutes of tape. It was, "Hiiii, Assemblymaaaan. You're Rangel, riiight?" That was usually it.

I can't overemphasize how hard it was to defend him on television, given the way he treated me. Yet for all the problems I had with Adam, I was more furious with the folks outside of Harlem who had shown no interest in my people—locally or nationally—but were the first ones to attack Adam Powell and judge him a discredit to his race. I hardly ever dealt with Adam—because he did not see fit to deal with me—but I always felt compelled to challenge those outsiders with: "What right have you got to be critical of our congressman?" Whether he was in the United States or whether he was in Bimini, under the Constitution *we* determine who we want to represent us. As if I could go sound off about whether any of *their* congressmen were a credit to *their* race! So I really became not only a supporter of Adam, but assumed a place on the cutting edge of his support on TV and in his petitions before the Supreme Court.

You have to remember how Powell was brought down in the House.

Adam had long been in the sights of Southern Dixiecrats and the growing number of conservative Republicans. But by 1966 he was also in the
crosshairs of a new generation of moderate to very liberal Democrats
looking to oust the decades-old institutional power structure built on
strict seniority, in which the majority leadership and committee chairmen ruled by nearly divine right. Adam Powell had pushed a record
amount of legislation through the House to accomplish socially progressive ends, but for these insurgent young Democrats the ends no
longer justified the means: audacious power projected under the rules
of the House. Adam's outstanding arrest warrant in New York, and an
ongoing investigation into how his office expense account paid for his
staffers' trips to Bimini, gave the Jacobins the ammunition they needed
for a showdown in the opening days of the 90th Congress.

Speaker John McCormack of Massachusetts tried to head off the
move to kick Adam from Congress by arranging to strip him of his chairmanship as preemptive punishment. But one member from California,
Lionel Van Deerlin, refused to back down on his promise to put a motion
on the floor to deny Adam his seat outright. That motion was about something much bigger than what Adam had done, and it passed 364 to 64.
Besides the open assault on the old seniority system, which would fall
shortly after, it was about members responding to their constituencies. It
was about "Did you vote for that nigger, or did you vote against him?"
There wasn't anything substantive about it. They simply didn't want to
have to go home and defend a vote for him, so they kicked him out.

The law is very clear: The Constitution says that the conduct of a
member is to be determined by the Congress itself. That means you cannot predetermine the behavior of a member before he is sworn in.
Every two years it's a brand-new Congress, with the exception of seniority. Whatever they thought Adam did in the last Congress should have
had nothing to do with seating him in the next one. To be sure, had
they allowed him to be seated, they could have used all of the charges
swirling around him to condemn his conduct and kick him right out.
We have done that quite a few times. But that's not what they did, which
is why the Supreme Court eventually ruled in Adam's favor. He did not
have to please the Congress to be sworn in. But that day nevertheless
became his unraveling. By the time he was vindicated and reinstated two
years later, he'd forgotten that he did still have to please Harlem.

I was one of the Harlem-elected officials who got on buses for Washington that day in January 1967 to bear witness to the spectacle and to
protest Adam's ouster. Once again, I was one in a crowd, outside the
Capitol this time, responding to the call of Adam Powell. My morally
outraged stance was consistent with the strategic position into which the

persecution of Adam Powell had forced most Harlem politicians. Our constituents were now incensed; there was no political gain in validating any of the critics' charges. They were after Adam for all the wrong reasons. Adam Clayton Powell had made his constituents so proud with the stances he had taken for decades. Running off to Bimini made most of us embarrassed and ashamed. But nobody was ready to hold him accountable in 1967.

———————————

In 1968, shuttling back and forth from his exile in Bimini, Adam ran for reelection against a group of rank incompetents. As unknown as his challengers were, Adam *really* performed poorly at the polls, to everyone's surprise. I can't remember how active I was in supporting Adam that year, my first reelection to the Assembly. Things were happening so fast. Tensions over Columbia University's expanding development plans in Harlem merged into the larger antiwar, antiracism, and pro-black youth revolution in the streets that spring and summer. The assassinations of Martin Luther King Jr. and Robert Kennedy, and Mayor Lindsay's performance on the hot streets of Harlem, made the Adam opera almost unnoticed in the larger scheme of things. There were so many fires to be put out, and other flames, like my agitating about corruption in the police department, to be fanned.

The fact that I would go to Bimini the following year to try to get Adam to come back really shows the limits of my political ambition at that time, as far as Washington was concerned. I only went because Governor Rockefeller challenged me. I had taken him on about Adam's situation and he threw the ball back in my court. There were other black politicians out there, with bigger names than mine, who might have done it, but many of them were Adam's people, and I was the one who had that special relationship with Rockefeller. Throughout my career I've tried to strike a balance between invading other people's political space and defending my own place in line. So, for example, when the mayoralty rolls around, the media and others never fail to ask me if I might be a candidate. I'm not even thinking about running for mayor. But I'll keep my name out there for a while, just so people who haven't done anything and think they can just come and ask for my support will have to wait until I decide to actually *say* I'm not a candidate. In my rules of this game, you work with the people ahead of you in whatever line you are on until they excuse themselves. Or, in rare circumstances, they are excused by their own actions or other events.

That's the only way I can explain why, until his position became politically untenable, I remained excited to have a congressman like Adam Clayton Powell. Even immediately after returning from Bimini, still stinging from the very personal degradation Adam inflicted on me, I didn't seek any publicity out of the experience. I didn't go out and get the easy "Adam Refuses to Come Home" headline above my picture in the papers. I still thought I was on the brink of starting that new law practice. But out of all the candidates who had run against Adam before, as the noncandidate I had already become the best known. I had been on television defending him for two years. Adam's absence, and my defense of him, gave me credibility. Had Adam decided to come home it would have fit in quite nicely with me practicing law and legislating in Albany.

But, of course, that was not to be.

I can't tell you how many times I've been asked to identify the moment I decided I would run against Adam. But I can tell you that once I made it, the decision itself was not as significant as you might think. The significant decision was when Percy Sutton and I merged a few years earlier. When we merged, the excitement was about winning. There was no long drawn-out process about where we were going. There was only the chess game we were playing to win, and recognizing both the threat and the opportunity presented by the new players Adam's abdication would bring to the table. The truth of the matter was that no incumbent should have done as poorly as Adam Powell did in his 1968 reelection. The turmoil in the streets that season obscured it, but nobody who counts votes for a living could fail to notice. It was very clear that Adam was vulnerable. That was one of the things I had gone to Bimini to tell him; these were real numbers, representing real people.

Adam's failure to come home brought a lot of people out of the political woodwork. As Percy and I saw the support some of them were getting, it occurred to us that we might be seen as *too* strong supporters of Adam Powell. Suddenly my seat looked imperiled, as Percy and I were now viewed as being the regulars of the Democratic "machine." This became especially clear when the West Siders in the district, the so-called progressives, were so upset with Adam Powell that they began reaching out for the most radical, anti-Powell candidate they could find. Fortunately, Percy Sutton, as Manhattan borough president, was always being mentioned by the press as the one to watch as the jockeying to replace Adam began in earnest. And when the media asked, " Mr. Sutton, your name is being mentioned . . . don't you have an interest?" he would reply:

"No, there's a young fellow named Rangel—he's being drafted."

"Rangel?" they asked.

"Yeah," Percy would reply. "He's in the State Assembly."

"Oh, *that* Rangel," the interviewer would say.

We got weeks of television exposure from those exchanges. Of course, the only ones drafting me were Percy and me. Floyd McKissick, the head of the Congress of Racial Equality, wanted to run. Often described as a "firebrand," he had been holding a regular series of community meetings from earlier that winter that were billed as seeking a consensus about how many people were not supporting Adam, and what they might want in a replacement. Everyone, but especially Adam himself, was invited. I think Floyd's idea was to constantly ask Adam to show up at this brownstone, and when Adam kept failing to appear McKissick would emerge as the candidate, with the backing of everyone attending. Then one night Adam actually showed up. Percy and I were there. In vintage Adam fashion he made an entrance, and then said in no uncertain terms that he was running for reelection. To make it clear that he was still the lion in this den, perhaps to counter rumors that he was dying of cancer, Adam dramatically opened up his shirt to display scars from the radiation therapy he was getting at New York Hospital.

The effect was probably more shock and pity than the awe Adam was looking for. Somehow, as God would have it, I was the one with the car. I drove him from 136th Street and Lenox to where, to my surprise, he was living on Seventh Avenue in a little apartment above Jack Duncan's funeral parlor. I knew Duncan was his friend, but I had no idea that was where and how Adam was living when he was in New York now. As we drove, he kept telling me how much money a congressman made, how they had just gotten a raise and improved pension benefits. He was teasing me, as if I were interested in the job. I felt awkward enough taking Adam home in my broken-down Ford Fairlane. But to see him go up the stairs to a tiny dingy apartment above a funeral home was to see the Adam Clayton Powell I thought I knew humbled beyond recognition.

I announced on February 20, 1970, and once we started we went all out. My brother, Ralph, was my right hand, and Percy was my left. We even had "Women for Rangel," mature professional women who were involved with throwing fund-raisers and supporting rallies. I wouldn't say that all my television appearances defending Adam completely inoculated me against charges of selling him out now that I was running against him.

But I would say that I didn't really need any inoculation in Harlem, because I'd known for years that Harlem was fed up with Adam Powell, and Harlem knew it, too. The major problem that we had all those years was that every time we got ready to replace him, these damn fools in Congress would do or say something stupid that would unite us behind Adam again. Kicking Adam out of Congress brought him more support than he had had in decades. Before I ran, I was on television saying, Hey, he may not be all that we want, but he's ours. After I announced, I didn't have far to go in saying that, unfortunately, he didn't want to be ours anymore.

I can't conclude that my run was more an act of political courage than plain political survival. But it did involve a great deal of risk. I give up my Assembly seat to run; both seats are up at the same time, so you can't run for both the Congress and the Assembly, you have to choose. If I had lost, I'd be out of office and going back to a law practice that I had just figured out would doom any hope of a comeback as an elected official. Of course, I knew I'd have two bites at the apple, because the Rockefeller people had given me the Republican line, so even if I lost the primary, I would still be in the fight. In fact, that's exactly what happened to Bobby Garcia in the Bronx that year—he ultimately got elected on the Republican ballot line.

As it turned out, I didn't need the Republican line. Even after the recount that Adam demanded, I won the Democratic primary in June by 150 votes. The slim margin gave Adam an opening to sue me on a technicality that would not be worth mentioning except for the fact that it went all the way to the U.S. Supreme Court. I won there, too. Hardly any of the political leaders backed me outright in the primary. But we always had the feeling that they were not vigorously opposing me. All I really had to do was dominate the vote in my own district, because it was the heart of the congressional district, geographically, politically, and numerically. After that, you might say that my margin of victory came from the reform Democratic precincts on the Upper, Upper West Side.

I've often said that if I had actually known Adam Powell, I could never have run against him. When I ran against Lloyd Dickens for district leader in 1963, Adam, who had never met me, was nevertheless calling me out by name as a candidate of the downtown bosses. My feet were swollen; I was broke as Billy B. Damn, sitting in my basement apartment, hearing the legendary Adam ripping into me by name. But that was what he owed the regular Democratic organization that supported him. I never took it personally, but it was just so bizarre to hear from the congressman every day that I was being supported by rich white folks.

Nobody that I know *really* knew Adam Clayton Powell. If I've said it once I've said it a million and one times: Anybody as used to the constant roar of the crowd in his ear as he was—in New York, in the Congress, wherever he went—and can then get on a sailboat and stay in that water for days, weeks, months, and years with no one around, that's a man for a professional to study and try to figure out. Just because you drank and smoked with him at Jock's or The Rooster didn't mean you knew Adam. I knew most of the gang Adam Powell hung out with, whether in the bars or the clubhouses. When I ran, they all made it clear they weren't going to be opposing me. Sure, they all formally endorsed Adam, but they did so with a wink and a nod in my direction. In the end, they had the same feeling I had about this man we didn't know: He's not all we want, but he's all we got, so leave him alone. Then, when someone said it was time to go, I was only repeating what other people had said: "Adam's gotta straighten up and come home; we need a congressman." It wasn't as though they loved me—they hardly knew me because I had just gotten into their political midst. For them to invest in a guy who had been in the Assembly for only three years, a guy they had barely heard of, said more about what they finally realized they didn't know about Adam than what they thought of me.

He was a very complex figure. He took his persona-defining slogan—"Keep the faith, baby"—from what St. Paul wrote in the Bible as he faced the inevitability of his execution by the Romans—he was ready for death, because he'd stayed the course and kept the faith. Adam just added "baby" to the end of it—it was, after all, the sixties. It wasn't exactly threatening, but it was a powerful statement of encouragement that carried a promise. It became the title of the Showtime television movie of his life that may well frame Adam's legacy. His sons, Adam Clayton Powell III and Adam Clayton Powell IV, born to Adam's second and third wives, Hazel Scott and Yvette Diago, made a point of telling me how hard they worked for ten years to get the film made. Attending the premiere at the Magic Johnson Theatre in Harlem, I jokingly told my buddy Percy Sutton that if the movie didn't turn out right I was getting up and walking out. Percy will tell you with a laugh, for a long time everyone applauded me for becoming the next congressman, and blamed him for getting rid of Adam!

When you see this movie, you see a drinking, womanizing pastor who courageously takes on the issues of black America, is politically crucified, and ultimately vindicated as he removes himself from all of life to Bimini. But my question about the movie, one that nobody seems to be able to answer, is: Why would these sons allow the story of their father to be told with such an emphasis on his womanizing? Always with a drink in his hand, always leering at women. I have to assume the sons had some control over this—they are both listed as executive producers—so how did this happen?

In the movie, Hazel Scott is played by Vanessa Williams. When they first meet, Adam's already married, and she makes her objection clear. He responds that his wife knew very well who she was marrying. Hazel takes up with him in this whirlwind romance and they marry. The son Adam III is born, and at some point Hazel, fed up with Adam, is taking the boy with her to Europe, where he would be raised. In the scene the father looks at the young Adam and says something like, "No matter what happens, son, remember that you're a Powell." And he goes out to the limousine, she waves, and so much for that son. (Adam III goes on to marry and has his own Adam IV, not to be confused with Adam Jr.'s second son of the same name.) From the motion picture, as well as recorded facts, Adam's women always seemed to overlap. Hazel Scott overlapped his first wife, Isabel, Yvette Diago overlapped Hazel Scott, and there was always room for Corrine Huff. It seems to me that as much as both of these sons loved their father, they really resented the way Adam treated their respective mothers. That's my theory, and I'm sticking to it.

Someone once told me, and I'm sorry that they did, that members of Congress should be very humble people, because almost all of them came to Congress as a result of a vacancy because someone died, or because someone suffered a national disgrace. I had never really thought about it. But you know, when you look at the record, and see the turnovers just since I've been in the Congress, death has cost the New York delegation the following members:

> William Fitts Ryan, September 17, 1972
> Benjamin S. Rosenthal, January 4, 1983
> Joseph P. Addabbo, April 10, 1986
> Theodore S. Weiss, September 14, 1992

So, I haven't died yet, and because I've been born again, politically, ever since the FBI cleared me, I don't expect to suffer a national disgrace. All of which maintains my humble belief that I really haven't had a bad day since.

7

Rangel (D-N.Y.)

We are now going through a revolutionary period in the history of this country that may actually be far more important than me being shot in the behind in Korea.

When I started this book project, it was Charlie Rangel hoping that some of my experiences might be helpful to other people, because clearly, in my own mind, they've worked for me. But what is far more important—more than the civil rights movement, why I went to Congress, or the constant struggle for decent health care, education, and affordable housing—is the status of the world today, the posture of the United States in it, and the importance of the difference that people, especially in the leadership of the Congress, can make.

It's about how people in the world today are answering the question: Are they better off today than they were twenty or thirty years ago?

The United States has demonstrated that she will display and deploy her economic and military power to influence the conduct of other countries in her favor. Through diplomacy and the world trade organizations it formed and directs, the United States is coordinating the commerce of smaller nations. It's ostensibly for our mutual benefit, but the truth is that these countries do not play on a level field with us. The international development finance institutions like the World Bank that set the criteria for participation by smaller countries are also directed by standards created by the United States with our interests first among unequals.

It took until the 1970s for the small economies of the Caribbean to begin to emerge from colonial status and establish a foothold in the global economy. Countries like Jamaica earned precious foreign exchange from the royalties paid by international mining companies for bauxite—aluminum ore—mined and shipped immediately from the island. Most of the Caribbean was entirely dependent on raw material, tourism, and some agricultural exports. Caribbean leaders sought to develop higher-value export industries, particularly in textiles and garments. However, tariff barriers made it economically difficult for them to export to the United States. I fought for the Caribbean Basin Initiative (CBI) in the early eighties in order to create a Caribbean export market in the United States by eliminating the tariffs on a preferential basis.

The CBI has been responsible for nearly two decades of unparalleled growth in trade between the United States and our close Caribbean neighbors. Unfortunately, such examples of using economic diplomacy for the common good have been overshadowed in recent years by the priorities set under the influence of the Bush preemptive war doctrine. Entering the war in Iraq based on erroneous information, knowing that all they really wanted to do was knock off Saddam, has forced us to go shopping around the world for friends, armed with carrots and with sticks. In order to pull together what was later called a willing coalition, they went to the poorest developing countries and said, "If you can't send a soldier, send a policeman." And, "If you don't have the money, can we give you some?"

Deals were made. I recall once being asked by the president of one of these small countries to please join him and our ambassador for a meeting they were having. I made it clear that I wasn't in that country on official business, or even dressed for it, but he insisted and I attended. The U.S. ambassador made it clear to this president that if he withdrew the handful of soldiers he had sent to Iraq, it would be very difficult for him to get a trade agreement with the United States, and that I was the senior Democrat who had made that decision. I was shocked and forced to clarify that I was opposed to the war and as far as I was concerned the deal for the trade agreement had nothing to do with his willingness to send troops.

We are a world power relying on techniques that are not much different from those the cops in Harlem used to use when they were dealing with numbers runners in the forties and fifties. It's just so basically crude. It threatens to shatter my story. Here I've gone from Lenox Avenue to sitting in the august halls of the Congress, only to see them bring Lenox Avenue into my government, as far as our role play on the world stage is concerned. We arbitrarily pick a regime to represent everything we don't like about the reaction in the world to our own long-standing policies, and make it a scapegoat for sacrificial slaughter. Not because it has done anything—to anyone beside its own people—but because their leader talks against us, and if we knock him off, the rest of the gangs in the neighborhood will be put on notice. It's intimidation, Harlem cops versus gangsters. President Bush would have the Congress and the American people believe that once democracy was established by force in Iraq the other countries in the region would simply fall into line. But that just didn't happen.

Obviously I've been talking about our dealings with Saddam Hussein. But do we have another plot being orchestrated, this time in Central and South America? Why all this attention to Venezuela's Hugo Chavez and his relationship with Fidel Castro? Is this where we're expecting a new front in the war on terrorism? Or is it really the Venezuelan oil we're coveting? Why were the peasants left out of the Central American Free Trade Agreement, and where will *they* be turning in Bolivia and Colombia? I don't have the answers, but I do know this: America's attempt to bring democracy and free market capitalism at the end of an M-16 rifle hasn't worked in Cuba, isn't working in Iraq, and certainly won't work in Venezuela.

One might legitimately ask, "How can America afford to be the liberators of all dictatorships?" How can we afford the hundreds of billions of dollars we're spending in Iraq, and how much will the same policy cost in Iran? And how much will we have to borrow in order to pay for the trillions in tax cuts we've given to the very richest Americans? We do all these things at the expense of the health and education of our own people. The tragedy of Hurricane Katrina is a perfect example: America knew New Orleans was not protected by the levees, and didn't do anything about it. Money to address the problem had long been requested, but was denied for budgetary reasons. We didn't have to suffer the loss of lives we took in the Gulf states from Katrina. And everybody watching on television saw what the victims had in common.

It wasn't their color; it was their poverty. How ironic that in the richest nation in the world we can say with sobering confidence that poverty, in and of itself, is a life-threatening condition in America. At a time when we're spending $5 billion a month in Iraq, and talking about rebuilding it—physically, politically, and socially—because it's our moral responsibility, we have 45 million Americans without health care.

Forget about my legacy for the moment. The legacy that concerns me now is that we've decided to answer questions of public health with private medicine. We've settled for answering questions of public education with increasingly private, for-profit incarceration. We've merged all questions of social and/or political disparity—and their victims' discontents—and answered them with a web of national security that stretches from the cop on the beat to the grunt in Afghanistan. Our leaders are so confident in their moral and political authority to do so that they only thought once about setting up torture-friendly prisons all over the world to circumvent the Constitution and other inconvenient principles of human rights we claim to hold dear. And it's not just a handful of people in the White House. It's the Congress, the American people, and even our churches, full of people claiming to be born again yet somehow above Christ's more progressive principles.

These are not the questions that I had to deal with when I first went to Congress. As daunting as those were, they were not as seamlessly woven into the political, economic, and fiscal fabric of domestic policy-making. The Great Society was not yet a dirty word in 1970, and no one imagined that it would be before the decade was through. Notwithstanding the winding down of the Vietnam War, our posture in world affairs was not anywhere close to the lethal cynicism and global reach of today's foreign policy. The seeds of today's global dystopia had only just been planted in 1970. Congressman Jack Murtha (D-Pa.), one of the most decorated veterans to ever serve in Congress, was only recently back from his tour in Vietnam. The war was over when he came to Washington in 1974, but the bitterness concerning how we got into that conflict, and especially how we got out, was far from done. But not in our wildest dreams would I or Jack Murtha have imagined it would come to him being denounced as a coward on the floor of the House because he insisted on a timetable for withdrawing our troops from Iraq.

You have to understand who Jack Murtha is to appreciate what happened to him in November 2005.

Nixon fought communism from the moment he entered public life. Then he went to China. Name someone in Congress who has not only led the charge for every war we've supported, every war we've carried out, but actually saw combat in two of them. John Murtha.

Show me someone who's had thirty-seven years in the marines, active and reserves. John Murtha. Pick out for me, of 100 senators and 435 members of the House, someone whose reputation as the Pentagon's best friend on Capitol Hill is unimpeachable. John Murtha. Tell me who has visited more of the broken bodies and minds of our brave veterans in hospitals all over. John Murtha. Who passes Arlington National Cemetery every day and thinks of our war dead? John Murtha. Biggest advocate for military spending? John Murtha.

If they polled the generals and officers as to their favorite congressman, who would win? Jack Murtha. He supported this Iraq war more strongly than even the average Republican. So when he introduced a bill calling for a firm timetable for substantially reducing our troop strength and moving them toward the periphery of the fighting, he gave invaluable political cover to every Democrat who, in their scramble to stake out credible positions against it, has had trouble explaining his or her initial vote for the war.

Though Murtha and I disagree on a lot of issues, we bonded easily enough in the thirty years we've served together. There's an amazing thing about combat veterans: We don't have to see eye to eye on civilian matters to become friends. We who have seen death, and lost friends in combat, can walk into a room and feel each other out, find the meaningful things to talk about and easily avoid the things that would tear us apart. Jack Murtha and I have traveled around the world together. I can think of no member of Congress held in higher esteem here at home or abroad. He usually sits in the same spot on the Democratic side of the House floor, and people just gather around him. When he started telling them his fear that the war was unwinnable, ears perked up. When Jack said, "You know, I think we're doing more damage than good," they listened even more. When he said that his friends in the military couldn't tell him that the war made any sense, and that we ought to get out and come up with a different view of how we maintain Iraq, it was a turning point in the politics of opposing the war, on both sides of the aisle. It was the beginning of bringing the Democrats together, finally, on a common front for addressing a war that is now clearly unpopular with a big majority of the American people.

And, of course, that meant it was bait that the Republicans just couldn't resist.

Knowing who John Murtha is, and what he represented, the administration and its attack dogs in and out of Congress could not keep themselves from pouncing on him. From somewhere overseas the president cames out and said Murtha sounded like Michael Moore. After Jean Schmidt (R-Ohio) effectively called Murtha a coward all hell broke out in the House. You could feel the tension in the air, and temperatures rising, after the vice president, someone who had actually avoided service in the military, actually challenged the patriotism of Colonel John Murtha. But in the end they couldn't touch him; their hypocrisy made Murtha a martyr with a cause.

Murtha became an international figure, and the face of something the administration did not know how to handle. Now, when Jack says these things, he gets standing ovations. Not to complain, but when I say it, as I've said since the war began, everyone says, "What's new?" And yet our attempts to put our conscience into resolutions about this war did meet near identical fates at the hands of the House Republican leadership.

When I called for reinstating the draft in 2003 the bill was buried immediately. I had no illusions about it being passed, but what I wanted was a national debate on the fundamental inequity in how we staff our wars. In a time of war I wanted a loud conversation about the de facto *economic* draft in place that puts the national sacrifice on the backs of poor and/or minority soldiers and their families. In October 2004, to make political points before the approaching election, and especially to quell Internet rumors that the administration in fact had plans for a draft, the House Republicans used their power to set aside the rules and bring my bill up for a vote without hearings or any possibility of debate. It went down 402–2. Even I wasn't one of the two who voted for it. But Jack Murtha was.

It was almost the same in November 2005. A group of Republicans looked at his resolution, focused on the words *immediate withdrawal,* and said, "Why don't we put out a resolution for immediate withdrawal of the troops, and force the bastards to vote it up or down." And so they put out a Republican resolution, sponsored by Duncan Hunter (R-Calif.), that cynically dared us to vote, in effect, for or against keeping the troops in Iraq, without any debate. Hunter went so far as to call his resolution "the Murtha bill." Murtha yelled loud and long, "That's not my bill, vote against it," and we all did, along with the Republicans.

As of this writing I can't predict what the unified Democratic line on the Iraq war will be in the 2006 congressional campaign. In fact, I can only hope that it will actually be unified. But I can say this: It's not rocket science. It's so simple to say, in a way that's both elegant and conservative. When I was a sergeant in the army, I could never challenge the Commander-in-Chief—no serviceman can. But now that I'm a member of Congress, if I ever believe that our military men and women are being placed in harm's way under false pretenses, I have a moral obligation to challenge the president. The president wants to paint his critics as unpatriotic underminers of our military morale whenever we have differences with him over the conduct of the war in Iraq. But the patriotic thing is to say and do what you think is right, even though it may be unpopular. I was criticized when I first spoke out about the absence of weapons of mass destruction, the missing connection with al-Qaeda or 9/11. But thank God more and more Americans now see that the president was wrong, and that it's time to stop the killing and maiming of thousands of our soldiers and countless Iraqis. The president's vague, elusive, and morally indefensible objectives are just not worth the price.

If indeed the American people were deliberately misled, because a handful of political operatives and theorists—in groups like the Project for New American Century—were looking for an excuse to knock over a guy they wanted to take out, sending a message to Iran and Syria in the process, then we're talking about something more than bungling. If we've sent the unfortunate cream of their generation to their death and disfigurement just to establish ourselves as the dominant power in the region, without saying as much to the American people, it's something beyond mismanagement.

The Congress owes the American people an investigation of the facts, to determine if this mismanagement rises to the level deserving impeachment. If so, as my story will show, it wouldn't be the first time I've sat in judgment of a president.

Let's rewind the videotape. I was shot in Korea in 1950, I graduated law school in 1960, and I was elected to Congress in 1970—it's all packed in there. And yet the remarkable thing is that I still had no plan. I had no blueprint. I guess I had one for a hot minute when I got to the Assembly—really more of an ambition than a plan—that I was going to become the Speaker one day. That's where I wanted to go. But then Adam changed all that, didn't he. Boy, did I have a classic "OK, now what do we do?" conversation with my brother the day after we won. As I've said, Ralph did nothing but work his behind off to get me elected, and we were inseparable.

"Going South, Charlie!"

"South, Ralph?"

"Yes, South, Charlie."

"Man, Washington is about as South as it's gonna get. Oh boy, oh boy!"

I am probably the least courageous person in the world when it comes to leaving New York. The net distance I've traveled in life, from where I was born and raised to where I live today, is three blocks. I grew up at 132nd between Fifth and Lenox, and I now live on 135th between Fifth and Lenox. I didn't go downtown; I didn't even go as far as Sugar Hill. All the while I was running for Congress it never really entered my mind that I would be moving to Washington, D.C. When last I worked for the federal government, on Lyndon Johnson's Selective Service commission, it was always about flying into D.C., going into the office, meeting with people who didn't live there either, and then getting on a plane and coming back to New York.

When I went to Washington for the first time with my brother, who had spent a lot of time in the South while he was in the service, he kept reminding me to recognize that I was not in New York anymore. We were walking in some part of the Capitol, and just as he reminded me for the tenth time, a white Capitol Hill policeman approached me, and in the deepest Southern drawl I could imagine, at least at that time, the officer said with a big smile, "Welcome to the Capitol, Mr. Rangel."

"Don't let that smile fool you," Ralph said when we were past.

We went to the cafeteria in the Longworth House Office Building. On the steam tables there was scrapple, hominy grits, and bacon with rind, along with the eggs and home fries. I was amazed that these white folks in Congress had all this Harlem food!

Ralph just looked at me and smiled. Even today, after seventy-five years, I can't think of one white Southerner I'd ever met in Harlem. My first Washington revelation was that what I had long thought of as soul food was really *Southern* food. I had forgotten that everything we had in our food culture they had, too, because that's where we came from.

Our Southern taste buds worked the same, but after that our tongues definitely parted ways. There was this chairman of the Agriculture Committee from Waco, Texas, named Bob Poage. When I first arrived I didn't want to ask a whole lot of questions. I was still covering my insecurity, and figured I was better off finding the answers myself. Poage was talking about an agriculture bill, and his Southern accent was so thick that I actually went down and sat right in front of him in the first row, in a vain attempt to try to figure out what on earth he was saying. Boy, was I relieved to later find out that hardly anyone in the House knew or cared about what Poage was talking about. He was truly a classic character of the old Congress. When he took the floor to speak, he had so much body movement that members said he was the only man in America who could wear out a suit from the inside.

Poage aside, you can see quite a lot from the front row. One day Bob Dornan, the fire-breathing California conservative who made a name for himself savaging what he saw as the moral bankruptcy of Ted Kennedy at Chappaquiddick, asked for a special order of personal privilege. The order gives a member time to stand at the microphone on the House floor and put anything they want into the Congressional Record. Some local paper had charged him with exaggerating his credentials as an air force fighter pilot to the point of lying. He was setting the record straight, with a flourish. His defense was quite convoluted, but from my front-row seat it was such exciting theater. Mind you, the place was empty way before he was done talking. But I couldn't leave; standing up almost in his face and walking out would have been so insulting. Afterward, I went to the cloakroom to make a call. He came in there, in tears, going on about how I was the only one in the House who had a sympathetic understanding of his situation! Moral: Be careful when choosing a front-row seat.

After absorbing the initial culture shocks of Washington, there was still the matter of Adam Powell's legacy to deal with. The first time I set foot on the floor of the House, I could hear people whispering:

"Who is he?"

"I don't know, but he's the guy who beat Adam."

For months I had no identity other than "the guy who beat Adam." Ironically, I hadn't completely beaten Adam Powell yet. I was still fighting him in court over the election. Or rather Adam's lawyers were still fighting me, using a legal technicality that would not be worth mentioning except that it actually made it all the way to the Supreme Court of the United States. Adam himself was never present in court, but his lawyers, in their attempt to call me into court to set aside the result of what was a very close election, tried to serve me by certified mail with return receipt requested. Meaning that I would have to go to the post office to pick up and sign for the notice if I wasn't home when it was delivered. The court ultimately ruled that I was not duly served, because I had no obligation to go and pick up that mail. My lawyers were Harold Fisher, Fritz Alexander, who went on to become the first black on the New York State Court of Appeals, and Pat Swygert, from a well-known New York law firm.

After we won, I found out that this outstanding lawyer Pat Swygert had also been a police officer in Washington D.C., and had graduated from Howard University Law School. He was the only real contact I had in Washington, so I was lucky that he agreed to be my very first chief of staff; I could not have made a better choice. I only had him for two years, as he went on to distinguish himself in academia and has been president of Howard University since 1995. His name lives on in my office, however, because his late brother Kenneth fell in love and married my secretary, now my Washington office manager, Brenda Swygert.

That was the legal end of my victory over Adam Powell. Adam himself died not too long after, in April 1972. But there were still a few lingering challenges to my legitimacy from would-be heirs to Adam's throne. There was Roy Wingate, of course, who gave me my only real primary contest in 1972. There was also the Reverend Calvin Butts, who assumed the leadership of what had been Adam's Abyssinian Baptist Church. There were some in the church who thought that their new pastor should also be the congressman, and admittedly there were rumors that even Reverend Butts thought so, too. But I'm pleased to say now that it would be hard for me to have a closer working relationship with Reverend Butts. He initiated the church's Abyssinian Development Corporation, which has played a leading role in rejuvenating the central

Harlem community. Whenever I visit the church, he says that Adam Powell was so great, it's taken the two of us to fill his shoes.

The initial rumors were fed by the feeling among some of the clergy that since Adam had been the pastor of Harlem's preeminent Baptist church, Abyssinian, that somehow the district was a "Baptist seat," and certainly not a "Catholic seat." The rumors proved to be untrue. Indeed, during the 1970 primary, the Ministerial Interfaith Association, an influential group of ministers from a number of denominations, came to my rescue with support. They were led by the well-known Reverend William James, who campaigned for me throughout the district. I never hesitate to attribute my close primary victory to their hard work and support. I haven't had a serious challenge, backed by any segment of my district, since. Over the years I've been blessed by a wonderful partnership with the churches, synagogues, and mosques in my district; they are now one of my strongest sources of support.

It was anything but downhill after getting elected to Congress. Far from an anticlimax, becoming a member of the House of Representatives was like a booster rocket igniting under me. My getting on the Ways and Means Committee in December 1974 at the end of my second term was like entering orbit. What, after all, is the world all about if it's not about taxes and health care and trade? Some 30 percent of all the legislation in Congress comes through Ways and Means; everything we're talking about today that really matters tends to be the jurisdiction of my committee. I may have hit Washington without a plan, but I still had Sergeant Rangel's old clipboard-wielding ambition: I wasn't there five minutes before I set my cap for an appointment to Ways and Means, with the hope of rising from there into the House Democratic leadership.

Little did I know that my ambition would bring me into conflict with a stiff-necked Polish-American representative from Chicago named Dan Rostenkowski, who was chairman of Ways and Means from 1981 to 1994. By the early eighties I'd risen as far as Deputy Majority Whip under the speakership of Tip O'Neill. But from the start, Rosty never tired of coming after me about where my loyalties lay, with the committee or the leadership.

"You can't do both," he would insist.

"Wait a minute. Tip's my buddy," I'd reply.

"He's my buddy, too," Rosty would say. "But damn it," he'd continue, "you can't do both. You're either a tax writer or part of the damn leadership."

If there was any one person responsible for any good I've done in the Congress, it would be Tip O'Neill, period. Rosty's love for the Ways and Means Committee led him to believe that I could not be a member and Deputy Whip at the same time. Years later, my failed attempt to be Majority Whip would prove him right. Once Rosty tried to block me from appointment to an important House-Senate conference committee, the place where differences between the houses on parallel pieces of legislation are resolved. As chairman, Rosty held the power of recommending to the Speaker which committee members went to the conference. Trying to intimidate me, he threatened to withhold my recommendation, even though, as a senior member, I would normally be appointed.

Rosty's problem was that I had refused to commit my vote to him no matter what the conference issues were. He made it clear that unless I agreed to vote his way before the conference he wasn't going to recommend me.

"Rosty," I said, "you can't do that."

"That's the way it's done, Charlie," he replied.

"But Rosty, I'm black. I can't explain to anybody why as a senior member I was not recommended."

"You're not playing the race card on me, are you?" he asked.

"Yes, I am," I said. "I'm the first black on this committee. How am I going to explain that I was supposed to surrender my vote to you no matter what?"

Remembering my protest, it's really strange today when I hear *myself* asking Democratic committee members for their votes before I, as senior minority member, recommend them for the conference. But back then my answer to Rosty was, "Dan, you know I was with you before, I'm with you now, and I'm gonna stay with you as long as I can." But the truth was that Rosty knew an appeal to Tip O'Neill was always my hole card.

I've fought to own every bit of privilege due me as a member of Ways and Means ever since I was appointed. I must say that my battles over conference committees with Rosty were nothing compared to the war with the Republicans running the Congress that still rages as of this writing.

Let's be clear: laws are drafted in regular committees of the House and Senate, amended and then voted on by the respective bodies. If passed, they will usually make their way in some form to the president's desk to be signed into law (or, rarely these days, vetoed). Laws get their final form in conference committees, from which it is quite possible for them to emerge with faint resemblance to the legislation initially passed by either body. Bills returning from conference cannot be amended, only voted up or down. It's safe to say that the active ingredients in the laws that govern our country, the net result of our national democracy, are added in conference.

Before the Republicans took control of the House and Senate, senior Republicans and Democrats would meet with their committee staffs and work out differences to be brought to the table for the bipartisan conference to consider. The committee chairman appointed the majority party conferees to a majority of the slots, and the ranking minority member effectively appointed the rest from his party. The doors might be closed, but everyone had some input into what was on the table. Some conferences were even held in open public meetings. But since Republicans took over, they call a ceremonial meeting to open the conference, quickly adjourn, then typically go off into secret meetings of their own. The fix—usually in favor of their chosen special interests—is added there. On one such occasion the conference was meeting in the Capitol. Bill Thomas of California, the current chairman of Ways and Means, was chairing the official conference. But reporters told me that he and the Republicans were meeting privately in his hideaway office in another part of the Capitol. I took my legislative papers and marched right in as though I was invited. They were so embarrassed that they just peeled off and left the room one by one, until the only one left was Thomas. There was nothing for him to do but adjourn the meeting.

Tip O'Neill's open friendship boosted my self-esteem. Though Dan Rostenkowski was considered a pretty rough chairman, I was more than able to hold my own as a result of it. Once, when the going got especially tough, I took my problem to Tip.

"Oh Charlie," Tip began. He must have been in his next-to-last term, after more than thirty years in the Congress. He was already working on his memoir covering all those years, and he assured me that "sooner or later, Charlie, you're gonna know what it's all about."

What it was all about was a relic of congressional myth and legend that goes back to the infamous 1968 Democratic Convention in Chicago. The convention chairman was Carl Albert of Oklahoma. The whole meeting was a nearly continuous melee inside the convention center, what with the big fight over the seating of the black delegates trying to represent newly enfranchised voters in Mississippi and the bitter splits on support for the Vietnam War. At the same time, protesters were battling Chicago police in the surrounding streets, and the chaos and violence seemed about to erupt inside the International Amphitheater, where the convention was being held.

I was there as a New York delegate, but I had no inkling of what was really going on. Richard J. Daley, the legendary late Chicago mayor, was having none of this. There would be order at a convention in Chicago under his watch. Daley ordered this small mountain of a young congressman—Rosty—to bring the convention to order. Rostenkowski went to the podium, yanked the gavel out of Carl Albert's hand, pushed him aside, and gaveled the convention into order. Carl Albert was a little man and Rosty was a big man.

Two years later, in my first Congress, the Ninety-second, Albert is elected Speaker of the House. Hale Boggs, the congressman from Louisiana, had campaigned and won the Majority Leader position. At that time the Majority Leader selected the Whip, but it had to be approved by the Speaker. Today the Whip is elected on his or her own—I know because I ran and I lost in 1986. Boggs's campaign manager was Dan Rostenkowski. They're both Catholics—so Boggs picks Rosty for the Whip job. Everybody supported it, because Boggs made certain that his supporters lined up behind Rosty, too. But when it came to Speaker Albert, who still remembered the '68 convention, it was "hell no" as far as Rosty was concerned. So Boggs went back and picked my longtime dear friend Hugh Carey, also Catholic, from New York. I'm in the Congress at this point, and I saw all of New York celebrating because, for the first time in a generation, a New Yorker had risen to a high House leadership position. There was something close to dancing in the streets, especially in Brooklyn, Carey's home.

But there were two guys from the New York delegation—John Rooney and Jim Delaney—who were not amused. They were as conservative and as right wing as you could get and still be Democrats. Delaney represented the fictional Archie Bunker's real neighborhood in Queens. I like to think that he *was* Archie Bunker, only not as charming. They went to Carl Albert and told him that Boggs had picked this left-wing, liberal, so-called Catholic from Brooklyn, and it wouldn't work for them. If they wanted a Catholic, they said, then damn it, they had to go through them. Albert said he didn't care who was picked, as long as it wasn't Rosty. Boggs dumps Carey, and tells Delaney and Rooney to go get another Catholic.

Who did they pick? Tip O'Neill. And just as Albert never forgot, neither did Rosty, setting us up on a kind of friendly collision course through our years serving together on Ways and Means. After hearing this story, every time Rosty gave me a hard time, I was able to believe that it wasn't about me, but about his sour grapes over not becoming Speaker. Tip had so many wonderful stories; he was always telling them in the right place and at the right time.

While Pat Swygert swiftly organized my Washington office, my wife, Alma, was making all the decisions about our newly acquired home in northwest Washington, D.C. She was the one involved with the car pools, babysitting pools, and all those domestic decisions I hated making time for. As I have said, in the heat of the race to succeed Adam Powell it barely occurred to me that I'd be relocating to Washington. So it went without saying that I had no particular vision for my family life as a congressman. Alma would supply that vision, but at first it was left up in the air as to whether she and the children would even move to Washington. Former New York governor Hugh Carey, who was already in the Congress when I was a freshman, brought that decision to earth. Our friendship had begun the year before, when Carey and I were both taking long shots at the presidency of the City Council office. We hooked up when I got to Washington and remain good friends to this day. Stepping back from our closely intertwined thirty-year personal and political relationship to take a historical view, I think Hugh Carey's performance during New York City's fiscal crisis of the 1970s alone puts him in the ranks of the greatest governors we've ever had.

But first and foremost he was a big, big family man, who had so many children and grandchildren that when he became governor in 1975, insiders joked about how the governor's mansion, a home I knew well before and after he arrived, went from an aristocratic Rockefeller compound to Albany's best-known nursery. One day, very early in my first year, Carey sat next to Alma and me on a bus returning from some congressional event. He confided to her his regrets for missing out on the tender years with his wife and oldest children, because he elected to leave them behind in Brooklyn when he came to Washington. He advised her that whatever she did, she should not stay in New York. "Don't make the same mistake I made," he told her. "Come down with your husband, and work with your husband." Afterward, when Alma said she wanted to come down and look for a house, I said, "Whatever you want."

We came across this dilapidated house on Colorado Avenue, just west of Sixteenth Street, in what native Washingtonians call the "Gold Coast," historically the most elite black neighborhood in postwar, post-1960s Washington, D.C. It was big, and beautiful—the floors were magnificent, not that you would notice for all the beaten-up rugs covering them—but dilapidated. The price was right, though we still had to borrow some money just to get in it. The older black woman who owned it was a recluse. After her husband, a former army colonel, had died, she let a lot of things go to seed on the property. But it had so much land around it that we knew it had been someone's grand house at some point. She had a dog named Zeus, and she insisted that we take the dog, too, because they wouldn't let her have it in the place she was moving into. "Sure," we said; our kids already loved it anyway.

Later, she finagled a way to get Zeus into her new place, breaking the kids' hearts, so we went out and got a cute little puppy, fresh from a German shepherd litter, and named him Zeus. We raised them all together for fifteen years; Zeus just knew he was our third child, and we felt he was, too.

Alma converted that house into a magnificent mansion. We'd go out to these garage and estate sales that frequently take place in Washington when diplomats are recalled to their home countries and are forced to leave their furnishings behind. I think 90 percent of everything we had in that house came from estate sales—furniture from all over the world, a lot of it from embassies. It was mostly quality stuff—half of it is now in my son Steven's house. We filled the place and still had plenty of room, with all that yard space and decking. The house on Colorado, which we sold in 2005, would prove perfect for all the socializing we'd be doing for years to come.

Herman Badillo, the first Puerto Rican–born congressman to represent a mainland U.S. district, was also in the 1970 freshman class. We campaigned for each other, naturally, because his East Harlem/South Bronx district bordered mine. After we won, as new members of Congress, we were supposed to enter a drawing, based on seniority, for the choice of office space. It's a big thing for freshmen, since we would be picking from the best of the leftovers. So I was shocked to run into Herman right after he should have "pulled" a number in the freshman lottery.

"Herman, did you pull?" I asked. "I got a great number . . . you better go pull."

"I'm not going to pull," Badillo says, "because I'm not staying here like you are, Charlie. I'm going to be the mayor."

I thought it was pretty cocksure of him, the way he handled it. But, true to his ambition, he didn't stay—if you count a mere three and a half terms in Congress as not really staying. He did run for mayor, first in 1973, and he ran and he ran and he ran again, but he never made it. In his second try, he drew off enough black votes in the 1977 Democratic primary to keep Percy Sutton out of a runoff with Ed Koch, who would ultimately win in November. The late seventies and early eighties were really the last hurrah for unapologetic, unabashed ethnic politics in the New York mayoralty. Black and Hispanic leaders especially were zealous about the cause of unifying behind one or the other of their own to take Gracie Mansion. Badillo seemed to think he was supposed to be first in line, but it was never that simple, and his style was not suited to the complexity of post–fiscal crisis New York. Rather than uniting people of color, Badillo's third try, in 1985, helped open up an unfortunate wound of political distrust between blacks and Hispanics in New York that persists to this day.

And it also gave Percy Sutton, David Dinkins, Basil Patterson, and myself our nickname: the Gang of Four.

The name came out of Badillo's frustrated attempt to corner the market on black support for what, combined with presumed backing from New York's Latinos, would have made him New York's first non-white mayor. Badillo was going for the support of the black community, and it appeared he had a lock on the backing of a committee headed by Brooklyn Assemblyman Al Vann that was charged with identifying a consensus candidate for unified support of black elected officials. The inside story, I believe, is that Badillo cut a deal with Vann, an influential player at the time. If Vann endorsed him, and brought black elected officials along for the ride, Badillo would back Vann for Brooklyn borough president. Now, I had previously gone out of my way to tell Vann to do what he had to do in picking a candidate, but not to embarrass me by taking a decision without my input, and then expect me to go along with whatever he and his guys from Brooklyn came up with. He let me down. I had no idea at the time of Vann's political relationship with Badillo.

So there we were—Percy, Dinkins, Patterson, and me—at this big meeting with all these ministers and Brooklyn pols. Badillo expected it to end with a blessing, but it didn't turn out that way. We felt as if we had been set up, so we made a pact not to participate in the discussion, but to lay back and see where the whole thing was going. I also knew that Herman "Denny" Farrell, now the incumbent New York Democratic Party chairman, was making his own last-minute play for the mayoral nomination. I didn't expect it to amount to much, but Denny stepped up and gave one of the most passionate speeches I've ever heard in his own behalf. Doggone if we didn't end up walking out of there endorsing Denny Farrell for mayor! The Puerto Ricans were furious. Badillo called a press conference the same night, saying he'd been stabbed in the back by black leadership, led by what he called "the Gang of Four."

We had never heard the term before. After Dinkins became mayor, he would often say that while some saw the title as derogatory, he wore it as a badge of honor. I can't say I disagree with him. During the Badillo-Farrell debate, the well-known minister Reverend Herbert Daughtry was an active participant in this very political discussion. Today we are very good friends, but I didn't know him well at the time. I asked him point-blank:

what made him, a Brooklyn minister, think he knew as much about choosing political candidates as the politicians? As a preacher, he replied, before he ever makes a political decision, he asks his personal Lord and Savior Jesus Christ whether he is doing the right thing.

"And you know what, Rangel?" he said. "More often than not He agrees with me."

I've never asked another clergyman that question again!

Badillo resigned from Congress during his fourth term to be a deputy mayor in the first Koch administration. His successor, via a special election, was Bobby Garcia of the Bronx, with whom I had served in the Assembly. We had also worked closely when, as a state senator, his district included part of my assembly district, both politically and as friends. As it turned out, however, he didn't stay with me in Washington very long either. Garcia was forced to resign in 1990 after getting caught up in the Wedtech scandal. Bobby plead guilty and went to jail, along with his wife, before being released after a successful appeal. He lost out politically, but he and his lovely wife, Jane, found Jesus Christ in the experience. Today he's a very successful Washington lobbyist, and very strong in his religion. I count them among my very best friends.

The South Bronx "Badillo" seat has been held ever since by Jose Serrano, with whom I couldn't have a better friendship. On the House floor we are considered brothers, and today his son, my "nephew" Jose Jr., serves as state senator for East Harlem. So, for East Harlem, it's a family affair. Congressman Serrano had a rocky road through the minefield of Bronx Democratic clubhouse politics, as an organizational outsider with passionately progressive tendencies. For a long time the joke was that his only real political friends were Al Sharpton and Fidel Castro, but he has since established a legislative record that's secured his recognition as an outstanding leader within and beyond his district.

━━━━━━━━━

My victory over Adam in 1970 actually made Charlie Diggs of Detroit the most senior African American in the House. Of course, that didn't stop Diggs from coming to Harlem to campaign for Adam and against me in 1970, but I understood that. Once I was seated, Diggs became my first mentor in Congress, and I became enough of a friend that when he decided to marry a woman from New York, at the historic Riverside Church, he asked me to be his best man. Charlie Diggs was really our man in Africa. He headed the Foreign Affairs Subcommittee on Africa, and spoke early and often against South African apartheid like no other member. He fell on hard times when he was forced to leave the Congress, but he was certainly ahead of his time in drawing America's attention to the importance of having African countries as friends.

In the spring of 1971, the number of blacks in Congress jumped by over a third, from nine to thirteen—all Democrats. As the most senior, Diggs counseled me and the other black freshmen—George Collins (Ill.), Ron Dellums (Calif.), Ralph Metcalfe (Ill.), Parren Mitchell (Md.), and Walter Fauntroy (D.C.)—on committee assignments and other strategies for increasing our effectiveness in step with our growing numbers. You must understand that in the twentieth century, until Diggs's first election to Congress in 1954, there had never been more than two African-Americans in Congress at one time. One represented the south side of Chicago—William Dawson from 1942 to 1970—and the other was Adam Powell. Three more African-Americans, Robert Nix of Pennsylvania, Gus Hawkins of California, and John Conyers of Michigan, came in between 1958 and 1964. By 1968, a year of radical change that brought Shirley Chisholm (N.Y.), Bill Clay (Mo.), and Louis Stokes (Ohio) to the House, the number tripled to nine.

Chisholm and I were the only two African-Americans out of forty-one members of Congress from New York. The story of Herman Badillo's "temporary" House office space illustrates the big problem that's historically plagued New York City's congressional delegations: Very few members went to Congress to stay in Congress. For a variety of reasons, Washington's greatest value was as a stepping-stone. The political organizations would park their man or woman in Washington for two or three terms until they were in line for judgeships or other plum appointments. Or, if you look at the number of New York City House members who have simultaneously run for the office of mayor, safe in the knowledge that they wouldn't have to risk giving up their seats to do so because the mayor is elected in an odd year, the same pattern appears. The net result: New York City's congressmen turn over more frequently than the congressional average, and they don't accumulate as much seniority as representatives from less urban parts of New York and other states.

The members of what would become the Congressional Black Caucus in 1971 didn't have that problem. Whether from big cities or, as would be more common after the impact of the Voting Rights Act began to be felt throughout the Deep South, small towns and rural areas, black members tended to come to stay. Unless, of course, circumstances forced them to make other plans. Though a New Yorker through and through, I immediately had this longevity tendency in common with the thirteen African Americans who were sworn in for the

91st Congress. Five of us went on to collectively serve for 142 years and counting. Two of us, John Conyers and myself, are serving still; we're two of the four most senior Democrats in the House. What turnover came among us was usually due to competition within the local Democratic organizations in a particular district. For example, Robert Nix, who became the fourth black in Congress in 1958, was always being challenged by opponents of the regular Democratic organization in Philadelphia; he was finally beaten by former congressman Bill Gray in 1978. Gray's voluntary departure in 1990 marked a small but significant countertrend in the long-term pattern.

I've got more to say later about the pros and cons of black longevity in Congress, now that we're up to forty-three black members. But in 1971, when we formally constituted the CBC, we had no idea what we would grow up to be. It grew out of an informal group of black representatives led by Charlie Diggs that periodically met with Speaker Carl Albert to discuss our concerns. Anticipating the jump in our numbers, Bill Clay drafted a memo to the group at the end of 1970 calling for a formal structure with officers and an executive committee. Clay's vision was of a caucus that would be the primary policymaking vehicle in the Congress for the interests of African Americans. To some extent, the caucus would also have authority to act on behalf of its members in a crisis. Over the years there have been periodic tensions around how much the caucus speaks for any single black representative, and how much any single representative can speak for the caucus as a whole. But the thing we were clear about was not wanting to be seen as speaking for all of black America.

Our biggest fear was that, by virtue of holding office in the national government, we would mislead people into thinking that we were the nation's black leaders in every area—from civil rights to economics to local politics. Our formation, two years after the death of Martin Luther King Jr., received an unprecedented amount of national and international publicity. All Americans concerned with continuing the advancement of African Americans beyond the triumphs of King's nonviolent, nonpartisan movement were searching for the next center of leadership. Our struggle had profound implications for majority-minority power relationships worldwide, and people all over the world were actively looking for the next chapter in our story.

We didn't want to become the custodians of all black American aspiration, because we knew that meant being responsible for all of black America's problems. We didn't want to create expectations that would far exceed our ability to perform. It was also important not to be seen as usurping the surviving civil rights leadership organizations like the

NAACP, the Southern Christian Leadership Council, and the Urban League. My vision was that we were part of the black leadership, but not *the* leadership. I really wanted us to be perceived as the legislative leaders, after my experience with Percy Sutton in the formation of the Black and Hispanic Legislative Caucus in Albany.

Our first test put us up against Richard Nixon, and in a way, passing that test is what put us on the map. It's important to remember the context. Nixon had been elected in 1968 on a platform of law and order that was a not-so-subtle racial appeal to what he called the Silent Majority of conservative whites who had had enough of the social upheavals associated with the civil and social rights movements to that point. Indeed, America as a whole was still reeling from the assassinations of King and Bobby Kennedy just a few months before the election, and the devastation of a number of urban centers not just by the riots that ensued, but by accelerating white flight to the suburbs. Nixon's silent pledge to his Silent Majority was that whatever they were fleeing, especially forced busing for school integration, would not be allowed to follow them. His Southern Strategy—cutting the Democrats off at the knees by pushing the politics of racial resentment especially hard in the Old Confederacy—worked.

Meanwhile, if white America was having a social anxiety attack, black America was in a full-blown crisis. Beyond the too familiar objective facts of racial disparity, and the emerging patterns of what we now call social pathology within increasingly isolated and concentrated black communities, it was really a crisis of leadership. The landmark federal and state legislation that had passed through Adam Powell's House, and the far-reaching federal and state court decisions that backed and even expanded their impacts, were still toddlers. Lyndon Johnson's executive order that put the phrase *affirmative action* into American social politics had not yet made its way into the fabric of public and private institutions.

The promise of all these laws, rulings, and orders was overshadowed by the frustration of sharply higher black expectations on the one hand, and the increasingly fearful white "backlash" of resentment against black demands on the other. Everyone knew where Nixon was now heading on these issues. But nobody knew where black leaders were supposed be leading *to* anymore, much less who actually was a leader. The civil rights model that brought us to that point was beginning to break down and enter what we now see as a slow but certain eclipse. But nothing had really emerged to take its place.

The CBC, I believe, was the first step toward institutionalizing the gains of the 1960s in the national government. Led by Charlie Diggs, our first move was an attempt to bring black America's concerns to the top of the national agenda, again, by taking them to the president. Nixon, by his very electoral strategy, we reasoned, was responsible for an environment that was indifferent at best and hostile at worst to African American issues. Nixon, of course, didn't immediately see it that way. Diggs began asking Nixon to meet with us in March 1970. It took two months for Nixon to respond—with a note of rejection signed by a White House staffer. Undeterred, Diggs and the other eight black members at the time began to work through new networks of black influence to get Nixon's attention. Black media coverage of the insult started a drumbeat in black America. The pre-CBC group made it clear that as far as we were concerned, in dismissing us the president was dismissing 25 million Americans who were black.

With the memory of the civil rights struggle quite fresh in all our minds, the black media began to focus on Nixon's attempts to cut back or kill the kinds of programs aimed at helping African America catch up. As explained in Congressman William Clay's book, *Just Permanent Interests,* Nixon responded with superficial press releases about the benefit of his programs for blacks. Diggs countered in late 1970 by appointing a "shadow cabinet" made up of black experts in various fields. Each bore a title corresponding to a Nixon cabinet post. Every time a Nixon official rolled out a new initiative, a shadow cabinet member would respond with a strong critique of the program from the black community's point of view.

As it turned out, Nixon, and key staff including John Erlichman, had a tin ear for drumbeats in the black community. So Diggs led us in more direct action: we boycotted the January 1971 State of the Union message. I had just been sworn in, and already I was walking out to make a point. All thirteen sworn black members participated in the boycott, leaving Senator Edward Brooke of Massachusetts, a Republican, the only black member of Congress in the Capitol that night. The bold move was heavily picked up by the Soviet news agency TASS, the BBC, and Communist China's Radio Peking, who between them saturated Europe, Asia, and Africa with the story. Still locked in an ideological battle for the hearts and minds of the world, as the war to stop Chinese-backed North Vietnamese revolutionaries in Vietnam dragged on, the Chinese and Soviet communists were especially pleased to have something with which to stick it to America, and the Nixon administration. The fact that our troops in Vietnam were disproportionately black was gravy.

We got our meeting on March 25, 1971. Ed Brooke set it up. We gave Nixon a list of sixty recommendations drafted by the best brain trust we could find. Among other things, we wanted him to stop trying to kill the Office of Economic Opportunity, and similar cabinet or near-cabinet-rank agencies that Lyndon Johnson had intended to carry the standard for the Great Society. Afterward, commenting on the meeting, Congressman Bill Clay (D-Mo.) told the *New York Times* that the CBC would have "no permanent friends, no permanent enemies, just permanent interests."

We were still careful to avoid any suggestion that we were "Super Negroes" looking to take over from all the work that had been done by the preexisting civil rights leadership. It wasn't humility as much as the fact that most of us were lifted to the Congress by the support of that leadership in the first place. And even though, collectively, we could get more attention than almost any one of them could individually, we still needed them to get support for our legislative goals and to secure our reelections. At the same time, however, we recognized a new mandate: to represent a black constituency that went far beyond the voters in the thirteen districts that sent us to Congress. At the time it is safe to say that most of black America did not have a representative in Congress whom they would call their own. Hispanic and Asian constituencies were even less represented by someone "of color." In an interview on NBC in New York after the Nixon meeting, I said that "black people throughout the country, whether they have a black congressman or not, now have a body to deal with. Not a black, a Puerto Rican, a brown, or a yellow man can now say he doesn't have a friend in the Congress."

In the Nixon meeting, each of us worked hard to be certain we weren't repeating ourselves as each of us got a turn at the president's ear. I used my turn to insist on recognizing drug use and addiction as a national crisis, and to begin to respond to it as such at every level, from border interdiction to treatment. I went to Congress as probably the member most concerned about illicit narcotics traffic and drug addiction. I knew a lot more about the issue than other congressmen because, as an assistant U.S. Attorney, I prosecuted drug cases exclusively. I had made drugs, and drug-related corruption of law enforcement, my signature issue when I was in the Assembly, and I ran hard on the issue against Adam Powell. My comment on Adam was that he was a good man, but, particularly on the drug issue, he had given up on Harlem. Even after I won, I would tell people that "I didn't beat Adam Powell, I ran for an empty seat."

My engagement with fighting drugs in 1971 and 1972 began putting good distance between me and Adam Powell's long shadow, because it quickly cut off discussions of what Adam might have done on other issues in 1964 and 1965. Things were bad, and the worst of the crisis, the crack cocaine epidemic of the early 1980s, was yet to come. Drug thugs were killing judges in the street. They were blowing up federal buildings in Bogota. In 1983, I co-sponsored the legislation creating the Select Committee on Narcotics Abuse and Control, with Congressman Ben Gilman (D-N.Y.). Lester Wolfe, a Democrat from Long Island, became chairman of that committee. Pursuing its mission, Gilman and I traveled extensively over the years, especially in Latin America. Every time he and I made a return visit to Colombia, somebody we met there before—the minister of justice or the national police chief or the general in charge of something drug related—had been assassinated.

Drugs affected every part of every life in my town. Senior citizens were assaulted by addicts, while addicts were fighting and killing one another and had taken over whole streets and neighborhoods. Worse, the corruption was making what was historically a bad relationship between the police and the community a lethal one, as, instead of protectors, the police became something of an enabling army for the drug dealers.

At first, even my friend Robert Morgenthau, when he was the U.S. attorney and I was a prosecutor, refused to believe how deeply the corruption had penetrated the New York City Police Department. I had to tell him that I'd played poker for decades with a number of career officers. When we started they were straight as arrows, at least when it came to drugs. They would admit taking numbers money, but swore they would never touch money from the drug trade. I told Morgenthau that I didn't hear them talking that way anymore. I didn't hear the old outrage when we'd tease one another about being corrupt. I eventually persuaded one of them to begin giving testimony, under condition of anonymity, and we started prosecuting policemen along with the dealers.

I remember vividly a case involving an undercover officer I'll call Smitty. A dealer he had been working on was brought into my office for questioning after his arrest. The prisoner was quite belligerent, denying everything and asking for his lawyer. I asked Smitty to come into the room. I'll never forget the look on the dealer's face. He was shocked, after years of doing business and hanging out with what he thought was his old pal.

"I just don't believe it," he said.

"Smitty," I said, "just show him your badge."

When he saw the badge, he knew the game was up. "Smitty, how could you do this to me and my family?" he asked. "OK, I'm prepared to plead guilty," he says. "But Smitty—just give me my money. If I'm going to jail, I have to leave something for my old lady."

Smitty looked at him and said, "What money?"

The defendant started to cry. "Smitty," he cried, "please don't mess with my money!" I saw the look on Smitty's face, and the defendant's, and I knew Smitty had taken that money. He went to jail for it.

In the early seventies Turkey was the biggest producer of opium in the world. When I was running for Congress it was easy for me to explain how the opium being grown in Turkey was then processed and transshipped in Marseilles, France—we had prosecuted the famous French Connection case in my office. The movie of the same name was a smash hit in 1971. I had picketed the Turkish embassy and even suggested boycotting all French imports as part of my campaign.

My aggressiveness on this issue earned a lot of support for my candidacy from the Greek-American community, and their undying friendship, because I was death on the Turks. At the time, Greece and Turkey were coming very close to war over control of the island of Cyprus. Greek passion against Turkey ran high; any enemy of their enemy was a friend. When the Cyprus-Turkey-Greece issue came up in the Congress, and I came down against Turkey, the Greek constituency joined me as though I were Greek. They were the wind under my wings, saying, "Listen to Rangel; he'll tell you who those Turks are." So when I went to Nixon about drugs, I didn't just have my Harlem thing together, or my federal prosecutor résumé. I had an international indictment against Turkey, and a mandate from a small but vocal nonblack ethnic American constituency. Though my time with Nixon was brief, I had the facts to make the international case against Turkey for their undisputed role in the production of heroin's raw ingredient.

A few months after the Nixon meeting with the caucus, a staffer named Patricia Bradley came into my office and said President Nixon was on the phone. I swore she was putting me on. I picked up the line and said "This is Charles Rangel," and that unmistakable dark-shadowed voice came back, "This is President Nixon." I was really floored. I told him that my late grandfather wouldn't have believed that the president of the United States would be calling me. Of course, my grandfather would be surprised at *anything* successful that I had done. As it was reported in the *New York Times,* Nixon replied that his father wouldn't believe he would be calling me, either. That's how odd it was seen for a conservative Republican president to be calling a black Democrat from Harlem. Then Nixon went on to tell me, in advance of the public announcement, that the government of Turkey had agreed to abolish all opium production, under an administration threat to cut off all Turkish military and economic assistance. At that time Turkey was run by a military government, and thus was highly motivated to comply. Nixon wanted me to know that I was persuasive in that March meeting, and that he had followed through. The call garnered my first big *New York Times* success story as a congressman. Two years later the *Times* would also report me as a member in good standing on Nixon's offical "enemies list" of political opponents.

Nixon was a tough son of a bitch on drugs. Henry Kissinger, who was secretary of state, and I worked closely together on what was the beginning of our international "war on drugs." Kissinger and I remain very friendly with each other when we meet to this day. The national passion behind the war against drugs, I'm sorry to say, has not had the same longevity. It hit its high point somewhere in Ronald Reagan's presidency, during the crack epidemic, and has since petered out. We never did win the war, of course. It took a place in the backseat as the larger efforts for black economic and social advancement in the age of affirmative action took the driver's seat. I've always felt that as you improve the quality of people's lives, the more they have at risk by dabbling in drugs. The more opportunities and options people have, the less likely they are to choose drugs. So, to the extent that African-Americans as a whole advanced sharply from the mideighties through the Clinton nineties, a lot of the drug-related bleeding was staunched. But to this day, when you tell a kid, "Don't do drugs because you'll lose your reputation and your job," and they know damn well they have no reputation and no job to lose, and that things will not get any worse for them being involved, no amount of "just say no" is going to work. To the extent we have more kids with more opportunities, we have a much better chance at defeating the drug dealers, who remain alive and well in business.

When I first went to Congress, though I was looking for a seat on Ways and Means, I ended up on the Science Committee for a short time and then moved on to Judiciary. Judiciary had long been chaired by the great civil rights advocate Emanuel Celler of Brooklyn, the dean of the New York delegation. But Celler was succeeded by my long and dear friend the late Peter Rodino, who represented Newark, New Jersey. I looked forward to contributing in the areas of civil and constitutional rights and fighting crime, since my war on drugs fell under its jurisdiction. But nothing much really happened until Nixon got in trouble over what became infamous as Watergate. The activity in the Congress began in the Senate, where North Carolina's Sam Ervin's committee led the investigation. Our charge, once the Ervin panel decided that there was enough evidence to bring an impeachment proceeding, was to act as a kind of grand jury. We would determine whether the evidence warranted voting Articles of Impeachment, similar to an indictment, that would then be turned back over to the Senate for a trial. We followed much of the same boring procedures the Senate did, until it got to the matter of the infamous Nixon tapes.

We commenced poring over the transcripts and sometimes listening directly to the conversations Nixon secretly taped between himself, his staffers, and other people. Soon, the secrecy we were bound to, for fear that damaging unrelated testimony about the president would leak out, caused an unbelievable amount of tension to build up within and between the members of the committee. Tip O'Neill, who was Majority Leader at that time, sensed the pressure on us. Tip felt it was only a matter of time before something blew up, so he came before us and made it clear to Rodino that unless we moved more swiftly, he would remove jurisdiction from Judiciary and appoint a special committee. Tip's underlying message was: either we vote the Articles of Impeachment or let him go, but get it over with. He feared that if we didn't it would become an issue in the upcoming midterm congressional races.

The politics of that committee were an interesting snapshot of the House at the end of the age of omnipotent chairmen and dominant Dixiecrats. We had conservative Democrats who, working with moderate Republicans, would ultimately sustain impeachment votes pushed by urban liberals like Robert Drinan, the Massachusetts Jesuit who was among the very first to call for Nixon's impeachment. We really worked hard, seven days a week, from day into the night, sometimes in study groups in one another's homes.

Though he wasn't on the committee, Louis Stokes, who was chairman of the Congressional Black Caucus at the time, was a mentor for me through all this. We had a real special relationship that included joking and playing cards together, relieving some of the tension. When it came to some of the serious matters before the committee, I sometimes felt awkward about letting people know what I really did not know. But I never had a problem confiding in Lou Stokes. He was the kind of person that no matter whom he was talking with, he would have you believe that your issue was the most important on his mind. He was very unique in that regard—he's someone I stay in touch with on political issues to this day. Stokes is now in the private sector, where he's very well respected on issues of public health.

Peter Rodino ran a pretty tight ship when it came to protecting the confidentiality of the taped conversations between Nixon and his staff. Only the parts that were considered relevant to impeachment were printed in the transcript. That meant the transcript was riddled with blacked-out conversations. In order to find out what was missing, members had to get permission from Rodino to go into the back room and hear the unedited tape. My curiosity being what it was, along with many other members, I frequently found myself checking out the scenes from the unraveling of the Nixon presidency.

In one particular scene I heard Nixon, clearly under the influence of alcohol, sharing with his staff a rumor that Supreme Court justice Thurgood Marshall was dying of cancer. Nixon told them that through his appointment power, his legacy would extend far beyond his eight years in office; he said he hoped that the "Negroes" would not expect him to replace Marshall with another black. He went on to say that Jewish people felt the same way about Supreme Court seats. But in Nixon's opinion, on this tape, having Secretary of State Henry Kissinger on hand was "enough Jewish for everybody."

The response from his staff was awkward but supportive. That put Nixon on a roll. He volunteered that the best candidates for appointment would be Democrats from the South, "because they think like we do, they vote like we do . . . and what the hell could the Democrats object to?" Finally, he started talking about Italian Americans. He seemed to have an odd sympathy for them as victims of discrimination. He said that some of them smelled bad, not because of poor hygiene but because of all the garlic they eat coming out of their pores. They didn't have the opportunity to go to the better schools, Nixon said. And, according to Nixon, you couldn't find an Italian American who wasn't somehow tied to organized crime.

Now, there happened to be a young Italian American Republican member on the committee from New Jersey. He was forever supporting everything Nixon did, and vigorously opposed the impeachment inquiry. I couldn't wait to usher him into the back room to listen to this tape. He thanked me very much. When he came back, I asked him what he thought.

"Sickening, absolutely disgusting," he said. Then he went right back out there defending Nixon! His name was Joseph Maraziti, and he only served that one term. He came from a solidly Republican district, but was trounced by the Democrat in 1974; most analysts said his rock-solid support for Nixon killed him.

Peter Rodino was so eager to be seen as fully American and not merely Italian American. He cried when he voted for the Articles of Impeachment, because he thought it was un-American to go against any president just because the evidence was there. That's the reason he deleted all that racist anti-Italian stuff Nixon was spewing. I said, "Pete, what were you thinking about keeping that stuff out?" He replied that it "was not relevant on the question of whether he violated the Constitution . . . just despicable, not related."

Barbara Jordan was one of the most articulate members I ever served with. She always sat in the same spot, though in the Congress there are no assigned seats. Not that it would have mattered: wherever she sat, the entire Texas Democratic delegation would surround her as though she were the queen bee. Many members who had guests visiting would ask her to leave the floor to greet and take pictures with their constituents. We never had an event—Fourth of July or Memorial Day— that Tip didn't ask Barbara to take the floor and express the patriotic sentiment of the House. She didn't spend too much time on the black-white issues; she rather resented being slotted in the black *or* female role. She believed in the Constitution and the individual rights it protects. For that reason she took that aspect of the investigation of Nixon's conduct a lot more seriously than I did. Nixon may not have known how Watergate started, but he certainly did know about and participate in the cover-up. As a former prosecutor, I was focused on what I saw as a clear path to his conviction. Barbara Jordan saw something larger, and we are all the better for her vision.

I suppose that Watergate gave me my first taste of truly national media exposure. It got me on television far more than I expected I would as a second-term congressman. I can't exactly recall how it felt at the time. But I do have an interesting perspective on it now.

In life, once you've known somebody, no matter how high they climb or what they attain, you just don't forget how you knew them "when." There was a guy who served in the 503rd Field Artillery unit with me. We were at Ft. Dix together and at Ft. Lewis. He was with me at Kunu-ri when the Chinese hit, and we survived the night on that mountain. He finally called me a few years ago for help with some problem. I said, "Blue, it's so good to hear from you—it's been over fifty years!" He agreed, and we told some war stories. Finally, I said, "Blue, how long have you known I was in the Congress?"

He said, "Oh, a long time, Rangel."

"Well, why haven't you been in touch with me?" I asked.

"Rangel," he started, "you were such a screw-up in the outfit; I just couldn't believe it was really you." I laughed and laughed, because I per-

fectly understood exactly how he felt. Each step of my accumulated no-
toriety has been as comfortable as the first, because I can never forget
how long a process of becoming it's been. To this day I don't spend a lot
of time worrying before doing interviews, or preparing written remarks.
I just do my homework and be myself.

Watergate and Nixon's fall are now very much part of history, with
many forests sacrificed for the record in books and the windy pro-
nouncements of politicians. Nevertheless, I'm still proud of the views I
put into the Congressional Record above and beyond the report of the
Judiciary Committee that voted the first of three articles against Nixon
on July 27, 1974. My witness, as history (published in the *Washington Post*
on August 26, 1974), has aged into the accepted facts of Nixon's fall that
journalists call truth. As prophecy, my remarks have an eerie ring at this
writing. Nearing the end of 2005, newspaper accounts of the Bush administration's encroachments on our civil liberties, democratic values,
and perhaps the Constitution itself seem to confront the Congress almost daily. Nixon's bad acts "threatened the system of law and justice"
much as the successful Republican plot to seal its hold on power by
stealing six Texas congressional seats, currently the subject of a criminal
trial there, threatens our system of democracy under law.

Nixon "substitut[ed] power for law, to define and attempt to im-
pose a standard of amorality upon our government that gives full rein to
the rich and powerful to prey upon the poor and weak." Today that
power runs "dark" prisons in paid-off countries, where loosely defined
"terrorists" can be tortured out of our moral and media sight, and beyond the letter (though not the spirit) of our law. Lobbyists for the rich
and powerful are having their way with the poor and weak victims of
Hurricane Katrina, preserving tax breaks for the wealthy while the
money for long-term relief and the rebuilding in New Orleans remains
stalled in the Congress. Some of these lobbyists' activities are also under
criminal investigation.

What Nixon did was "demean the importance of national security
by using it as a handy alibi to protect common burglars." What Bush did
was to exploit real fears for our national security after 9/11 to protect
and advance the agenda of the influential coterie of handlers who believe American military and economic domination is not a means to
prove our values worldwide, but an end in itself.

"We have reached a state in our national life where responsible
members of Congress argue that the president does not have to account
for his actions to anyone or recognize any higher authority." He doesn't
have to appear before audiences that are less than 100 percent supportive. He doesn't have to let the public see coffins of dead soldiers

coming home. He doesn't think he has to share review of decisions to spy on Americans suspected of terrorism (by the same agencies that dropped the ball before 9/11, condone torture, and reserve the right to abuse and then deport legal permanent resident aliens at will) with the judicial branch. And, when it comes to matters like Iraqi weapons of mass destruction and evidence of Iraq's complicity in 9/11, he doesn't have to level with Congress about what he knows, and how and when he knows it.

"Thus," I said in partial conclusion, "we stand on the brink of total subversion of our Constitutional government. . . ." I threw in something about the specter of dictatorship, too; thank God that hasn't happened—yet.

As I've said, I had my eye on the Ways and Means Committee from the first day I set foot in the Congress. A lot of people, including my CBC mentor Charlie Diggs, wanted me to aim for Adam Powell's footsteps and a seat on Education and Labor. But I had really had enough of trying to follow Adam. Wilbur Mills (D-Ark.) had been chairman since the Eisenhower administration. He was often called "the most powerful man in Washington," for his ironclad grip on the committee and his mastery of the tax code that it wrote. He would be brought low within four years, when police caught the very married Mills drunk in a car with an Argentine stripper. They had apparently been fighting, down by the Mall after midnight; contrary to the urban legend, it was she who tried to escape by jumping into the Tidal Basin, not Mills. But when I first got to Washington, I thought Wilbur Mills was a god walking among us mortals.

Mills had this froggy baritone croak that seemed to come out of some Arkansas swamp deep in his throat. It made my gravelly voice sound merely sandy. For months Mayor John Lindsay and Governor Nelson Rockefeller had been putting in good words for me with Mills for a shot at the committee. Whenever I would see him on the floor of the House it was always, "We-e-e-l-l-l, y-a-a-ah-ung man, you kno-o-o-w-w-w I've ga-ah-ah-t some ve-e-e-r-r-r-y go-o-o-o-d reports on yo-o-o-ou from our people in Alban-e-e-e. Ah-a-a-n-n-d, of cour-r-r-r-se, from ah-u-r-r-r people in City Hall."

Hell, I thought that's the way you were supposed to talk. So I'd come back with, "Tha-a-a-nk yo-o-o-o so-o-o-o much, Mister Chair-r-r-r-m-a-a-an." I didn't realize his speech had as much to do with the deep influence of alcohol as anything else. It taught me a lesson about just how well someone can function, in a powerful position, and still have this problem.

As it turned out, Wilbur Mills would have nothing to do with my getting on Ways and Means. Though he somehow politically survived the October 1974 Tidal Basin incident and was reelected, something possessed him to appear on stage with the stripper, who worked under the name Fanne Foxe, in a Boston burlesque house that December. Afterward, he checked himself into the Bethesda Naval Hospital for an apparently much-needed rest and rehabilitation. While he recovered, the Democrats reformed former titans like Mills out of power, and in the process cut me into the game.

It started over breakfast with Hugh Carey at the end of that crazy summer of 1974. Gerald Ford stepped into the White House following Nixon's resignation, and he nominated my friend Governor Rockefeller to be his vice president. That left Albany wide open for a short, sweet Carey campaign to replace him. I used to always joke about what a great governor he'd be, and he asked me at that breakfast to sign on to his campaign. Now, he also happened to have a seat on Ways and Means he wasn't going to be using anymore. Somewhere in that conversation I must have mentioned it, because it's consistent with what I would do today. Years later, Carey loved to tell the story about how I was one of the first on his gubernatorial bandwagon, but only after he agreed to back me for his seat on the committee. I guess I did shake him down, but I swear I don't remember doing it. I probably was awkward in bringing it up, and he just ran with how "of course" I'd be the best man for the job. However it went down, all I know is that with his eye on the governor's chair he had no reason to give me a hard time about it.

So, on the strength of Carey's informal recommendation as the incumbent in one of the committee's "New York seats," I had my chair on Ways and Means—for about five political minutes, that is. As soon as I had the delegation's informal backing, Otis Pike, who had represented Suffolk County on Long Island for fourteen years at that point, decided to leave his position on the Armed Services Committee at the last minute and challenge me. He was apologetic, but he was tired of waiting for a shot at the Armed Services chairmanship. With his seven terms of seniority to my two there was no contest—I was bumped. But Charlie Rangel had a friend in Tip O'Neill, and they created a seat for me. When you've got friends in high places—Tip was Majority Leader then—they just create another spot and you keep on keeping on.

My appointment, in December 1974, capped an incredible year for the House Democrats in general and for me as a black member in particular. The post-Watergate midterm election delivered a Democratic landslide—a 289 to 145 majority in the House—that, combined with major reforms in the seniority system and the rules, promised to break the hold of conservative Southern Democrats and moderate Republicans and clear the way for bringing truly progressive legislation to the floor. My seat on Ways and Means was one of twelve added to the committee, bringing it to thirty-seven from twenty-five members. Nine of the original twenty-five were conservative Southerners; ten of the twelve added seats went to moderate to liberal representatives like me. In January, Al Ullman (D-Wash.) would take over the chairmanship from the disgraced Wilbur Mills of Arkansas. After six years of Nixon's creeping conservatism, there was now talk of everything from raising taxes on the wealthy to ending tax breaks for Big Oil to national health insurance. All these things, if they flew at all, would fly through Ways and Means.

The year Nixon resigned was also a milestone for the CBC as a group, and a number of its members individually. Yvonne Braithwaite Burke, a beautiful, dynamic Los Angeles lawyer, became the second African American named to the powerful Appropriations Committee, where she joined Louis Stokes in pushing for a number of affirmative action measures that created unprecedented opportunities for black businesses in the seventies and eighties. (Years later, former Egyptian president Anwar Sadat, enthralled by her beauty, caused a number of CBC jaws to drop when he said Burke reminded him of his mother, except that his mother was darker in complexion.)

Andrew Young (D-Ga.), who was elected from Atlanta in 1972, became the first black named to the "exclusive" House Rules Committee. Taken together, our appointments to entry-level leadership positions in a newly Democratized Congress represented one rail of a new track being laid for African Americans in the pursuit of power in Washington. We were coming into position to leverage our individual clout for the benefit of our interests as a group. Where once we had only Adam Powell, a powerful committee chairman accountable to no one but himself, we now had a growing number of blacks simultaneously seeded in multiple leadership paths and voluntarily accountable to the CBC.

On the group track, I had succeeded Louis Stokes as CBC chairman in January 1974. Though I would be pinned down for much of the year by the Judiciary impeachment proceedings, I did raise our profile by calling for equal time for a "black response" to Nixon's State of the Union message that month. Addressing rising unemployment and the disparate inflationary impacts on black communities from the 1973 oil shock was high on my agenda. I also took the opportunity to be very deliberate about publicly positioning the caucus as a player within a larger legislative body, and not a civil rights group. I told the *New York Times* we would become more tightly focused on being effective legislators "rather than trying to be Jesus Christ to blacks."

The payoff, I believe, from our two-track approach was reflected from the start of the Ford administration, in August 1974. Remember, it took Nixon thirteen months to grant Charlie Diggs's initial request for a meeting when the caucus began in 1971, and in the end he dismissed almost all of the recommendations we made. Since that time, three caucus members, including me, had sat in judgment of Nixon on the Judiciary Committee, and in that national spotlight helped carry the ball for his impeachment. We'd also voted on whether to confirm Ford's elevation to vice president after Spiro Agnew was forced to resign; all three of us had said no. In October we would clearly be playing an important role in Rockefeller's confirmation as Ford's vice president. So I was greatly pleased, but not entirely shocked, when, just days after taking office, President Ford called me, as CBC chairman, to ask for a meeting to discuss our concerns.

Two weeks later, we walked out of the White House meeting smiling and assured of one thing: the CBC was now recognized as a leadership constituency at both ends of Pennsylvania Avenue.

Internally, the Black Caucus is a very, very competitive organization. Its members are more strong-willed than most, because they come from districts that are noncompetitive in terms of national elections. It was true even in the seventies, and it's even truer today, when no more than about three seats are truly contested. It's hard to say if that's good or bad. Secure black seats accrue valuable seniority no matter the fortunes of the national Democrats or Republicans. We turn over much more slowly than the rest of the Democrats, increasing our relative power even in good times for the party, and especially in bad times, like the late seventies and eighties when we lost the white South. On seniority alone, had the Democrats retained control of the House in 1994, we would have had four full committee chairmanships—Armed Services, Judiciary, Ways and Means, and Education and Labor—and eighteen subcommittee chairmanships to the CBC's credit. It would have meant power that far exceeded the black share of the U.S. population. Though they deny it, the Republicans quietly made our potential ascension, complete with our pictures, the poster child for what would happen if whites voted for Democrats that year. It's not the only reason, but it's no coincidence that the Democrats haven't had a House majority since. We've slipped a bit since then, mostly due to retirements. Age has been a factor in some cases, but the prospect of trying to legislate in the minority indefinitely has played a larger role. Still, with the Democratic majority elected in November 2006, African American representatives are in line to chair three to four full committees—including Judiciary, Homeland Security, and Ways and Means—and sixteen to twenty subcommittees.

Viewing the Black Caucus's position is like peering through the looking glass at the postwar history of the Democratic Party in the South. When I got to Congress, the Democratic majority in the House was dominated by racist white Southerners who never turned over, because Republicans hadn't been competitive for a hundred years and blacks couldn't vote. When the national Democrats finally broke with the segregationists and their immediate heirs, white Southerners from the Old Confederacy (not to be confused with certain Southwestern populists) saw that their future would have to be connected to blacks, and it was just too awkward, politically, for them to adjust. The Southerners began to retire or switch parties in droves. These retirements, which got an extra push from sweetened pension benefits in the seventies, accelerated my swift rise in seniority on Ways and Means.

The Voting Rights Act also enhanced the trend, by encouraging states to concentrate black voters in newly drawn minority "super majority" districts that were well over 65 percent black. The net effect was good for the CBC and good for the emerging Southern Republicans, but bad for the Democratic Party as a whole. The creation of black seats, especially in the South, dramatically increased the number of African Americans in the Congress, but at the cost of a net loss of Democratic seats in the Congress. I don't think it went unnoticed by the national Democratic leadership that as our numbers increased, Democratic seats decreased. Everybody knew that black politicians often fought for those seats in an alliance of convenience with state and local Republicans. It's hard not to blame the trend for the loss of our majority.

I truly believe that a genuinely competitive Republican Party—that is, one that sincerely competed for black votes—would allow African Americans to achieve a lot more politically, and therefore economically. It would cause the Democrats to be far more responsive to the political needs of a group that has already gained leadership in the Democratic Party, and it would cause the Republicans to quickly become quite dependent on a constituency it now ignores.

As things now stand, however, it's very, very hard for me to see how the Republicans could ever be sensitive to the needs of a group that consistently, and overwhelmingly, votes against them. Groups that are much smaller than African Americans manage to attract the competitive attention of both parties. You see it in competitive seats in California all the time today—Republicans making big concessions on liberal positions to woo just enough Jewish or Hispanic voters to gain the margin of victory. Those concessions could and should be coming to African American communities, too. But it's no secret why today's Republican machinery makes a much greater effort to get Jewish, Hispanic, and other minority votes than black votes. The reason is rooted in a kind of racist algebra; by their calculation of risk, they have too much to lose by association with a perceived black political monolith.

I'm proud to say that the CBC remains a vital force for black America in the Congress. But we must remain no less aware of its limitations than I was in 1974. We have to accept the fact that the black members of Congress do not generally speak with one voice. It's not that we don't get along, or can't get our acts together. We simply cannot speak as one because, most of the time, our primary responsibility is to speak for ourselves, and even better, to speak for larger coalitions in the Congress, especially the party leadership.

The CBC has to be very selective about the formal group positions it takes. We tend to limit ourselves to stances that each member is ready and willing to defend when an interviewer or political opponent throws it in his or her face. There will always be issues that require us to take a joint stand, but they seem to be fewer and farther between, and riskier. Granted, it's a gamble that we sometimes have to take. If we want to organize to be powerful in our stands, we also have to accept the fact that when we do, some people will say, "I didn't vote for him," or "They don't speak for me." Increasingly, however, we don't see the need to roll those dice. Take the Iraq war, for example. Quiet as it's been kept, four CBC members voted to give President Bush the authority to wage preemptive war, despite the overwhelming opposition to the war by African Americans as a whole. The point is that there is no official caucus position on Iraq. But when people see our overwhelming individual opposition to the war, they just assume we got together and took a vote.

Today we may very well be at that long run point of diminishing returns to ethnic block politics, at least in Congress. Our districts are increasingly pressed by the faster-growing Hispanic populations, and we will continue to lose our old, noncompetitive seats to Latino challengers. If the Republicans continue to refuse to compete for African American votes, then African American political leaders will have to learn anew how to compete for power within the Democratic Party, without aiding and abetting the current Republican electoral majority, until such time as the Republicans may be forced to come around. And believe me, the more we learn to look, feel, and act politically like other ethnic groups, the more the old Republican calculation of net loss will shift to net gain. And they will come around.

To rework the classic political wisdom, African Americans must make permanent friends of those who support and can advance our permanent interests in social justice and equality of economic opportunity. Some of those new friends will be white Southerners who were not born when Nixon launched his Southern Strategy, and several of them will be Latinos.

Some of our friends will even be Republicans. In 1974 I ran with their unanimous endorsement in New York County for the second term in a row. In 1974 I gave Nixon hell, was courted and consulted by President Ford, and helped my Republican friend Nelson Rockefeller get as close as he ever would to his dream of being in the White House.

I still had both feet on the up escalator to the top of the Democratic leadership.

And I haven't had a bad day since.

8

Into the Leadership

I have a beautiful story about a guy named Max Rabb. As chairman of the Select Committee on Narcotics in the eighties, with a special interest in international efforts against the drug trade, I led a number of congressional delegations to Rome. Max Rabb was the U.S. ambassador to Italy, and boy did he and his wife, Ruth, treat me and the delegation like royalty. Max and I really hit it off. What a combination, a kid from Lenox Avenue and a distinguished diplomat who was an ambassador's ambassador if I ever met one.

Even after he returned to the States in 1989, with our political relationship past, he kept in special touch with me. When my friend Frank Guarini left the Congress in 1993, he headed up an Italian American foundation whose top members would meet once every two months or so for dinner. His friends became my friends, and I'd meet with them, too. The group included Bill Fugazy and, though it was basically an Italian American group, George Steinbrenner . . . and Max Rabb. At first I assumed he was Italian—after all, he'd been our man in Rome for eight years—but I later learned that he was Jewish. He and Ruth were part of the gang, and his fond support of me didn't miss a beat from the Roman embassy days. He was a partner in a big-time New York law firm and sat on a number of boards. He was always so very excited about the least little legislative success I might have had. No evening would end without him touching on me and my future, with a twinkle in his eye. He was always planning things he wanted to be doing with me. Sometimes he'd just stare at me, as if seeing into another time or place, and say, "You shouldn't just be in the Congress . . . let me tell you about what I could do for your career." And all the while I still just thought he was a very kind former ambassador.

Then one day I picked up *King of the Cats*, the Adam Powell biography by Wil Haygood. As I read about Adam's impact during the Eisenhower years, the name Rabb kept leaping off the pages at me. Not my beloved Max Rabb, but Maxwell Rabb, of Brookline, Massachusetts. It told how he became a special assistant to President Eisenhower, with the special assignment to take care of the political needs of my predecessor, Adam Clayton Powell. Eisenhower was always looking for a way to repay his political debt for Adam's audacious support of the Republican incumbent in 1956. But Ike didn't want to be connected to Adam politically in any way—no pictures, no nothing. Maxwell Rabb would stand in the gap as Eisenhower's back-door liaison to Adam Powell. Together they began the desegregation of Washington, D.C., and veterans hospitals around the country, and a number of other measures in relief of discrimination that Adam never got credit for. The relationship allowed Adam to go to Africa, representing not just black America but the United States of America. And all of this without the connection getting much publicity, because Eisenhower didn't need it.

I told this story in the synagogue at Max's funeral in 2002. Even as I was saying it, I could not believe that you could find someone so selfless as to be completely satisfied, maybe even fascinated, to identify vicariously with my career and aspirations, and never, never, never say how important he was, or how instrumental, in making those dramatic national changes through my predecessor. I remain in awe at the humility that prohibited him from ever saying, "Hey, I knew the guy you succeeded," when it would have been so natural and politically expedient to do so. He could have been patronizing, but he wasn't. He could have never let me forget the great things he had done for my district, my people, and my country, but he didn't. And when I finally confronted him with my revelation, he was almost embarrassed.

"I had a job to do," he said. "And I'd love to do a job for you!" he added.

That was Max Rabb. Unbelievable! All Max ever did was to praise me in ways that almost felt awkward, ways that took me back to my grade school teacher Nettie Messenger and everyone else who ever believed in me before I believed in myself. And all because he saw in me the continuity of my community being served. When I think about his faith, it puts all my ambitions into context. My story cannot be just about a big-shot congresssman on the fast track to fame and fortune; my story must be part of a larger, slower procession toward justice for a people. And that procession, my Max Rabb story reminds me, is about individuals, human and flawed yet, at their best, bound by ties of friendship and interest in the common good.

On the average, of course, it was politics as usual as I made my way into the national Democratic leadership in the eighties and assumed a position near the center of influence in New York City politics. I realize that I may be in danger of wearing out the word *friendship* in talking about political relationships. I hear myself calling people "buddy" over the phone, or saying "Yes, my friend," all the time. There's no question that the word has been abused. When I talked about being friends with Henry Kissinger earlier, I used the term as loosely as can be. Kissinger and I are, in fact, very, very friendly when we meet. I would say the same of Senator Orrin Hatch (R-Utah). We are friends by the standard that I know that if people were talking about me in their company, they would have my back. They would say, "I don't agree with everything he says, but Rangel is a decent guy." I know it because people have come up to me and said, "How is it that you have such a great supporter in Henry Kissinger?"

Then, too, by any standard, no one can say that Percy Sutton is not my dear friend, though we've never had dinner together, or been to a bar together. In fact, I can't remember ever being at his house. Yet after my own brother, I've never had a better friend. Same thing, pretty much, with David Dinkins. In New York, I'll admit, such friendships tend to be rare, if not precluded, in a world based on the two-year election cycle for the State Assembly and the Congress. Yet Harlem has been so very different from the other boroughs, and even the rest of Manhattan. The Sutton-Patterson-Dinkins-Rangel kind of political friendships are hard to find in Brooklyn. In Brooklyn, such friendships never last more than two years. All politicians see their job as situating themselves for candidacy two years hence. Therefore, all friendships come with only a two-year warranty. When she was in office, the late Shirley Chisholm had new enemies and new friends every week. And the amazing thing was they were *the exact same people* as the week before, just recycled! As I survey the political battlegrounds, in Brooklyn I see the political machinery being torn apart by every ethnic group in the borough. As I write, the so-called Chisholm seat, held by Major Owens for more than twenty years, could be inherited by a young white city councilman because the black leadership is so divided. In the Bronx there is such a tradition of family dynasties and succession that someone told me that's where the expression "Leave no child behind" comes from. But Harlem has had a tradition of political families that goes beyond blood.

Harlem's political stability is not just a function of a stable population. A lot of it has to do with whom we have in public office. Assemblyman Keith Wright has a strong community base that no one challenges. City Councilman Bill Perkins was challenged in 2003, but it wasn't serious, just a testing process that we understand as appropriate to our democracy. No one will be challenging State Senator David Patterson, the Senate Minority Leader, anytime soon; the consensus in our community on his value is just too strong. Now that he has been tapped as the candidate for lieutenant governor, running with New York Attorney General Eliot Spitzer, we have the opportunity to effect yet another orderly succession for his Senate seat, in the Harlem tradition. We have a political team here that works together. We understand that when elected officials spend most of two years protecting their backs—or trying to—constituents are not served. We do our homework, and we don't use our resources to fight one another. I'm proud of my place near the center of this consensus.

We'd like to think that Harlem-style political amity can be extended to contests beyond our borders, but that hasn't always been the case. In 1977, everyone was telling my dear friend Percy Sutton, who was then borough president, to run for mayor, succeeding the incumbent, Abe Beame. Years earlier, when Beame was the comptroller with his eye on Gracie Mansion, he and Percy agreed that if elected, Beame would only serve one term, clearing the 1977 field. Beame's mayoralty was shaky from the start. I told Percy that he was sitting in the catbird seat, but who knew where people would be in four years? We decided to go and visit all his supporters, just to see how strong they were. Though I was in Washington, I spent a lot of time going door to door, from supporter to supporter, with Percy, giving it all that I could.

At the end of the tour we thought we had it in the bag. Then, for whatever reason, Beame broke faith and decided he would run for mayor again, and Percy's support just crumbled. Percy ran anyway, with me as campaign manager. It was an exciting campaign, a great campaign—but we lost. However, because we were Harlem, we were still very much in the game. The close primary resulted in a runoff between Ed Koch and Mario Cuomo. I had served with Koch in the Congress, and he asked me to secure the backing of the Coalition of Black Elected Democrats, which includes all black Democratic elected and party officials.

The group designated Percy and me to go and meet with Cuomo and Koch, and then make a report as to whom it should endorse. When we met with Cuomo, he took great pains to explain that he was color blind, and therefore could not promise a certain number of positions for blacks in a Cuomo administration. He said that he himself wasn't even Italian; he was just an American. The very idea that blacks would need particular political support was racist, Cuomo told us. Percy just looked at me, stunned. Years later, when Cuomo was governor, he still couldn't explain his performance that day. He would joke that the interview was really an apolitical discussion. Meanwhile, Percy was silently begging for candidate Cuomo to say something, anything, to justify his not having to support Ed Koch, with whom he'd had a lot of difficulties during the primary campaign.

"This is bad," he said. I looked at him, and we left.

When we went to see Koch, all he wanted to know was, "What do you want?" "Sure, we're gonna have a black deputy mayor," Koch promised. "What do you need? How are we gonna work this out?" he asked. But Percy had had a very bad experience in the campaign and in the debates with Koch, so he was very reluctant to endorse him. Then we learned that a handful of blacks—from the Bronx, I think— were standing on the steps of City Hall endorsing Mario Cuomo for mayor. The fact that Cuomo knew, as did Koch, that we were still in the process of getting a black leadership consensus on the mayoralty, yet still would allow this to happen, led Percy to say, "I'm off Cuomo, just make one report." The black Democrats all came out for Koch, and he won.

Now, there are some who say this is a fine example of black bossism in politics, where the black powers that be all get together and "deliver" the black community's support to one white man or another. I've never heard anyone in the black community call it bossism. All I've heard it called is black political leadership. It was black officeholders—not our staffs or the people who were not elected—deciding who we were supporting for mayor, as we were elected to do. We are the ones our community had voted for. What could be more democratic and less bossism than that? I would have to ask those critics to answer this question: Why did they vote for us in the first place? The answer: To vote on things they couldn't vote for. To be their eyes and ears so that if they couldn't get to the president or governor or mayor, as most of them can't, they could certainly get to us. That's why Percy founded the Black and Puerto Rican Caucus when he first went to Albany, which was the template for the Council of Black Elected Democrats. Critics should recognize that these are legitimate, small "d" democratic organizations, not platforms for demagogues. If, as in this case, *the community* is seeking a consensus as to which of two white people, the Jewish guy or the Italian guy, would be best, they will look to the people who know these guys, the people they elected.

The process isn't perfect, but, at the end of the day, it is our elected leadership organizations that will be held accountable. Take our endorsement of Ed Koch—please! His feuds with the black community began not six months after he took office. The newspaper clippings over the Koch years show dozens of headlines resulting from some Koch confrontation with the black community, followed by a Koch peace initiative, and then an uneasy truce . . . until the next confrontation. Through it all, I tried my best to do my job—to represent the concerns of my community while accepting responsibility for making the Koch relationship work—but it was tough. I remember standing up with Koch at a 1979 community "constituent hour" meeting in Harlem where Koch, in peacemaker mode, was actually shouted down. Later that year, things were so bad that a number of black leaders and some elected officials were spearheading a petition drive to place a mayoral recall provision in the city charter. Ed Koch and I had many private and public disputes during his terms in office. The recall movement did actually get going, only to fail when it was determined that a majority of the signatures were not valid. The net effect was to spur Koch to become even more forceful in asserting himself, as if to prove, in his words, that he would never be anybody's "punching bag."

Of course, all this took place as Koch was forging his reputation as the feisty mayor who led New York out of the darkest days of the fiscal crisis and began to restore its reputation as the preeminent, indispensable American city. But the truth is that it would be some years before many black New Yorkers would see any kind of renaissance that they could believe in. Working with Governors Carey and Cuomo and with me in the Congress, Koch oversaw programs that, in the long run, sparked massive rebuilding and restoration in the South Bronx, Harlem, and a number of Brooklyn neighborhoods that had suffered the most in the seventies decline. But in the short run, it was the Koch administration that decorated the bricked-up openings of abandoned buildings with painted-on curtains and window frames. And, long run or short, his personal style of confront first, kiss and make up later, was tailor-made for antagonizing the black community.

Koch was basically a conservative, who has since proven my long-held feeling that his values would be more comfortable in a Rudolph Giuliani Republican Party. He was also totally insensitive to the yearning of black New Yorkers for respect, and their rising aspirations for empowerment and control of their own communities. He took calls for "diversity," the code word for black opportunity that was coming into vogue in the eighties, as a direct challenge to his authority. He refused to accept my advocacy for a larger black slice of the pie. He refused to want to look like anything except smarter than, stronger than, more powerful than blacks. Blacks, in turn, were not supposed to challenge his benevolence. Yet for all this, the battles with Koch were never really personal. They were a modern form of ethnic political theater that, however regrettable, I understood. Even today, Koch can still get a laugh out of me by joking that "you know, you never did support me, you were just against Cuomo."

I wish I could say the same for Mario Cuomo, who, ironically, I backed for governor in 1982 over Koch because Koch was so toxic in the black community at that point. Let me be clear: By the time his three terms as governor were done, Cuomo had been very, very good to me, as far as my effort to establish the Harlem Trade Center. And when my Empowerment Zone legislation was finally signed in 1983, I was able to convince Governor Cuomo and Mayor Dinkins to put up $100 million as part of the incentive package, sealing New York's participation, and the launch of the Upper Manhattan Empowerment Zone, the catalyst for the second "Harlem Renaissance" that's still transforming my community with new investment, a new middle class, and new hope for our future.

But I still don't get the meaning of Mario Cuomo and his remarkable, dead-end career. A few years ago he wrote a book in which he dispensed wisdom and advice about the error of the Democrats' ways, having lost the Congress and the White House in four out of six elections since 1980. I was surprised to see it taken seriously—most people seek wisdom and advice from people who have won, not those who have lost, as Cuomo lost the governorship of New York in 1994. About that time, Mario Cuomo's son Andrew, who had run the Department of Housing and Urban Development in the Clinton administration and had well-known ambitions for office in New York, paid me a visit. While his father's book was on my mind, I shared the following story with him.

When Hugh Carey became governor, though I was in Washington, I was an unofficial member of his inside cabinet, a part of the inner circle. When his lieutenant governor, Mary Ann Krupsack, decided she would bolt and challenge Carey for governor after his first term, they had a middle-of-the-night meeting, and damn if they didn't replace her on the ticket with Mario Cuomo. I raised hell with them. In my opinion, Mario Cuomo had done nothing to merit getting on the very short line to the governor's chair. What had he done? He arbitrated a nasty dispute between residents of Forest Hills and advocates seeking to build public housing there.

Meanwhile, we in the African American community believed State

Senator Basil Patterson deserved consideration. The whole idea that Cuomo was slam-dunked for the governor's chair while Patterson was overlooked didn't sit well with us. Twenty-four years later, Andrew Cuomo didn't do much to redeem his dad when he challenged our Carl McCall in the 2002 primary.

Percy Sutton never forgot how Mario Cuomo left him hanging in the mayoral race. Nevertheless, it didn't stop him from moving on. Percy bought a failing AM radio station, WLIB, and was forced to take on its FM twin as part of the package deal. The AM station had a weak signal near the end of the dial, but its mostly R&B music programming had long been a fixture among black New Yorkers who could pick it up. At a time when FM radio had just established itself as the premiere platform for music, especially rock, in clear stereo, there was no black-oriented, much less black-owned, presence on the frequency-modulated dial. Percy rebranded it as WBLS-FM, and within a short time it became one of the most listened-to stations in the nation, with a young following that went far beyond the black audience while retaining a uniquely black identity.

From that success, Percy started buying stations all over the country, building Inner City Broadcasting into a diversified media company with eighteen stations in seven cities. He bought the Apollo Theatre, dark and bankrupt, in 1981, and it almost became his life. He went all over the world for the marble, the crystal chandeliers, the carpeting. I helped get it federal, state, and city landmark status, and when it still didn't work out as a for-profit venture, I was able to get grants and other public funding for it as a nonprofit foundation, keeping it alive today.

So my partnership with Percy is in its fifth decade. We remain different at our cores. Percy's father was a school principal, and his mother was a teacher. I never really knew my dad. When Percy and I met in the 1960s, scuffling on Lenox Avenue and fighting in Korea were all I really knew. Percy's about ten years older than me, and a world apart in sophistication and certain skills. He learned to fly planes in Texas, where he grew up, and was a part of the famous Tuskeegee Airmen during World War II. To me, just leaving Texas—or Mississippi or Georgia or the West Indies—to seek your fortune far away denotes a person who is willing to take risks. That's just not me. I fought against the misery and pain of poverty most of my young life, but I could only do it from right here in New York. There's hardly a day that goes by that I don't say that if the doctor told me tomorrow that I had to leave New York City for my health, my only question would be, "How much time in New York do I have left?" Unlike Sutton, I've never wanted to be anywhere else for more than three days. Nor do I see any kind of destiny taking me away. But then again, I didn't see Washington claiming the better part of my adult life, either.

My rise into the Democratic leadership, in Congress and nationally, was a direct result of an extraordinary relationship with Thomas P. "Tip" O'Neill of Massachusetts, who was Speaker of the House from 1977 through 1986. There is no other way to say it. It began with my election to chairman of the Congressional Black Caucus in 1974, when it became my mission to get more African Americans slotted on key committees. That meant introducing them to Tip, who was then Majority Leader, and persuading him that it was in the best interest of the Democrats, the Congress, and the country to have these people placed on important working and leadership committees. My initial push coincided with the major reforms of the seniority system in December 1974 that generally increased the influence of liberal Democrats. That's when Yvonne Braithwaite Burke joined Lou Stokes on the Appropriations Committee, and Andrew Young became the first African American on the Rules Committee.

On many occasions, when I was trying to make the case for opening doors to minorities, having been denied opportunities to serve in key positions in the past, Tip was not only sympathetic, he empathized and repeatedly shared his experience of how the Irish had been treated in Boston when he was coming up. He always had a story about the scorn and ridicule they had suffered, to underscore the sincerity of his willingness to work with us. I can't recall any black members challenging the idea that Tip was one of the most compassionate members of Congress, much less Speakers, that we'd ever served with. A lot of Tip O'Neill was explained by the fact that he never had any money, nor did he aspire to it. He just really loved people. In every story, no matter how complicated the issue, whether he was fighting against the Vietnam War or to expand health care, he'd always talk about some kid or some old person in Boston, and make the virtue of compassion the bottom line of the story.

He never, ever took a congressional trip without inviting me. For at least twelve years, usually around Easter, we were off somewhere abroad—Egypt, Russia, Israel and Greece, Africa twice, and a few times to Ireland. And like any other group experience you have abroad, when you come home you talk about it, you share memories, and it forms a special bond between you. Tip and I were both Catholics, like a number of the other members of our regular traveling group, which included Rostenkowski and his friend Marty Russo from Chicago, Silvio Conte, a liberal Massachusetts Republican, and my late friend Jim Scheuer, who was Jewish. Because it was Easter, we always found a way to wrangle the services of a Catholic priest to say mass on Sunday morning, no matter how much we'd partied the night before.

When it comes to travel, there's economy class, there's business class, there's first class, there's luxury class, and then there's traveling with the Speaker. Remember, he's third in the line of succession to the presidency. We were welcomed at castles and palaces and mansions in capitals around the world, at the invitation of the legislative leaders or the monarchs of all these nations. Corporations tripped all over themselves to throw lavish receptions for us everywhere we went. But Tip O'Neill was just as comfortable watching a baseball game with most of our same group in the basement of my house on Colorado Avenue. He was the same guy at a castle in Spain, or just sitting around on the House floor and telling stories from his big political heart in the pauses between his duties as Speaker.

He was the same regular guy to the end. Tip had a modest home in Boston with his lovely wife, Millie, and shared a Washington apartment with his friend Edward Boland, another Massachusetts Democrat, for over twenty-five years. A few years before he retired from Congress, however, he bought a $1 million condominium and sent for Millie to enjoy it with him.

"Tip," I said, "how the hell can you afford to buy that? You haven't got a pot to piss in!"

"Charlie," he said, "I thought you'd understand, being on Ways and Means."

"Understand what?" I said.

"Damn it, I don't own anything. All I did was sign my name. I'm seventy-three years old. I got my little house in Boston. I'm not thinking about having any equity in this—the only thing I'm paying is the interest and writing it off; they can keep the damn condo!"

His funeral, at the age of eighty-one, was just as consistent, simple, and beautiful. He went off in a little neighborhood parlor that was freezing cold, with people all out in the street afterward, making their way to services in a plain little Boston church. That's the way he wanted it.

Tip was a guy who came up the hard way and always remembered it. He always wanted to help somebody who went through the rough days like he did, and there's no question that I was one of them. Although Tip was from Boston and I was from Harlem, we really came from the same place. We came from a world where ethnic urban pols come up poor and climb the ladder of opportunity through public service, doing what they have to do to care for their families, and their neighbors' families, going along to get along and waiting their turn for the power to advance their community's interests. Except that, in the Congress, I didn't really have to get into line and wait my turn; Tip kind of pushed me to the front of the line. And even if he didn't, most people thought he did, and treated me better for it.

Tip was my big brother throughout his speakership. Even after his retirement I still felt his presence. Dan Rostenkowski was really a two-fisted, John Wayne type of chairman, but he never really intimidated me, because even when I didn't see Tip physically, I always felt as though he had my back. Rosty was also a big-city ethnic pol, as was his father. But somehow his story diverges from mine and Tip's after that.

Rosty's father was a big-time Chicago alderman who had changed his name from Rostenkowski to Rosen, until they told him that he was only being selected because he was born Rostenkowski. Rosty was known as a workhorse with a fierce loyalty to the party and the process. His upbringing in the Daley political machine was not entirely unlike my mentorship by J. Raymond Jones in that sense. That made us fit as allies and combatants, too; either way, we knew the rules. When we got into our running battles, I was steeled by my respect for the House and its traditions. I knew the importance of getting along, and what you had to do to get along. But I was black, and I was from Harlem, and I had succeeded Adam Clayton Powell. There was no way in hell for me to say I wasn't going to be included in a legislative conference unless I met some Rostenkowski precondition about my vote. If the boys on Lenox Avenue thought that I could be excluded from an important meeting like a conference just because I didn't give my vote up in advance, I wouldn't be able to come back home!

Rosty kept insisting that I couldn't be a Ways and Means tax writer and climb in the leadership, too. In 1979 I was elected chairman of the Health Subcommittee, which controlled President Jimmy Carter's initiatives to curb hospital costs and establish a national health insurance program. The same year I was also appointed to the Democratic Steering and Policy Committee, which nominated committee chairmen and set the majority legislative priorities.

"You can't do both," he'd say.

"I can do both, Danny, I am doing both," I'd come back at him.

"You've got to be focused on which track you want to go," he'd insist. "And I'm telling you, you could be chairman of this damn committee."

As if to prove his point, and cement my loyalty, shortly after he became Ways and Means chairman in 1980, he made me chairman of the Oversight Subcommittee. It was the only subcommittee that could pass bills to the floor without having the whole committee's approval. He gave it to me knowing that if he had bills he didn't want the whole committee to look at, he could count on me to get them out for him. He also gave me legislation on low-income housing and other measures for the poor, including tax credits for job creation. Over the years that put my name on bills that preserved the deductibility of state and local taxes—critically important in high-tax states like Illinois and New York—and measures that sought to hold the line against the Reagan administration's cuts in programs like Social Security, Medicare, Medicaid, and welfare (AFDC). All of these bills aimed to help Chicago, as well as all other big urban areas like New York, freeing Rosty to be the big shot on international trade and such, and to deal with the CEOs at the time in our economic history when the term *global economy* was coming into vogue.

But in 1993, when the cloud of the House Post Office scandal got Rosty into a tough primary fight, he jokingly told me, "If you're ever being challenged in a primary, don't spend a whole lot of money on your literature."

"What the hell are you talking about?" I asked.

"Remember all those 'Rangel bills' you had and were thanking me for?" he asked. "Well, they're Rostenkowski bills now," he said.

When Tip O'Neill made me a Deputy Whip in 1983, it probably sealed Rosty's worst suspicions about where my loyalties lay. Indeed, with my position on Ways and Means secure, it was only natural for me to run for Whip in 1986, as the first big step toward one day becoming Speaker myself. Why did I think I could become the Whip? Why not? When I was blocked at the last minute by Otis Pike for my Ways and Means seat, Tip just created one for me, right? I thought I was bad, in the old Sergeant Rangel, self-promotional sense; the written rules needn't always apply to me. It was pretty clear that the next Speaker, succeeding the retiring Tip, would be Jim Wright of Texas. Tom Foley of Washington was in line to move up to Majority Leader from Whip. That meant the next Whip should have to come from the Northeast, or a major part of the Democratic constituency would be left out of the leadership tripod: Speaker, Majority Leader, and Whip.

In my mind, it was all lined up. When I would go to the New York delegation, the second largest in the Congress, it would be nothing more than a wink and a blink. In the Black Caucus, up to twenty-one votes strong in 1986, well, how could they vote for anybody but me? Same thing with the small but growing number of Hispanic members. We're all in this together. Everywhere I went, I thought, who was gonna tell me no?

So I had no idea, as I well understand now, that the race was not about my arrogant calculus. It was not to the swift. It was about . . . *the money.* I had no idea of the allegiance people attached to those who gave them money—in this case former congressman Tony Coelho of California. No idea! When I talked with people, they would gush about what a great Whip I would be. Then, when they said in the next breath that they were supporting Coelho, because he had helped them in their campaign, I couldn't believe their candor—at first. But I understand it now. Coelho was chairman of the Democratic Congressional Campaign Committee. Not only was he raising millions for the Democratic candidates for congress, he was also deciding which members received funding.

Today money isn't just the mother's milk of politics; it *is* their politics. But I had never needed money to hold my seat, so the whole idea of me making a commitment to someone because he or she gave me money was beyond me. Even black members, from our traditionally safest seats, are not immune. Once, during a key Medicare vote, as I begged Democrats, black and white, Jew and gentile, to stick with the party because the Republicans could not win without Democratic defections, I had black Democrats tell me that white doctors supported them in primaries when blacks didn't. They told me that they had to support this hospital or that one in this fight, even though it was out of line with the common good, because it supported them when the party didn't.

One day in the heat of the campaign, one of the members from the Southwest came to me and told me what a wonderful Whip I would make. He praised my ability to work with all the various regions and factions in the Congress. When I thanked him for his support, he made it clear that he wasn't supporting me, he was supporting Coelho. I asked him how he could possibly be supporting him after all the nice things he had just said about me. He said Coelho had been very helpful to him financially during his campaign. "You mean, he gave you money?" I asked. "And that's why you're supporting him?"

"Look, Charlie," he said. "You're my friend. If you want to make me out a whore, you can. But I'm telling you: I'm supporting Coelho." No one had ever said it that plainly to me before, but I understand it now.

It's obscene what money has done to the Congress. Just look at the number of millionaires in the Senate these days. The percentage has increased so much in the last twenty years that I think it's safe to say that you have to be one to be a senator. The Senate was always a rich man's club, but look at the rising number of millionaires in the House, and the mounting cost of the average congressional campaign. In 2004, Martin Frost of Texas told me it was going to cost him $3 million in his race. Three million dollars! He came close, raising $2.8 million. But he was beaten by Republican Pete Sessions, who almost matched Frost, *a twelve-term incumbent,* by raising $2.5 million. Of course, the now infamous Republican gerrymander that targeted a half-dozen Democratic seats in Texas didn't help Frost either. But that, as the indictments against Tom DeLay for his role in financing those races prove, was about money, too!

I never really employed a fund-raising person before I became the senior Democrat on Ways and Means, because I never had a serious challenge to my seat. But being on Ways and Means this long has given me a special responsibility to assist other members in raising money for their campaigns. That responsibility not only takes me all over the country, all the time, but causes me to have up to four big-money birthday parties every year, depending on which restaurant is available. So I was terribly disappointed by how Coelho's money raising caused me to finish a distant second in the Whip race. But if I had problems with Coelho's fund-raising in 1986, I certainly don't have a problem vigorously fund-raising for the Democrats running in 2006.

In 2004, rumor had it that Adam Clayton Powell IV, the son who was born in Puerto Rico, was actually going to challenge me that year. I didn't think it made any sense. He doesn't like to work that hard, and he's already had a couple of jobs, having been in the City Council before winning his current seat in the State Assembly. I wasn't vulnerable; I'd never felt more secure in my office. It didn't make any sense, yet people he'd discussed it with kept coming to me. One of them even said Powell promised to support him for the Assembly seat he'd be giving up, in return for his support against me. Knowing what I know about giving up an Assembly seat to run for Congress, I was convinced that

Adam IV didn't have the nerve to risk his seat to challenge me. When he heard that, he let it get back to me that even if he didn't win, he had enough money to hang out, and maybe run for the City Council again in 2005, and whenever I decided to quit, it would be his seat.

It would make sense, if he were merely talking up his ambitions to be a congressman. But this whole business of talking about giving up his seat, raising money, asking people to give him money so he could run, and then not run and use it to go for the City Council instead, it's just not right. Lo and behold, I got an invitation to a fund-raiser for Adam's "exploratory committee," an appeal Adam made because one day he wants to be the congressman. Checks payable to "Powell for Congress." He ended up raising about $69,000. My fund-raising people were elated—the threat, however less than credible, gave them an excuse to go out and raise about $2 million! And you know what? Powell never did run that year.

I was giving a speech in Georgia that was all about rural poverty when I was summoned to visit with the governor. I got my first impression of Jimmy Carter from the big stretch limousine he sent for me; it embarrassed me no end, given the subject of my speech. It turned out he had some kind of relationship with a rock band; they volunteered to come and take me to the mansion.

As Carter's dark horse candidacy overtook and then lapped the Democratic field from the far outside in 1976, his indispensable black supporter was Congressman Andrew Young, my colleague in the Congressional Black Caucus, whose Atlanta district actually had a white majority. Young represented Carter to black America as the model of a "New South" white politician: a fusion of traditional Southern conservative and Christian Democratic values, minus the Dixiecrat segregationist baggage. Early on, as increasingly marginalized liberals attacked, Young defended Carter in the *Village Voice*, saying, "Carter is one of the finest products of the most misunderstood region of our nation. You are probably right in questioning Jimmy's doctrinaire liberalism, but progressive politics in 1976 must be based on a tough mind and a tender heart and a loving sensitive spirit."

Young's support of Carter, combined with the end Carter put to the national aspirations of George Wallace, was enough to put me on his side in 1976. In truth, Carter was inevitable well before Election Day. But from almost the day after, Carter began battling with Congress, especially with Tip O'Neill in the House. There were always fights between Hamilton Jordan, Carter's chief of staff, and the Democrats. Always. Jordan actually thought Carter could govern while ignoring the House of Representatives. His attitude made for a very rough honeymoon. How do you, as president, dismiss one half of Congress that your own party controls? I guess the explanation was that Carter was really a naval officer and not a politician. Moreover, Carter thought his mandate came from the American electorate, not the liberal-leaning Democratic leadership in the House, a belief that had some truth to it.

Tip, who was new as the Speaker, had to take on the executive branch to get some respect and recognition that we had to work together. But I don't think they ever closed the political culture gap between the Massachusetts liberal and whatever it was that Carter and his "Georgia Mafia" represented in politics at that moment. Tip used to tell the story of the first time he went to the White House for breakfast. They asked him if he wanted some grits. He said he'd never tasted any, but he'd try one.

It seemed as though the accumulated weight of decades of American foreign, fiscal, and economic policy sins came crashing down on a Carter administration that was uniquely unprepared to collaborate politically with anybody. The Carter years were difficult for me because they were difficult for the Congress. Tip O'Neill and President Carter did not have the best relationship. However, Joe Califano, who was Secretary of Health, Education, and Welfare, and I had the greatest of friendships. That relationship took me to the White House a great many times to work out the details of complex legislation. So I was especially hurt and dismayed when Carter abruptly dismissed Califano in 1979, part of a larger purge of over thirty administration officials that year. Califano's campaign against smoking caused me a lot of embarrassment, because whenever I went to his office he could smell the smoke in my clothes and he would lecture me about it. But ultimately it probably saved my life, as I would quit for good a few years later.

Jimmy Carter also accepted Andrew Young's resignation as UN ambassador a few months after Califano's firing, to the deep dismay of most black political leaders. Still, Young stayed with Carter in the run-up to his crushing reelection defeat at the hands of Ronald Reagan. By the time the election came, Carter had everything from runaway inflation to soaring gas prices to sky-high interest rates going against him. The matter of the hostages being held in Iran was a lingering fatal blow. By the end, things were so frayed between Carter and the rest of the Democrats that his own vice president was quoted calling him a "queer duck" at the Democratic National Convention, and was considered a possible challenger for the nomination. It was in this context that, in frustration, Andrew Young called Carter's inner circle "smart-assed white boys." Black Southern politicians like Young were the primary endorsers of Carter's politics; I think we all were disappointed. It was Young's way of saying the administration was not listening to him at all, that he was on the outside while these "smart-assed white boys" ran the show, to the exclusion of those who brought Carter to the White House in the first place.

On the other hand, we had no choice but to be with Carter against Ronald Reagan and all his looming presidency would portend. Reagan, for all his outward charm, campaigned as someone who was antiblack, pro-Confederate, and conservative. With the hostage crisis deliberately being stretched out through the election—the Iranians would not let them go until Carter left office—you could feel the tide of political history turning, but that made Democratic unity more important than ever. My support for Carter put me on the other side of David Dinkins, who was backing Ted Kennedy. In fact, I made the cover of *Newsweek*, with a picture of Kennedy and Carter with me in the middle. Kennedy finally withdrew, but waited until the last minute to endorse Carter at the convention.

In the end, of course, it didn't make a whole lot of difference. I had a much better relationship, even on the way to another punishing Reagan defeat, with Carter's vice president, Walter Mondale. When I first came to the Congress, I got a call from then Senator "Fritz" Mondale indicating he shared my concerns about the rising problem of drug abuse. Though he hailed from Minnesota, a state still not associated with such so-called urban problems, he wanted to work with me on this issue, with the hope that we could team up to introduce companion legislation on our respective sides of the Capitol. From that we became friends, and regularly visited each other's homes. In 1976, when Jimmy Carter was trying to determine who his vice presidential candidate was going to be, I had my fingers crossed for Mondale. One night during the 1976 Democratic National Convention, the first of two in a row held in New York City, I had gone to the Cafe Carlyle to see and hear the late Bobby Short. I had to go to the men's room, which is off the Carlyle lobby. And in the lobby, surrounded by Secret Service people, was Mondale.

"Fritz?" I started.

"Don't tell anybody," he said in a low voice, as if anyone could miss the new phalanx of security around him. "I've just been selected! I've just been selected!" he said, excited as a schoolboy on his first date. Eight years later, when Mondale decided he was running for president, a lot of the early planning meetings took place in the basement in my house in Washington. I also brought a lot of Congress members to various social affairs at the vice president's residence that Fritz threw to allow people to get to know him better.

The problem for me in 1984, of course, was that Jesse Jackson was making his unconventional, historic bid for the Democratic nomination the same year I was making my debut as an insider on the ground floor of a leading presidential candidate. Of course, I wasn't the only one with a problem. Jackson's run put black pressure on the entire Democratic Party, from within as well as from without. From the inside, it generally forced the party to be much more open in its courting of the black vote—the only constituency that didn't defect to Reagan in 1980. It also made the party much more sensitive to black demands for a bigger voice in Mondale's front-running campaign. In that context I was named a Mondale national co-chairman in July of 1984.

Nevertheless, I was still the congressman from Harlem, the capital of black America, in a year when Jesse's run electrified African American communities from coast to coast. I had to watch my back. Early on I had a series of meetings with David Dinkins and Percy Sutton, who backed Jackson, and a number of district leaders and other public officials, about how to handle the obvious conflict. Thanks to Harlem's tradition of rational, constructive, and pragmatic politics, and my long, deep friendship with these men, the Jackson run proved to be another bad day that I didn't have. They assured me that I owed it to the community to stick with Mondale, and told me not to worry about them taking care of Jackson in New York. And so it was almost a miracle that I went without criticism for supporting my longtime, dear friend Fritz Mondale.

The late Ron Brown was Jesse's campaign manager. Our connection went back to my Hotel Theresa days, when I worked for his father as a young man and Ron was just a kid. Before taking on the Jackson campaign post, he called to ask my advice. I told him he'd never get better experience than by managing a national campaign. When Jackson withdrew from the race, among my many responsibilities in the Mondale campaign was managing the integration of the Jackson people into the Mondale effort. I had mentored Brown since his beginnings at the Urban League, and helped him get into St. John's Law School, but this added a new layer to our close friendship.

I didn't have a personal relationship with Jesse Jackson before that campaign. But since that time we have developed a mutual respect, and worked together on many national and local programs. And his close relationship with Percy Sutton has really kept our friendship and partnership alive. That said, and our good personal relationship aside, what was the 1984 Jackson message, anyway? Besides the dramatic prime-time convention speech, what was the practical political objective? To be sure, there were many excellent collateral benefits. Ron Brown became so well known that he later took on the whole Democratic National Committee and became its chairman. I was especially proud when, from that position, he made himself indispensable to the only successful counterattack on Republican rule in twenty-five years. Bill Clinton himself says that he never would have been president without the brilliance of his former commerce secretary.

To be sure, there definitely was a "Jackson Effect" on African American political involvement nationwide. Everywhere he went he inspired and mobilized a new generation of talented and ambitious folks who seemed to say to themselves: "If he can get up and run for president, and rock the Democratic Party to its foundations in the process, surely I, too, can run for public office in my hometown." My friend David Dinkins never tires of reminding audiences that Jackson's run was the wind beneath his wings when he sought to become New York's first African American mayor just five years later. Not everyone can aspire to and become mayor of such a great and large city as New York. But David Dinkins has become the model for how to be a great mayor. The Dinkins administration will long be remembered for its innovative community policing programs and a sharp increase in housing. Dave Dinkins will always be America's gentleman mayor.

Jesse Jackson continues to be a constant source of inspiration for African Americans seeking public office. As Jesse himself is fond of saying, he's a tree shaker, not a jelly maker. So it's not necessarily a negative thing to point out that his legacy includes no lasting political organization. Jesse Jackson's political gift is to get people excited, enough to motivate some of them to pick up the ball and organize themselves, often to very great effect.

From the beginnings of the Congressional Black Caucus, black leadership in the post–civil rights era, which coincides with my time in Congress, has run on two tracks, the group and the individual. I run for Congress as an individual, but I'm elected by a group that can variously expect me to represent the interests of the individual district and the interests of the race. Quite frequently they expect me to represent both interests simultaneously, cutting down my room to maneuver as an individual, and sometimes threatening to put me in political hot water.

In the 2004 campaign, I threw my support behind General Wesley

Clark, even though Reverend Al Sharpton, also a candidate, had made it clear that New York—meaning black New York—was *his* home base. When I brought Clark up to Harlem in December 2003 for the grand tour, a story in the *Daily News* picked up on the potential conflict and asked, "So Who's in Charge in Harlem?" It went on to talk about the conflict between Rangel the insider and Sharpton the outsider, and suggest that Sharpton might be stepping on my turf. A few days later, veteran New York newscaster Gabe Pressman asked me about a report that Sharpton had threatened to retaliate politically against any and all black politicians who had abandoned him. I told Pressman and his audience that while I had read that report, I hadn't heard that from Sharpton or his people directly. Having dealt with that, I went on to talk about what I wanted to talk about, the illegitimacy of the Bush presidency and why I thought General Clark was the man to beat him.

The media still finds it expedient to reduce the politics of the black community to the absurdity of "who's in charge," as if we were nothing more than a tribe that must have one chief. I resent it but I understand it, and I don't let it get in the way of the complexity that is my political reality. As a better story, the *New York Times* pointed out earlier that season that there is now a much greater diversity of political opinion, and a vastly greater sophistication, within the black electorate today than when Jesse ran in 1984. The limb I crawled out on for Mondale that year has grown thick enough to be another trunk of a tree representing the strength of black political diversity today. At the end of the day, I'm still a professional legislator who is delighted to be the next chairman of Ways and Means, and I look forward to working closely with the next Democratic president ot the United States, as soon as that victory might come. That's not a black or a civil rights issue, that's my leadership as an individual in the Democratic Party and a member of the national legislature. There was no way to look at the Sharpton candidacy as anything more than a vehicle for his ability to represent the issues and interests of the black "group" in the primary debates, as only the gifted Reverend Al can do. No matter how much Al Sharpton and I have appeared to differ on political issues, we have always ended up on the same page. As Sharpton often says, "A choir is made up of many voices." But we weren't talking about his potential inauguration any more than we were talking about the election of Jackson. True, Mondale didn't get elected either, but he was the party's candidate.

In the end, I am held accountable every two years as an individual, based not on my stewardship of the interests of the entire race, but on the interests of the 15th Congressional District of New York. As I see it, my power to advance those interests, and my individual advancement in the leadership of the Congress, are one and the same. I lose sight of this truth at my peril, I believe, though it has sometimes brought me close to grief when it has conflicted with the group agenda of the Congressional Black Caucus.

In 1986, the year I lost the Whip race, I also lost my mentor Tip O' Neill, who retired at the end of that Congress. To be honest, losing that race was a body blow for me. I wasn't completely sure if the money factor was determinative or just an excuse people gave to cover the fact that they didn't love me as much as they said they did. It made me wonder—for a minute, anyway—about who my friends *really* were, and who was just pretending. Such self-examination is useful, but only up to the point where it becomes the kind of self-doubt that is toxic to a politician's will to lead: the will to make decisions, alliances, and deals. Fortunately, however, I still had enough going for me that the setback did no lasting damage to my self-esteem. I still had my seniority, and I was still on the Ways and Means Committee.

We have a Ways and Means reunion in Washington, a kind of Democratic fund-raiser that, as the senior Democrat, I call together every year. It's for all the present and former Democratic members, so the current lobbyists can not only see the current members, but all the old members, and the old lobbyists, too. We always set the date around Rosty's schedule, because he's the star attraction, dominating the conversations by retelling all the old war stories so well, spinning lies into legend to the members' delight.

One of the legends concerns my race against Tony Coelho for Whip. I know Rosty says he supported me. But I also know that support wasn't very visible. Now, Rosty would respond that I lost that race because, instead of staying on the phone and contacting members, I was off gallivanting with him on some congressional trip. "What the hell do you mean 'gallivanting'?" I would protest for my part of the story. After all, it was Rosty who invited me to go on that trade trip, and in order to keep his "support," I accepted! Meanwhile, I thought, with other members of the committee along for the ride, I would solidify my support with them, too.

There were two members from Alabama, Ed Jenkins and Ronnie

Flippo, on that fateful 1986 trip during my campaign for Whip. One night, in the hotel in some foreign country, the three of us were at the bar going over all the gifts and things we had bought. And they were telling me they loved me, and how powerful the Ways and Means Committee was going to be when I became the Whip, and how they would be able to come to me with their problems and have my favor. And the more they drank, the more I drank. And the more they promised, the more I believed. And the next morning, sobered up and sheepish in Rosty's presence, they came up to me and said, "Hey, Charlie, did we commit to you last night?"

Tip O'Neill would always tell me about how badly the Irish were treated in Boston when he came up. But Rostenkowski could never admit how badly the Polish people were treated in Chicago. Chicago is the most racially polarized, if not downright racist, city that I've come across. When I went out there in 1983 to support the late, great Harold Washington for mayor, there were no blacks willing to say they supported Jane Byrne, the major white candidate in the primary, and virtually no whites who'd say they were supporting Washington. I had my first run-in with the Chicago Democratic machine when, as chairman of the CBC in 1976, I had to come to the defense of Congressman Ralph Metcalfe, who had actually been a loyal member of the Daley organization. Metcalfe was not the most militant black member Daley sent to Congress, to say the least. But his son became a victim of a brutality incident at the hands of the Chicago police. Metcalfe thought the matter was mishandled, and when he complained to Daley, Daley withdrew his endorsement and backed another candidate against him.

When we took on Daley over it, his people tried to pass the buck, saying that the endorsement was withdrawn by members of the organization in their dual capacity as union officials. So we went after the head of the then still powerful AFL-CIO, George Meany. Meany arrogantly refused to meet with us. Instead, he sent a white guy, accompanied by a black subordinate. We told that white guy, who was as arrogant as his ultimate boss, that we were strong enough to vote against every damn bill labor wanted. We told him we were confident that our constituents would understand that our vote had nothing to do with the merits of any particular bill. Our constituents would understand it was our response to the AFL-CIO's insult to the black community by turning on Metcalfe, who had a 100 percent pro-union voting record.

Well, as if we had snapped our fingers, we got Meany's proper attention. I can't begin to tell you the elation we felt when these Chicago labor leaders turned about-face, and had this big press conference supporting Metcalfe, who went on to win easily.

━━━━━━━━━━━━━

When I say I haven't had a bad day since I left Korea, I mean it with my whole heart. I didn't plan it this way, but that's how it continues to unfold. I didn't know that Tip O'Neill and I would hit it off so well. All I know, and truly believe, is that you do the best you can at whatever your job is. If you get the impression that Dan Rostenkowski was difficult to work with, there's no question that he was a rough chairman. But he was also fair, trustworthy, and whatever promises he made, you can bet your life those were promises he kept. Somehow, as much as I would like to become the chairman myself, I'm reluctant to think I might have to use some of Rosty's more strong-armed tactics to maintain the loyalty of my members. I have found it much easier to allow the members with jurisdiction in the subcommittees to work these things out among themselves, and then give their views to the remainder of the Democrats. We may disagree, but we will stick to it until we can report, with some degree of unanimity, to our leader. Why? Because ultimately it's the leader who will have to persuade the entire Democratic Caucus. Since I've been in the minority I haven't had any carrots or sticks to move my members. If and when I get in the majority, I hope I won't have to use them; but you never know.

A few years ago, I took the House podium to talk about about Tip's wife, Millie O'Neill, who had recently passed away. I spoke for about thirty minutes. Nobody was on the floor, and I had no idea that the O'Neill children were watching in the gallery. Oh, the lovely letters I got, for remembering the wife of someone whom 75 percent of the House didn't even know. In my tribute, I said that anything I've ever done in a gentlemanly, civil, and professional way in this House of Representatives, I owe to Tip O'Neill. He would take me in and raise hell with me sometimes, or just talk with me about whatever I was doing. At the end of each discussion, for all of the militancy and baggage that I might have brought with me to the job, Tip O'Neill would be right.

I told the empty chamber about going into his office one day, full of fire about the injustices taking place against minorities on the very same House floor, under his very leadership. When I walked back out, they asked, "What did Tip have to say?" My answer: Tip O'Neill had told me of all the problems the Irish had in Boston, and what his family was up against, and how cruel the white Anglo-Saxons were, and about all the discrimination against Catholics.

I said he had me in such tears that I forgot what my issue was in the first place!

Forgetting, completely, what is good and useful to forget is one of my best political traits. That's what Tip taught me about never having a bad day since.

9

Chairman in Waiting

Soon after we lost the majority in 1994, I was in a local market. There was a butcher behind the meat counter, just wiping his hands on his apron, and staring at me and smiling. That's not that unusual, so I just smiled back. At that, he came around from behind the counter and said:

"Didn't you used to be somebody?"

That's the way it goes, and the way it went. There was no way to see it coming, and I wasn't losing any sleep looking for it to come. I lost all the sleep I was going to lose over such things in 1980 when Reagan and Reaganism came in. It was really a surprise to me. Right after the election I woke up in the middle of the night, and I still didn't believe it. I really thought it was a bad dream—it was terrible, but nowhere near as bad as the 1994 rout.

I was still not the senior member on the Ways and Means Committee. My aspirations for the chairmanship were twice removed, in the person of Sam Gibbons of Florida and and J. J. Pickle of Texas, numbers two and three, respectively, behind Rosty and ahead of me at number four. I used to jokingly say of Sam Gibbons's son that I would get him to run for his dad's seat, and name a library after Jake Pickle if he'd only retire.

Now, when Rostenkowski got into trouble, and it appeared he would not be returning to the Congress, it was natural for everyone to believe that Sam Gibbons would assume the chairmanship. What I did not know was that my friend the late Bob Matsui of California had an interest in jumping the line to the chair. I first realized it when I discovered he was making contributions to Democrats on the committee who otherwise had no problems raising funds or getting reelected. Then one day he came out and made it clear to me that if *I* did not run, he would like to be considered as a candidate, with my support.

I said, "Bob, this doesn't make a lot of sense." Matsui was the son of

Japanese Americans who were interned in World War II. He grew up in an American concentration camp. "Like you," I said, "I've faced a lot of prejudice in my life. But the only thing I have is the seniority system." I could only recall three or four cases during my time in Congress when senior members were denied a post that was due them based on seniority.

"Bob, just think about it," I said. "If you were to run and lose, you could never use seniority as a factor to succeed as chairman." I made it clear: I was not giving up my turn, based on seniority, *when my time came.*

Who knows why he did it? The ego of public officials, especially on Ways and Means, defies explanation, and I include myself in that group. He may have already asked Jake Pickle. He may not have liked Sam Gibbons, because clearly he thought he was more able to serve. But he knew he had to get by me. As the Congress was closing, Tom Foley, who was the Speaker, chaired a big meeting of senior leadership, a kind of pep rally for all the chairmen and other leadership as we prepared to do battle in what would be the rout of the 1994 campaign. Foley was lauding all the chairmen for all the great things they had done that term— he even went out of his way to say something kind about me—but he completely passed over Sam Gibbons, who was now acting chairman.

It's fair to say that no one even noticed.

Sam Gibbons was not the most popular member of Congress. Tip O'Neill once told me, "Charlie, my boy, you'll become chairman of Ways and Means long before that damn Sam Gibbons does." Gibbons had once run against Tip for Speaker, and Tip never forgot it. Sam was about as buddy-proof a member as I've ever seen, leading many others to disrespect him with impunity. But I had to support him, out of the utmost respect for the seniority system, and my own self-interest in its preservation. Normally, the most senior member after the chairman would be the first one tapped for the House-Senate conference committee on a Ways and Means bill. But Rosty would constantly fail to appoint Gibbons to these all-important conferences. I'd say:

"Sam, if I were you, I'd fight Rosty on that damn conference committee slot. You know, I couldn't take it if he was talking to me like that. If I differ with him, and he takes me off a conference for it, I have to make a big deal out of it. And I'm willing to make a big deal out of it now because you've been excluded. I'll go to the well with you."

Gibbons said he really appreciated it, but he didn't want to fight Rosty. "Sam," I said, "I'm not just doing this for you, I'm doing this for me, man. Because if he can treat you that way, that's going to happen to me, too!"

So there I was at this meeting. Matsui and his buddy Jim McDermott of Washington were sitting well in the back, taking in the scene. Whether Gibbons was going to stand up or not, I had to make my move.

"Mr. Speaker, you know we've been saying a lot of good things about the chairmen, and the fine job they've done. But I think we've overlooked Sam Gibbons, and the fine work that he's done as acting chairman of Ways and Means. He's done a hell of a job," I said, drawing a polite round of applause.

"And I also want to say that there have been some newspaper reports and some talk that he's being challenged. I want you to know that my name has been mentioned as a possible challenger to him when we come back. I want to set the record straight: Not only am I not challenging him, I'm going down to Tampa to campaign for Sam Gibbons." That brought cheers on top of the applause.

"And when we're campaigning," I kicked it up a notch, "he can campaign saying he's gonna be the next chairman of Ways and Means." Now they were really cheering. "And I want you to know, there is no one on our committee who is prepared to challenge our Sam Gibbons!"

McDermott, who is still my buddy, later told me that as the meeting roared for Gibbons, Matsui stuck an elbow into his ribs, pleading: "What the heck should I do?"

McDermott said the best thing he could do was to keep his mouth shut.

And that he did. He became one of my most supportive Democrats on Ways and Means. Tragically and suddenly, God took Bob from us, but his wife, Doris, overwhelmingly elected to succeed him, has done a great job. Sam got a standing ovation not only for the great job he'd done as acting chair, but as the next incoming chair of Ways and Means. Then my friend J. J. "Jake" Pickle of Texas made it official: He would not seek reelection to the 104th Congress for a sixteenth term. My place in the line to the chairmanship, just one seat away, was now secure. As far as I could tell, I had done my job.

After the twelve-year siege of Reagan-Bush, the charismatic Bill Clinton was halfway through the first term of a promising presidency. The Senate, lost to us for half the Reagan-Bush years, was solidly in our hands. I had just turned a spry sixty-four years old, and as my Gibbons maneuver showed, I was perhaps more nimble than ever after twenty-four years in Congress. My battles with Rosty were won, and Sam Gibbons would eventually show his appreciation for my loyalty. The war was over, I thought. The plague of Reaganism had passed. How was I to know that a more virulent strain, personified by Newt Gingrich and the Contract with America, was about to lay us low? It was rolled out, like a big legislative Trojan horse, just six weeks before the congressional elections. It was fiendishly brilliant, and while I can't give Gingrich and Dick Armey, the first Republican Majority Leader since the Eisenhower administration, all the credit, in the end we lost fifty-four seats, the second biggest congressional turnaround since World War II.

The guts of that Trojan horse were taken nearly verbatim from Reagan's 1985 State of the Union address. The core of that speech, the heart of Reaganism, venerated the new Republican mantra of cutting taxes on wealth and slashing government spending on "entitlement programs." Where once "entitlement" merely referred to the fact that a program's spending level was a function of the number of people entitled to its benefits, like the number of people old enough to get Medicare or poor enough to get Food Stamps, "entitlement" became identified with a newly revived, all-purpose political scapegoat: the undeserving poor. The massive budget cuts the Gingrich-Armey Congress pursued with a vengeance in 1995 were the cutting edge of Reagan's 1985 vision of boosting growth and balancing the budget by cutting regulation on corporations, taxes on the wealthy, and spending on the poor. Of course, Reagan put a much friendlier rhetorical face on it, with a much more reassuring delivery. "Every dollar the federal government does not take from us," Reagan said, "every decision it does not make for us, will make our economy stronger, our lives more abundant, our future more free."

It was a classic performance in the Reagan theater of political misdirection, with the symbolic virtues of faith, family, and freedom all dressed up in the spotlight, while the real meaning, and the mean economic and ideological interests driving the policies, were well hidden far off stage. I tangled with Reagan the very next day over the way he tried to politicize Mother Clara Hale in that speech. Hale House, a Harlem home for babies born addicted to heroin, had been an unsung fixture of necessity in my district since 1969. Even as he proposed freezing—the same as cutting in a time of inflation and population growth—social spending, Reagan had Hale sitting next to his wife, Nancy, in the House Chamber. His salute to her as "an American hero" on national television may have been long-overdue praise, and the exposure granted her fifteen minutes of hard-earned fame. But I told the *New York Times* that in staging her appearance, Reagan had used her as nothing more than a prop, a cruel hoax when Hale House barely subsisted, for lack of federal funding, "in an area that is so infested with drug traffickers, because of the lack of Federal action, that traffickers sell without fear of arrest."

When Reagan decided to adopt the Caribbean Basin Initiative, a program of aid and trade initially drafted under Jimmy Carter, he invited members of Ways and Means to the White House to push for its passage. When we met, he was holding a short stack of three-by-five cards with the positions that had been taken and not taken by each of the Democrat and Republican members. I, of course, was a big supporter of the initiative. But he looked straight at me and said, "I want you to know, Congressman, that if you don't support this, the blood will be on your hands." Everyone laughed, because obviously he had singled out the wrong guy. It wasn't that he thought I was somebody else, he really just didn't know one member of Congress from another.

There wasn't that much of a connection between the Black Caucus and Ronald Reagan. At least Nixon cared enough to refuse to meet with us, at first. I don't think Reagan even gave that much of a damn about us at all. I can't think of any bill that we worked on, or anyone in the CBC, that had a special relationship with him. For Democratic legislators, the Reagan-Bush years were mostly one long rear-guard action to preserve as much of the fabric of the American social safety net as possible from the relentless pressure of Reagan's charisma pushing the passage of budget cuts. We Democrats may have gotten a bit too comfortable for our own good in those years. We were in power in the House, and regained the Senate in the middle of Reagan's second term. It may have lulled us into the belief that our bargains with Reaganism were sound, and made from a position of strength. In retrospect, perhaps we didn't have the strongest kind of leadership on our side at the time. And Reagan was so good at throwing in strategic spoonfuls of honey, like dropping low-income Americans from the tax rolls completely, to cut the sour taste of his larger agenda in our mouths. And to be sure, there really *was* a need for tax reform, and a genuine bipartisan feeling for working with Reagan on it.

Reagan, and later George H.W. Bush, had a great partner in Dan Rostenkowski. At one point Rosty was even advising Bush on how to get reelected, though of course it didn't pan out. Most people in the Congress knew that he had this great private admiration for Reagan and Bush Sr. The result was that both presidents got much of what they wanted, and Rosty got many things he wanted. For the most part, Tip O'Neill left Danny alone to negotiate directly with the White House on these major matters of social spending policy that fundamentally altered the fiscal relationship between the federal government, the states, and the society as a whole.

So, while the Reaganites mostly held the Black Caucus at bay, I was able to piggyback some of my issues onto bills that Rosty was able to pass as chairman of Ways and Means and then, working closely with Senator Howard Baker of Tennessee and the Senate Republicans, get to Reagan's desk for signing. It increased my dependence on maintaining a good working relationship with Rosty in those years, but it paid off when, for example, it came to extending the tax credits that fueled so much low-income housing construction in New York and elsewhere in the eighties and nineties. The provisions, replacing a law I spearheaded in 1974, were signed by Reagan in 1986 in no small part because of the Rosty-Reagan relationship. My legislative language protecting the federal deductibility of state and local income taxes was also included in that sweeping Tax Reform Act of 1986. Tom Downey, a promising junior member from Long Island, also played a key role in getting this provision passed. The administration's initial plan to do away with the deduction was a dagger deliberately pointed at the heart of high-spending, high-taxing states like New York, according to Reagan himself. Even Governor Mario Cuomo called me a hero that year for rallying Democrats to hold the line on that one.

The Rangel-Rosty relationship was also strong enough to get a key tax provision—disallowing a tax break for U.S. firms doing business with apartheid South Africa—into a larger budget bill in early 1987. The story of the South Africa "Rangel Amendment" really began in the summer of 1986 when, under the floor leadership of my CBC colleague Ron Dellums (D-Calif.), the Black Caucus managed to pass a package of trade sanctions against the apartheid government of then prime minister P. W. Botha. The caucus members carried the ball in the debate on the House floor, and when the person sitting in the chair declared that the Democrats had the votes to pass the sanctions bill, no one in the opposition dared request that the votes be counted. Instead, it was passed on a voice vote, sparing opponents the embarrassment of putting their unwillingness to "do something" about South Africa on the record. The Republicans couldn't afford to be seen blocking the long-overdue moral judgment of the American people that apartheid was wrong and had to go.

Reagan's infamous veto of that sanctions bill was just as famously and almost immediately overridden. The legislation's objective was to compel South Africa to free political prisoners, repeal laws enforcing the racist system, and negotiate with the African National Congress. But one year later, as the State Department prepared an assessment of the Comprehensive Anti-Apartheid Act of 1986, as it was titled, a *Time* magazine article reported that South Africa had done none of the above. The South African economy, it said, had proven "relatively invulnerable" to the sanctions, including a freeze on new investment there by U.S. firms and a ban on a number of South African imports. Something more was needed, and I saw an opportunity to deliver a decisive blow through the tax-writing power of the "awesome and powerful" Ways and Means Committee.

The Rangel Amendment didn't get that much press when it passed in December 1987, but by the spring of 1989 it had the masters of apartheid in South Africa howling and lashing out in pain. The measure increased the tax rate on profits made in South Africa from 58 percent to 72 percent, a 24 percent hike that truly made a difference. Even Nelson Mandela commented on it, noting that in South Africa it was not just known as the "Rangel Amendment" but "the bloody Rangel Amendment." Mobil Corporation, the largest U.S. investor in South Africa, had long resisted pressure that caused some 170 American multinational firms to divest their South African holdings between 1985 and 1989. But in April 1989, citing the new bottom-line impact of my amendment, Mobil finally withdrew. To the end it insisted that the pressure from anti-apartheid protesters and shareholders had nothing to do with the decision to pull out. In truth, the bottom-line reality that they couldn't afford to stay there took them off the hook of appearing to make a moral decision to leave, or continuing to defend their presence. It was no longer about black or white for Mobil and all the big names that joined the exodus from South Africa. It was about green.

And that was fine with me. Mandela was freed from prison in triumph ten months later.

———

It hit me when, as part of a congressional delegation, I went to Mozambique in 1974 to celebrate the end of their long struggle to gain independence, after five hundred years of Portuguese rule. The minister of finance for the new government persisted in asking me what I was doing there. I kept answering that I was vicariously enjoying the liberty and freedom they had just won, after generations of colonial oppression. But my answer kept missing his real question. Finally, he took me aside and told me a little story. He said that the Portuguese and the French had frequently bombed their schools and hospitals during the armed struggle, often killing their women and children. When the bombardment stopped, he would sometimes come out afterward and stare at the casings on the spent, lethal ordnance. He said he would never forget how the words *Made in the USA* stenciled in yellow letters on the heavy metal jackets stared back at him.

"Comrade," the recent freedom fighter asked me, "are you made in the USA?"

"Damn," I thought to myself. That was the first time I really realized that I was an American. Black folks can say anything they want about being an African American, or claiming the continent as Motherland, but at the end of the day they're still Americans. And unless you can change America's heart and will toward the treatment of Africa, from the African's point of view, that's all you are. Now that I've authored the Africa trade bill and the Caribbean Basin trade bill, now that the Congressional Black Caucus is the "must stop" for all the African diaspora leaders to make when seeing about their interests in the United States—just like world Jewry comes to court the U.S. Jewish groups—I really feel we're getting somewhere. We're not there yet, by any means, but we are getting there.

When Adam Powell was the face of black America in Africa in the 1950s and early 1960s, he made a point of representing himself as 100 percent American. Malcolm X projected a different persona, one that was openly divorced from an American identity. Like Garveyites before him, Malcolm saw "black American" as something of an oxymoron. I guess I fuse aspects of both perspectives, Adam's and Malcolm's, in my interest in Africa and the Caribbean. It must be the part of my uncle Herbert, the Garvey admirer who lived in the Bronx, that rubbed off on me. Of course, he wasn't a real Garveyite—he drank too much liquor to be *any* kind of real "ite"—but he would maintain the intellectual pose so he could be the man in the barbershop arguments. I try so hard in dealing with the African nations to get them to realize that however much or little African blood we have in our veins here, they need to come and adopt us, because we are as close as they will ever get to finding representation in a kinship relationship with the United States, as all the European countries and Israel have found. They need to adopt us because, left to ourselves, we will not do it alone. The fact of the matter is, we have largely had any genuine cultural, political, or even emotional connection with Africa and Africanness ripped from our hearts and consciousness by history.

Reagan's Caribbean Basin Initiative, and the role of Ways and Means in trade matters, took me to the islands quite a bit in the eighties, and gave me the credentials there that I still have today. George Dalley, my Washington chief of staff, whose beloved late wife hails from Jamaica, is the one person most responsible for my bonding with the cause of our Caribbean neighbors. There was also a relationship that I built with an ambassador from Haiti, Georges Salamon, going back to the 1970s. Salamon eventually arranged for me to meet with the infamous dictator Jean-Claude "Baby Doc" Duvalier. Dalley went with me, in an effort to get Baby Doc to open up the prisons and establish the court system. My heart has gone out to Haiti, the poorest nation in the Western Hemisphere, ever since. And, all too often, it's been returned to me broken, as it is today.

I first became very close to former Haitian president Reverend Jean-Bertrand Aristide in 1991 after he was ousted in a military coup led by General Raul Cedras. After his expulsion from Haiti, Aristide ultimately found asylum in Washington. I would meet with him often during what would prove to be a three-year struggle to restore the island's first democratically elected president to office. Because I'd had a history in working with Baby Doc, before he was overthrown by the military, I met several times with his Duvalierist successor, Cedras. Weeks after Clinton's election in November 1992, I went to Haiti and warned Cedras that American resolve to side with the poor Haitians fleeing his repression would certainly stiffen when Clinton was inaugurated. And I made it my business to press President Clinton, early in his first term, to commit the United States to doing the right thing by the Haitian people.

And so I became an Aristide adviser.

When he was finally restored in 1994, with the might of the U.S. Navy at his back, I went to Haiti and heard for myself the roar of the crowds of poor people hailing Aristide like a savior. Unfortunately, it wasn't long after the shouting died that the shooting and suffering resumed full force. In the end, I must doubt that I ever really knew Aristide. It will always be hard for me to see how someone so soft-spoken and sweet-talking in French, with such a religious background, could be as bad as even his former supporters now say.

There's no doubt that Aristide proved to be a terrible disappointment. He was unable to build any of the institutions of democracy Haiti so desperately needs in order to move forward. As profoundly distrustful as he was of anything he didn't personally control, Aristide may have simply been emotionally incapable of letting these institutions emerge, much as he was incapable of working with his opposition to support national programs for the common good. Soon, what little political system they had broke down, and the international community that rallied to return him to democracy began to cut off funding. Quite frankly, for all the hopes and dreams his Haitian supporters initially placed in him, life was no better under his presidency than under the various dictatorships that preceded him. When the issue of releasing funding came up in Washington, I tried, along with strong CBC Aristide supporters like

Maxine Waters, to persuade the Bush administration to see the Aristide glass as half-full and free the money. But Aristide's unwillingness to play ball with his opposition made it easy for the administration's point people on this—Secretary of State Colin Powell and national security adviser Condoleezza Rice—to steadily back away from their already limited enthusiasm for Aristide.

As the rebellion that would finally drive him from office in March 2004 approached the crisis stage, John Conyers of Michigan, the dean of CBC, arranged for a meeting with President Bush. We were concerned because, as Haiti slid into anarchy, Aristide called us frequently with increasing anxiety about his regime's future and, indeed, his own personal safety. We had a small crisis of our own that day when we arrived at the White House and Bush's chief of staff, Andrew Card, and Condoleezza Rice said the president wasn't going to be available. When Conyers realized that President Bush was actually in the building, he made it clear, in no uncertain terms, that we would not be leaving without seeing him. Card was incensed. He looked at us with utter contempt, but as he walked out of the room, Ms. Rice gave us a wordless gesture that told us everything was going to be all right. When she and Card finally produced President Bush, he assured us that, as disappointed as the administration was with Aristide, it would recognize the rule of law that said he was president until 2006. They said we would not support the rebels.

Soon after, however, our ambassador in Haiti told Aristide that the United States could no longer guarantee his safety. On that very night in February 2004, I was on the phone with Powell for hours, seeking reaffirmation of his commitment to Aristide's safety. Powell was trying to work with Jamaican prime minister P. J. Patterson on a diplomatic solution involving new elections. Aristide had agreed to share power, but the opposition, basically a diverse group of political professionals who once supported him in the original showdown with Cedras, had had enough of him and refused.

Meanwhile, the so-called rebels—branded freedom fighters by Aristide's opposition—continued to advance toward the capital. Many of them were former army members who, turned out by Aristide, fled to the area bordered by the Dominican Republic. A lot of drug money may have fled with them, because they came back into Haiti with new guns and new uniforms. Their return in growing force, mostly to the cheers of people in the towns they overtook, led Powell to conclude that Aristide would have to go. As with everything else about him, in retrospect, the truth about the circumstances of Aristide's departure remains shrouded in the fog of the tortured statements of diplomatic posturing.

The U.S. chargé d'affaires in Haiti said Aristide was already packing when he came to inform him that the United States couldn't protect him anymore. But soon after he left for Africa on the U.S.-provided plane, Aristide called the whole thing a political kidnapping. Powell insists otherwise, with some pride, because Aristide boarded with his own personal security people—though not before he signed a letter of resignation with U.S.-approved language.

Aristide may not have been kidnapped, but he was definitely shoved, even if it was for his own good. In a hearing held shortly afterward, under my examination, a right-wing State Department guy named Noriega, a former aide to Jesse Helms who generally held black folks in contempt, conceded that the resignation was definitely coerced. He said Aristide was told he'd be killed if he didn't leave, and he couldn't leave without signing a U.S.-dictated resignation.

From there the whole thing became a semi-tragic farce of Aristide's emotional high maintenance, and his inability to grasp the practical diplomatic reality of the situation. He wanted to go to South Africa, but when he got on the plane he had no idea where they were taking him. The Bush administration would have us believe that the RSA refused to accept him. But what really happened was that the South African president, Thabo Mbeki, was in the midst of a difficult reelection campaign himself, and had already caught political hell for being the only head of state to go to Haiti to recognize its two hundredth anniversary of independence, at great expense to South African taxpayers. Mbeki made it clear that he'd receive Aristide, but not before his elections. The French government arranged for the Aristide asylum tour's first stop, in the Central African Republic. Given the historical legacy of French colonial rule in Haiti, Aristide was greatly agitated to get off the plane and see all these French-speaking black soldiers around him, holding him nearly incommunicado. I talked with him several times while he was there, and Maxine actually went and visited him and confirmed my feeling that he was quite traumatized and somewhat disoriented by it all.

With our support, Prime Minister Patterson was persuaded to give him temporary haven in Jamaica until we could work something out with South Africa. But he wasn't in Jamaica long before he called me and said that the Jamaican foreign minister was pushing him off on Nigeria. Maxine and I immediately got on a conference call with Prime Minister Patterson. We were told that Colin Powell was putting a great deal of pressure on Patterson to get Aristide out of the Caribbean, lest his presence encourage his supporters in Haiti. There was also good intelligence that Aristide's life was in danger there. Yet Prime Minister Patterson said he was outraged that after thirty years of friendship—our relationship went back to my support of his political mentor Prime Minister Michael Manley in the 1970s—I would think he could be intimidated into welching on our deal. It was Aristide who was talking about going to Nigeria, Prime Minister Patterson said. The intelligence was correct, but it was Aristede's call as to whether he wanted to stay.

I told Prime Minister Patterson that I didn't always understand Aristide as clearly as I would like, but one thing was clear: He didn't want to leave Jamaica. Aristide said he didn't know why Nigeria was picked. Prime Minister Patterson said he expended a lot of his own credibility to negotiate a temporary asylum with the president of Nigeria until Aristide could get into South Africa. By the time we'd finished talking, he made it abundantly clear that he would straighten things out with Aristide. But he also made it clear that we had to help him with Rice and Powell.

I finally got a call from Aristide saying he'd been accepted in South Africa. He was ready to go, but he would never leave the country without letting them know that he had to talk to me and Maxine. He was very pleased that Mbeki had followed through on the invitation.

Again, I have to admit that there's still so much of the truth that seems unknowable about Haiti. But I do know that there are only two classes there—the very rich and the very poor. It's easy to believe that the whole thing was really the former working with a conservative Republican administration in Washington to get rid of Aristide, the only champion of the latter, however flawed, to emerge in generations. It was so easy for me to be friendly with Aristide when he was a simple, courageous parish priest uniting the poor. He gave me hope that for the first time in Haitian history a real democracy could be born. It was so easy for me to join with all the international leaders calling for his restoration after his first overthrow. But politics in Haiti is literally murder. It's burning and killing, and then kicking your opponent after they're dead. And Aristide's party is as guilty of committing these atrocities as any other. His opponents would say he's a cold-blooded murderer who can never be allowed to return.

My personal feelings for Aristide—a kind of sympathy tempered by doubt—have very little to do with the dilemma that his situation poses for me. While some still argue for his vindication, the international community is once more funding badly needed services and infrastructure in Haiti. It's clear to me that none of this assistance—for schools and roads and hospitals—would be taking place in a Haiti attempting to restore Aristide. In the choice between vindicating Aristide and preserving the Haitian people, I have to go with the people—their lives are far more important to me than the ideological principle of the rule of law at this point. My relationship with Aristide was intense, but not deep enough to allow me to be certain that he was innocent of all wrongdoing in the bloody conflict in Haiti. But I was a friend of Haiti before Aristide, and I'm a friend of Haiti now.

They used to allow members of the House to speak for an hour on any subject they wanted. But unlike today, they didn't allow the TV cameras to pan the chamber in the early days of C-SPAN, lest they record all the empty seats. So what Newt Gingrich would do was get up there and let it fly before the cameras, yammering at an empty House, trusting the magic of television to make nothing look like something.

"I say this, that . . . I challenge the Democrats! If there's one Democrat here that can deny what I'm saying about their distortions, their frauds, their dishonesty, let that person stand now, and I'll stop talking . . . Of course—not one of you has risen!"

Tip O'Neill put a stop to that nonsense, by coming on behind him to tell the cameras that "the House of Representatives is not in session at this time." But that, of course, was when Gingrich and the Republicans were still in the minority. It's funny but also true that "minority" or "majority" are not just designations based on relative numbers, but they are cultures, too. If being the majority for most of the post–World War II period made Democrats a bit too complacent in their assumptions about power and how to use it, being the minority ultimately bred a Gingrich-DeLay-type Republican culture in which seizing power and consolidating control—by any means necessary—is an end in itself. To crib from Vince Lombardi, winning isn't just everything for them, it's the only thing. Much as it has been said that you can take a boy out of the country but you can't take the country out of the boy, an election took House Republicans out of the minority, but it didn't take the minority—the mean, almost paranoid craving for revenge and control—out of the House Republicans.

The first fight I got into in the Congress—some twenty-four years after I first set foot in Washington—was with Bill Archer of Texas, when he became the Republican chairman of Ways and Means after we lost the majority. The first bill he brought up before the committee was to wipe out tax preferences for minorities acquiring television and radio stations. We really got into it with each other verbally. He said he was color blind. I said he picked a hell of a time to become color blind, waiting until I got there—representing the interests of minorities who had historically been deliberately shut out of these opportunities because of their color—to lose all sense of color. The whole thing degenerated into finger-pointing about who was playing the "race card" on whom.

Before the fight I had already agreed to have dinner that night with our new chairman and his wife. I couldn't possibly just not show up, but I knew they were upset with me over some of my earlier statements. For perhaps the first time there was a communication lapse between me and some of my staff, and something went out from my office likening Archer's stance and style to Adolf Hitler. It had not been cleared with me—that kind of language is just not my language—but I knew it was senseless to try to dissociate myself from it. It was on my stationery and over my name. My staffer was already crushed that he had done this to me, and I didn't want to make his life any more miserable than it already was. So I went to the dinner, and I approached Archer's beautiful wife.

"You know," I began, "when your husband told me he was color blind, I was outraged at his claim that he could not distinguish colors. I thought it was a purely political thing to say. But since then I've found out that he has problems with reds and greens and blues, and that you pick out his clothing."

"Yes, it's true," she said.

"So . . . he really is color blind?"

"Yes, he is," she said.

"Well, he never explained it that way to me," I said, smiling.

"You're outrageous," she laughed, breaking the ice that was setting in at the start of my tenure as the committee's senior minority member. But there was still a lingering cloud that darkened the entire three terms he served as chairman. We had a polite but really formal relationship. Archer was relentless in pushing the Republican agenda of shrinking government, not as a matter of fiscal responsibility but as a matter of ideology. When the government, on Bill Clinton's watch, ran up a record surplus near the end of his second term, Archer led the charge for spending it on tax cuts primarily benefiting the wealthy and particular corporate interests.

Archer's chairmanship did afford me an opportunity to add another dimension to my legislative skills. By challenging him as I did, I was able to build up the prestige associated with being the ranking member. Learning to maneuver from our position of weakness, fighting all those regressive bills they tried to pass, became my strength, and made me a real leader in the House. And Archer never, never, never allowed himself to go on TV with me. That usually meant they would put us on separately; half the time they just did me and not him. It's been the same way with his successor in the chair, Bill Thomas. The exposure has raised my profile in terms of my party's national leadership, too. Between being the ranking member and being on television so much, I became one of the highest fund-raisers for the Democratic Party. At my annual birthday fund-raiser in 2003, for example, with 890 people in attendance, we raised $400,000 in one shot.

Of course, I'd rather be in the majority again, but ranking minority membership has had its privileges and accruals. I became a bigger fish in the smaller, minority pool. Let's face it, the House Democrats have had a tough time figuring out how to navigate in the minority. But I've been steering myself as a minority all my life. I like to think that my party has come to truly appreciate what I've been able to do in terms of keeping our flag above the water. I have the overwhelming support of the House Democrats, because I get so many chances to talk back on TV. Afterward, I have so many Republicans who come up and say, "You got us again, but you were civil about it." Even in defeat, I still pick up the pieces. I'm still Sergeant Rangel, somehow leading what's left of our side over unknown terrain in the dark. And it's been much more challenging—and even rewarding—than when it was merely about jockeying with people within my own party for position, because there's so much more at stake.

I was able to get the support of Newt Gingrich for my African trade bill when he was speaker. Tom DeLay was one of the first to write and call me after my 2003 knee accident, though I think that was merely political. I am understood to be a partisan Democrat, but the reason they respect me, I think, is because I have not been personal in my attacks. Even in my more recent donnybrooks with the current Ways and Means chairman, most observers see me as the victim of his difficult personality.

Even the administration and the House Republican leadership have been objects of Bill Thomas's ill temper. My big run-in with Thomas came in 2003. There was a $90 billion pension bill before us that the Republicans, still sneaking around as if they were in the minority, decided to rewrite overnight without any input from our side. In the morning, Thomas moved to waive the formal reading of this bill that we hadn't even seen. It's a common enough maneuver, waiving the reading, but it requires unanimous consent. I objected, but he continued to push the waiver. I had to point out that he was violating the rules of the House by doing so. He asked if I was going to insist on the objection, and when I said yes, he had no choice but to read the bill. It was late on a Friday, and reading the whole thing would likely delay any action until the following week.

Needless to say, he was miffed, but that wasn't my problem. I was miffed myself. They started the reading. I left the peppery Pete Stark of California to insist they keep on, and then I took the rest of my Democrats into the library to huddle.

It wasn't a plot. I didn't have a plan. Thomas just irked me by saying that he wasn't going to give us time to read the bill. So I went into the back to use the time to figure out what we were going to do about this bill we hadn't seen. We weren't there five minutes before Thomas sent his chief of staff in to ask us to evacuate the library. The chairman, she said, may need the library for the Republican members.

"What are you talking about?" I said. "The Republican members are out there listening to the bill being read. You tell the chairman that we're not leaving."

Five minutes after that she comes back with a Capitol Hill policeman. "I'm so sorry, Mr. Rangel," she says. "But the chairman asked me to get the police to ask you to leave the library."

"Officer," I said, "just what are you going to do if we don't leave the library?"

He said he hadn't the slightest idea, and decided to go get a lieutenant. The lieutenant didn't want any part of this either, so he went and got the sergeant at arms, the House's top law enforcement official. Declaring it a matter for the members to decide, the sergeant at arms immediately punted it right back into Thomas's lap. The bells rang, calling us in for a vote. When we got to the floor the press was following me around as I told the Majority Leader that we ought to bring charges against the chairman for abuse of power. And that took up the next five hours, nailing their asses to the cross. All the Democrats were congratulating me, backslapping and all that. But that's what I learned how to do after decades of being a legislator. That's how we make an appeal to what is right and decent, and without anger. I did it for the framers of the Constitution, who intended that we would treat each other in a civil way. We call each other gentlemen to avoid being cantankerous. And no one person, Democrat or Republican, should ever call law enforcement on a colleague.

The drama, of course, had actually slipped into slapstick before we even left the library. At some point during the gesture of the reading, Thomas tried to cut it off and move to a vote. Stark, who was then seventy-one but still agitates with the testosterone of a seventeen-year-old, started sparring with Thomas over procedure. As things heated up, another committee member, Scott McInnis, tried to tell Stark to "shut up." I'm sure he now wishes he hadn't. Stark, according to the record, came back with: "Oh, you think you're big enough to make me, you little wimp? Come on. Come over here and make me. I dare you. You little fruitcake. You little fruitcake. I said you are a fruitcake!"

Clearly, Sergeant Rangel left the right guy to cover our rear flank.

In his subsequent embarrassment, Thomas tried to argue that he called the police to bring things to order after Stark's fighting words. But everyone, even Republicans, saw through the idea that Stark was really going to brawl with McInnis, who was twenty years his junior. A few days later, under some pressure from his own leadership, Thomas made a tearful apology, admitting that he only called the police to break up our meeting. He promised to do better at promoting civility and to exercise better judgment. But responding as the representative of the wounded minority, I got the last word. I took the floor and said that the problem I had was bigger than Charlie Rangel and Bill Thomas. I said it was bigger than Democrats and Republicans.

"We have been left a legacy to govern for the people, in this House of Representatives. We don't have the right to destroy this institution. Nobody does, not me, not Bill . . . where is Bill Thomas? Oh, there he is. Now, it took a lot of courage for that man to come here and say he's sorry. But he's not apologizing to me, or to Democrats. He's apologizing for trying to stain this institution. And you and I, Democrats and Republicans, we must make certain that when we leave here, that we leave the same thing that our forefathers who built this institution left to us."

The Republicans were up on their feet, along with the Democrats. Republicans came up to me afterward saying, "Damn, don't you give up, Charlie, you stick to it; I've never heard a speech like that." Privately, any number of Republicans were telling me Thomas deserved humiliation for the way he treated people. But I just don't believe in publicly kicking people when they're down.

Sure enough, the day after his apology, Thomas tried to turn on me again. We were at the White House, and President Bush asked me about getting a Medicare bill through. I told him that with his help, and a spirit of bipartisanship, I felt we could get the job done. As he left the meeting, when reporters asked what he thought of my remarks, Thomas said I was very good at talking about bipartisanship when the cameras were rolling, but when the cameras are gone, so is the bipartisanship. The next morning, his comment was all over the papers. There was also a formal conference committee meeting on the matter. As you may recall from an earlier chapter, since they gained the majority in 1994, the Republicans have shut Democrats out of these crucial meetings in which the differences between the House and Senate versions of bills are resolved. So when I was called to speak at this sham conference meeting, I said:

"Mr. Thomas, there's a statement attributed to you in the press this morning that I am only bipartisan when the cameras are here. So, it shouldn't surprise you that I'm looking forward to the success of this conference because the cameras are, in fact, here. And if you see fit to let me know where the *real* conference is going to be, where the *real* decisions are being made, I want you to know that whether there's a camera there or not, I will be there to try to get a bill out."

Everybody laughed. "Well, Mr. Rangel," he said, "I'm glad to see that at least you found a room where the cameras are today."

Now, he's supposed to be on good behavior, right?

"Well, with you, Mr. Chairman," I said, "it's always one day at a time."

Consensus may really be the watchword on my survival. Certainly, I could not be a leader in the Congress on taxes, Social Security, and trade—albeit a Democratic leader—without an instinct for consensus. My politics and those of my party are so different that every time I speak out publicly, I have to know that I've got the core of my party with me. Some people, however, will doubtless still be left shaking their heads, swearing that Rangel must be speaking for himself again. For example, as a potential chairman of Ways and Means, I've made it abundantly clear to big and small business that my door is wide open, but they have to come through it talking about education. I tell them I can yield on a lot of their issues in which my district is not particularly emotionally involved. The liberal part of my party might have an ideological problem with some of these concessions, but if you can exploit the glaring need for decent education and employment opportunities, I'll take the hit as the price of politically practical consensus. Because as long as these Republicans keep saying that education is not an issue for substantial increased federal funding, then I believe that it's in the best interest of business to step up to the challenge of providing for an educated, productive workforce, because it will serve to increase their profitability, productivity, and competitiveness.

I, for one, want American business to have a fair advantage over foreign business, so they're not going to have a great problem with me on matters of trade. I'm ready to give something up, but they've got to give up something for the larger good in return. That's what my support for the Caribbean Basin Initiative, Chinese free trade, the African trade initiative has been about. These things help these countries, but they also benefit American business. They may break me away from the majority of my party, but on my committee I have more than a consensus among my own members.

Consensus is also a very human and social process of having one's cake and sharing it with any number of politically self-interested parties. Politics has been called the art of the possible. Making consensus, creating such a political work of art, is the best way to describe my role in Hillary Clinton becoming the junior senator from New York, a platform that has put a serious run for the White House within her reach.

When I first came out for her, everyone said I was crazy, but I knew different. Not because I knew she would win in a walk, though I had every confidence in her. What I knew was that Hillary Clinton for Senate from New York wasn't about my madness, it was about her method. Whenever I think of it, I always remember that I went steady with my wife for seven years before we tied the knot, and to this day she has me convinced it was all my idea. So it was with Hillary; I knew when I drove up that she was ready to be asked to the prom. I knew my job, what we used to call "front running" back in the Harlem clubhouse days, would be to go out and get people to say which side they were on and bring the information back, the way a dutiful prom date fetches glasses of punch.

I was in Chicago, at a 1999 rally supporting the reelection of Senator Carol Moseley-Braun. Hillary Clinton was the big draw, and she was good, as she always is. Afterward, I was telling people how good she was, and someone said that she should be running for senator—from Illinois. I don't know if they were just flattering her, or if they were really afraid that Ms. Moseley-Braun was going to lose, which of course she did. Whatever the case, they allowed me to believe that Hillary had political ambitions, and I immediately jumped on it.

"I hear that you're interested in running for the Senate," I said to her.

"What are you talking about?"

"Some people tell me that they were thinking about drafting you right here . . . that you might have a political base here."

"I have no idea what you're talking about."

"Well, let me just tell you this: You can be the Senator from Illinois or the senator from New Hampshire or the senator from Kansas. But the *real* senators are from New York—that's where you should be running from."

And I could tell then, from the awkwardness of the smile on her face, that there was some interest. She was picking out a corsage for me to pin on her.

Before that rally meeting was over she made certain to turn me over to her chief of staff, who immediately began grilling me about how serious I was. "What about the New York delegation? What about fundraising? What about labor?" Now, to be sure, I hadn't talked to *anybody* about Hillary Clinton for Senate at that point. Nobody. But there I was, my psychic clipboard at the ready.

"Why don't you and I start talking about all those things," I said to her, "and let me start filling you in on what's there for her."

"That would be great," she said, enthusiastically. And that's where it began.

It's a kind of political thought process and telephone tree I learned at the feet of Ray Jones in the 1960s. It's the type of thing that experience teaches you. Nothing less and nothing more. I cannot imagine a guy running a school who doesn't do this before he promotes someone to be principal, or anyone in a church making a policy move before finding out what will fly with each and every deacon. Somebody on the Hillary team would ask, "Who in the hell do you think would support the first lady?"

"I don't know," I'd say, "but her popularity is overwhelming."

"The New York delegation, you think?"

"Yesss," I say, "the congressional delegation."

So at the next delegation meeting I'd say, "You know, if Hillary Clinton were to announce for the Senate from New York, what do you think?" And they say, "Hey, she wouldn't run . . . but if she did she'd be a hell of a candidate." Then, since I'm meeting with labor leaders anyway, I say to them, "Hey, if the congressional delegation came out in support of Hillary Clinton, what do you think?" Then I go to the people who always give to the Democratic Party, and I say, "If she had labor and the congressional delegation behind her, could you support her?"

And when I go back to the Hillary camp, and they ask, "What about this guy?" or "What about that guy?" I would go to that person and say, "What have you got against Hillary Clinton?" We used to call it front running; today you call it connecting the dots. And when you're a senior person in the campaign, operating from a position that can't be challenged, then people know you're not just out there taking a poll. You're authorized to ask these questions and convey the answers to the top. Some will respond, "Oh, not right now, but if you did have this one piece, or that one in place . . .," and I go looking for those pieces. And when I can finally make some of these endorsement statements public, knowing I can't be challenged because I talked personally with all these people, it adds up to something that's not exactly a draft but grants a minimum necessary level of comfort, an insurance policy, so that the candidate—Hillary in this case—knows they're not about to jump into an empty pool.

You might think I was being used, but nothing could be further from the truth. It was such an exciting opportunity, a no-loser. If it turned out she didn't run, she didn't run. But I could go around and tell everybody "what if?" And they would say what I expected them to say: "Are you crazy? Do you know what you're talking about?" And then I would have the thrill of sculpting a work of political possibility from the name "Hillary Clinton." It was like someone asking Michelangelo, "What do you mean you're gonna put a masterpiece on that ceiling?"

I started on my delegation. "If you want to beat Giuliani's butt," I said, "we gotta have a superstar, and I've got one for you: the first lady."

"Give me a break, Charlie," they said.

"All I want to know is, if we had her, would you be with her?"

"You bet your life," they said.

The union leaders loved being consulted about their support so far in advance of the politicians making the choice and presenting them with a done deal. It was the same with the progressive money men like Jonathan Tisch and Edgar Bronfman Jr.

Finally, while I was dealing with some legislation concerning the Empowerment Zones, I had a big meeting set with President Clinton to talk about the meat and potatoes of the bill. I had stayed up all night cramming facts and figures so I could go into the meeting with him with no staff, like policy wonk to policy wonk, and he would come away thinking I was the smartest SOB that ever came up from the Hill. When I got there, Clinton was waiting for me with a bunch of senior staffers, including chief of staff John Podesta. "Hot damn," I thought, "we're going to get into something today." But before we were all seated, the president asked them to step outside for a minute so we could talk privately.

"This is the day," I thought. We sat down, he crossed his legs, and he looked at me and said, "So tell me, how do you *really* think Hillary will do in New York?"

Once her name was out there, any husband, any friend from Arkansas, would want to hear what the heck was going on from the senior Democrat from New York. Did I talk to the county chairmen? Did I talk to the members of the delegation? What labor leaders did I call? Did I talk with Tisch, and other heavyweight fund-raisers? It was no big political meeting. It was really about "You're not gonna leave my gal out there, right?" and to let me know that he knew who the players were. I guess he also knew that wherever their careers might be taking them, his was hitting an end in Washington and hers was going to take off somewhere. Of course, I had no way of knowing he'd end up with his office just a block from my district office on 125th Street.

They said I was crazy, but I ended up with the once and future king and queen, respectively, as a neighbor and political godchild. In a sense, I helped the Democratic Party in exile find asylum in New York.

———————

All of my staff is dedicated and brilliant. Let me tell you about some of them. Vivian Jones goes back to my days at Weaver, Evans, Wingate & Wright. She was my administrative assistant when I first practiced law. She's a true friend with not only great skills—one of the last people on the planet who can take shorthand—but a great understanding of the nuances of dealing with politicians and constituents. I'm pleased to say that there are people who call up and want to speak with Vivian instead of me.

In Washington, George Dalley, Pat Swygert's successor, has been a friend to me and my family, and has handled problems in Washington and New York, but especially internationally in the Caribbean. Brenda Swygert was with me before she married Pat Swygert's brother, and remains with me, though she lost her beloved husband, Ken. Many people have said that if Brenda ever left Charlie Rangel he would absolutely fall apart. She needs no records, no diaries, no research. I can ask her who did such and such in 1974 and she just retrieves it from memory. Her mind is photographic, and her looks are photogenic.

Emile Milne has been my press secretary for decades. I've been so lucky to have a guy who possesses not only journalistic capabilities, but a knack for knowing my mind. I give him an idea, and when I get it back, it's still my idea, only improved.

Whatever there is to know about computers, Wendy Featherson knows it. She's dedicated, smart, faithful, and loyal. And my "new" Washington staffers—those with less than twenty years—including my personal assistant Annie Minguez, are cutting out their own reputations for exceptional service.

And, of course, I must remember my recently retired political adviser George Henry; he's the one person most responsible for this book's coming to be.

My New York chief of staff, Jim Capel, is well known to all of the politicians in the city. His political savvy is legendary in New York City. He knows exactly which people I need to call, which meetings I have to attend, and when I need to attend them. He's been with me so long that

I probably take the benefit of his political thinking for granted over the years. I haven't had many real campaigns, but whenever I've had a campaign manager, I can hear Jim's words coming out of his ears.

Tina McRae is my New York Brenda. Her personality is at once charming and dynamic; no one answers a phone, and makes all comers big and small feel respected if not loved like Tina McRae.

New York handles a great deal of immigration matters. Maritza Sanchez has become an expert in immigration law and heads those efforts in the office. One of the most exciting aspects of my district is the rising prominence and accomplishment of our Dominican community. I don't know what I'd do without the leadership of Maisotis Munoz to keep me up to speed on their issues.

Dan Berger is bright, energetic, and hard-working. Joined by Elbert Garcia, while new to the staff, they make an outstanding contribution to our work. Holding down and keeping me up on doings in "El Barrio" of East Harlem is Johnny Rivera, who shares his experience with me and is a great community adviser. Michelle Sherwood is our expert on education and health issues affecting the district. Her sharp mind and unfailing good humor make her a pleasure to work with and a credit to Harlem.

The guy who keeps me and my schedule together is Albert Beckett. He's the one who makes my train run on time in New York; we've been together since 1970.

I met the late Pope John Paul II about six times. As chairman of the drug committee, I was always meeting in Rome with international agencies fighting organized crime. On one trip I was talking with the wife of former Italian president Amintore Fanfani. "Of course," she said, you'll see the pope before you leave." I wasn't planning on it, but she insisted. So I told the other committee members; they were excited because half of them had never met the pope. When I met him, I started to tell him that "President Fanfani's—"

"President Fanfani?" he cut me off. "President Fanfani? Nooooo; Madame Fanfani," he said, and we had such a laugh.

I told the pope how no one who knew me then would have thought that this former altar boy from Harlem would be leading a congressional delegation at the Vatican. The pope went on to say that he knew who I was, and all about my reputation as a drug fighter. He said that whenever I wanted to see him, for moral support or prayers, he would welcome my call. I'm afraid I no longer believe in Catholic or even Christian theology and dogma the way I once did. Traveling all over the world as I have, and being exposed to so many different faiths, all I want to be able to do when I get to heaven is to have a little time with St. Peter to explain who I am. I've pretty much shaken off the effect of being raised with the mystique of the nuns and the priests and the bishops and cardinals, much to the chagrin of the Catholic hierarchy, in the person of the late Cardinal O'Connor.

I was on the plane with Cardinal O'Connor, going to Cuba to see Castro with the pope in 1998. Now, O'Connor and I had already had a long . . . not love-hate but love-difficulty relationship. He felt very strongly about my pro-choice position on abortion. But he also felt equally as strong about my independence in championing causes for the poor, to the point that I took on the Church for what appeared to be its silence on the question of Bill Clinton's policy of abolishing welfare as an entitlement. O'Connor would have me in for high-level meetings with bishops and such, presumably to talk about these issues, only to first spend time squeezing on my presumed Catholic guilt, talking about how he prayed for me to return to the fold—that is, their control. When, during one of the many parades in New York, I broke away from the tradition of elected Catholic officials literally kissing his ring as we marched past St. Patrick's Cathedral he made a point of telling the press, "Oh, he's the one who thinks he knows more about the Church and my job than I do."

I was critical of the Church's silence on the Haitian crisis of a few years earlier, as it played out with such tragic consequences in a predominantly Catholic country. At the time I had actually gotten more traction organizing the Jewish religious community to identify with the plight of the Haitian boat people who were being turned away from the Florida coast, much like the Jewish refugees on the SS *St. Louis* were turned away in 1939. When I challenged Cardinal O'Connor at that time, he made a show of having masses for the Haitians, said in Haitian Creole. But I had to push and push him to go beyond the ceremonial and throw the Church's weight behind the Haitian refugee cause. Now, on the plane with the pope's historic mission to communist Cuba, O'Connor made a point to come to the back of the plane to visit with me.

First he thanked me for coming, and said that he looked forward to meetings he knew I had scheduled with Castro. My name, he hastened to tell me, had come up in his conversations with His Holiness the Pope. Then he tried to weave in the idea that I was so good, it was such a shame I wouldn't come back to the Church and set an example.

"You know," he said, "you really do good work, looking out for the poor like you do. Have you ever thought about coming back to the Church?"

He went on to explain that now that I was a member of Congress, making national and international decisions, I needed a better understanding of my obligations as a Catholic on that level. He said it was unfair for me to even approach that responsibility with only an altar boy's understanding of the faith. This was not the first time the Cardinal had tried to encourage me to reenter the fold. I tried to deflect him with a little apostasy.

"I am so impressed with other people's belief in other than Jesus Christ, and purgatory, and getting into heaven . . . quite frankly I'm not prepared to take any gambles that my Catholic ticket is the only one that will be received there."

Somehow, though, he interpreted this as a reason to issue a serious invitation for me to return to catechism.

"Well," I started, "I really only have a kid's understanding of the Church, and the catechism and all."

"But you should come back, and learn more," he said. "You have an obligation to the Church."

I still felt a little awkward, so I tried telling him a story.

"Cardinal," I said, "did you hear about the astronaut who went into space, and somehow his ship went beyond its orbit and actually passed through heaven? After it circulated through heaven it made it back and landed safely. There was a big press conference, and he was asked, 'Did you really go to heaven?'

"'Yes,' he said.

"'Did you see God?'

"'Yes,' he answered.

"'Could you tell us what God looked like?'

"'Well,' said the astronaut, 'I was going so fast that I didn't really get the best look. But I'll tell you one thing: She's black.'"

And at that, Cardinal O'Connor just got up and left me; I don't think he spoke to me again for the rest of the trip.

His silence was a perfect metaphor for my problem with the Church. When you find the tax burden shifting from the rich to the working poor; when you find the federal government giving up responsibility for welfare, education, and health care; when you find Washington saying it has no moral responsibility for social services, that it's on local or state government or the private sector, you would expect the Church to be screaming with outrage. Not just about the unborn, but about the born. About what is happening in the Middle East and about AIDS in Africa is where the Church should be shouting, not at the victims but at the people with power.

Whether they talk to me or not, I'm determined to talk to them about a morality above and beyond their faith and their dogma. Once, during a Ways and Means hearing, a Catholic priest from the South made the comment about how much courage it took for him to come to Washington and testify on behalf of the poor. Afterward, because I was Catholic, I took him aside to ask him what he really meant.

"You know, Father, that was such an uncharacteristic remark. What's so courageous about you—married to the Church, celibate with an oath of poverty—what's so courageous about you testifying for the poor?"

"You know, Rangel," he said, "I've been following your remarks. I am a shepherd of the Church. You would ask me to take a two-by-four and hit my flock upside the head. What you don't understand is that if I did what you ask me to do, I'd lose my flock and my church. What I'm telling you is that poor folks don't buy stained-glass windows. Poor folks don't buy hospital pavilions. Poor folks don't buy libraries for universities. And poor folks are not selected as trustees or board members."

So much for organized religion. I'm simply too outraged by their consistent and historical lack of moral outrage when the basic tenet of their religion is "Thou shall not kill."

Even though I've been blessed with independence in the Congress and immunity to political pressures, what's emotional to me is this war in Iraq. It's emotional to me that people can be as indifferent to the actions of a president in taking a preemptive strike against a nation that has done nothing to us, and indifferent to his distortion of the truth in implying that Saddam Hussein was responsible for 9/11, to the extent that we cannot even talk about it,. It bothers me that poor whites, blacks, and Hispanics are being slain every day for this lie. It bothers me that I've seen fifty-eight-year-old National Guardsmen off to Iraq, and that reservists who had no intention of fighting anybody are going for a second and third time, which is breaking up marriages.

It bothers that this whole country—but especially the Church—was not outraged when blacks were being pulled out of their homes and lynched for so many decades, that we closed our eyes when six million Jews were being exterminated in the Holocaust. And we knew it. And the pope knew it.

So there I was, in St. Patrick's Cathedral, as Cardinal O'Connor finished up this Creole mass for the poor, suffering Haitians. Don't you know that he asked me to come up to the altar for a press conference? *With him?* I noticed there was even a mike set up at one of the side altars. I had seen the reporters, and I knew this was a dramatic event, filling St.

Patrick's and such. But to invite me to the altar was almost too much. Because I was an altar boy, there are certain things, certain rituals that are indelibly engraved in my mind. I just don't mess around on the church altar. I don't even walk up onto the church altar. A press conference? At St. Patrick's? And he even introduced me, in that "voice of God" tone of his: "And I hope that Congressman Rangel will join with me at the conclusion of this mass, as we share what the Holy Mother the Church is doing to help these people. . . ."

The biggest fear I've ever had is starting to believe my own feeling of self-importance. But bigger than that fear is not taking advantage of where I am, after forty-plus years in politics; realizing that it's not self-importance but my obligation to use what my community has given to me for thirty-four years on their behalf. It is the power to determine just how far I can push the envelope, because they have said I am all right with them.

When you ran off to Africa, they said, and it didn't get us any jobs, it was OK. You ran off to Haiti—hey, we don't have any Haitians—they said it was still OK. When you called for the draft, not that you wanted any more of us going to Iraq, but just to shame those who sent us, it was OK, too. You don't have to worry about political consequences, I hear them say, because seventeen times we've said, "Go back to Washington, and do what you have to do."

"So now is not the time to say you don't want to get involved. Go ahead, Charlie. Step up to that mike, and do what you have to do."

And I haven't had a bad day since.

10

Political Epilogue

Someone recently asked me point-blank: "What do you want to come out of this book?" All I could answer was that the period in which we're living has altered the arc of my political career, and therefore shaped this account of the meaning of my political life, far more than I ever imagined when I began. In the first place, we are in a war that is so unlike anything we've ever been involved in. I attend so many affairs now where people come up to me and say, "You're the only voice against the war." That's not exactly so, but there's no question that there aren't many prominent people against the war who get the kind of access to television that I do. I even get Republicans coming up to me now saying, "You are so right about Bush—we shouldn't be in this war. I'm changing my registration."

At the same time, I am increasingly called upon to prepare the Democratic alternatives to the administration's plans to keep cutting taxes on the wealthy, without regard to our mounting budget deficits. Now, somewhere down the line there may be a confrontation between me and my Democrats on this. My party may want me to stake out a politically convenient plan that's positioned just enough to the left of what the Republicans are talking about, the kind of triangulation that made Bill Clinton such a thorn in Newt Gingrich's side.

But the beauty of all this is that I can't lose. I've got the numbers on my side.

We're losing money hand over fist, hemorrhaging cash on the war and on tax cuts and on interest payments on the national debt. Yet I'm supposed to come up with something that's Republican lite, "me too, but not that much." If I'm to be the leader, I will have to get with my Democratic colleagues to come up with something better. Because I don't think I'll be doing the party or the country any favors by keeping us committed to going down the same road, only with some speed bumps added so we can say we were thinking of the middle class. Many of the tax cuts suggested by the Republicans are very attractive to many Democrats. Even though they increase the deficit, there's an old legislative saying: "If you have to explain your vote to your constituents, you have a problem." The real problem, however, is that we Democrats are going to be held to the standard we place in our alternative legislation. We cannot afford the luxury of being irresponsible in trying to be "Republican lite."

There used to be a time when all the responsible economists and businesspeople were always talking about the deficit, and the debts we're passing on to our kids and our grandkids. In order to restore integrity to the programs that we want, we would either have to cut defense, which may not be strategically practical, or raise taxes, which is always politically unpopular. But if I participate in getting us deeper into debt by signing on to yet another compromise with an economic view I don't believe in, I may be saving these programs today for burial in a fiscal mass grave tomorrow.

At this time we find this administration is still committed to not taxing anything except wages. Its zeal for cutting taxes on capital gains, estates, corporations, and the wealthy is unparalleled in my thirty-five years in Congress. At the same time, the administration and congressional Republicans continue to reduce aid to the states, money that the states must in turn replace by hiking regressive property and sales taxes. At the end of the day, then, the entire tax system is being shifted to the state, local, and regressive and away from the national and progressive. This shift in Republican tax strategy—paying for tax cuts by borrowing—now shatters the myth that the Democratic Party is one of "tax and spend." All of the tax cuts that we Democrats offer as alternatives are more progressive, and they are offset by cutting spending in other programs over which our committee has jurisdiction. That makes *us* the fiscal conservatives today.

My job is to make certain that while asking Democrats not to support the cuts in social programs and the continued tax cuts for the wealthy of this country, we Democrats on the Ways and Means Committee give them something to vote *for*, and are not merely opposing Republicans for opposition's sake. And I'm going to do just that between now and November 2006. But if we lose our credibility—as unbiased economists scream that everything we've done since 2000 is contrary to sound economic policy—then we'll all be tarred with the same brush: gross fiscal irresponsibility. So Democrats must be sure that we are right in whatever we're doing, and whatever we get behind. Because soon— very soon—there will be nobody left saying that the Republican fiscal program, such as it is, is right. Oh, the administration may say things are picking up, that the GNP is growing and employment is steady. But damn it, they can't get away from that deficit! Even the Republicans who supported the Medicare prescription bill are complaining about who is going to pay for it.

My point: What an irony for a guy from Lenox Avenue, from the heart of Harlem, to end up not only being a leading voice on the immorality of the war, but the voice of fiscal sanity in the House of Representatives. Imagine, me, doing the job that the old Chamber of Commerce, Main Street Republicans used to do, because the rest of their party have truly lost their minds. These are the times that shape my political epilogue.

It's safe to say that the Republican philosophy has always been an interpretation of the Constitution that says if certain rights and obligations are not directly spelled out for the federal government, then they are retained by the states. And they truly don't believe that social services are a federal obligation; they think state and local governments should bear those responsibilities. Federal taxes, in their view, should be so low that mayors and governors, who have access to people's corporate and individual incomes, will have to be the ones to lay on taxes for social spending based on local preferences. So in Florida, for example, they might want more care for the elderly, in California more care for the younger. There would be different tax structures for different social services, like the way many states use regressive lotteries to fund education.

To bring all this to pass, the Republicans in Washington persist in their efforts to dismantle what we call in Washington budget-speak "entitlements." Simply put, "entitlement" means that if you meet the criteria Congress sets for receiving certain benefits, you're entitled, and that the amounts people get, and the number of people getting them, are not subject to debate. The Congress says that if you are a certain age, you're entitled to Social Security, entitled to disability, entitled to widow's benefits. If you're sick and you're poor you are entitled to Medicaid; if you meet other criteria you're entitled to Medicare for your health needs. Historically, the Republicans have fought against these programs from their inceptions. In their view, government assistance saps the will to work and corrupts the moral fiber of the recipients. In their view, social services can always be better provided by the private sector, and if they can't, then they probably ought not to be provided. For all the lip service they give to Franklin Roosevelt, they fought his Social Security plan every step of the way. Republicans don't want people to remember that, on the same ideological grounds, they opposed the

GI Bill of Rights, the last of all the New Deal legislation, and by some measures the one that had the greatest impact.

Fortunately, Roosevelt was pretty much unassailable by 1944, when the GI Bill was signed. The relief and economic momentum coming out of World War II, and the immediate impact of our armed forces turning on a dime from soldiering to higher education and suburban home ownership, made the New Deal untouchable for two decades. The attack on the house that Franklin Roosevelt built for America in the thirties and forties only began in earnest after Lyndon Johnson renovated it in the sixties to include those who had been unable to take full advantage of the New Deal entitlements: blacks and other racial minorities. I was in the Congress when the Nixon administration began the effort to dismantle the Office of Economic Opportunity (OEO), the centerpiece of the Great Society program that focused on America's poorest communities. Though OEO reached at least as many poor whites as blacks, Republicans used resentment of the civil rights movement to racialize antipoverty programs to great political success, especially in the South, ironically, where so many poor whites lived.

Nixon's maneuver became an all-out fiscal and ideological assault under Ronald Reagan, going far beyond the racially identified Great Society programs. When Ronald Reagan's budget director David Stockman wrote that the federal budget was a beast that had to be starved into submission, he crystalized the demonization of the central role of national government in protecting the health, welfare, and living standard of average Americans, which is now the catechism of the modern Republican faith. Starving the beast meant cutting off the flow of tax revenue to Washington by any means necessary. As a thirty-year member of the tax-writing Ways and Means Committee, let me make one thing clear: The whole idea of reducing taxes on the wealthy is not because the rich have been screaming and lobbying for it. It's because, as a matter of right-wing ideology, the Republicans just don't want the money to be in Washington.

The Republicans don't want the federal government subsidizing the poor and the sick, because, since Roosevelt, they really don't think the Constitution gives it the authority. It's not even principle—a basic truth or moral standard—it's ideology, a group of ideas reflecting the aspirations of a group, a class, or a culture. Unlike standing up for a principle, when you're fighting for an ideology you don't have to let the facts or the truth stand in your way. When President Bush attempted to persuade America and the Congress on his plan to "save" Social Security, everyone knew he was trying to convert a public responsibility to a private "everyone get a job and provide for their own savings" initiative. The president insisted that Social Security was bankrupt. It wasn't true. He was using that to frighten people into ending federal responsibility for Social Security and into taking the money out of the Social Security trust fund and putting it into private accounts.

Fortunately, the Social Security pillar of our New Deal house is anchored in political bedrock. But the Great Society renovations are still quite vulnerable, after a twenty-five-year Reaganite siege. As I write, the Republicans still don't want Medicaid as we know it. As for Medicare, they are very candid about their vision of having the private sector compete with itself, as if there could ever be a truly competitive market for this kind of good. They are not about to let the conclusions of health care economists get in the way of what the health care and drug industry lobbies have to say.

To some extent, the same situation applies to the remnants of every New Deal–Great Society initiative. Despite all the returns to federal government investment in the health, housing, and education of the American people since World War II, we see more and more federal programs falling farther and farther behind the changing needs of the people in a global economy. As I write this, federal support for housing under the Section 8 program is in great jeopardy, and so are many other programs.

Perhaps worse than stifling existing programs, the Republicans have come very close to extinguishing the very impulse of fairness and social and economic justice that inspired the programs' creation in the first place. When George H. W. Bush trashed "the vision thing" as a kind of figment of the liberal Democratic imagination, he really wasn't kidding. So, as we Democrats make one more bid to return to power, they charge us with being "tax and spend" liberals. But what else could we be after so many years of untax and cut? What else could we do when they have already cut trillions of dollars out of revenue to the Treasury; spent close to one-half trillion dollars and counting in an unjust, unwarranted war; unnecessarily suffered the economic casualties of Hurricane Katrina; and forced us to pay an enormous part of our national budget just to cover the interest on all our debt? We have borrowed more money under both Bush administrations than under all the other presidents of the United States combined!

Our first job as Democrats must be not to do any more harm. True, we have to remain vigilant in getting rid of programs that don't work. But as Democrats, we have to be prepared to truly believe that education is not just a headache we're stuck with. In my opinion education and heath care are national investments, as important to our national security as nuclear bombs, planes, and armed forces. True, our education system has historically been local in funding and control, while health care provision has been mostly private. But from a point of view of national security, when you look at the threat posed by the economic advances of totalitarian China, and our steady loss of share in key sectors of international trade, it's clear that our technological edge is the only thing keeping us competitive. That is why it's critically important today to make taking people out of poverty our number-one national priority. Why? Because poverty is disproportionately visited on our most valuable resource, people under the age of twenty-one. To compete with massive, faster-growing economies like China and India, or better-educated, socially secure economies like Japan and the European countries, we will need all our young people heading for higher education and training instead of the military, prison, or jobs flipping hamburgers.

This vision is not new, but with Hurricane Katrina the connection between poverty and national security was finally televised. Most of the people who died in Katrina—a natural disaster that became an unnatural national tragedy—died because they were poor. It did not go unnoticed that blacks were disproportionately poor and suffered a greater share of the pain. But Katrina, like poverty itself, was at least partially color blind. If she were a terrorist armed with a WMD, instead of a hurricane, the results flowing from our failure to address glaring social needs would be similar. Those who are too poor to follow directions, to have the habit of reading or writing or otherwise do those things necessary to defend the good of the community, will cause the whole system to break down because they lack the education and sophistication and means to protect themselves. In my Democratic vision, if you can see all the catastrophic costs of rebuilding New Orleans and the Gulf Coast as negative consequences of underfunding education, infrastructure, and income security, everything looks different.

A decent education is directly correlated with a minimum level of economic success, and a personal investment in our larger social values of home, family, and community. It means young people are less prone to involvement in those things that are so corrosive to vulnerable communities, and ruinously expensive for government at all levels. As I spoke in an effort to stave off yet another money crisis at the world-famous Boys Choir of Harlem in my district in 2006, I had to remind Mayor Mike Bloomberg and the media that we spend $100,000 per year just to keep one kid locked up in the city's infamous Rikers Island detention center. One kid, $100,000, and there are many, many thousands there. Imagine if we were investing even a fraction of that in the education of every kid in New York. Fortunately, we have some great people in New York like former mayor David Dinkins. In his love for the institution, he has assumed the chairmanship of the Boys Choir. Together we intend to save it for Harlem and the world.

———

What does it mean when people think I might just become the next chairman of Ways and Means? The power of this chairmanship is in setting the terms for the relationship between the interests of the people and the private-sector stakeholders in our society. The CEOs don't come and ask how I am going to treat their companies. They come and ask what role we'd like them to play. They don't come to negotiate, they come to support—to get along by going along, one fiscal quarter at a time. Today they blindly support the ideological views of the Republicans because they want to make it to the next quarter without being disturbed. In my view, they can be amazingly flexible about how they get to that next quarter, as long as they have input into how things will shape up. I can see them in my office supporting national health and educational programs, as long as they have a say in the details.

I've met with the president of one of the top three American automobile manufacturers, who talked about the huge share of the cost of building a car that goes to providing health and pension benefits for each worker. I asked him if he wouldn't be better off by supporting a national health insurance program—the kind his company's Japanese and European competitors have—so that part of the expense would be shouldered by the general public. And if he got behind a new federal initiative to provide real support for education, I asked him, wouldn't that give him a more educated, more productive workforce? If you followed the principles of the Democratic Party, I told him, the government would assume responsibility for health and education, and you in the private sector could focus all your energies on research and development, with our help, to compete with Asia and Europe.

His response was simply to say that their decisions are made on a quarterly basis. What matters most is being able to make credible quarter-by-quarter projections over a five-year time frame. More than just raw profits, Wall Street wants predictability. I have no problem with that. My job on Ways and Means is to marry the narrow financial interest of shareholders in predictability with the long-term interests of our multinational corporations in the health, education, and welfare of the people who create and purchase their products. It's my humble opinion that the presidents and CEOs not only have a moral responsibility to protect the interests of the people of the United States, but that it is one and the same with their fiduciary responsibility to do the right thing for their stockholders. If the Chinese can do it cheaper, though we need the jobs and the technology to stay in the United States, the corporation has a responsibility to the people and the shareholders to support the programs that will restore or maintain our advantage in productivity.

There's no CEO who can dispute that, if present trends continue, the Chinese will exceed our ability to compete unless we completely shift our priorities away from guns and bullets and toward books and education. Yet unless progressive Democratic leadership in the Congress superimposes this vision on the corporate imagination—much as the Republicans have blessed the profitability of outsourcing, running trade and budget deficits, and selective direct subsidies for certain industries—we cannot rely on the private sector to do the right thing.

In 1955, a former GM chairman defended the firms' oligopoly pricing power in a Senate hearing with the argument that cheaper Chevys would just put employees at competitors out of work. He summarized his view with the now infamous boast, "What's good for General Motors is good for America." But the truth is that he made that boast before a Republican-controlled Congress under a Republican president inclined to see it his way. The fact is that there are many things that might be good for General Motors; it's the job of Congress to identify which things are also good for America and guide them toward it.

Again, when I talk to the CEOs, even if they're for the war and against the draft—believing that those who volunteer for military service bear full responsibility for the national blood sacrifice—they have to concede the need to invest more in the health and education of our most vulnerable youth. Because even if you look at them as mere cannon fodder, they're unusable if they're on drugs, have criminal records, or are without education. We have to educate them because the military is far more technical now than it was twenty years ago. Any way you slice it, there's nothing more patriotic than investing in the education, health care, and productivity of all our people.

What can be obvious to the corporate and military bottom line is not as easily made clear to many other stakeholders in the status quo. When you're talking about reversing the trends of the last quarter century, and flowing some measure of control over education and health care to Washington, you're talking about many millions of jobs and billions in budgets in the hands of mayors and governors, teachers' unions and other organized interest groups. There is now a substantial constituency for the dismantling of the federal government administration of health care delivery. When you put, as we did with the Medicare prescription program, $13 billion into HMOs organizing to compete against the federal system, creating more health care entrepreneurs in the process, some members of Congress have difficulty voicing opposition.

Change is hard. It's much more difficult to increase taxes than to cut taxes by trillions of dollars. At the end of the day, if the Republicans have their way, they can always say, "Well, it was a good argument, but how are you going to pay for it?" And if there are only three ways to pay—borrow more money from Asia and Europe, increase taxes, or cut other programs—what are we going to do? We have to get the public to put its foot down and say enough is enough. When you are in leadership, and in authority, you can craft and send that message out. But just because you lead people to the water of reason and truth doesn't mean they will automatically drink. We've got to identify their thirst first, or the beneficiaries of these very social policies, and a new worldview, will continue to vote against their own best interests.

I had hoped, for example, that Hurricane Katrina would focus a demand across racial lines to eliminate poverty. Katrina clearly showed that a lot of poor white folks lost their lives, not because they were white, but because they were poor. Why, then, would poor white folks not be looking for a better Social Security system, and a better educational system? Somehow the poor in this country have come to place more hope for change in their relationship with religion than engagement with changing the political structure. Now, the Republicans have been able to turn out a great many Evangelical Christians to vote for banning abortion and stopping gay marriage, imposing certain Christian values on other people's lives. But when it comes to their own economic interests, this group has more confidence in going to church than going to the polls to vote Democratic. The tragic irony, of course, is that the Republicans have not delivered on the "moral values" agenda or their economic security, and have no politically viable plans to do so.

I don't pretend to know how to change their minds. One way, perhaps, as *New York Times* columnist Tom Friedman has suggested, would be to translate the term *tax cut* as used in Republican speeches into a phrase the American people will finally understand: *spending cut on services that matter.* I do know one thing. We used to have a similar state of apathy with old folks, but once they wised up to what Social Security really means for them, they became unbeatable defenders of this New Deal pillar. President Bush spent the best part of his short work year in 2005 trying to tell them about how the system needed change, and promising them that their benefits would not be changed. Their response? "Hell no, keep your hands off our Social Security; you're not changing it for us, or for our kids and grandkids."

On the domestic front, I think the sinking of the Bush Social Security reform was the first direct hit scored in the battle to take back our house. The most important indicator of a pendulum swinging back is the low number of people who believe the president on anything. As I write this, the polls have his approval ratings in the mid-30s, and still heading south. A CBS News poll in March 2006 put the share of Americans who say President Bush is not honest or trustworthy at 52 percent. When that happens it doesn't matter what he's talking about anymore. It's now gone beyond being misled about the war in Iraq, beyond disappointment with the people he appointed to FEMA, beyond disgust with the people indicted in his Office of Management and Budget, beyond suspicion of his ties to the Jack Abramoff scandal. It's even beyond the shock of his determination to illegally wiretap Americans in the name of the war on terror, while failing to scrutinize the sale of the management of key American port facilities to a company owned by the United Arab Emirates.

At this point, a great many Americans just don't believe the president, period—meaning they are not likely to believe him on the issues that haven't made the headlines yet. One of those things is the coming budget crisis forced by the high cost of borrowing money. At my Town Hall meetings, I often say that I don't have any problem with borrowing money. I don't mind paying back what I borrow. But what really gets to me emotionally is paying the interest and service charges on what I borrow, while not seeing the principal being reduced. It is staggering to think about the obligation each child of my grandchildren's generation will have to shoulder in taxes when they grow up, not to eliminate the debt, but just to pay the interest. When that amount becomes larger than the sums we're investing in transportation, infrastructure, environment, basic science, education, and health care, our nation has a serious economic problem. The Republicans keep trying to say that we will grow out of it. But when you look at people being laid off, or retiring without pensions, it's an increasingly hard argument to sell to them. Especially when nobody believes the face of your party anymore.

I really believe we're in a parallel moment with 1994, the midterm election year in which the Democrats had lost the confidence of the people. The Republicans came in with a slogan, a Contract with America, and America said, "Yeah, let's get rid of these guys who have been running things for forty years." I think we've reached the point now, with the war, the incompetence, and the lies that have been told, when the people are ready to listen to another version and another vision of the American dream. They hear the Republicans talk about a prosperous economy, and see that they're really talking about the coupon-clipping class. They see the willingness of Congress to use its power as a sword—tacitly supporting torture and the killing of innocents in Iraq and Afghanistan—rather than as a shield to protect the American people. I think the people are prepared for a change, and in leading that change I think we have the responsibility to pick up the pieces of the programs that have been working, like affordable housing and Head Start, to try to get this nation going back in the direction where the people are protected, rather than the corporate structures or the so-called private sector. Who is this private sector, anyway, and where in the Constitution are its special rights enumerated?

Is America ready for Charlie Rangel in the chair of Ways and Means? In 1994, right after we lost power in Congress, *Congressional Quarterly* magazine did an article asking "Is Charles Rangel Too Liberal to Chair the Ways and Means Committee?" It ended up concluding that liberals and conservatives have different ways of achieving the same goal: a better and more prosperous America. It was very, very complimentary to me. I, for one, am very excited for what my chairmanship would mean for America. Just take a look at the major areas of my jurisdiction.

On trade, I helped draft the Caribbean and the African trade bills. I didn't vote for NAFTA, but I did support our trade opening with China, as well as agreements with Chile and Jordan. The only difference that I have with the Republicans on this—the firewall between us—is that I believe we should have international standards, albeit minimum standards, for the workers in these foreign countries. They should be able to get a minimum wage, and to organize and form unions. There should be no child labor and certain other things that Americans just don't believe in. I'm not saying other countries should have our standards, but there must be some international standards.

On Social Security, quite simply, I believe America is with me in keeping the private sector's hands off of it. America proved it when the president tried to reform it.

On Medicare, I'm not going to have any problem persuading my constituents in the United States of America that when you get old and have paid into the system, you should be entitled to health care.

As for taxes, we should be able to raise as much revenue as we need to fulfill our national responsibilities, and raise it in a way that encourages economic growth but makes certain that the system is, and is perceived to be, fair and equitable and based on one's ability to pay. It's religious and moral: from those to whom much has been given, much is expected. That's all it's about.

America and the Congress do not have to worry about Charlie Rangel. I've been here for thirty-five years, most of them on the committee. No one has ever credibly accused me of demagoging on the issues before it. A politician running for statewide office in New York recently said to me: "I want a partnership with you. Everyone thinks I'm right on the issues, but they don't like me. But with you, they don't care whether they agree with you or not—they like you. We ought to have a partnership."

It was very flattering. But I think it's fair to say that even though I've had my knock-down, drag-out confrontations with the incumbent chairman, Bill Thomas, when I say I haven't had a bad day since, it means that Bill Thomas has never given me a bad day. I see no reason why any of the competing voices in the new people's House to come should give me a bad day either.

As we move forward in the new Congress, I am so pleased to have Democratic minority leader Nancy Pelosi as a partner. She has been able to bring the diverse segments of our caucus together and keep them united, without losing the principles of our party. Her leadership allows all of us to believe that she respects our views and values our unique contributions. She's dedicated, hard-working, and a true believer in the principles that have made our country as great as she is. Still, as good as America is, Nancy Pelosi believes we can do better, and we will.

I'd rather be right and a patriot, than a demagogue and a Democrat.

As I go across the country fund-raising, I ask Republicans to ask me the hard questions and tell me where I'm wrong. Tell me where I go wrong when I ask why is it that government involvement must always be inferior to the private sector? Especially when you consider the dozens of private sector top managers who are now languishing in jail, and the dozens more who will soon be going to jail. They don't argue with me much on this point. Republican members of Congress can't really argue with me either, but they do have their self-interested, sometimes bought-and-paid-for, priorities. Again, it is so easy, politically, to vote consistently to reduce the size of federal entitlements, and to cut taxes on the wealthy. It's just so seductive. I've had members of Congress support the repeal of the estate tax, a tax that only reaches estates over $100 million.

I asked them, "How could you do that? Do you know anybody in your community who would benefit from it? Have you even read about anyone in your community who would benefit?" They say no on both counts, then add, "But maybe one day we'll be rich, too."

It has been said that their constituents feel the same way about the wealthy and their wealth. But as for the Congress, I think the main reason a representative of working- or lower-middle-class Americans supports this kind of tax cut is that they hope to get campaign contributions from the ultra-rich. I'm leading the fight against the repeal of the estate tax because I believe that this tiny fraction of Americans have such a large share of the wealth that they ought to pay an equitable part of that to the federal treasury for the benefit of the vast majority of people in my district, and indeed the vast majority of people in every congressional district. Yet there are many people in the Congress who will vote at least indirectly against their constituents' interest in progressive taxation to provide for their needs. The fact is that there aren't a lot of citizens jumping up and down about taxing the rich. They're much more interested in the supermarket tabloid headlines about how the rich spend their money than about their obligation as citizens to share their money. Members of Congress know this. People don't give a damn about obtaining a measure of social equity from the rich. They're concerned about their own welfare, and they don't make the connection between the two.

We Democrats have our work cut out for us, because the ordinary voter doesn't vote on issues like repealing the estate tax. The ordinary voter isn't asking me about my vote against dramatically reducing corporate dividend taxes, or about capital gains taxes. Now, I understand that no one likes the tax collector. Nobody should. But when you're dealing with thousands of pages of tax code, deductions and tax cuts and credits and such, people just want to know one thing: Are you cutting taxes or are you raising them? Because they don't seem to care *whose* taxes we're cutting or raising, it has become political wisdom to embrace *any* cut that comes down the pike. But the mountain of federal debt piling up proves that it's fiscal foolishness; honest leadership requires us to tell the people the truth, and get out in front of a movement for change.

Republicans say they've been voting for change since 2000. But what we have today is not the change they were looking for. They weren't looking for war. They weren't looking for an expansion in the number of poor people in this country, especially poor children. They were not looking for cutbacks in health care. It has been said over and over that they were looking for a change in moral values—defined by whether women had access to abortion or homosexuals could marry—as dictated by their Christian faith. But what about the moral values that Jesus actually commanded?

I call it the Gospel of St. Matthew. In Matthew 25:31–40, Jesus explains to His disciples that when He returns He will reward all those who fed Him when He was hungry, who gave Him something to drink when He was thirsty, who gave Him a roof over His head, put clothes on His back, took care of Him when He was sick, and showed concern for Him when He was in prison. Then Jesus predicted that the people who consider themselves righteous will ask: "Lord, when did we see you hungry and feed you, or thirsty and give you something to drink? When did we see you a stranger and invite you in, or needing clothes and clothe you? When did we see you sick or in prison and go to visit you?"

Jesus answered them with, "I tell you the truth, whatever you did for one of the least of these brothers of mine, you did for me." Jesus then condemns all the self-righteous people who didn't recognize Him in their obligation to the poor, the sick, the homeless, and the imprisoned to Hell, but that's not my political concern or an article of my personal faith. All I'm saying is that Democrats must lead a new politics of moral values, the values that are consistent with the best impulses America ever had. We have to rebuild our house according to plans that Jesus would recognize whenever He might return. When the Republicans talk about reforms of Medicare or Medicaid that are really cuts, we need to remind the moral-value voters of what Jesus said. When people can't afford to heat their homes in the winter or cool them in the summer, when they have to choose between filling a prescription and eating, we have to remind them that after "Love the Lord your God with all your heart," Jesus said the second greatest commandment was "Love your neighbor as yourself."

The voters might not be hearing this from the pulpits right now. But this is what I'm talking about in the next election. I don't think it's moral to invade a country based on misinformation or prejudged facts, with the result of thousands of Americans and tens of thousands of Iraqis killed. I don't think it's moral to then declare victory by lying about what the objectives were in the first place, when you have no WMDs, no capture of Osama bin Laden, no connection between Saddam Hussein's Iraq and al-Qaeda. I know the facts of the issues are complicated, but I don't think people vote on the stuff of policy wonks and think tanks. I think people vote on a feeling, a gut reaction to the people and the party in power. I think it will all come down to one thing: Do you trust them?

It seems to me that every religion conveys the thought that humankind has an obligation to support the lesser of our brothers and sisters, as St. Matthew said. That is why it amazes me how silent the churches, synagogues, and mosques have been on the war in Iraq. But I must say that for the first time, in a 2006 budget reconciliation, I was pleasantly surprised to see the outrage of the religious community at the proposal of $30 billion in cuts to programs for the working poor at the same time they were reducing federal taxes by $100 billion and increasing the deficit by $70 billion.

With India and China emerging as strong economic competitors, I don't think it's going to be too difficult for Democrats to convince the private sector that our workforce has to be better trained, and certainly be kept in better health, if we're going to maintain our competitive edge. So among the major legislative thrusts that we should have are universal health care and a marked improvement in the nation's educational standards.

The war is almost too emotional for me. The closest I come to having a bad day is hearing people like Vice President Cheney say that to be critical of the war is to undercut the morale of our young people fighting in Iraq. But I go to the funerals, I talk to their parents. They're proud of their youngsters, and they want people to say good things about the courage and patriotism of their husbands, brothers, sons, and daughters. *But they want us to get the hell out of there, too.* They don't believe that a cockamamie constitution, imposed on a land hopelessly divided into three mutually suspicious tribes—Shiite, Sunni, and Kurd—is worth the loss of their children. And they don't believe the president when he says we're stopping terrorism here by knocking off Saddam Hussein over there.

When it's somebody else's kids fighting the war, and you hear the president say we won't bring one soldier home until we have victory, it's easy to give him the benefit of the doubt. It's easy to accept the loss of American lives, the shattered bodies and lives, when you don't identify at all with the kids or their families. I have called for considering a return to the draft not because I support war but because I insist that the burden of war be spread equitably across our society. Right now there's no relationship at all between most members of Congress, the Executive Branch, or the corporate management class and the blood being shed in this war, because their kids are not being placed in harm's way. But for those of us who can relate, as my colleague John Murtha has said so many times, this war is very, very hard to take. He's been over there a half-dozen times. Every week he visits the kids in the hospitals, and every day he passes the dead in Arlington Cemetery. If he has a weakness, it's his love and affection for those people who put their lives on the line. But for the people in charge, it's hard to believe they have any idea of the pain and suffering it takes to go to war, much less an unwinnable conflict of such dubious beginnings.

It's been fifty-five years since I've been in war. Every time I go to a soldier's funeral, I'm always hoping that the bereaved families have never misinterpreted my strong political opposition to the war as flowing from anything except a love and respect for those who stand where I have stood in battle, especially those giving up their lives. And so, recently, as I arrived at the funeral of a young Dominican soldier in my district, I was moved by the way the crowd of mourners were waiting for me outside of the church, because they thought that the presence of a member of Congress was providing some kind of dignity to the loss of this young father, brother, and son. As I walked in, it felt like I was being carried by a surging tide of family and friends, taking me to see their boy. And they were saying, "Tell them, Congressman, that my husband was a hero. Tell them my brother was a hero. Tell them in Washington what he fought and died for."

Most of the fallen heroes in my district have been marines. But as I moved slowly to the casket, instead of a marine in the usual sparkling blue uniform with the red stripe and white cap, I saw a dead soldier who was about twenty years old. He had on the same brown uniform, with the brass buttons and the olive drab green tie, that I had worn with such swagger more than fifty years ago. When I saw how much he looked like me when I was his age, my knees buckled. As I have said, when I first went to Korea in 1950, I wasn't afraid of any North Koreans. I wasn't overly impressed by the sight of the bloated, stinking, uncollected bodies of dead South Korean soldiers left by the side of the road as we made our way north. But when we saw the dead bodies of those black soldiers from our own 2nd Infantry Division, stacked like cordwood in the back of those trucks passing us heading south, well, we all collapsed. The sight of that young Dominican put me right back to my beginnings as cannon fodder in a questionable war.

A few years ago, I led a group of veterans—what's left of my outfit that went overseas—back to Korea for a commemoration of the fiftieth anniversary of the war. Not the end of the war, mind you, or the winning of the war, because technically we accomplished neither of those things. Hell, at the time we didn't even call it a war. What we went back to commemorate was really the anniversary of the North Koreans overrunning the South. It was so hard to revisit the pain and misery we went through, for something that doesn't even sound like it's patriotic anymore, something that doesn't make you feel like a genuine warrior. We didn't win anything in Korea, and the war is still technically on. The 2nd Infantry Division is still stationed there; they have not left Korea since we went in July 1950.

The general gave a dinner in my honor, and they had GIs there for us to talk with. They were white, and they were black, and they were Hispanic. They had on our fatigues, our Indian head insignia patches. They were us fifty years ago. Not one of us didn't cry at the recognition of ourselves; we couldn't imagine that we had once looked that way. And that's why the indifference of the architects of our foreign policy to the sacrifice of our youth outrages me so. The president and his men have neither the personal experience for identification nor a relationship with the communities that send young men to war. Wherever I go raising campaign funds, in the ballrooms and in the boardrooms of Wall Street, I ask people who support the war if they would continue to back it if their kids were eligible for a draft. They all say no. I still haven't figured out how these people can remain so numb to the deaths of the people who do go to Iraq, and the suffering of their families. But quite frankly I think even that is changing. Not as dramatically as I had hoped in 2004, but it is changing.

I'm similarly disappointed, yet hopeful, in the social and political aftermath of the Hurricane Katrina disaster. There were a lot of very negative stories written about me in the fall of 2005, when I said that in the wake of Katrina, President Bush could do for the cause of social and economic justice what the infamous Theophilous Eugene "Bull" Connor did for the struggling civil rights movement in 1963. I meant everything I said. The Alabama Public Safety commissioner is best known for his indifference to the aspirations of African Americans, and his willingness to confront black and white protesters with the most violent means at his disposal.

Connor represented the average American's passive acceptance of the lynching and murder of blacks in the South for over a hundred years. These murders had not outraged the conscience of America, just as the killing of Jews during the Holocaust didn't outrage America when it was happening. The victims were too far removed, by race, religion, and geography, to be identified with. America gave the segregationists and Hitler the benefit of disingenuous doubt. But when people saw the bodies of the Holocaust victims, or when people saw Bull Connor's raging dogs biting children on television, something happened that led them to say, "Enough is enough." They knew all along it was terrible, and subconsciously they knew it was wrong. But it took something more to bring them to the point of outrage, to say that *we* shall overcome, and march.

I thought about this American moral outrage as I saw those bodies floating in the waters of New Orleans, white poor people lined up trying to get gasoline to get out of town, and black people being stuck trying to get to the Superdome. And about Gene Taylor, a white congressman from Mississippi, saying he wished Katrina had hit just three days later, because "my people would have gotten their checks, and had enough money to get some gasoline and get out of town, too."

And just as Bull Connor showed a total indifference to the unarmed people he had hosed and mauled by dogs, and to the historical moment of Birmingham in 1963, I saw President Bush, not showing up for three days, not concerned about reports that the levees had failed. He was indifferent to the incompetence of "Brownie," the FEMA director. He actually seemed to care more about his attire for the Katrina photo opportunities than poor white Mississippians begging for water.

I thought that after seeing what happened in the Asian tsunami the year before, Americans watching Katrina would say to themselves, "I didn't know people were that poor in this country. I didn't know that poverty could be so fatal." I thought they would see that if this could happen in a natural disaster, then it would certainly happen in a terrorist attack. I thought they would see that poverty is real, and that we must do something about it. That people shouldn't die just because they're poor, and they shouldn't be poor just because they're black. I thought an enraged America would give us a clear mandate to resume the war on poverty that Lyndon Johnson started and from which the Republicans cut and ran.

That didn't happen, but it doesn't mean that America wasn't sensitized; all it means is that we Democrats failed to harness that sensitivity into practical politics of change. America didn't demand a Great Society. Lyndon Johnson, an old schoolteacher, used the teachable moments from Birmingham and Selma and the 1964 riots to lead us to reach for a Great Society. As I write this, I believe it's still not too late to revisit that lesson, and apply it to today's challenge.

11

Personal Epilogue

I was the only one from my childhood living with Grandfather when he died in 1965. He was on his third or fourth wife. I don't think he ever got around to saying he loved me; I don't think he had to. It was enough to have surprised the hell out of him by going to law school and then becoming a politician, because I was the last one he ever expected to make something of myself.

I was still living in the basement at "Seventy-four," because I just wasn't ready to go anywhere. It was just him raising hell all the time, and my diabetic stepgrandmother. I was disciplined enough never to scream and yell back, because he was Charlie Wharton, the CEO of Buckingham Palace. I don't know whether anyone would take his kind of abuse today. But in the old days people could get by with that; all that screaming and yelling was his "nature," they would say.

When I think of him, I think of all the people who would come up from Accomac, Virginia, with no place to stay, and how he always had a pot on the stove and a room for them. I've always known he was a good man, notwithstanding him sitting on the stoop like Scrooge and not letting anybody play ball near the house or otherwise mess with his most valued treasure. He was a poor elevator operator who owned a house. That was all. Unlike at my father's memorial, I knew the guest of honor at Grandfather's funeral. I couldn't say anything about how Grandfather loved everybody, because people would have laughed. You can joke more now than you could then. Still, my sister and I really missed him, and so did my mom.

I have found myself at funerals listening to people talk about the loss of a mom or dad who trained and guided them toward their careers. I have heard myself telling people, crying for their lost fathers, that it might help their pain to know that I never really knew a father, never had that comfort or guidance or experience shared with me. I never really had anyone to help me make decisions as to what I should do with my life and how to do it. I always hoped it would be a comfort to them to realize how much of their pain was due to the abundance of love, now lost, they had in the first place. I remember when my mother told me my father had died, there was some question as to whether I'd even come home from the army to go to the funeral. I thought it to be hypocritical to mourn someone I didn't even know. My mother never knew her mother. She lived a very rough life as my grandfather undertook to raise her and her brother alone. She married a man who was not the nicest, but the first adult man who might have taken her away from it all. She gave me more than my share of love, but it was a very rough life, tagging behind her erratic moves and being exposed to things I shouldn't have as I was shared back and forth among my relatives.

Still, I never got a chance to feel sorry for myself; there were too many other kids on Lenox Avenue with similar stories, and worse. Survivors. I often wonder, in my getting married and having children, what I brought to the table in terms of knowing love, and my will to be the model for the loving father I never had. I was a lawyer and a politician for a few years before I was a husband and a father. It could very well be that my first real love was the one I fell into with a larger family, a political family, and a larger constituency. It is a love I find myself almost unwilling to give up.

I have not told many stories about my personal and romantic life between the army and my marriage in 1965. But I will allow that in relationships I was always content to borrow and share. I never had or wanted any "thing" of my own, because I couldn't afford to have any emotional ties or obligations. I was going to school, and I made it very clear that if I didn't succeed it would not be because I fell in love with somebody; it would be because of me. In fact, I used to run away from the word *love*, much as my grandfather did, for fear that it would become too familiar, and thus fall into contempt. Especially when so many people were just abusing the word, saying "I love you" when what they really meant was "I love you . . . for this evening."

I knew that I was getting a second chance in life, and no relationship was going to derail that. This may have contributed more to never having a bad day since than I care to admit. I've never had a broken heart, because I never let anyone or anything be in a position to break my heart. Whatever heartbreak I had was as a kid; I left it on the battlefield at Kunu-ri and I never went back to look for it. Keeping my heart out of the way of hypocrisy and harm may have become my ultimate, unexamined defense mechanism. I left my heart with that hand truck in the gutter. Next thing I knew, I was committed to becoming the one thing that would seal my grandfather's respect for me. But somewhere after that—perhaps from the first time I walked into Lloyd Dickens's political club—nothing else seemed all that competitive. From that day on, seeing the reception that I received from elected officials as well as Democratic party officials, I knew that I would be embarking on a political career.

There's no question that my dedication to my profession has had its impact on my marriage. But there is absolutely no question in my mind that my wanting to be the father I never had has richly rewarded me with my loving daughter, Alicia, who has provided me with two grandsons, and my son, Steven, the lawyer, who is not only my son but my buddy, my friend, and my landlord in Washington. I don't know if I'd want to do anything differently. I may well have missed much in terms of having a larger, more comprehensive and balanced direction for my life. But the reward of living when I could be dead, the opportunity to get an education, and the privilege of meeting far more people in this country and around the world than most has more than made up for it.

I must confess that since Korea I haven't prayed for anything except my mother and my brother's recovery from illness. But I haven't hesitated to thank God every day for all that's worked out right. I do believe that puts me in a better place, psychologically. You can't think clearly if you always feel you've been singled out for a heavy burden. At the same time, I don't feel guided by a sense of having a calling or a mission. But if I did, it would be to show how thankful I am for living past that night in Korea.

I'm still just a guy from Lenox Avenue. I can look out my apartment window today and see the steps of "Seventy-four," where my grandfather sat. I'm on the national stage, but it's only because people understand that what I say I truly believe in. In my heart I believe that, in a world with so many people with the wealth, and lawyers and lobbyists to represent their interests, I have to thank God by doing the right things for people like the ones outside my window. I know people I've gotten out of jail appreciate it. Even people I have *put* in jail never fail to say I was fair, which amazes the hell out of me.

I was surprised, a few years ago, to hear Speaker Denny Hastert telling a group of new members that it's not just about understanding the law, it's understanding and respecting the people of the Congress. "You should talk to people like Charlie Rangel . . . and get to know these people," he said. Democrats came to me after and asked what the hell I did for Hastert to make him say that. But I felt proud that I'd carried myself over the years in such a way that I had a reputation like that.

Some people would have me believe that I'm really conning myself about people liking me. They would say it's all political—because I have the office—and that all these people are not sincere in their praise for how helpful I am, how good I am, and how glad they are to have me as a friend. It's not like the love of your family, they would say, it's just political support. They have a point, but so do I. If people can "love" me that way until I die, what difference does it make? As far as I'm concerned, they don't really have to be sincere—as long as I can believe them. I treat you kindly because you treat me kindly. The fact that you might not be sincere doesn't bother me. Nor does the fact that your kindness is political, and not, say, spousal or filial.

I'll admit that *friend* is a word we politicians overuse. Everything on the phone is "Yes, my friend," or "How are you, my friend," or "Let me call my friend such and so." In my everyday communication, to hear me talk, you would think that "friend" was nothing but a term of political expedience. I have never shared as much as a casual meal with a great many people I call "friend," including even Percy Sutton. Everything we've ever eaten together has been on one campaign trail or another. Yet I would only count my late brother as a better friend than Percy. David Dinkins and Basil Patterson fit the exact same bill—friends with whom I would feel comfortable entrusting my entire reputation. The only difference with all the rest of the legendary and lesser-known people in politics I've called friends—Hugh Carey, Nelson Rockefeller, Roy Goodman, John Lindsay, Frank Guarini, Mario Biaggi, Ben Gilman, Tip O'Neill and so many others—is in degree.

That doesn't mean that when I leave public office I will not be prepared to see a lot of this love disappear. Percy Sutton tells the story of how sometime after he ran for mayor and lost, and was finally out of public office, he spotted an old and dear friend working his way toward him through a crowded reception hall. The friend had a big familiar smile on his face, at first. But as he approached, Percy saw that smile dissolve into a look of recognition that Percy was no longer an elected official. The guy stopped to talk to someone else, and never made it across the floor.

Veteran politicians are fools to deny the truth in that story.

Every political career will come to an end, including mine. I know that life will be different when that end comes. I recognize that being in Congress gives me an opportunity to have a lot of "friends." But I've never thought about what life would be without public office, because I still consider myself to be a public person. I simply haven't prepared myself for a retirement of fishing and golfing and boating. I never acquired the restful skills those pastimes require. A vacation to me means a bag full of work and some music and a couple of good books. I've enjoyed social affairs in Miami, Ft. Lauderdale, Martha's Vineyard, and Sag Harbor over the years. But even if I wanted to, I have no idea how I could slow my engine down enough to put my life into retirement gear.

Since we lost the majority in Congress, the younger Democrats on the Ways and Means Committee have strongly supported my efforts to fight the good fights in the minority and endure until we return to power and I get the chairmanship. Of course, their political lives will be dramatically transformed when that happens. I want it as much as I did in 1994, when I thought I was close enough to taste it. But chairman or not, I can't imagine anyone getting more satisfaction out of each day of work. When we failed to take back the Congress in 2004, I had this big party after Election Day. It should have been a bad day, but I talked about how it had been a great try, and that there would be other opportunities. Missing the brass ring for the fifth time in ten years was probably the roughest time I've ever had politically. But I joked about how I went home and slept like a baby—crying all night. And since then I've only tried to move forward. To be honest, I've felt sorrier for the people who wanted more than I did for myself.

I cannot imagine my disappointment being any less than Nelson Rockefeller's at never running for president, or John Lindsay's ultimate political repudiation. But unlike them, where it was all or nothing, my quest has always been achievable by working hard and excelling at what I'm doing. The chairmanship has been close enough to touch and far enough away for me to forget it. As of this writing, I am touching it again. Yet I never forget that, for all my hard work, I'm in position to triumph because of things over which I have no control and for which I can take no credit: the fortunes and misfortunes of others and the action of time itself.

Being unwilling to test my ability to deal with upstate New Yorkers, I never had the ambitions of a Rockefeller or a Lindsay. Just thinking about the challenge of wooing the farmers and the suburbanites made me say, "Hey, I'm OK in this congressional seat; if it can get me to the chairmanship one day, that's more important to me than being a junior senator." And if that goes for New York State, then you know it goes for national office. I would never be out there campaigning for vice president.

I play three-dollar poker, and I'm good at it. I know nine chances out of ten in three-dollar poker, I'm gonna come out a winner. But I don't go to the game without limits. There is a fundamental divide between the natures of legislative and executive office. Executive jobs, with all those commissioners and department heads to worry about? And my reputation rises or falls based on their performances? You're not in charge of your destiny. People can go out and do what they want to do, and you have to turn around and explain it, like Bush had to explain Michael Brown at FEMA. I'm sorry, that's too much wear and tear. I don't know how I'd be able to avoid bringing my problems home every day. No, no, no . . . God's been very, very good to me, just like it is.

For many years I have thought that if I did not succeed in attaining the chairmanship—if the Democrats did not get back the majority—I would take the last few years of my life to explore some other exciting venture. But somehow I never found out what that exciting venture would be. I always believed we were only a few votes away from majority. But right after the 2004 Bush reelection, and seeing the widening of the number of seats that we needed, I began to think I'd be very comfortable announcing in the early spring of 2006 that I would not be seeking reelection.

But as I write this, all I can see is the expanding mess of the war in Iraq, the lack of reasons given for the war in the first place, the weapons of mass destruction that didn't exist, and the lack of sincerity amid the mounting loss of life. I see the daily exposure of the administration's bare backside as the emperor is revealed to have no clothes, the unwillingness to admit mistakes, and the determination to seek a victory they can't even describe at the cost of more American and Iraqi lives. The corruption scandals surrounding DeLay, Scanlan, Rove, Scooter Libby, and Abramoff are blooming like weeds on a dung heap after the first spring rains. The deficit, and the legacy of debt we're leaving to our children, is soaring and the gap between the rich and the poor is widening. I see the president's popularity down in the thirties and heading south, and I hear more people than ever before saying we can take back the House.

I'm sorry, but this is not the time to fold 'em. It just wouldn't make sense for me not to wrap up this book with looking forward to my last two years in Congress as the chairman of the Ways and Means Committee.

At the end of my next term I'll be seventy-eight. If I don't do it now, then I never will. Claude Pepper, when he was my age, used to tell the story of some broker who was trying to sell him on some long-term investment. "Young man," Pepper said, "at my age, I don't even buy green bananas."

I'll take my late friend's wisdom and pass on talking about 2008. My passion is still there, no question, but I don't know if it's strong enough to survive another two years of Bush and the Republican majority. I do know, as a good poker player, that I am not the ultimate dealer in this game.

As I've spent time basking in the sun on the beach at Punta Cana in the Dominican Republic, where I have a little house, facing a big ocean and beholding the beauty of the Caribbean Sea in total relaxation, I've thought of telling God not to worry about me if it turns out there's an overbooking or backlog on people waiting to get into heaven. I'll be OK right here until it's time for me to come. The older I get, the more I think of how I can make my case with St. Peter in order to get into heaven with some decent accommodations. I often joke with my priests, ministers, and rabbis that when they see me there negotiating, please don't interfere or try to help. They'll have enough problems making their *own* cases. But I promise, if I get in, I'll put in a good word for them.

I've spent all of my life preparing this case. It will include the Caribbean Basin Initiative, the African Growth and Opportunity bill, Empowerment Zones, and the Rangel Low Income Housing Credits, among so many other things in the Congressional Record. And if St. Peter's not overly impressed with my legislative record, then I'll just have to tell him that I did the best I could.

And if I succeed in getting a room with a view, then I can truly say that I haven't had a bad day since.

Index